'some good corne, meatly woodyd, and weil pasturyd'
Dodderhill through the ages

Derek Hurst, Kate Allan, Lyn Blewitt, Chris Bowers, Della Hooke,
Colin Jones, Cas Morris, Helen Peberdy, Stephen Price,
Cheryl Stewart, Jenny Townshend and Mick Wilks

First published 2011

© Copyright of authors.

All rights reserved. No part of this book may be reprinted or reproduced or utilised in any form or by any electronic, mechanical or other means, now known or hereafter invented, including photocopying and recording, or in any information storage or retrieval system, without the permission in writing from the copyright owner.

ISBN 978-0-9569637-0-3

Typesetting and origination by Orphans Press, Leominster, Herefordshire

Printed by Orphans Press, Leominster, Herefordshire

Contents

List of figures v
Foreword (*by* Chris Bowers) viii
Acknowledgements xi
Notes for the reader xiii
Introduction (*by* Derek Hurst) 1
    Scope of the project..1
    Defining Dodderhill (and Wychbold) 1
    Geology and topography 4
    Dodderhill – the name 6
    Note on fieldwork 6
Earliest times (*by* Derek Hurst) 9
    Pleistocene era..9
    Earlier prehistoric (*c* 10,000–800 BC) 10
    Later prehistoric (Iron Age; *c* 800 BC–AD 43) 12
Roman (AD 43–410) (*by* Derek Hurst) 16
Post-Roman and middle Saxon (AD 410–*c* 900) 25
    The early medieval landscape of the Droitwich to Bromsgrove region (*by* Della Hooke) 28
    Wicbold – mother church, 'villa regalis', and vill (*by* Lyn Blewitt) 38
Late Saxon (*c* 900–1066)..54
Domesday Book (1066–1086) 55
    Wychbold – the Domesday Book evidence (*by* Lyn Blewitt) 55
Medieval (1066–1550) 61
    The medieval landscape of Dodderhill (*by* Derek Hurst) 63
    Manor of Wychbold (*by* Jenny Townshend) 68
    Parish and church (*by* Helen Peberdy and Derek Hurst) 71
    Other religious institutions (*by* Lyn Blewitt) 74
    Water mills (*by* Cheryl Stewart)..77
    Meet the locals (*by* Derek Hurst) 80
Post-medieval (*c* 1550–1800) 82
    Astwood (*by* Cheryl Stewart)..88
    Hill Court (*by* Helen Peberdy) 108
    Local administration through the manor court (*by* Jenny Townshend) 109
    Parish and church (*by* Helen Peberdy) 111
    Quaker burial ground (*by* Helen Peberdy)..113
    Lives revealed – some insights based on wills (*by* Jenny Townshend)..................114
    Farming (*by* Jenny Townshend) 116
    Sheep and the cloth trade (*by* Jenny Townshend) 124
    Food in probate inventories (*by* Jenny Townshend) 128
    Vernacular buildings (*by* Stephen Price) 134
    Education (*by* Carolyn Morris) 148
19th century..150
    Parish and church (*by* Helen Peberdy) 151
    From manor to mansion: the ownership of Impney (*by* Lyn Blewitt) 153
    Education (*by* Carolyn Morris) 156

20th century *169*
　　Parish at war (*by* Colin Jones and Mick Wilks) *169*
　　National farm survey during the Second World War (*by* Kate Allan) *177*
　　Education (*by* Carolyn Morris) *190*
Conclusions (*by* Derek Hurst) *200*
Bibliography *202*
Index *211*

List of figures

Figure 1   Location of Dodderhill parish: based on the 1843 tithe map
Figure 2   Geology of Dodderhill parish
Figure 3   Topography of Dodderhill parish: relief and drainage
Figure 4   Dodderhill parish: areas of fieldwork carried out during the project
Figure 5   Finds washing under way in 2008
Figure 6   Mammoth and mammoth tooth discovered in north Dodderhill
Figure 7   Sampling the Mesolithic deposits at Impney
Figure 8   Mesolithic flint core from Kennets Hall
Figure 9   Mesolithic/early Neolithic flint core from fieldwalking at Astwood
Figure 10   Penannular drainage gully encircling a roundhouse at Stoke Lane
Figure 11   Late prehistoric ceramic salt container (briquetage) from Droitwich
Figure 12   View northwards along Roman road at Crutch Hill
Figure 13   Early Roman marching camp opposite Chateau Impney
Figure 14   Roman soldiers parading at Wychbold
Figure 15   Large tank at Upwich in the early Roman period
Figure 16   Bays Meadow villa at Droitwich
Figure 17   Fieldwalking in progress in 2005 (WSM 34766)
Figure 18   Piece of circular ceramic baking plate of Roman date
Figure 19   A typical array of fieldwalked pottery arranged in rows by date with other finds
Figure 20   Brine-boiling hearth at Upwich of early/middle Saxon date
Figure 21   Territorial units in north Worcestershire
Figure 22   The uplands fringing the ?original northern border of the Hwiccan kingdom
Figure 23   Estate centres in the Droitwich-Bromsgrove region
Figure 24   Place-names and land use in the Droitwich-Bromsgrove region
Figure 25   Early medieval charter-bounds and medieval forest boundaries in the Droitwich-Bromsgrove region (plus tree species recorded in place-names)
Figure 26   'Watch Hill', Stoke Prior
Figure 27   Church of St Augustine viewed from parish boundary of Dodderhill, and looking north across location of Upwich brine well
Figure 28   Former parochial affiliations in the vicinity of Droitwich, as alluded to in mainly later medieval sources
Figure 29   Site of Hanbury minster
Figure 30   Silver penny of Alfred the Great issued c 875–80 and found next to Upwich brine well
Figure 31   Copper alloy stirrup terminal found in Dodderhill and dating c 1020–c 1100
Figure 32   Domesday Book entry for Wychbold in 1086
Figure 33   Brine extraction at Upwich in c 1300
Figure 34   Dodderhill parish: medieval places and structures
Figure 35   View looking towards Dodderhill church from the salt-making area of Upwich in c 1300; showing original form of the medieval church
Figure 36   Detail of indenture of Thomas Carewe, lord of the manor of Wychbold, dated 20 January 1584

Figure 37 Early 17th century manuscript map of Droitwich showing part of Dodderhill parish
Figure 38 View looking north across Wychbold in *c* 1600
Figure 39 Reorganisation of fields in Wychbold based on 1671 documentation compared with 1843 tithe map
Figure 40 Late medieval ceramic drinking cup manufactured in the Hanley Castle area
Figure 41 Sagebury farmhouse
Figure 42 Wychbold Court as shown on a postcard dated 1903
Figure 43 Sir Thomas Nott 1606–81
Figure 44 Steps leading up from the cellar of Hobden Hall
Figure 45 Drawing of Hobden Hall by A Aldham in *c* 1870
Figure 46 Hobden Hall farmhouse as it is today
Figure 47 Moors farmhouse in July 1968
Figure 48 Sagebury Cottages in 2010
Figure 49 Cheese rack with shelf supports still in position at Astwood Court Farm *c* 1985
Figure 50 Astwood Court Farm
Figure 51 Possible site of Astwood mill near Hobden Hall
Figure 52 Astwood Manor Farm in 1947 as drawn by William Albert Green
Figure 53 Survey and map dated 1722 of Astwood estate of John Wild, as drawn by Joseph Dougharty
Figure 54 Causeway Meadows Farm: plan dated 1845
Figure 55 Causeway Meadows Farm: view of a now demolished timber-framed part of the house
Figure 56 Causeway Meadows Farm: as pictured in the 1920 sale catalogue
Figure 57 Hill Court as featured in 1928 Droitwich town guide
Figure 58 Dodderhill church at the end of the 18th century as illustrated by Nash (1781–2) showing Civil War damage
Figure 59 Percentages of inventories showing crops
Figure 60 Size of herd
Figure 61 Traditional churning of butter
Figure 62 Mill Cottage: apex of cruck truss
Figure 63 Tudor Cottage: view from the south-west
Figure 64 Tudor Cottage: fragment of wall painting depicting King David
Figure 65 Wychbold Court (west elevation)
Figure 66 Astwood Court Farm: rear (north) elevation
Figure 67 Astwood Court Farm: panelled parlour with 17th century overmantel
Figure 68 Mere Hall, Hanbury (rear elevation)
Figure 69 Christmas, Rosemary, and Laburnum Cottages, Wychbold
Figure 70 Redhouse Farm
Figure 71 The Old Cottage, Sharpway Gate
Figure 72 Ridgeway Court Farm
Figure 73 Designs for farmhouses by William Pitt (1796) from his *General view of the agriculture of the County of Stafford*
Figure 74 Hobden Hall
Figure 75 Piper's Hill Farm
Figure 76 Rashwood Farm
Figure 77 Sharpway Gate Farm
Figure 78 Sapper Oldham of the Ordnance Survey trying to make sense of the overlapping boundaries of borough and parish in 1881
Figure 79 Impney Mill as copied in pencil in 1825 from an original sketch by Miss P Amphlett

Figure 80 Engraving of the Coventry Hospital in 1833
Figure 81 Plan dated 23 August 1845 for National School in Dodderhill
Figure 82 Mrs Sutton in 1930s and Joan Serrell in 1950s outside Overstreet Cottages
Figure 83 Rashwood School 1905
Figure 84 Location of known sites and buildings with wartime associations
Figure 85 Typical 1941–2 Primary Farm Return record: Astwood Manor Farm
Figure 86 National Farm Survey map showing 1941–2 land holdings in the vicinity of Brine Pits Farm
Figure 87 Plot of Dodderhill land holdings as mapped by the National Farm Survey of 1941–2
Figure 88 All crops by acreage (1941–2)
Figure 89 All crops (excluding grass) by percentage of acreage (1941–2)
Figure 90 Type of cereals by percentage of acreage (1941–2)
Figure 91 All livestock (1941–2)
Figure 92 Type of cattle (1941–2)
Figure 93 Type of sheep (1941–2)
Figure 94 Type of pig (1941–2)
Figure 95 Type of poultry (1941–2)
Figure 96 The schoolroom at Rashwood in 1913
Figure 97 A class at Rashwood in 1952
Figure 98 Rashwood School in 1965 showing the new extension
Figure 99 Members of the Dodderhill Parish Survey Project with Mick Aston at the *Making Time Team* lecture event at Avoncroft Museum

Foreword (*by* Chris Bowers)

Think of a Worcestershire parish split by the busy M5 Motorway and marked by two high transmitter masts. Here is the parish of Dodderhill, just north of Droitwich, which, on the surface, is a community with rural roots, but also one which has a growing community of new residents.

Dig a little deeper, as members of the Dodderhill Parish Survey Project have done, and much more about the history of the parish will be revealed. Our research began with the tantalising mention of a Saxon royal residence at Wychbold in three contemporary charters, and our hope to find the location of this building. Now more than ten years on we are no closer to finding that elusive place, but we understand that the likelihood is that it was a compound of timber buildings including a large hall, long since gone, where representatives of the king held court.

The group's first formal efforts to gain more understanding of the history of the area were made by attending a WEA (Workers' Education Association) course on landscape history in March–April 2000, led by an archaeologist and sponsored by the Droitwich History and Archaeology Society. The group of students then held public meetings in the local Wychbold Community Hall where local people were encouraged to share their knowledge. One of those local people was Robin Skerratt who, as the son of the local policeman, had lived in the village as a child. Soon the group organised a coach tour with Robin sharing his childhood memories as we stopped beside local buildings and properties, and with the profits of the coach trip opened a bank account and established themselves as an independent group. The 'Dodderhill Parish Survey Project' was born! (The story told on the coach trip became a 174 page book *Memories of Wychbold before the motorway* (published in 2001), parts of which have since been reproduced on the website – but more of that later!)

As time went by a small core group began meeting and an application was made to take part in the Local Heritage Initiative (of the Heritage Lottery Fund), administered by The Countryside Agency. The application was successful and a three-year project, 'Discovering Wychbold's Past' (September 2000–December 2002) became a reality with a grant of £3625. *Dodderhill Parish History Notes* (2002) recorded the first research findings made by group members.

At the end of that initial project, a second larger application was made for a Local Heritage Initiative grant, and a second project 'Delving Deeper into Dodderhill's Past' (May 2003–May 2006) was set in motion with a grant of £24,992 which enabled the group to continue with their research and also to employ specialist workers. *Dodderhill Parish History Notes 2* (2006) recorded the group's new research findings and updated those previously published.

This book is the end result of a successful third grant application (November 2006–2011). Gaining a third grant was a much more daunting task as it was a requirement of the Heritage Lottery Fund to have a wider educational brief, which would include not only members of the local community, but also local school children, local historians and a much wider public audience, and which was to include creating a local history website. It seemed appropriate that this third project should be entitled 'Sharing Wychbold's Past'. Members of the group were required to produce a detailed application submission which identified how and what we would achieve, and this has proved an invaluable tool for achieving our objectives, by providing a framework for the many many hours which have been spent researching, and sharing our knowledge and understanding with others.

The group has continued to research and transcribe historical documents and, with the permission of local property owners, has employed specialists to research historic buildings and undertake dendrochronology (tree-ring dating) and to use geophysical techniques in order to locate ground anomalies in the search for hidden features. Members have also continued with a programme of fieldwalking to discover pottery and other finds which have enabled the group to map human activity in the landscape over thousands of years.

In addition to this work to increase the knowledge and understanding of the local history of the parish of Dodderhill, our four-year project 'Sharing Wychbold's Past' has involved us in the following exciting challenges:

- bringing eminent historians and archaeologists (including Mick Aston of 'Time Team') to speak to a wider audience;
- working with Wychbold First School where a Saxon shelter was built with the children's help and Saxon life became part of the curriculum with skilled historians in the lead; and where archaeological test pits were dug in the school grounds, and Roman soldiers (from the Roman Military Research Society) 'took over' the school and 'trained' an army of young soldiers;
- welcoming Roman soldiers to the village fete where they camped and marched in the adjacent field;
- creating a database to log all data regarding field-names listed on the 1843 tithe survey, and those identified in wills, inventories and deeds, which has listed around 1500 local field- and minor place-names (mostly now otherwise lost), and 2000 personal names dating mainly from the 13th–19th centuries;
- designing and publishing a poster-sized illustrated parish map and displaying several large copies at strategic points within the village;
- designing an illustrated 2010 calendar for delivery to every household in the parish;
- planning two historical footpath walks through the village and publishing their routes as a leaflet, downloadable from the website, as well as leading guided walks;
- collecting, enlarging and laminating a number of photographs and illustrations for use at public events;
- creating our website, which challenged everyone, not only for the technical skills required but for the choice of accurate and easy to understand text with the use of appropriate illustrations, and;
- finally, the publication of this book.

This new publication updates our research and includes many new facts and observations. For example, it is now possible to say with certainty that Dodderhill apparently contains the earliest example found so far in Worcestershire of a significant new building style of *c* 1600. It is a culmination of many years of research, undertaken by members in their 'spare time'. The number of hours spent by each person indicates just how absorbing this research project has been. Like any research project, we present what we currently understand to be true, while understanding that new evidence and research could modify these conclusions.

On behalf of all who have been involved in our research project, I hope you will enjoy sharing in the history of our parish.

Chris Bowers
Co-ordinator, Dodderhill Parish Survey Project

Note on authorship

Individual authors are identified to their appropriate sections; where not specifically identified the work is authored by Derek Hurst, who also collated and edited the volume. Copyright of illustrations and photographs is otherwise individually credited, where appropriate. We have all tried to be as accurate as possible, but, where mistakes remain, these are our own.

Acknowledgements

This project would not have been possible without the encouragement, support and enthusiasm shown to the researchers by so many. Our thanks in particular go to:

- Worcestershire Record Office, Nottinghamshire Record Office, Cheshire Record Office, and National Archives, and their staff, for enabling the researchers to gain access to vital documents;
- Worcestershire Historic Environment Record;
- the Bromsgrove Historical Transcribing Group (Gillian Ansfield, the late Beth Bucknall, Annette Chubb, Jean and the late Aubrey Edwards, Pam Gough, Margaret Must, Madge Vaughan, and Audrey Wheeler), and members of the project for extracting essential information from those documents;
- the eminent historians and other speakers who have made our meetings so interesting, and provided information which helped shape the development of our project;
- the staff and children of Wychbold First School (head teachers, Peter Bravo and Rachel Hughes), members of Worcestershire Young Archaeologists' Group, Wychbold Community Hall Committee, St Mary de Wyche Church and St Augustine's Church, Dodderhill;
- the numerous volunteers who happily joined in fieldwalking;
- Derek Hurst, archaeology advisor and consultant;
- Stephen Price, building researcher, and;
- the families and friends of our researchers.

Chris Bowers would like to thank the following: Alan Baker for his considerable assistance and support in preparing the grant application to the Heritage Lottery Fund; Roger Peberdy for his assistance with the website; and Frank Hazzard for various illustrations during the project.

A debt of gratitude is owed to many during the preparation of this volume, including as follows: Derek Hurst would like to thank Robin Jackson for his comments on the worked flint, as well as Emma Hancox, Maggi Noke and Oliver Russell for information from the Worcestershire Historic Environment Record, and Darren Miller for comments; Lyn Blewitt would like to thank Jean Brettell for kindly permitting access to and the transcription of two conveyances, and access to other documents, including maps of the Impney estate, and Christine Jackson for transcribing and arranging digital copying of the conveyances; Carolyn Morris offers special thanks to Joan Moore and Audrey Hackett for confirming her suspicions as to the whereabouts of Dodderhill's first school, and to Kate Allan for finding Elsie Hughes; and Kate Allan is very grateful to William B Booth for crucial help during the struggle with data, and then for assistance with statistics and the creation of pie-charts. Stephen Price would like to thank: Peter Walker, Nicholas Molyneux and the late Paul Williams who helped with building recording and interpretation; members of the Dodderhill Parish Survey Project Group, in particular Chris Bowers, Cheryl Stewart, Jenny Townshend and Derek Hurst who were especially supportive; Dr Nat Alcock and Bob Meeson for sharing the results of their research on Mere Hall, a house which has close architectural and historical connections with Astwood Court Farm; Robin Whittaker

(Worcestershire Record Office) for providing background details about the 1985 photographic survey of Dodderhill; and Andrew Harris for kindly agreeing to the use of the results of his fieldwork which forms part of the Hereford & Worcester Record Group's archive in Worcestershire Record Office.

Many, therefore, have contributed to the project over the years it has taken place, whether through encouragement or active participation, and all provided momentum propelling the work forward. These included in particular Joyce Gill and Stuart Miller who, unfortunately, were not able to see the final outcome of this research, but whose efforts and support should not be forgotten.

Members of the group are especially indebted to all those landowners and householders who have given the research project access to their properties (including R Aylett, A & J Baker, R Cartwright, N Cole, Mrs Everett, J Finch, B & J Gill, T & H Hill, I Hollingsworth, C Jackson, J Kriss, C Laird, D & T Mace, R & C Morris, Mrs D Townsend, R Tracey, T Walder, Westwood Farming Partners, S Williams, and H & J Wylie). Without their support our research project would not have made much headway.

Various specialists contributed to the work reported in this volume, notably the following: Arthur Davis (illustrator of the reconstructed historical scenes), Dr Pam Gough (bio-geographer), David Guyatt (document transcriber), Carolyn Hunt (illustrator, Worcestershire Historic Environment & Archaeology Service (WHEAS)), Martin Bridge (dendrochronologist), and Shona Robson-Glyde (WHEAS) and Paul Williams (historic buildings specialists).

Dodderhill Parish Survey Project members: Kate Allan, Lyn Blewitt, Chris Bowers, Derek Hurst, Cas Morris, Helen Peberdy, Cheryl Stewart, and Jenny Townshend.

Notes for the reader

Prices are stated as in the original source, and conversion rates to modern decimalised currency are as follows: 1 shilling (s) = 5p; and c 2½ old pence (d) = 1p.

Medieval monetary values are difficult to gauge without knowing the average contemporary income at different levels of society, and the values of some basic commodities. The following prices may help to provide a very rough guide to the value of medieval currency in terms of its purchasing power, and so enable the scale of the sums stated in this book to be better appreciated (daily incomes mainly after Dyer 1989, and 2002, and prices after Rogers 1866 and 1882):

century	daily income		wheat	ale/beer/cider	salt
	labourer	craftsman	(per quarter)*	(per gallon (4.5l))	(per bushel)*
13th	1d	2½d	5s–6s	½d (cider)	4d
early 14th	2d	4d	4s	1d (ale)	5d–6d
early 15th	3d	5d	5s	2d (beer)	6d
early 16th	4d	6d	8s–12s	2d (ale)	9d

*A quarter weighed about 450lb (204kg), and a bushel 56lb (c 25kg).

Abbreviations

BCA	Birmingham City Archives
VCH	Victoria County History
CRO	Cheshire Record Office
NA	National Archives (Kew)
WRO	Worcestershire Record Office
WHEAS	Worcestershire Historic Environment & Archaeology Service
WHER	Worcestershire Historic Environment Record
WSM	Worcestershire Sites and Monuments (record number)

Introduction (*by* Derek Hurst)

Scope of the project

The broad aims of the research carried out by the Dodderhill Parish Survey Project in 2000–2010 have been to collect, analyse, and report on data relating to the past history of this parish. The project has aimed to be comprehensive in the range of techniques applied, and so has seen the commissioning of dendrochronology, building recording, archaeological fieldwalking, survey and excavation, geophysical survey, finds identification, and reconstruction illustration, as well as undertaking its own original historical research; this has meant going from contending with muddy fields one day to finding our way around the National Archives at Kew in London on another, and so ranging from pot sherds to original documents, both being equally authentic voices of the past, but now located in very different places. Each year an eminent speaker was also invited to deliver a public lecture, in the expectation that this would inspire work on the project, by bringing about fresh insights, as well as providing an opportunity for those speakers to make a contribution of their own to this local research.

Periodically bulletins were issued reporting on the progress of research (*Dodderhill Parish History Notes* in 2002 and 2006), and initial results have also been uploaded to the website created during the project (www.dodderhillhistory.org.uk). The final and more substantial overall reporting stage represented by this book has been tackled very much as a collaborative exercise by group members, and was based around discussions at regular meetings, followed by allocation of topics to individual authors.

The project has also generated an archive which comprises:

- a copy, or calendar, of all Dodderhill written historical documents identified during the project;
- copies of aerial photographs taken by the RAF in 1946 as held in the National Monuments Record at Swindon;
- a listing of all place- and field-names, and personal names recorded during the project, and;
- detailed reports on individual surveys undertaken during the overall project.

This archive is currently being held locally by Cheryl Stewart (Mill Cottage), and detailed specialist reports will also be passed to the Worcestershire Historic Environment Record (WHER).

Defining Dodderhill (and Wychbold)

Today Dodderhill is but one of 210 Worcestershire parishes. Its roots lie in the distant past, its earlier history being bound up with an estate that went under the name of *Wicbold* (literally 'the hall at Wich'; or as later, Wychbold). The origins of this estate and its associated buildings are lost in the mists of time but, when the name is first seen in 7th century historical sources, it is clearly a place of importance, and becomes the place where Mercian kings took up residence when in the area. The name could not be clearer as representing the chief place at *Wich* (ie Droitwich), and *Wich* was also the place-name element that bound together the different related parts of the whole that constituted the salt-making business, suggesting that at this time Wychbold had a lot to do with this industry.

It is presently considered that what eventually became Dodderhill parish was the vital core of the former Wychbold royal estate, and it is this which forms the focus of the present study. This means that some former components of greater Wychbold, such as Elmbridge and Westwood, are not included here except in passing reference. Indeed the use of the terms Wychbold and Dodderhill seems to have been the source of some confusion to outsiders in the distant past, and so it is unsurprising that care is necessary in the use of these names. For instance, in 1274/5 it was being carefully explained that Dodderhill was not an inhabited settlement but was just the name of the hill near where the church was situated, the church being in Wychbold (CPR Lett II, 381). The concept of a parish named Dodderhill, therefore, seems only to have emerged here later in the medieval period. The size of the area concerned will not have helped, as it was apparently necessary to use smaller units in very large manors when collecting tithes; these were called yields and were to be found in Dodderhill, King's Norton, and Alvechurch, all large parishes with dispersed settlement. For what became Dodderhill parish the yields were Astwood, Wychbold, and Impney, suggesting that these were the primary places when this system was adopted, while the operation of local administration showed Wychbold at its head.

The remnant of greater Wychbold which finally became Dodderhill parish, when looked at on a map, does seem to have a coherent shape in respect of both its natural and historical landscape in that it:

a. comprises a considerable length of the River Salwarpe and its valley, including valuable meadows, and;

b. takes in land on either side of the old Roman road (now A38) and, therefore, seems to have been deliberately set out to embrace a long length of this road which was probably always crucial to the salt production in Droitwich.

Perhaps far from co-incidentally, both these aspects of its setting turned out to be advantageous, the one being exploited by a disproportionate number of late Saxon mills, and, very unusually for a king's highway, medieval Wychbold also had a toll-house, presumably intended to profit the manor while raising funds for the maintenance of this important road.

For the purposes of this study Dodderhill, therefore, has been taken as that area shown in the 1843 tithe map (Fig 1), which did not include Elmbridge (suggesting that their separation had already occurred at an earlier date, though this was not formalised until 1877). Dodderhill parish later lost Huntingdrop to Hanbury and Crowfield to Bromsgrove in 1880, and its southern end in the borough of Droitwich was added to adjacent town parishes in 1884 (*VCH Worcestershire* III, 59). Crutch to the west had probably become extra-parochial in 1178 when assigned to Westwood nunnery, and in 1541 became part of Hampton Lovett ecclesiastical parish (*ibid*). Dodderhill parish has, therefore, been defined, for the purposes of this project, as it was in the mid 19th century, though occasionally fieldwork in adjacent fields bordering the parish boundary has also been included.

INTRODUCTION

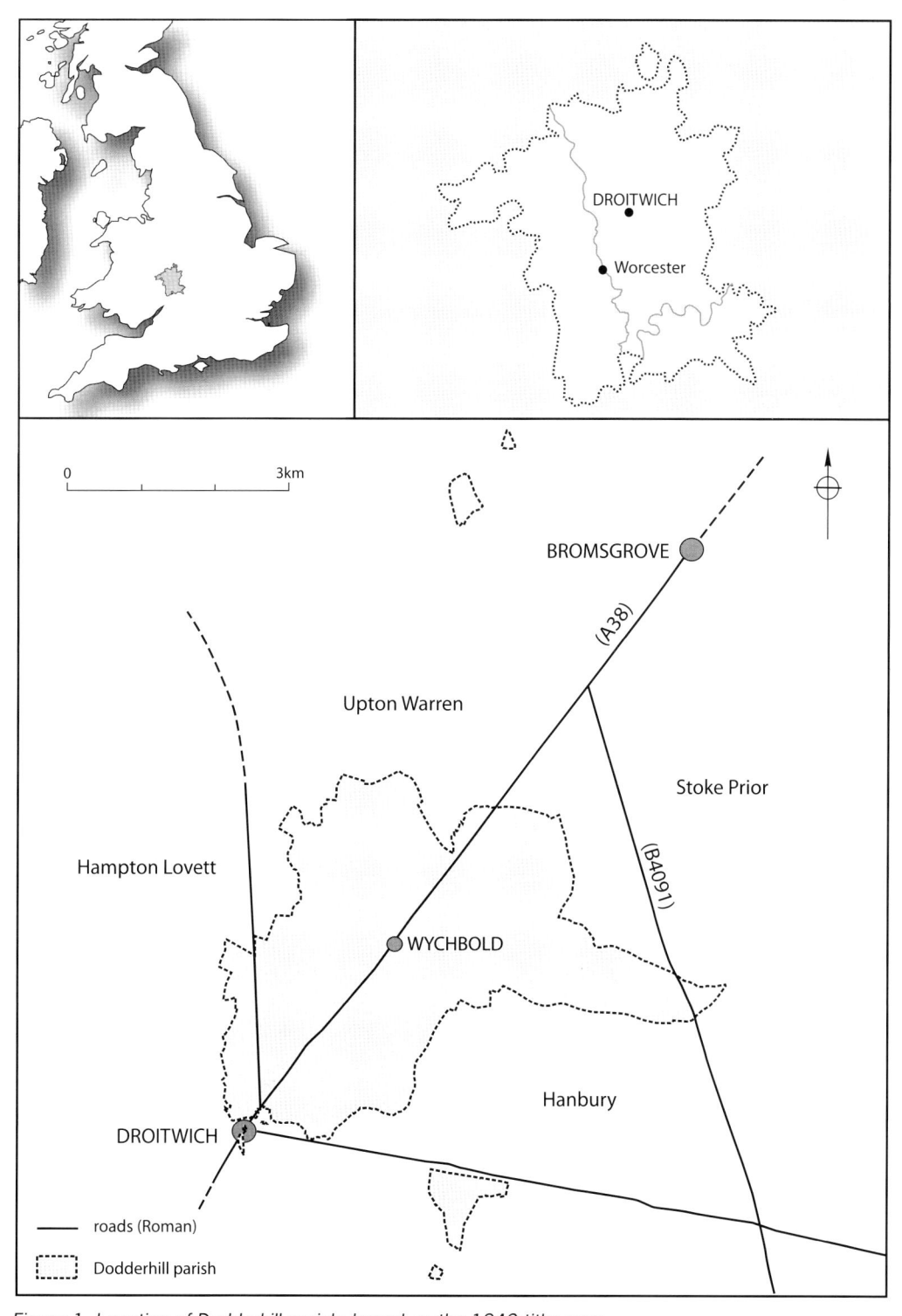

Figure 1 Location of Dodderhill parish: based on the 1843 tithe map

Geology and topography

Surface geology comprises either river terrace deposits (well-drained sands and gravels favourable to habitation and early cultivation as they provide light soils) or Triassic Mercia Mudstone clays (Mitchell *et al* 1961; Fig 2), the latter giving rise to heavy, but potentially fertile, soils and much harder to cultivate without a heavy plough. The area is drained by the River Salwarpe and its associated brooks, which jointly drain the higher ground to the north (Fig 3). Deep underground, and in a line through the centre of the parish from Stoke Prior to Droitwich, there is the subterranean brine run that gave rise to the Droitwich salt industry over its thousands of years of production. It is the higher ground around Droitwich that provides the artesian pressure to make the brine erupt in springs. Though normally regarded as a part of Droitwich the main brine springs at Upwich were, in fact, historically within the boundary of Wychbold (and, therefore, later, Dodderhill parish).

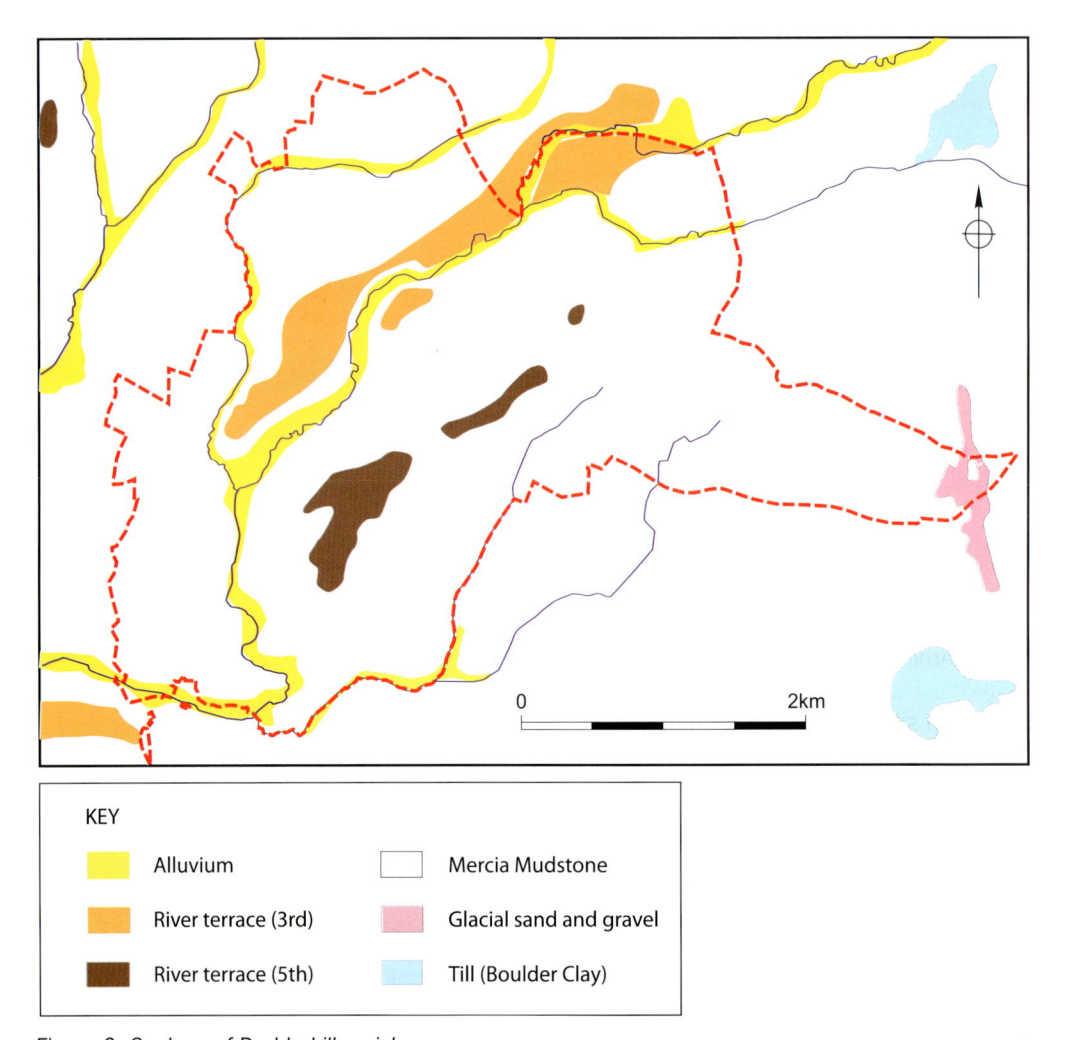

Figure 2 Geology of Dodderhill parish

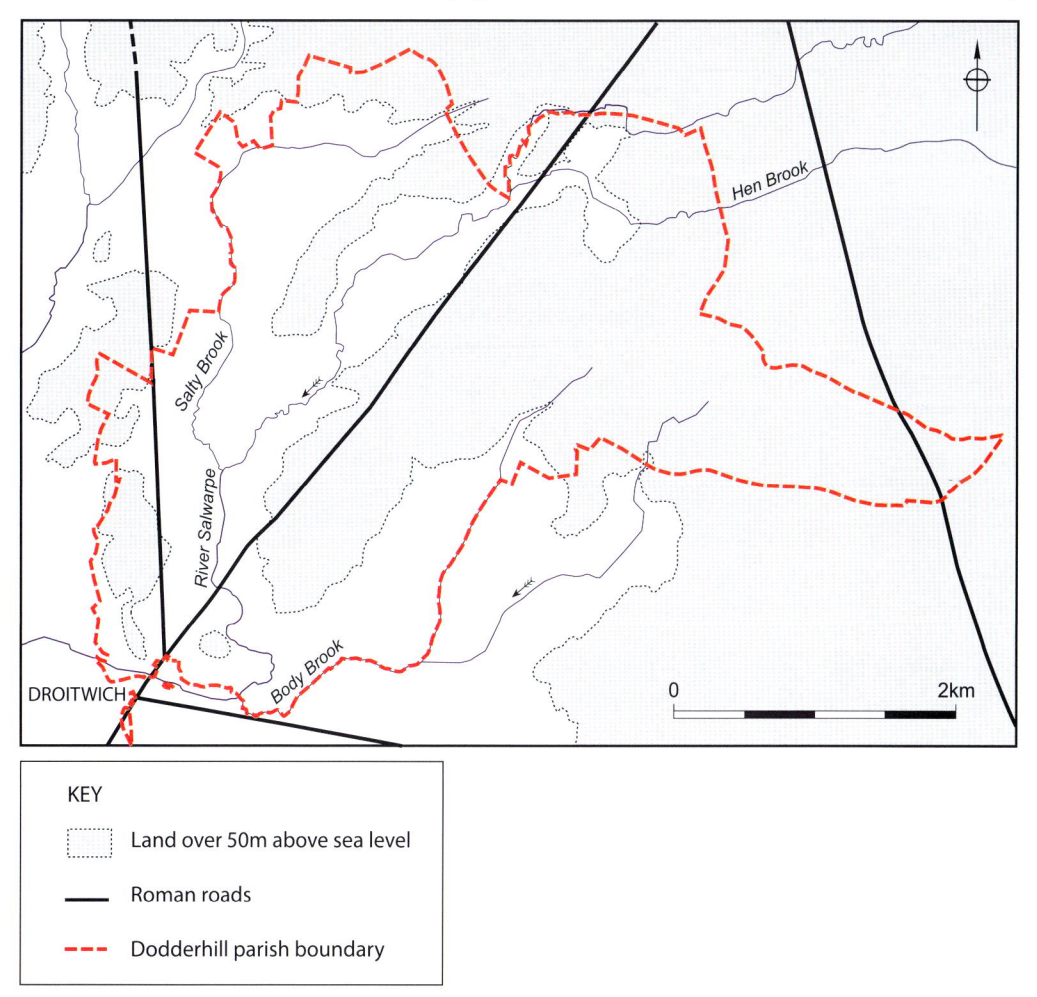

Figure 3 Topography of Dodderhill parish: relief and drainage

It remains uncertain whether the brine run gave rise to any other areas of salt making elsewhere in Dodderhill, apart from those located within what later became the medieval borough of Droitwich. The name Brine Pits Farm does seem to offer firm evidence that there were other production sites beyond the borough confines, but, so far, any historical proof to corroborate this has proved elusive. It has been claimed by some, for instance, to be the site of the ancient and historically attested site of *Helperic* mentioned in Domesday Book (Thorn & Thorn 1982, note 1,3a).

As another aspect of its environment it is also worth considering the climate of Wychbold. Local rain-fall levels are comparable with the rest of the Severn valley and about 10% higher than in the south-east of the county, with the clay soils of this central region being well able to withstand this, in contrast with the sandy soils to the north with their colder climate (Buchanan 1944, 427 and 432). This suggests a favourable combination of circumstances of benefit to farming. Otherwise little seems to be recorded about the special local qualities of the Wychbold area, though a general Worcestershire survey in the 1930s recorded that its pastureland was appreciated for the grazing of cattle and sheep (Buchanan 1944, 461–4).

Dodderhill – the name

Dodderhill was originally the name given to a hill overlooking the River Salwarpe valley, and its earliest surviving written source dates to the late 11th–12th centuries (Mawer & Stenton 1927, 281); the derivation of the name is uncertain but it is clear any earlier Celtic name had been replaced. The name Dodderhill has been explained as incorporating a personal name *Dudra*, literally 'Dudra's hill', but another possibility is that *dodra* was Old English (R Coates, pers comm) for a plant known today as Dodder; two types of Dodder are found today, one (*Cuscuta epithymum*) on heaths in England, and the other (*Cuscuta europaea*) is rare and localised and found on common nettles; both plants are notable for being parasitic and, therefore, growing on other vegetation (McClintock and Fitter 1956).

Note on fieldwork

The fieldwork undertaken by members of the community during the project (Fig 4) was largely fieldwalking, but there was also test pitting in collaboration with pupils of Wychbold First School (in the school grounds; WSM 38562), and also with Worcestershire Young Archaeologists' Club (at Astwood New House; WSM 39898).

The fieldwalking early in the project tended to be general scanning of fields, and only later in the project was carried out systematically using a 20 x 20m grid for the collection of finds so that finds could then be plotted, and distributions examined. As a result only very generalised comments could be made about fieldwalked assemblages collected up to 2005/6, whereas for 2007–10 detailed plots of finds were available.

A total of about 9000 finds, weighing approximately 117kg, were collected and processed (ie washed and identified; Fig 5) during the fieldwork, including nearly 6500 sherds of pottery dating from the ?Bronze Age to modern times. The results of the identification and analysis of this multitude of finds are summarised below, and more detailed reports are available through the WHER (Hurst 2010a–f). Only through this painstaking collection and study of finds over increasingly large areas can new sites be discovered and the past landscape of Dodderhill be pieced back together, especially in the case of the more distant times when only new and local archaeological discoveries can improve our understanding.

INTRODUCTION   7

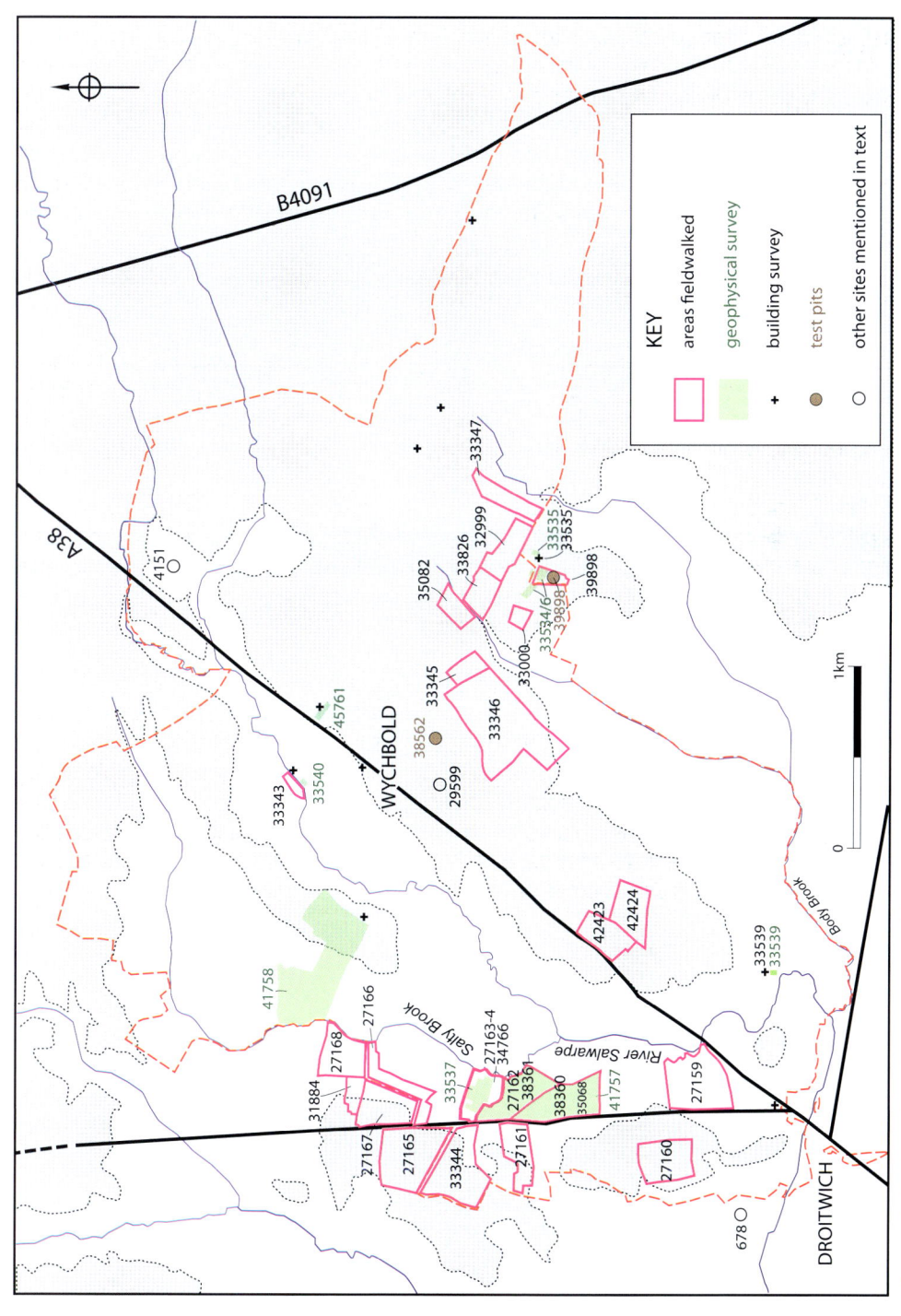

Figure 4 Dodderhill parish: areas of fieldwork carried out during the project (WSM numbers indicated)

Figure 5 Finds washing under way in 2008 (photograph by D Hurst)

Earliest times (*by* Derek Hurst)

Pleistocene era

Our history of Dodderhill opens with dawn breaking over a scene where animals are quietly grazing. But these animals are not those familiar to us; instead they are mammoth, woolly rhinoceros, reindeer, and bison, which are roaming the uneven grassland spreading as far as the eye can see (Fig 6), in a land now warming up after years of extreme cold when Ice Age glaciers had dominated the landscape. In the foreground there is a shallow pool, where these same animals can be seen drinking their fill, and the surface of the pond is swarming with many different types of flies and beetles. This very detailed scene can be constructed with some certainty from rare evidence discovered in the north part of Dodderhill during gravel quarrying in the 1950s. Today an expanse of water has returned (this time in the aftermath of gravel quarrying), and so now the species *Homo sapiens* can see much the same landscape as before, except that now this is a temperate world with trees and hedges, and instead of Ice Age animals, there are sailing boats (Upton Warren Sailing Club) and bird-watching hides (Christopher Cadbury Wetlands Reserve). Much has changed after 42,000 years.

It was during the extraction of gravel in the 1950s that archaeologists became aware of this very rare find of a rich organic deposit sandwiched deep down in the gravels, and associated with large amounts of animal bone (WSM 4151; Coope *et al* 1961). The organic deposit turned out to be the well preserved remains from a pool of water, which was even more unusual as it turned out to have been slightly brackish, being fed by the underground brine springs which were destined to have such an impact on the human history of the area in future times. Just adjacent we should also envision a predecessor of the River Salwarpe, though unrecognisable from its current placid state, as it would have been swollen with melt-waters from the glaciers further north. The river occasionally flooded the ponds and so washed in the detritus of bones

Figure 6 Mammoth and mammoth tooth discovered in north Dodderhill (photograph by D Hurst)

off the surrounding land surface. It has been these remains that have subsequently allowed this detailed faunal scene from many millennia ago to be reconstructed.

As time elapsed this scene was eventually to be transformed again, as it proved that this was just a temporary amelioration of the climate. The bitter cold returned, the glaciers again fixed their icy grip on the landscape, and in the face of such terrible conditions the animals retreated southwards once more. The remains of the pools, including clues to life in this remote era, were sealed under fresh gravel, and thereby safely preserved for future discovery.

More than another 30,000 years were to pass before, what we now know as the Ice Age, finally gave way heralding the present (no doubt equally temporary) period of warmer weather which we now enjoy, and which commenced about 10,000 years ago. This has since allowed temperate vegetation to become fully established across the region, providing, this time, the conditions suitable for the emergence of natural climax vegetation of broadleaved woodland, and cold weather animals like reindeer will have passed through again but, this time, they continued northwards as the landscape of our area warmed up even more than before. Such conditions allowed human activity to follow apace as hunters moved northwards accompanying this fresh warming of the climate, and the northward spread of prey animals. Whereas previous evidence of human activity, if it was present, had been scoured from the landscape by the ice, this time the scene was now set for the present act of our human drama. This time the impact of humans on the landscape, even where unrecorded in written sources, is there to be read through archaeology, and so we can now start to tell the tale of Dodderhill in much greater detail.

Dodderhill's history has, therefore, started with a startling site of great significance for the region, and it is surprising how many other highlights of interest there are to be described in what follows.

Earlier prehistoric (c 10,000–800 BC)

Mesolithic

Surprisingly the first period of prehistory for which human activity may be expected to be found in this region is also notable in Dodderhill for some very well preserved deposits of considerable regional rarity (Fig 7; though these have now been sadly damaged in the course of recent modern development). In the earlier part of the Mesolithic period (c 10,000–4000 BC) peat deposits accumulated along the River Salwarpe at Impney, such deposits being key to revealing the surrounding landscape and extent of human activity through the evidence of pollen (WSM 31799; see below). In addition there has been the rare discovery of *in situ* Mesolithic worked flint in quantity only a short distance away and close to the brine springs in Droitwich (Bradley 1989). Both these sites are markedly focussed on the banks of the River Salwarpe suggesting the high potential for remains of this date to survive in the base of this river valley. However, both sites have also now been compromised by recent development.

Radiocarbon dating of the Impney peat deposits confirmed their Mesolithic date at around c 9500–6000 BC. Pollen found in these deposits can be used to indicate aspects of the contemporary vegetation and, therefore, landscape history including human activity. At Impney the results showed a consistently rather open grassland with woods of pine and birch, and signs of burning (Greig 2005). The burning perhaps represents residues from camp fires, presumably indicating encampments in the vicinity. By *c* 7500–6000 BC the pollen sequences show that the mainly grasses and herbs now included cereal, with a range of tree pollen (Pearson 1999). This is extremely odd in that cereals would not normally be expected in this period when hunter-gatherer communities are, by definition, living off the land. Though this is the first instance in Worcestershire, outside of the county the presence of cereal pollen has also been noted previously in deposits at several sites of this period, for example in Oxfordshire, where wheat pollen was recorded in deposits dating to *c* 4800 BC. It presently remains unclear whether at Impney this represents very early experimentation with cereals, or whether it is just contamination with later material (*ibid*). Regardless of that uncertainty the Impney landscape differs markedly from that detected elsewhere in Worcestershire, such as at Hartlebury (Brown 1984) where wildwood dominated during the Mesolithic period, and there was no significant deforestation until late Bronze Age/early Iron Age times.

Figure 7 Sampling the Mesolithic deposits at Impney (copyright of Worcestershire County Council)

An interesting observation on the plant remains in the peat was abundant seeds of a bulrush species (*Schoenoplectus lacustris* ssp *tabernaemontani*) of a type normally found in coastal locations in brackish waters, and, therefore, indicating local brackish conditions (Pearson 2005, 12).

Aside from any uncertainties about the interpretation of the results of this work, the fact that there are well preserved profiles through peat deposits of early prehistoric date at Impney means this must be a key site in the region for understanding the environmental context of the Mesolithic period. This is particularly the case as a period of approximately 1000 years was represented by a relatively deep formation of peat, and there is a further 0.85m of even earlier peat below the level dated to the 8th millennium BC.

Looking more widely Mesolithic flint scatters have also proved to be a feature along the Salwarpe tributaries in Dodderhill, including well to the north at Kennets Hall (Fig 8), and such

Figure 8 Mesolithic flint core from Kennets Hall; used to produce small parallel-sided flakes for the manufacture of microliths for a multiplicity of applications (photograph by D Hurst)

widespread evidence for this usually elusive period may suggest a higher than usual population in a favoured area for hunting.

Neolithic/Bronze Age

Elsewhere across Dodderhill parish a scatter of worked flint has been noted (Fig 9), with heavier concentrations (ie WSM 27159, 27163; Fig 4) sometimes occurring, including on the edge of Droitwich, usually in close proximity to the River Salwarpe and its small tributaries (eg Salty Brook); while blank areas (eg WSM 27162, 27165) have also been noted suggesting, therefore, that the denser scatters might indicate significant evidence for early activity/occupation. A possible early Bronze Age funerary barrow was noted on the Stoke Lane excavation site but discounted as being too small (Jones and Evans 2006; see also below), and a single sherd of possible Bronze Age pottery (?fabric 6; Hurst & Rees 1992) has been noted from a site along Crutch Lane (WSM 27163).

Long distance routes in this period are often identified as following the higher ground, thereby avoiding the wetter ground in the valleys and allowing easier movement, and just such a ridgeway may have traversed Dodderhill from the south-west to north-east. Generally worked flint would be expected in association, and this has been noted in Dodderhill, but, because of the general prevalence of flint in the area, no special significance could be attached in this case. Perhaps a ridgeway such as this should be a focus for future study, to see if it was really associated with heightened levels of prehistoric activity.

Figure 9 Mesolithic/early Neolithic flint core from fieldwalking at Astwood (WSM 35082) (photograph by D Hurst)

Later prehistoric (Iron Age; *c* 800 BC–AD 43)

Following a period of climatic deterioration in the later Bronze Age (Burgess 1974) cold/wet conditions prevailed in the Iron Age until *c* 150 BC (Lamb 1995). Then a gradual warming of the climate began, which would have been favourable to agriculture, and could have stimulated food production. With the increasing availability of iron better implements could also be made, which may have also aided food production, and so this period is generally thought to have been a time when population increased, eventually to such an extent that it led to tension, the results of which are now still visible in the landscape in the shape of the hillforts often thought of as characterising this period.

The Iron Age provides the earliest certain occupation sites that have yet been identified in Dodderhill, though not earlier than about the 2nd century BC. It is quite difficult to interpret this evidence at the Stoke Lane site (WSM 29599; Jones and Evans 2006) on the south side of Wychbold village, as so little of the site was dug and it could be argued that the excavation strategy was flawed if the objective was to gain as great an understanding as possible from such a rare discovery. It seems this small settlement had existed for some years as the houses (Fig 10), which were built in the typical roundhouse style of the period, were renewed several times; few other features were recorded in the part-excavated rectangular enclosure within which the main structures sat. A small ring-ditch of 6.5m internal diameter could not be assigned a contemporary function by the excavators; it is possible that such a feature marks an Iron Age burial mound, and a similar feature has now also been recorded near Bewdley (Hurst et al 2010). However, so little of the site was excavated that the small amount of finds could well be very misleading; the limited data indicated that occupation commenced in about the 2nd century BC and it is taken to have continued into the late Iron Age.

Other Iron Age activity has been recorded on the hill of Dodderhill itself, where there was a cluster of shallow pits and postholes on the hillside to the east of the church (McAvoy 2006, 3–7) associated with briquetage (ceramic material relating to salt; usually fragments of container). Though interpreted as evidence for salt making there were none of the storage tanks nor clear evidence for heating seen elsewhere, so perhaps this is better interpreted as settlement, though no definite building was identified. The dating here rests on a single sherd, and the generally small amount of material may suggest a relatively short period of activity.

Figure 10 Penannular drainage gully encircling a roundhouse (excavated with baulks of fill remaining) at Stoke Lane; one side of entrance showing in foreground right (photograph by C Bowers)

Salt production

Some evidence of Iron Age salt making was recovered from the base of the river valley below Dodderhill where a possible hearth was located at Upwich (Hurst & Hemingway 1997, 9), though the best evidence for this industry lies just outside Dodderhill parish on the south bank of the river (eg Woodiwiss 1992). Despite the generally large scale of salt production in the Droitwich area, there is locally, so far, surprisingly little indication of contemporary habitation, apart from a possible roundhouse at Bays Meadow (Barfield 2006, 93), prompting the idea that salt making was a seasonal activity carried out by workers who normally lived elsewhere. The only site that, on current evidence, seems to present a case for dense occupation is at the fortified hilltop site at Hanbury; where, for instance, just a single small trench revealed multiple features (Cook et al 1998). However, care must be paid to attaining more precise refinement to the dating of any Iron Age activity, which is otherwise too broad to be of use for establishing any other than a very broad chronological sequence. Currently much of the Iron Age activity described here seems to be from the later middle Iron Age (3rd/2nd century BC) onwards, which does not obviously tally with the evidence from consumer sites which show Droitwich salt arriving from earlier in this period (see below). On the face of it this suggests that there is still much more to learn about the prehistoric production of salt in the Droitwich area.

Despite the difficulties of understanding how Iron Age society of the area was organised during this period it is clear there was some engagement in highly productive industrial activity, which resulted in a widely 'traded' commodity, salt. The salt quantities must have been considerable, and its distribution was extensive (Morris 1985), since it can been mapped through the presence of the ceramic salt containers (briquetage; Fig 11) found at consumer sites, providing one of the best examples of evidence for industry and product distribution for the period.

In fact Dodderhill seems to have been situated in an area where Iron Age industry and trade were well developed from the beginning of the middle Iron Age (ie 4th century BC). Just adjacent, Droitwich has revealed a wider than usual range of ordinary domestic pottery types (Morris 1992) confirming its widespread contacts through salt. However, the presence of this domestic material here is quite problematic in the light of the poor evidence for occupation. Various scenarios are possible. Possibly people came from far and wide to make their own salt, or, more likely, to collect it, and so brought local pottery with them in their baggage which they were happy to leave behind once they were loaded with salt for the return trip. Traders carrying the salt from Droitwich out into the region are perhaps the least likely, given the present evidence, as there would be little point to their bringing other pottery back to Droitwich when this was already readily available locally, as shown by other sites in the wider region of the middle Severn valley.

Figure 11 Late prehistoric ceramic salt container (briquetage) from Droitwich; used to package the salt, and as found at consumer sites (copyright of Worcestershire County Council)

Other Iron Age activity in Dodderhill

A watching brief on a pipeline (1990–2) heading north-eastwards from Astwood, on the face of it, found little. In Astwood only two sherds of Iron Age pottery were produced and these were only tentatively identified as being of this date (Morris 1994, 177). Elsewhere, in north Worcestershire (eg Dinn & Hemingway 1992), similar survey on large infrastructure projects, has drawn a blank in identifying Iron Age settlement and any obvious signs of associated agricultural activity. Such outcomes tend to indicate little contemporary arable agriculture in this area, and possibly indicates that pastoral farming was dominant. Extensive fieldwalking during the project has not increased the number of Iron Age sites in Dodderhill, though there is the extra difficulty of locating such sites this way because associated pottery may be dark-coloured and friable. Aerial photography may have located another, possibly contemporary, settlement site (WSM 2171) just in Hanbury parish; this has many similarities to the Stoke Lane site suggesting that rather isolated (enclosed) farmsteads may be locally the primary type of rural settlement at this time. Taking all the evidence together it presently seems increasingly likely that sites of this date are relatively infrequent in this part of the county.

In the tribal context of late Iron Age Britain central Worcestershire is considered most likely to have been within the territory of the Dobunni, usually regarded as having a centre at Bagendon (near Cirencester, Gloucestershire), as coin minting equipment has been discovered there.

However, the situation seen through coinage really only reflects the last generation or so of the Iron Age, and may not necessarily reflect earlier political arrangements, especially if the emergence of coinage itself reflects deliberate political affirmation. Accordingly the socio-political context of the impressive Iron Age sites built earlier in the Iron Age in this region cannot be stated with any certainty, though it is clear that, however such sites as the great hillforts came into being, they indicate great forces at work in society. Hanbury is the nearest such monument to Dodderhill, and was presumably a key site in this area for at least part of the Iron Age; the further select investigation of such sites is necessary for advancing the better understanding of this period.

Late Iron Age coins for the first time provide us with historical evidence for the political situation, a generation or so before Roman invasion. Several Iron Age coins found in the local area do indeed reveal a Dobunnic allegiance, and confirm that it lay within the territory of this tribe. And since we know that Droitwich salt was enjoying widespread distribution in this period, the apparent lack of coins from other tribes may suggest that its salt was largely supplied to people within this one territory by the time of the later Iron Age. Taken together with other contemporary finds of coins (all also of Dobunnic type) to the east of Droitwich, specifically in the vicinity of Hanbury, these could all be taken as a relative concentration of such finds, the only other area of Worcestershire where this clustering of coins occurs being the central south and south-east parts of the county (source: WHER). Any interpretation, however, remains currently problematic.

Roman (AD 43–410) (*by Derek Hurst*)

The conquest of Britain was initiated by the emperor Claudius in AD 43, just as the Roman empire was expanding finally towards its maximum extent. Some southern British tribes were already allied with Rome and so the advancing armies would have made plenty of ground before they encountered any real resistance. In the very broad direction of Dodderhill substantial resistance seems to have been in the South-West (archaeological evidence) and towards Wales (documentary evidence). However, there seems little reason to envisage native Dobunnic resistance since no hillfort in this region has yet shown definite evidence of a Roman assault; it should be noted in this context that the dating of the 'massacre deposit' in the entrance-way to Kemerton camp hillfort on Bredon Hill is by no means proven, though the 1938 report places the event in the context of the Roman invasion. Generally the more recent available evidence is that settlements already functioning in the later Iron Age, such as at Stoke Lane in Dodderhill (Jones and Evans 2006), carried on uninterruptedly into the Roman era (see more below).

New roads were quickly constructed, initially for military purposes, and these carved their way past Droitwich heading northwards on the way to either Greensforge (Crutch Lane; Fig 12) or Metchley (Birmingham; A38) forts; and eastwards (Hanbury Road) on the way to Alcester (Warks) also possibly a place with military origins, and southwards to Kingsholm fort (Gloucester; A38). Another road considered generally to be of Roman origin was a loop that bypassed Droitwich on the east side of Dodderhill parish (B4091; Margary 1973, 284). This system of roads meant that some much older routes, often routes following ridgeways, as possibly in the case of Dodderhill, were largely supplanted.

Archaeologically ancient roads have been little excavated as they often remain in use today. However, in Dodderhill a section has been observed across the Crutch Lane Roman road in *c* 1970 in the vicinity of Dodderhill School; this was incomplete but showed that the road surface was at least 24 feet (8m) wide and that side ditches were present for drainage, a mixture of clay and small stones being used for the metalling (Bond & Babb 1971) – the same road was observed at Chaddesley Corbett, north of Dodderhill, to be fully 34 feet (10.4m) wide (Margary 1973). Where observed by Bond & Babb (1971) undated pits were found under the road suggesting that the road had potentially obliterated pre-existing features – perhaps the M5 was not the first such road scheme to pass through the area!

Two well-dated early Roman sites were entirely Roman in origin, and were both constructed by the military. The earliest, that predates the main Roman road north of Droitwich (later A38), was a (marching) camp (Hurst *et al* 1988; Fig 13). Such a site would only have been occupied for a very short time, possibly just overnight, while

Figure 12 View northwards along Roman road at Crutch Hill (photograph by D Hurst)

the unit was en route elsewhere, presumably in this case heading northwards. It may well have been the first appearance of the Roman army in the area as part of the advance to secure the conquest of Britain. The first stage of this campaign was marked by the strategy of establishing a network of legionary bases and other forts, and the Droitwich camp may well represent one of the troop movements when pushing forward from these secure positions.

Slightly later in date, a Roman fort occupied the hilltop on Dodderhill (St Joseph 1938; Whitehouse 1962), and this was established sometime under the rule of the emperor Nero, the excavated finds suggesting that its garrison was present in the years c AD 61–8 (McAvoy 2006). This may represent consolidation of the area after the failed uprising of Queen Boudicca of the Iceni (East Anglia); though it is also possible that the fort represents special protection of the salt production area (see more below). In plan Dodderhill fort is an unusual construction, as it has offset entrances and the regular playing-card fort plan has been adapted to the shape of the hill. These characteristics have been taken to indicate the identity of the unit which may well have been part of the 14th legion (*Legio XIV*). The layout of the twin rampart defences has also been taken to indicate that the garrison had a contingent of archers and so this would have been an auxiliary fort (*ibid*). Its internal area of about 6 acres suggests that it was home to about 500 soldiers.

Figure 13 Early Roman marching camp opposite Chateau Impney: north-east corner of camp, cut by A38 (photograph by W A Baker)

The Roman soldiers on Dodderhill enjoyed a life-style which was supported by a well-organised military system of provisioning, as they used, for instance, pottery vessels that were distinctly different types to those used by the local population (Fig 14). Through their quartermaster they had access to wine (imported in amphorae of which pieces were found), and so their remoteness from the Mediterranean world did not mean deprivation of its pleasures. The only concession to use of local ceramics was that the soldiers resorted to using local cooking pots, presumably because these were hidden away in the kitchen, and so did not, therefore, interfere with the display of superior equipment which went with Roman soldiering. Acquiring these pots locally may also have saved the soldiers from having to carry such heavy items in their kit when they moved.

Soldiers stationed for a while must have meant a good supply of coinage for the local

Figure 14 Roman soldiers parading at Wychbold (The Roman Military Research Society) (photograph by C Bowers)

economy, which previously had been largely based on barter, as the native late Iron Age coinage had mainly been high denomination gold and silver issues, and may have been used for specific social purposes rather than for general exchange. The use of Roman coins for everyday transactions would have served to stimulate trade, and might have helped to bring together traders into the Droitwich area making it a ready focus for settlement. Peaceable interaction with the local population seems likely, since overall there are few Roman forts known in Worcestershire, and none superimposed on Iron Age hillfort sites (as in Dorset for instance), and there is no evidence for local conflict in the invasion period (as, for instance, at South Cadbury hillfort in Somerset). However, too little is yet known about the condition of local society immediately prior to AD 43 to judge why the presence of the alien Roman force was apparently so readily accepted; it is just possible that this was seen by some as an opportunity to replace an unpopular local aristocracy and also participate in a society offering a better future.

In fact in Worcestershire it is possible to perceive a rapid acceptance of goods in a thorough-going Roman style with the rapid establishment and success of a new pottery venture based in the north Malverns area. This turned out large quantities of pottery vessels in a wide range of new shapes (usually referred to today as Severn Valley ware), and helpfully to the archaeologist the new colour of preference was bright orange. The large quantities and bright colour of this material makes Roman sites much more visible to the fieldwalker than sites of earlier date, and marks a departure from the rather sombre tone of much previous pottery. But, at the same time, there is also much continuity from the pre-Roman period, and small farmsteads continued much the same without any new building in the radically different Roman style and materials, though possibly because the expertise to build in any new way was not yet accessible rather than out of any antipathy towards Rome. The Roman state now levied taxes to pay for the military occupation, and carrying through the process of Romanisation of the province of Britannia, and so financial pressures on the vanquished must have been considerable, the impacts of which will have depended on the general state of the economy and the levels of funding needed to maintain instruments of state such as the standing army.

The character of civilian settlement in Worcestershire during the Roman period is still to be established with greater certainty. At the present, evidence suggests that it varied in character across the county. South Worcestershire eventually, probably in the later 3rd–4th centuries, achieved a high level of villa estates presumably based on successful cereal farming, and more in keeping with the character of Roman settlement on the Cotswolds. Further north into central Worcestershire economic activity remained predominantly agricultural, except that industry marked out some places, for instance ceramic production at the north end of the Malverns, iron smelting in Worcester, and salt making at Droitwich, with the consequent heavy demands for fuel, especially firewood. Here small farmsteads, and related field systems, seem to be the principal signs of life in the countryside, but these have only relatively rarely been encountered giving an impression of thin settlement. Almost in contradiction of this the widespread occurrence of Roman pottery suggests that agricultural activity was fairly general. However, once again it is difficult to chart agricultural trends through a major period, as data is presently not amenable to close questioning; though some expansion of arable is likely to have followed the adoption of more efficient Roman farming equipment and methods, especially under the incentive of taxation. The impression of low population levels in the central Worcestershire countryside (small single farmsteads and occasionally more developed sites of unclear function; see below) might suggest a heavier reliance on pastoral farming, but the extent of arable farming achieved in the medieval period by a relatively low population should also be borne in mind, especially under the impetus of population growth and favourable economic circumstances in peaceful conditions.

Using the new roads would have made it easier to reach more distant places, and must have opened up fresh opportunities for commerce, presumably vitalising markets, where transactions could also now be quickly done in coin. It is presently unclear that this resulted in reaching more distant markets, except in exceptional cases such as where the local Severn Valley ware pottery was being delivered to the military on the Antonine Wall (Scotland; Webster 1977). Markets are usually assumed to have been centred on the main towns, though in the absence of any identified market places at Droitwich or Worcester (the 'forum' of the more major Roman town, the nearest of which was at Gloucester), this cannot yet be readily confirmed – though large numbers of coins at the Bays Meadow villa might suggest that it functioned as a market-place. However, it is clear that incoming goods from other areas in the Midlands, and even from much further afield including the Continent, were now available, and so local industries must have been faced with competition from further afield than before. Former political boundaries evaporated and barriers based on tribal affiliations were apparently removed, so that a more cosmopolitan style emerged, though, as stated above, the area still had its own regional character, including its own distinctive products, in addition to more subtle variations in rural and urban life-styles.

Mediterranean Roman civilisation was essentially urbanised, with the countryside ideally being seen as either the preserve of the rich landowner, or of the plantation-style farmer using slave labour; Roman Britain generally developed its own hybrid style of Romanisation, and the latter was more evident in the town than the countryside. To experience the fuller flowering of Roman life some distance had to be covered, and the aspiring Dodderhill Romano-phile would have had to have travelled as far as Wroxeter, Gloucester, or especially Cirencester, where large public buildings and facilities (such as public baths) were available, including at the latter public entertainment at the amphitheatre. In the case of Droitwich the convergence of Roman roads was more to do with the manufacture and distribution of salt than with bringing the traveller to any new attractions, but it could also have served to facilitate the collection of taxes at a central place.

It is still quite difficult to bring Roman civilian life in the countryside of Dodderhill into focus. The best place to start is the former Iron Age site at Stoke Lane (Jones and Evans 2006), which may have continued to be occupied into the Roman period, though the evidence from the main enclosure is not so very convincing. Most of the Roman pottery from the vicinity of the occupation area comes from the tops of features, so the occupation could well have ended in the Iron Age with the Roman pottery arriving through subsequent agricultural activity. More clearly of Roman date was the laying out of new long ditches radiating from the old Iron Age enclosure showing that this focus for farming remained visible in the landscape. However, these new boundary ditches were relatively ephemeral, compared with the size and depth of the Iron Age enclosure ditch. The new Roman road (now the A38) passed by the site just to the west on a completely different alignment to these boundaries revealing its intrusion into an earlier landscape. Interestingly, field boundaries in the area today are much more in alignment with the Roman road suggesting that any earlier orientation of fields was eventually totally replaced. The impression of a wider farmed landscape by this period is supported by pollen evidence from relic channel deposits of the Body Brook by Impney (Mann 2007), which suggests that clearance of all trees had taken place by the 1st/early 2nd century AD in some parts of the Dodderhill area.

Salt, being such a useful substance at the time, is likely to have continued to have been made regardless of the turmoil of invasion. The excavations at Upwich (in Vines Park) in 1983–4 revealed a large tank (Fig 15), the planks lining its sides having been hewn from trees felled in about AD 61–5 (Hemingway and Hurst 1997), a date which corresponds very well with that of the occupation of the Dodderhill fort. The tank was most probably used for the collection and purification of the brine being extracted from the nearby springs, and, on the face of it, this might be taken to imply clear army involvement in salt production. However, the archaeological sequence suggests these planks were reused in their final position in the early 2nd century, and so it may just have been material scavenged from the nearby fort long after its desertion. Therefore, it remains unclear whether the Roman military took an active interest in the salt production. Though like other mineral resources the salt springs would presumably have been confiscated by the Roman state, and would then normally have been handed over, at a price, to a private entrepreneur to profit from, if not worked directly.

Figure 15 Large tank at Upwich in the early Roman period; post and horizontal plank construction against an earth bank forming the tank sides (copyright of Worcestershire County Council)

The Roman role of the main brine springs at Upwich became clearer with the 19th century discovery of a villa complex nearby (Fig 16). Though now just outside the Dodderhill parish boundary, the Roman villa at Bays Meadow probably housed the franchisee assigned by the Roman state to exploit the salt making (WSM 678; Barfield 2006), and so it is likely that the occupants of this building dictated the course of Roman Droitwich (its Roman name being *Salinae*, literally 'the salt-works'). Up to the middle of the 2nd century, when this villa was built, it seems the salt business had been run by an absentee entrepreneur. Then the most lavish building was erected in proper Mediterranean Roman style, and apparently no expense was spared. For the next century and a half it seems to have prospered and several exceptional and high quality finds confirm this (*ibid*). The delay in its appearance until the mid 2nd century may have given time for the market to have become more fully developed together with the money economy. Great wealth could then be more easily realised. Though, so far, it has proved difficult to locate the area of contemporary salt production, which seems, therefore, to have been relocated away from where much of this had been carried out in the Iron Age.

Figure 16 Bays Meadow villa at Droitwich (land later in Droitwich St Nicholas parish) (copyright of Worcestershire County Council)

Despite the difficulty in identifying Roman salt-making features it is clear that activity continued at the villa and also, opposite, on the south bank of the River Salwarpe, where a trackway and buildings have been excavated (Woodiwiss 1992). But there were signs of trouble by the end of the 3rd century when the main villa building was burnt. This occurred after ditch and rampart defences had been built around it suggesting that its owners had had some warning and felt sufficiently vulnerable to erect major defences. It is note-worthy that such defences have not been seen at other Roman sites in this area, and so the burning of the main villa building could be interpreted as an expression of anti-Roman feeling aimed at the most obvious symbol of Rome in the area. If so, it was not very successful, as a new large building was erected (interestingly in a new style, which was, arguably, more of a hydrid of native and Roman).

The numerous artefacts of this period certainly indicate that people were now living in the vicinity of where Droitwich was later established, and occupation included domestic grain processing alongside the new road (now A38; Hughes 2006). So far the evidence points to the south side of the River Salwarpe as the main focus beyond the villa for civilian settlement. However, formal burials occurred on the north side of the river; two inhumation burials at The Gardeners Arms (WSM 4093) and a small inhumation cemetery a little distance further west (WSM 6000) may mark a large cemetery at this location, and may indicate that Vines Lane was also originally a Roman road, as Roman cemeteries were usually situated alongside roads. Radiocarbon dating of one burial suggested this was of very latest Roman or early post-Roman date.

Occupation at the Bays Meadow villa lasted well into the 4th century, when the site was finally totally deserted. Curiously at a later date the boundary of Dodderhill parish, which was to include the core of the Wychbold estate and, therefore, the next seat of local administration, seems to have deliberately excluded the old villa site, which must still have been quite evident as an earthwork.

Most of the Roman activity described above was located at the extreme south end of Dodderhill parish, which might be as expected given that this was the area of the nascent salt industry, and this has been a primary focus of archaeological endeavour. In order to balance this the Dodderhill Parish Survey Project has deliberately attempted to look beyond and into the surrounding Romano-British countryside, and the results of field survey during this project hopefully provide an inkling of this wider landscape. The following is a summary of these results based on, firstly, the investigation of a small farmstead at Ford Cottages and, secondly, an overview of all the fieldwork data relevant to the Roman period.

Ford Cottages site (WSM 27163, 34766 etc) and its environs (especially WSM 38360, 38361)

Fieldwalking and geophysical survey have demonstrated a small farmstead location just east of Ford Cottages (Hurst 2010b; Fig 17). Dating of the pottery indicates the site was occupied from the mid 1st century AD right through to the second half of the 4th century (Roman pottery concentration of 0.268 sherds/m^2). There was a wide variety of pottery, including imported samian (tableware from Roman Gaul) and Black-burnished (cooking) wares (from Dorset), the former usually regarded as a marker for a more Romanised outlook and eating habits, in common with the mortaria (mixing bowls) also present. However,

Figure 17 Fieldwalking in progress in 2005 (WSM 34766) (photograph by D Hurst)

the bulk of the regular pottery in use was the local Severn Valley ware, its range of food preparation, storage and eating vessels covering most other domestic requirements. Imported amphora, generally rare in the West Midlands, occurred in a small quantity.

The next field to the south (WSM 38361) also contained Roman finds but at lower concentration (average sherd density was now down to 0.013 sherds/m^2). This pattern of distribution was entirely compatible with this material being derived from the farmstead site to the immediate north-east. Again, where dating was possible, this generally fell as later 1st/2nd–3rd century. This scattering is usually attributed to the spreading of domestic waste from an associated farm-yard midden into the surrounding arable fields.

Continuing southwards into the next field there was a clear impression that the spread of material was still emanating from the same occupation site, the concentration of Roman pottery dropping again (WSM 38360; 0.0011 sherds/m^2). An unusual find here was a large piece from a flat circular ceramic plate (Fig 18; c 270mm diameter) made in the Malvern area, and probably representing a specific method of cooking in a small clay oven. Finally, a geophysical survey was carried out in both fields (GSB 2009) and this did not reveal any obvious features confirming the interpretation of the fieldwalked finds as representing a scatter from a single centre. Furthermore, in this vicinity, scatters of Roman pottery were also relatively sparse to the west of Crutch Lane (eg WSM 27161, 27165) with the same farmstead possibly implicated as the main source.

Figure 18 Piece of circular ceramic baking plate of Roman date found during fieldwalking (WSM 38360) (photograph by D Hurst)

Other possible Roman settlement – fieldwalking evidence

Of the other fields fieldwalked during this project only one other area produced any significant quantity of Roman finds which could be taken to be indicative of settlement (ie WSM 33345). Elsewhere quantities could be very low, for instance in the Rashwood (WSM 42423, 42424) and the Astwood (eg WSM 33826/32999) areas, the latter confirmed by test pits at Astwood New House (Hurst 2010). Even where considerable excavation has taken place at Impney very few Roman finds have been noted and only one possible feature of this date (Griffin *et al* 1999). A small amount of early Roman pottery was suggestive of occupation at Crutch Farm where mid–late 1st century drinking vessels were noted (Blewitt 2002). Extrapolating from such an incomplete and random survey is fraught with difficulty, but it does seem, on present evidence, that there were relatively few Roman occupation sites in the general neighbourhood.

Comparison with Hanbury

Comparison with fieldwork data from the adjacent parish of Hanbury is instructive as once again Roman finds were very widespread, though here usually at very low concentrations. As in Hanbury imported (samian ware) and regional pottery (Black-burnished ware) and mortaria (mixing bowls taken to be highly indicative of Roman cuisine) were all found at Dodderhill in the usual small quantities compared with the ubiquitous Severn Valley ware, the latter being local to the area and available in a wide range of forms (accounting for 85% and 88–98% of the Roman pottery assemblage at Dodderhill and Hanbury respectively).

At Hanbury a total of twenty Roman sherds was taken to indicate a likely occupation area (Dyer 1991, 16), which seems very low as a threshold to defining settlement. With due consideration, in Dodderhill a much higher threshold was thought better for determining settlement sites, and this was set at about 20–25 sherds per 1000m^2 (equivalent to about 100 sherds per acre) with a minimum assemblage size of about 75–100 sherds. A similar figure emerged (unpublished data) from fieldwalking over a Roman villa near Broadway (Childswickham; Patrick & Hurst 2004). On this basis only two sites emerge as settlement sites in Dodderhill area (east of Crutch Lane at WSM 34766 and on the east side of Wychbold village at WSM 33345). This tends to further confirm a landscape that was seemingly, at the time, only sparsely populated.

In Hanbury all the Roman sites eventually succumbed to desertion, and in Dodderhill this pattern was also the case, with no sure indication that occupation continued beyond the end of the 4th century. The presumed farm to the east of Crutch Lane had been a fixture in the landscape for at least 300 years (possibly 10 generations) and had been proven to be a good site with adjacent water and on a south-facing slope so as to enjoy the sun to the maximum. The earlier finds here of Mesolithic and Bronze Age date tend to reinforce this picture of a favoured situation. At a time when food supply should have been as much a priority as usual, if not more so with the withdrawal of Roman authority and protection, the sudden termination of this settlement exudes a rather sinister air.

Overview of fieldwork results

The more definite of the Roman farmstead sites (WSM 27163) was set well back off a Roman road and was relatively isolated, with any other site at a minimum of c 1km away (at least on the same side of the road). It is also striking that areas just beyond the central area of Roman Droitwich were apparently without obvious evidence for more intensive use at least on the north and east sides of Droitwich (ie where evidence is available).

Roman pottery was found on eighteen out of twenty-one sites and was, therefore, present at most sites (85%) where fieldwork took place (eg Fig 19). Two possible sites of occupation were recognised, one of which was confirmed by geophysical survey. These results suggest that Roman occupation was sparse in Dodderhill, whereas the extensive scattering of Roman pottery tends, in contrast, to suggest that contemporary arable agriculture was very widespread; though of course, given a span of

Figure 19 A typical array of fieldwalked pottery arranged in rows by date. Left to right: 19th/20th century, 17th/18th century, medieval (one sherd), Roman (four sherds), with other finds (all periods) at top, including clay pipe (photograph by D Hurst)

350 years, it is not clear how much land was actually under cultivation in any given year, or indeed whether pasture was also being manured periodically.

End of Roman Dodderhill

Returning to the wider picture, present evidence tends to suggest that the social and economic fabric of this part of Roman Britain received a severe set-back in c AD 300. In the Dodderhill area the most dramatic sign of this was the sudden destruction of the main villa building at Bays Meadow. It seems that there was a general breakdown in the Roman peace that accompanied the secession of Britain from the rest of the empire, though this was only temporary and, with the removal of the pretender Carausius, Britain was once again returned to its provincial status. Such troubles may well have disrupted agriculture and been a sign of things to come; natural woodland regeneration in Hanbury is considered to have taken place after the end of Roman Britain (Dyer 1991, 27), but possibly it commenced earlier, as there are few signs of any very late Roman pottery in the countryside hereabouts.

The degree of ultimate Romanisation of the area is in question, as for several generations following the conquest the preferred house style remained the prehistoric roundhouse with its thatched roof. Only the household clutter in it reflected a more Romanised outlook, and that may have been because the large-scale producers of objects such as pottery could more or less impose this through their dominance of markets. To truly adopt the Roman life-style (which was rather out of place in this rainy island anyway) required a substantial income and outlay, and perhaps it was aspired to by many but only achieved by few after generations of saving. The majority made do with the *pax Romana* which at least allowed them to carry on the daily grind without constant fear of assault and robbery, and may well have been an improvement over previous times when the hillforts at least give an appearance of endemic warfare. However, before the truth behind such monuments can be revealed much more archaeological investigation of the region needs to take place.

No Worcestershire Roman rural site has yet shown much continuity beyond c AD 400; instead new settlement sites appear with new styles of building (eg at Ripple; Barber & Watts 2008) and old sites, despite their apparent advantages were avoided (eg Bays Meadow villa), very possibly deliberately. Whereas after the disruption in the later 3rd century, a semblance of normality had eventually returned, Roman Britain, just a few generations later, finally came to a shuddering halt. Disruption seems to have been extreme, as long-occupied sites were abandoned, and the obvious signs of Roman civilisation evaporated. A period of great material prosperity was totally suspended and commonplace objects like pottery were now apparently in short supply. Any conventional assessment would conclude that standards of living had plummeted, and lives must have been totally reshaped in the process of this cultural transformation. The people of Dodderhill, like everyone else in the region, must have been swept along by this tide of change, and they must have been looking forward to the future with trepidation given all this disruption to their material lives.

Post-Roman and middle Saxon (AD 410–*c* 900)

The native Romano-British population in the Severn valley continued after the Roman departure without any serious disruption from Anglo-Saxon incursions until at least the 6th century and, though evidence is hard to come by, this has been demonstrated archaeologically at Wroxeter (White & Barker 1998). However, eventually, regardless of ethnic background, the material culture of the area, as elsewhere, reflects the new Anglo-Saxon outlook, and such evidence has been discovered at Upwich (Droitwich), where salt production was still being vigorously pursued (Hurst 1997a). During this time the area later known as Worcestershire formed part of an independent territory under the banner of the Hwicce (see Hooke, this volume), until it was eventually absorbed into the major English kingdom of Mercia in the mid Saxon period (by the 670s; Maddicott 2005, 26). By then even any lingering British (ie pre-Roman) or Roman cultural traits, as signified by speech and material culture, had become entirely transformed and were now purely Anglo-Saxon in character, and without any obvious local adaptation.

Some have seen the radical shift in language as a sign of the enslavement of most of the native British, or their prior flight (Coates 2007) when the Anglo-Saxon advance westwards reached this part of the country. If flight occurred it may have been over the River Severn and westwards, into areas where native British culture had probably remained strong even during the Roman period judging by the linguistic legacies there. More locally to Dodderhill, apart from at Droitwich, the impact of these momentous political and cultural changes, however brought about, remains unseen in the first decades after Roman withdrawal. Continuity of salt making at Droitwich may suggest that the countryside roundabouts continued to be farmed, but, in that case, apparently from different locations yet to be discovered, again signifying major change. The recent surprise find of probably 6th century pottery in the top of a Roman ditch just beyond Droitwich to the south (WSM 42444), indicates a domestic presence in the vicinity, though also perhaps the failure to maintain the Roman landscape, since the Roman drainage ditches were now silted up.

Just beyond the south-east boundary of Dodderhill there may be a clue preserved in a place-name to what happened to some of the original British inhabitants. In Hanbury the place-name 'Walmer' (literally 'the pool of the Welsh'; Dyer 1991, 20) is suggestive of a surviving enclave of British who seem to be living remotely from any larger settlements (it is situated on the edge of both Wychbold and Hanbury), and possibly on poor land, which had not yet been drained for agriculture. This may imply some specific survival of the original population by taking refuge on the poorest land in order to leave the way open for the Anglo-Saxon war-lords – certainly the display of weapons was a feature of those few sites in the area where burials have been investigated (eg Beckford; Evison & Hill 1996), though as yet the ethnic background of such individuals has not been determined. But it has also been observed that *walh* communities were almost invariably associated with estate centres, and has been suggested (Hooke forthcoming) that they had a special role within the estate structure. The only British name to come through this period is Crutch (Welsh *crug* (barrow) or its Brittonic source), which was attached to the most striking landmark in Dodderhill; its solitary survival is testimony to the otherwise overwhelming nature of the eventual Anglo-Saxon presence.

Anglo-Saxon 'grass' tempered sherds were reported from the site of the Roman fort but on checking the project archive the relevant sherds could not be located – only four sherds seem to be concerned and they were interpreted as the last identifiable evidence for post-Roman agriculture since they were found in the tops of Roman features. At Upwich such pottery seemed to have a *terminus post quem* date of *c* 6th century AD (Hurst & Hemingway 1997, 24; Lentowicz 1997), where it was found in association with brine-boiling hearths.

Salt manufacture can be seen to have continued in this period in the vicinity of Upwich, which was the principal brine well of later periods. As a result some of the best Anglo-Saxon remains so far excavated in Worcestershire form part of the history of Dodderhill. These are the hearths used to boil brine arranged in an orderly fashion along the original north bank of the River Salwarpe (Hurst & Hemingway 1997; Fig 20).

Figure 20 Brine-boiling hearth at Upwich of early/middle Saxon date (copyright of Worcestershire County Council)

By the 7th century the ownership of some large tracts of land in the vicinity begins for the very first time to be revealed in pious royal gestures associated with the foundation of a minster church. In 657–74 a huge estate at Hanbury was granted to Abbot Colman (a Celtic name) and was probably part of an existing royal estate covering a large part of north-east Worcestershire (Dyer 1991, 19) with associated salt rights perhaps proportional to the extent of its woodland.

Salt production in *Wic*(h) (ie Droitwich), including presumably at Upwich (then known as the 'great pit or well' when first mentioned in 691; Finberg 1972, 86), seems to have been prospering at the end of the 7th century into the 8th century, as the Mercian kings granted salt rights to more new monasteries of the area (including at Worcester and Evesham). Such generous gifts served to bind Church and State together, but practically it may also have served to take pressure off royal woodland, as well as expanding the industry in the process, as the king may not have necessarily reduced his own exploitation of the brine at the same time.

Wicbold was first mentioned in a charter dated AD 692 (Finberg 1972, 87), when there was an assignment of land there by King Aethelred of Mercia to Oslaf, a former thane and now a monk at the church of Worcester. By 716/17 land of Worcester church on the north side of the river Salwarpe (?Upwich) was being exchanged with the Mercian king for land for new salt production (salt-making houses) on the other side (Finberg 1972, 90), perhaps suggesting that Upwich had become separated from the adjacent Wychbold, and perhaps now was being re-united. *Wic* was presumably already taking shape with new buildings spreading across the ruins of the Roman remains.

That *Wicbold* retained the *Wic* connection inherent in its name is shown by the special status of its being recognised as a royal vill by the early 9th century (Maddicott 2005, 32); and the royal witan met here on occasion. A royal residence may well reflect the special attention that the Mercian kings gave to salt production here, which could be seen as a deliberate policy where economic growth is now being based on production of commodities and their toll in preference to war and distribution of booty (Maddicott 2005, 8).

Various elements of the Dodderhill landscape had also emerged by the 8th century: Hen Brook, Sharpway, and Piper's Hill (*langandune*, literally 'the long hill'; Stoke Prior charter). It is noticeable that Hanbury, Stoke Prior and Dodderhill each have part of the latter hill which is the highest area in their territory, suggesting that agreements had been reached in the distant past to share equitably the natural landscape resources in the region. There was also a reference to a 'wheat clearing' (or wood) at the bottom of the *sceap weg* on the Stoke side, with 'hollow way' (Hooke 1990, 66) being a reference to the adjacent Roman road (now B4091); the latter would only have been so-named after its Roman construction had become worn out, as now it was presumably carved deep into the landscape through heavy use and lack of maintenance of the original metalling. This road might stand as a metaphor for the state of the Roman legacy in the area, which might have stood intact sufficiently to shape the new era, but, without maintenance, finally crumbled away.

By 836 the Mercian kings were trying to take back some of their former generous gifts, as Wiglaf, king of the Mercians, negotiated with Hanbury monastery for the surrender of some of its lands in return for freedom from impositions such as feeding the king and his servants (Dyer 1991, 19) and the maintenance of the royal palace (?at Wychbold). In passing there is a reference to the still wooded character of the area surrounding Hanbury which would have extended westwards into Dodderhill. Rather than now fostering industry through gifts to others there seems to have been a realisation that valuable resources had been too easily released from royal hands in earlier days; now that the country was coming under Viking attack no doubt resources were needed back in royal hands so that they could be directed to guarding against this dangerous new foe.

This era may have been accompanied by woodland clearance and some expansion of arable farming in the middle Salwarpe valley above Droitwich as the salt-making centre was devastated by flooding and deep deposition of mud in the 7th/8th century (Hurst & Hemingway 1997, 28), the classic cause of which being poorly managed arable cultivation leading to soil erosion. Incidentally this presumably gave rise to the naming of the river as 'the thrower up of yellow-brown material' (or the Salwarpe as we now know it) implying that it was a major characteristic of the river to behave in this way. Since the river weaves through Wychbold/Dodderhill before reaching (Droit)Wich land management in this area could well have been heavily implicated in this event. Such disruption could have had serious consequences for the economy of the area, and this may be one reason why having a watchful official eye locally on the salt making might have seemed eminently sensible. It may have also encouraged the sinking of new brine wells just off the bottom of the river valley where the flooding was at its worst.

In the 9th century the royal residence at Wychbold was clearly now the hub of royal administration for the area, and decisions signed and sealed there could relate to distant property in the Thames valley (eg Gelling 1979, 104, no 207). Such a place would have been designed to serve as a point of assembly, as well as where taxes would be collected and administration was carried out; such a site would usually be identifiable from both documentary sources and/or from archaeological evidence. The latter would comprise the presence of a large, and, therefore impressive, hall, typically 18–30m in length and 6–9m wide, with the typical thatched roof of the period, and the principal structural elements being very substantial squared posts up to 0.6m across, and walls of either daub or planking, with the entrances being set centrally in the long sides of the building (English Heritage 1989). Other immediately adjacent buildings would usually indicate a settlement where the ordinary folk lived and worked. There could also be associated enclosures, including one enclosing the whole site. Sometimes, as at

Cheddar, a royal residence continued in use into the post-Conquest period, but elsewhere such sites were absorbed into later settlements after the high status of the palace was lost. These royal centres were usually placed in fairly low-lying locations, or on a hilltop overlooking a river next to good communications and on well-drained ground. Such sites are typically associated with higher numbers of finds than most other types of site of the same period, and this should mean they are prone to be discovered archaeologically.

Such sites often had a prehistoric and Roman phase, and even an Anglo-Saxon phase which was of 'normal' status, and at Cheddar the medieval church was closer to a former Roman villa site than to the mid Saxon palace. It has been noted elsewhere, including in the Severn valley, that high status later Saxon sites tend to be placed apart from, but in proximity to, the main settlement, as in the case of Kingsholm near Gloucester and at Holm Hill at Tewkesbury (Reynolds 2003). This generalised description of the location of such sites has several elements that are quite indicative of 'Dudra's hill' (Dodderhill) being a likely site for such a complex, however, as yet no clear clue as to the exact whereabouts of the royal residence has come to light. Few archaeological finds of the 8th–9th centuries have also come to light, apart from a silver penny of Alfred the Great minted c 875–80 found at Upwich (Lentowicz and Seaby 1997, 96; Fig 30), and possibly pottery.

The marketing of surplus salt would have stimulated economic activity across the region, as well as spurring on ancillary trades and rural fuel production to higher levels. Salt-ways emanated from the town from the later Saxon period testifying to the scale of salt production that was being achieved. Participation in this industry was a sign of royal favour and it enriched the institutions of both Church and State, and its commodity status invited the role of markets in the new towns that were soon to develop.

The early medieval landscape of the Droitwich to Bromsgrove region (*by* Della Hooke)

Early medieval/mid–late Anglo-Saxon territories

A folk region documented in part of north Worcestershire in the early medieval period was that of the *Husmeræ*, a people recorded in an 8th century charter, the focus of whose territory appears to have lain in the Stour valley close to Kidderminster. A second territory can be identified immediately to the east of this but it is not clear whether this also fell within the *Husmeræ* territory or that of another, unnamed, group (Fig 21). A landmark, *usan mere*, on the boundary of *Hellerelege* (Fig 25) suggests that both

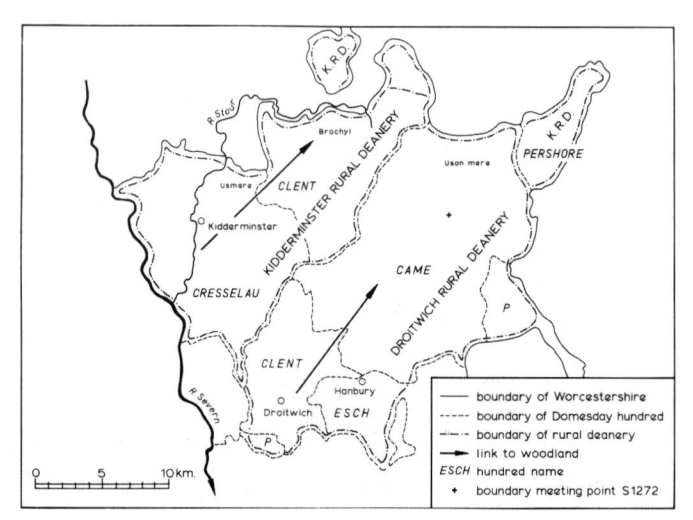

Figure 21 Territorial units in north Worcestershire (from Hooke 1985a, 81, fig 21)

belonged to the *Husmeræ*. Again this second territory had a riverine heartland drained by the River Salwarpe; Droitwich, Roman *Salinae* and, in the early medieval period, the chief inland salt producing area within England, had been established beside this river. It was within this region that Wychbold was located. These territories lay within the Anglo-Saxon kingdom of the Hwicce, itself focused upon the Severn basin, but by the 7th century this kingdom had been subsumed into Greater Mercia. The origins and extent of the Hwiccan kingdom have been discussed elsewhere (see Hooke 1985a) but it seems to have developed out of the late Iron Age territory of the Dobunni, and once extended further south-eastwards to include Wychwood, and southwards to include the region around Bath. Perhaps in compensation for these losses on its southern and eastern borders, its northern boundary seems to have been pushed north-eastwards, a kingdom boundary that became fossilised in that of the later diocesan boundary (*ibid*, 5–7, fig 2).

Within these folk regions, their territories perhaps in part fossilised in those of the later rural deaneries, central estate foci remained prominent (Hooke 1985a, 98). Just as an Anglo-Saxon minster was to be established at Ismere, probably the later Kidderminster, in the north-western *Husmeræ* territory, so also in the eastern folk territory a minster was to be established at Hanbury, located within the ramparts of an Iron Age hillfort (*ibid*, 91–2, fig 24). Such a location may have been a symbol of power within the new Christian/Anglo-Saxon administration. The royal centre, however, seems to have been located at Wychbold and the presence of a palace or assembly building is suggested by the fact that several charters were signed here (eg Sawyer 1983, 293, 298). Although a Mercian charter (Sawyer 1968, S 220) granting land in Hertfordshire was signed at a meeting of the *witan* (a public assembly) held at *Saltwic* in 888, seemingly referring to Droitwich, it is Wychbold in the parish of Dodderhill that was described as a royal *tun* in 815 and 831: one Mercian charter granting land in the district of Faversham in Kent was signed 'in vico regis qui dicitur Uuicbold' (S 178), and another granting land at Botwell in Middlesex was signed 'in regale villo quæ nominatur Wicbold' (S 188). These documents recorded the granting or leasing of rights over land and would have been signed in the presence of the king or his representatives and/or leading churchmen. The *bold* suffix of Wychbold might indicate a superior building. No signs of a palace building have, however, yet been found. Wychbold is literally 'building by or belonging to *Wich*', the latter either the 'dirty' or 'noble' *Wich* (or Droitwich, as named from the 14th century), alternatively referred to as *Saltwich* (Watts 2004, 705, 195). As a centre of salt production the place would indeed have been 'dirty'. Around and within Droitwich there were several identifiable and separate areas of salt making – including Netherwich, Middlewich and Upwich (Hooke 1981). The *wic* suffix itself refers to 'a place of trade' or 'a place with a specialised function', and so suits Droitwich very well. The brine here wells up naturally and was evaporated in leaden vats over wood-fuelled ovens.

Folk territories of the kind referred to above almost always included areas of complementary resources – apart from their more heavily cultivated heartlands they included more marginal regions which offered the valued resources of wood and pasture. These often lay some distance away but were linked by communication links that were often made up of drove-roads and it seems that at an early stage domestic stock may have been actually moved to seasonal pastures away from growing crops during the summer; in autumn distant woodlands provided mast (acorns) for fattening pigs (Hooke 2008b). Communications in this region ran from south-west to north-east, as did the Roman road from Worcester to Metchley (Birmingham). The minster of Ismere had rights in the woods of *brochyl*, possibly Brockhill near Wollescote in Old Swinford (Hooke 1990, 61–3; S 89), carrying its rights into the wooded Clent Hills, while those from the Droitwich area extended north-eastwards towards the Lickey Hills (Fig 22). The latter were clearly functioning up to the time of the Norman Conquest for the royal manor of Bromsgrove had been sending wood as fuel for the salt furnaces of Droitwich in exchange for salt: the manor receiving '300 mitts of salt, ... they [the salt-workers] used to be given 300 cartloads of wood by the keepers of the wood in the time of King Edward' (Domesday Book, fol. 172b, see Thorn & Thorn 1982). Wychbold sat at the centre of this exchange.

Figure 22 The uplands fringing the ?original northern border of the Hwiccan kingdom viewed from the Lickey Hills; view eastwards from Cofton Hill

Although Droitwich was the most important salt-producing centre in the early medieval period (Nantwich in Cheshire is a second centre appearing in later documents), Bromsgrove was the dominant manor in this region at the end of the early medieval/mid–late Anglo-Saxon period (Fig 23). Bromsgrove rarely appears in earlier charters although a charter of AD 804 (S 1187) expresses the intention of one Æthelric, son of Æthelmund, to bequeath a substantial holding of 11 hides located there and on the manor of Feckenham to the bishop of Worcester for life with, upon his death, reversion to the Church. Some years later (822 x 823) another charter (S 1432) records how King Ceolwulf of Mercia had requested that the land at Bromsgrove and Inkberrow should be returned by the community at Worcester. Before the Norman Conquest, Bromsgrove and Feckenham numbered among the possessions of Earl Edwin, some of whose holdings, at least, seem to have represented estates held by the earlier Hwiccan rulers (*VCH Worcestershire* III, 72). These charters give the earliest form of the name as *Bremesgraf*, 'Breme's grove'. Although a Worcester monk had allegedly claimed rights over Wychbold in AD 692, these were recorded in a charter (S 75) judged today to be spurious and, besides, Wychbold was described as a royal *tun* in the 9th century where several royal charters were signed (see below). Nevertheless, the Worcester monk Hemming records how the estate was

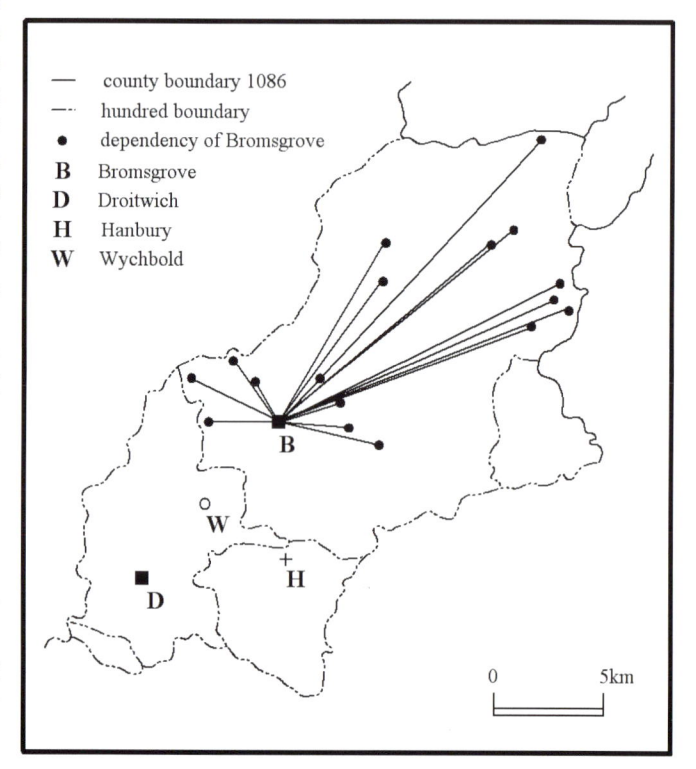

Figure 23 Estate centres in the Droitwich-Bromsgrove region

seized from the Church by Edwin, who was to be killed fighting against the Welsh in 1039 (*VCH Worcestershire* III, 59). The estate was then claimed by Earl Godwine (whose daughter King Edward had married), and was granted after the Conquest to Osbern son of Richard, who held the manor in 1086.

These early medieval wooded regions were not, however, areas of dense woodland. One of the main usages was as wood-pasture and the browsing of animals would have ensured that the woodland remained relatively open. Indeed, in wood-pasture regions extensive areas of heathland would have formed a landscape mosaic, with actual woods surviving in more inaccessible locations. The woods were also carefully managed, especially as they provided the essential fuel for the salt-works, and the *graf* of the name Bromsgrove might indicate coppicing (Gelling & Cole 2000, 226–8). So important were the acorn (or, in some mainly southern regions, beech mast) harvests for pigs that the woods of Domesday Book were often assessed in some circuits not in leagues

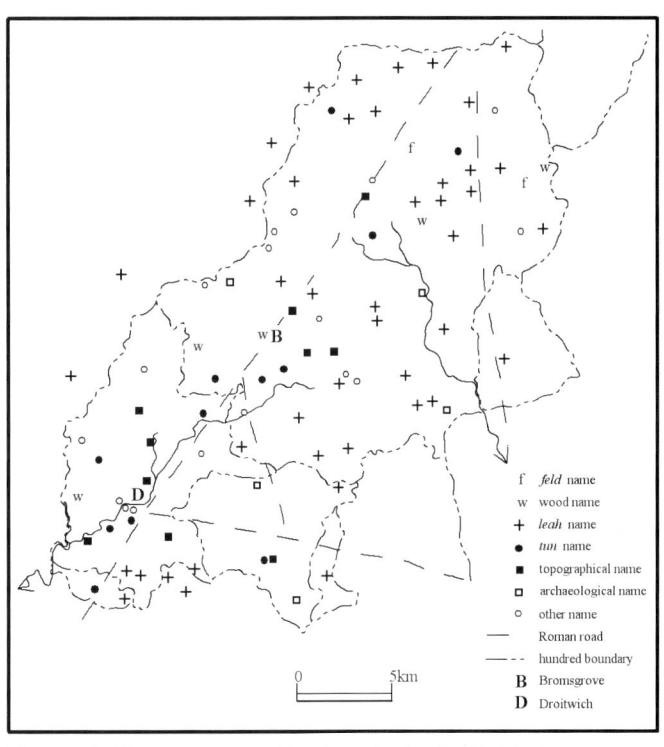

Figure 24 Place-names and land use in the Droitwich-Bromsgrove region. Apart from leah *names the emphasis here is upon names recorded by 1086 plus any later parish names*

but for their value according to the number of pigs they could support. The use of woods for pasture in this way is probably indicated by the use of the *leah* term in place-names (Hooke 2008a) and a concentration of such names can be observed in the north of the area on the sandstones, breccias and marls of the Clent-Lickey foothills (Fig 24). However, much of this area, especially in the east and south, was underlain by Triassic clay soils (Mercia Mudstone) and woodland seems to have been present across much of the region. Other *leah* names occur in the south-east, which was to become part of Feckenham Forest in medieval times (Fig 25). The oak and the ash were familiar trees in this context and already some trees were being pollarded in order to produce wood and timber growing out of the reach of browsing animals (Hooke 2010, 139–41). Worcestershire was, indeed, one of the most heavily wooded counties at the time of the Domesday survey – Rackham (1990, 50) has estimated that it was 40% wooded at this time, third only in the percentage of land area under woodland after the Weald of south-eastern England and Gloucestershire west of the River Severn (the Forest of Dean).

In contrast, *tun* names, usually indicating villages, are found in the south of the region and along the axis of the Roman road (Fig 24). Some topographical names are also likely to have referred to early estate centres but such names could be coined at any time in the early medieval/mid–

late Anglo-Saxon period and many smaller settlements that took the name of local topographical features only find their way into documents at a relatively late stage (eg Dodderhill, 'Dudra's hill', is not recorded before the late 11th century: Mawer & Stenton 1927, 281).

The early medieval/mid–late Anglo-Saxon countryside: the evidence from charters and place-names

Occasionally, more intimate glimpses of the early medieval/mid–late Anglo-Saxon countryside are offered by the boundary clauses that accompany some charter grants. Although the charters themselves are in Latin, the bounds are usually written in Old English. They provide an enormous amount of detail about the landscape of the time, supplementing the thinner but more ubiquitous evidence of place-names. There is an abundance of charter evidence for Worcestershire where the cathedral scriptorium was never destroyed by Danish raiders and where much material was collected and copied by the monk Hemming and other scribes in the 11th century (Ker 1948), the original manuscripts surviving in the British Library. Unfortunately, this region had rather fewer charters accompanied by boundary clauses than other parts of Worcestershire.

It is the charter evidence, combined with that of place-names, that helps us to recognise the landscape regions of the county. The Vale of Evesham was an area of prime agricultural development already by late Iron Age times and it is here that one finds most of the charter evidence for the emerging practice of open field farming: furrows often separated the fields of adjoining townships and reference is made to strips and furlongs (Hooke 1985a, 216, fig 49). Village nucleation was slowly progressing, although still incomplete in the early medieval period (Hooke 1985b), and this region was the one most affected by the enclosure movement of the 18th and 19th centuries. In contrast, the western strip of Worcestershire beyond the River Severn was much wilder and less developed. Here one finds references to *haga* enclosures which were associated with the retention and capture of deer (especially in the area of the later Malvern Forest) and there is strong evidence for the existence of parallel drove-ways leading westwards, routeways typical of a wood-pasture region (Hooke 2008b). Central Worcestershire, on the other hand, where Wychbold lay, was a kind of 'in-between' region: the *leah* woods had been pushed back towards the boundaries of the individual estates and settlements bearing the habitative suffixes of *tun* and *cot* represented small villages and hamlet communities. Hedges are numerous, clearly intended to protect crops from woodland animals (one is described as 'roe-deer hedge'). Droitwich stands out because of its presence as a salt-producing centre.

The Droitwich region

Here the Droitwich region with the middle and upper Salwarpe catchment are described, together with Bromsgrove, so as to provide a context for Wychbold in this period, when so little historical and archaeological evidence is generally available. There are only three groups of pre-Conquest charters with attached boundary clauses within the main Droitwich-Bromsgrove folk region: Cofton Hackett/Alvechurch and *Hellerelege* to the north-east; Salwarpe and Martin Hussingtree close to the confluence of the Salwarpe and the Hadley Brook to the south-west; and Stoke Prior and Tardebigge at the headwaters of the Salwarpe (Fig 25). In addition, on the fringes of the region, there are boundary clauses for the Church of Pershore estates of Beoley and Yardley.

There was still a considerable amount of woodland on the two most southerly estates of Martin Hussingtree (S 786; Hooke 1990, 196–8; two separate early medieval settlement centres) and Salwarpe, for the Salwarpe charter (S 1597, S 1596; Hooke 1990, 397–402) records two *leah* woods, Pulley and Oakley in the far east of Salwarpe parish, and Westwood to the north of the River Salwarpe, between that river and the Doverdale; another wood lay in the east of Martin Hussingtree. Marshland was recorded along the north-eastern boundaries of both estates. There was still half a league of woodland (with a park) recorded on Earl Roger's estate at Salwarpe in Domesday Book. The arable land of these estates normally lay well within their boundaries and is seldom mentioned (see below). There is little indication

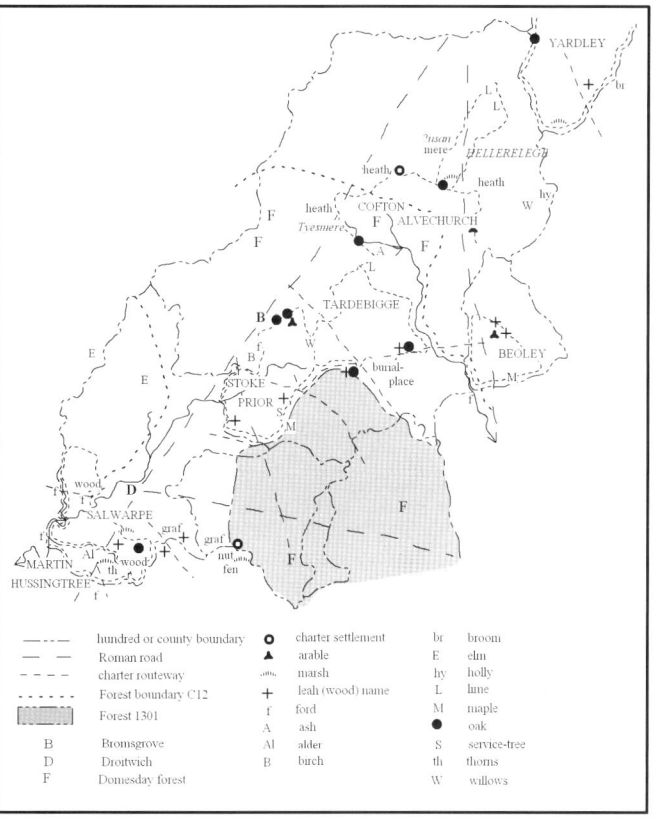

Figure 25 Early medieval charter-bounds and medieval forest boundaries in the Droitwich-Bromsgrove region (plus tree species recorded in place-names)

in the charter-bounds of the land for the seven ploughs recorded on Earl Roger's manor but this probably lay within the parish area away from its boundaries. A road running south-eastwards is noted in the Martin Hussingtree charter as a *stræt* or 'made-up road', elsewhere recorded as a major salt-way (only the ford carrying the main Worcester to Metchley road over the Martin Brook is noted in this charter), while two *col* fords noted in the Salwarpe bounds were probably routes used for carrying charcoal across the Salwarpe, suggesting that this may have been used in some processes at the Droitwich salt-works – at least one route ran eastwards from woodlands located on the ridge between the River Severn and the Hadley Brook where the place-names Chatley and Hadley suggest available woodland (some surviving); the route crossing at the northernmost ford (*wicforda*) led directly eastwards towards the Droitwich salt-works.

Moving northwards, the Stoke Prior charter (S 60; Hooke 1990, 65–9) is a forgery in which the church of Worcester attempted to strengthen its claim to the 10 hides which formed the whole of the parish when it only possessed a genuine charter for the 5 hides of Aston (S 59) that it had been granted in AD 770. The bounds of the later spurious charter are quite detailed and refer to two *leah* woods and a hart's slough (miry place). The woods, one described as a 'bitches' or 'thieves' wood', lay on the south-eastern boundary close to where this was crossed by a WNW–ESE routeway. The other was 'wheat wood', perhaps referring to a catch crop grown either when the wood was cleared or in an open patch within it; it lay beside another routeway, the 'Sharpway', leading to another Roman road crossing the southern boundary. The latter is the route which gave its name to *Holewei* 'the hollow way' in Hanbury, recorded in 1086, giving its name to the settlement of Hollow Court, and this route crossed the parish north-westwards towards the Roman Worcester to Metchley road and was indeed referred to as the *holan weg* 'hollow way'. A possible finger-post and a crucifix oak are noted close to the east–west route (the first may have marked a road leading towards Bromsgrove; for the latter, see below). Arable land is noted in the reference to '*bennic* acre' at the northern tip of the parish. Many of the landmarks used were, however, prominent topographical features occurring along the boundary. These include the River Salwarpe, various brooks, and valleys, one of which is referred to as 'a trough' (admirably describing the local terrain and the deeply incised brook near Stonehouse Farm) and another as a 'coomb', and two hills. The precision of the bounds is again illustrated by the way that the bounds run to 'the front of watch hill to the middle part of watch hill … from mid watch hill brook to the middle part of long hill' (Piper's Hill), which exactly describes the line followed (Fig 26). Descriptions of trees standing at prominent locations are also a feature of this boundary clause (see below). Although a forgery, the boundary was obviously described by those with good local knowledge, probably walking along the route.

The exact bounds of the two northern charters, both pertaining to estates held by the church of Worcester, cannot be securely identified on the ground although *Hellerelege*, granted in the early 8th century to the Church (S 64), probably included the 'bishop's wood' in King's Norton (Demidowicz & Price 2009, 8–9). It is not unusual for boundaries to be less easily followed in areas of marginal land. A lease of lands by the Church in the 9th century included 'Cofton' (S 1272) and was accompanied by a boundary clause that certainly covered Cofton Hackett and the northern part of Alvechurch (Hooke 1990, 135–42). In these two sets of

Figure 26 'Watch Hill', Stoke Prior

bounds *leah* woods, heathland and marshland are noted, although references to single trees suggest a relatively open landscape over much of the area. Deer are noted in the references to a 'roe-deer's lair' and 'a hart's wallowing-place' on the south-western Alvechurch/Tardebigge boundary. Where the bounds ran 'along the *heagan*', this may have been a reference to a *haga*, an unidentified deer enclosure within Alvechurch, perhaps the predecessor of the medieval park there. It is again the Cofton Hackett/Alvechurch charter-bounds that refer to ploughland near the estate boundary (*eardland* 'ploughland' is recorded on the northern boundary and *ceolferdes æcer* 'Ceolferth's acre or ploughstrip' on the north-eastern boundary). As in Stoke Prior, these areas of arable may have been associated with small settlements nearby, for in marginal or woodland zones small scattered settlements, some even located close to boundaries, were features of the landscape (Hooke 1985b). Indeed, in this set of bounds, *Hopwudes wic* and *cybles weordig* are likely to have been actual farms established close to the boundary – the first, possibly a dairy farm belonging to Hopwood, remains unlocated, but the second lay on the edge of West Heath. The Roman Ryknield Street may be being referred to in the *stræt mere* 'lake beside a road' on the northern boundary of Alvechurch where the following landmarks refer to the shaw (?narrow woodland strip) and the spring of the heathy wood (later Headley Heath). Another 'hollow way' is recorded at the north-western corner of Cofton Hackett parish. This lay close to the Worcester to Metchley Roman road but may have described the detour afforded by Groveley Lane as it cuts through the Lickey ridge. References to heathland occur several times in this area, indicating the nature of the vegetation cover over much of the Lickey upland.

While the boundary clauses in their references to woods and marshes, therefore, tell us something about land use and vegetation cover in the area, references to so many individual trees are also of interest, indicating the species found in the area. An 'alder brook' ran along the boundary of Martin Hussingtree and Salwarpe, the alder being a tree common in damp places; a 'thorny marsh' and a 'thorny wood' are recorded on the boundary of Martin Hussingtree and a 'sedge marsh' on the boundary of Salwarpe, while one of the Salwarpe *leah* woods was an oak wood. Limes were growing in the far north of the area with a 'spreading lime-tree' recorded on the boundary of *Hellerelege* which perhaps gave its name to the settlement of Lindsworth nearby. Another lime-tree was a landmark on the boundary of Alvechurch while an apple-tree, several willows and a birch-tree appear within the estate, plus an interestingly named 'Penda's oak-tree' at another unidentified location. The Stoke Prior charter mentions not only a service-tree and a rough-barked maple-tree, a white birch-tree and withies (willows) growing along a brook, but no fewer than three oak-trees – one 'ivy-grown', one associated with someone called Alebeard and, interestingly, a 'crucifix oak'. The Tardebigge charter refers to the same 'withy brook' and to the 'great lime-tree' of the Cofton Hackett/Alvechurch charter but adds another 'crucifix oak'. Two additional boundary clauses describe the bounds of the Pershore Abbey holdings of Yardley and Beoley in the 10th century (S 786; Hooke 1990, 219–25). Beoley may be 'bee wood', referring to the fact that wild bees were a valuable source of honey in the early medieval period while the name of Yardley suggests a wood from which yards or rods could be obtained, perhaps implying the practice of coppicing. Again marshland is recorded on the southern boundary of Yardley, while *leah* features include a *burh leah* in Beoley (probably referring to an Iron Age fortification or *burh* here) and a 'white' wood in Yardley (?perhaps referring to birches). Individual trees include a maple-tree on the southern boundary of Beoley (not far from Mappleborough Green in Studley which also takes its name from the maple), two oak-trees, an apple-tree, a 'boundary' thorn, and a 'broomy hollow' on the Yardley boundary. Again, several routeways crossing the boundaries of these estates can be identified. The term *geat* in these charters may refer either to a 'gate' or a pass through a ridge; in Beoley the 'maple-tree gate (or pass)' marks the point at which the Roman Ryknield Street crosses the southern boundary, while the 'stone gate' was the narrowest crossing-point of the eastern boundary ridge.

References to crucifixes are of interest because they are relatively rare in charters and place-names (Blair 2005, 479, n242). When the two crucifix oaks are plotted they are found to have stood beside trackways leading towards the church of Tardebigge and a further 'holy oak' is recorded in the 13th century on another routeway running in this direction from the south. What may have been a pagan burial lay beside another routeway coming from a south-easterly direction. Although it may be fanciful to suspect a special reason for this it does seem to suggest that the Christian church may have had a reason to place crucifixes in these particular locations. Is it possible that Tardebigge had been associated with some earlier heathen cult? The church that was established here was to be dedicated to St Bartholomew 'the caster-out of devils' (a new church was rebuilt upon an earlier site in the 18th century). There is even another pagan name – Grimley, referring to the god 'Grim' – in the parish, but it has been suggested (Mawer & Stenton 1927, 360) that this may refer to an in-comer from Grimley in west Worcestershire into the area.

The Domesday evidence

By the 10th/11th century a shire system had been established across the west midland region, the shire of Worcestershire demarcated around the burh of Worcester fortified in the late 9th century by Æthelred and Æthelflæd. Hundreds, as administrative units, had also been recognised before the Norman Conquest, possibly based upon an older system of regions paying tribute but regrouped and influenced by later landownership. Most of the folk region postulated above fell into Came Hundred but with a detached part of Clent Hundred around Droitwich and Wychbold to the south, and a small part of Esch Hundred lay around the old minster centre of Hanbury. Detached portions of Pershore Hundred lay in the north-east and east taking in the Church of Pershore's estate of Yardley and Beoley (the former, at least, possibly a later intake to the region). In the south, another former Pershore estate, Martin Hussingtree (by then granted to the Church of St Peter's, Westminster), also formed a detached part of Pershore Hundred (Fig 21).

Bromsgrove in the hundred of Came was a royal estate in 1086 that had been a manor of Earl Edwin, possibly inherited from the early Hwiccan kings, and it owned 13 salt-houses in Droitwich with 3 salt-workers (Thorn & Thorn 1982, 1,1a). This manor is entered as having 7 x 4 leagues of woodland on its appurtenant estates in 1086, woodland which extended north-eastwards as far as Moseley, King's Norton, Wythall etc. Many Worcestershire manors held rights in salt-houses or 'houses' at Droitwich: among the royal manors, King Edward the Confessor had held 11 houses at Droitwich and rights in the brine-pits with no fewer than 54 salt-houses at Upwich, 17 at Helpridge and 12 at Middlewich; Earl Edwin had had 51½ salt-houses; other royal manors with property or salt-houses in Droitwich included Suckley, Kidderminster and Tardebigge, Feckenham and Hollow (Court) – the latter two had been leased to various thanes in the time of Earl Edwin. The church of Worcester's manors of Worcester, Hallow, Holt, Northwick, Phepson, Crowle, Hanbury, Hartlebury and Alvechurch held salt rights, as did St Peter's of Westminster's manor of Hussingtree (the villagers here were paying 100 cartloads of timber a year to the salt-houses at Droitwich but the source of the wood is not clear – although a *leah* wood was recorded in the 10th-century charter, no woodland was recorded on the Domesday manor); St Mary's of Pershore's manor of Pershore; and Evesham Abbey's manor of Ombersley. Manors with salt rights belonging to Norman landowners by 1086 included Wychbold, Halesowen, Astley, Elmley Lovett, Wychbold, 'Osmerley' in Alvechurch, Doverdale, Belbroughton, Upton Warren, Witton, 'Thickenappletree' in Hampton Lovett and Chaddesley Corbett; others held land in Droitwich itself. In 1086 Wychbold, Osbern's manor, had rights in 26 salt-houses at Droitwich and 13 burgesses there. Beyond Worcestershire were other manors holding salt rights and the salt-ways linking these to Droitwich can be reconstructed (Hooke 1998a, 8, fig 4). Clearly some had originally, like Bromsgrove and Hussingtree, sent wood to the salt furnaces, although by 1086 the Herefordshire manors were instead sending payment (probably obtained from the sale of wood closer to home). The most distant estate was Princes Risborough in Buckinghamshire and it is interesting to note that here the king probably already had a hunting park (*VCH Buckinghamshire* II, 260–7) for in medieval times salt was essential for preserving the venison carcases (Birrell 2006, 180–4).

The Domesday entries for the estates in the region under discussion here show that the most intensively cultivated part lay around Droitwich in the south where plough-team densities reached three per square mile – not as many as in the Vale of Evesham but still a relatively high density for the county (Monkhouse 1971, 240, fig 78). The numbers of ploughs recorded on the individual Domesday manors can be deceptive, however, because of the grouping of statistics under capital manors. Thus, there were six ploughs working on the Hussingtree manor of St Peter's Westminster and eight ploughs on the Salwarpe manors, with another in Chawson, but the combined holdings of Bromsgrove (including King's Norton) had a total of 77 ploughs and Alvechurch with its outliers a total of sixteen ploughs (and another six on the second Cofton manor). At many places in the region it seems that the Domesday commissioners felt that there was scope for further extension of the arable and that more ploughs could be employed – at Elmbridge and Hampton Lovett it was considered that the number of ploughs could be almost doubled: in the case of Elmbridge from ten to twenty and at Hampton Lovett (split into two holdings) from eight to fourteen. One wonders if this might infer a loss of arable since Roman times – traditional Iron Age farming had often laid a greater emphasis upon stock rearing outside the main regions of intensive agriculture.

The woodland, too, is amalgamated and recorded in Domesday Book under the capital manors with woodland 7 leagues long and 4 leagues wide at Bromsgrove (with four hawks' eyries) and 3 leagues at 'Willingwick' and Chadwick, all royal land, with another 4 leagues on the church of Worcester's manor at Alvechurch. Beoley, in a joint entry with Yardley, had woodland measuring 6 x 3 leagues. Also in the north, Frankley had woodland 1 league long and ½ wide, Selly Oak with Bartley Green had 'a wood 1 league long' on each of its two manors, Northfield woodland ½ league long and 3 furlongs wide. Further south, woodland seems usually to be recorded more in much smaller quantities, although Wychbold had 1 league of woodland, Elmbridge 1 x ½ league, and Salwarpe with its outliers 1½ leagues. More typical of that part of Clent Hundred in the south of the region is Upton Warren with woodland totalling only 3 x 2 furlongs and Horton with 'a small wood' while many manors had no woodland recorded at all (like Hussingtree which still had to supply wood to the salt-works). It is said that at Hanbury in Esch Hundred the woodland, measuring in total 1 x ½ league, had been put into the king's forest and in this part of the region a park and 'all the woodland' of Hollow Court had been 'put outside the manor', that at Shell 'in an enclosure', similarly implying forest. Already the core of Feckenham Forest to the south-east had been established and these manors bordered upon it. However, outlying woods elsewhere had also been declared subject to forest law for the same restrictions had been placed upon the woodlands of Woodcote Green, 'Willingwick' and Chadwick (on the king's manors). The king had also placed half of the woodland on the church of Worcester's manor of Alvechurch (with its outliers Cofton Hackett, Wast Hills, 'Tonge' and *Ovretone*) in his forest, including the additional woodland of 3 x 1 furlongs on the separate manor of Cofton taken by Urse of Abetot; also the woods on the same Church's manor of 'Baddington' in Stoke Prior. Of the three parks recorded in the Worcestershire folios (in addition to a number of less formal 'hays' which are likely to have been enclosures for capturing deer), two lay in this region – the king's enclosure at Hollow Court described in the Evesham folios as 'a park for wild animals' ('Ibi est parcus ferarum'), and another at Salwarpe ('in parco') recorded under the entry for the Church of Coventry's holdings and again ('ibi parcus') under the entry for the holding of Earl Roger. These were for the localised hunting of deer. The eyries recorded on the royal manor of Bromsgrove were also sources for the taking of young hawks to be for trained for use in fowling and hunting.

The forests were being established, therefore, by the Norman kings immediately after the Conquest but often these gave official recognition to areas that had already been used for hunting by Anglo-Saxon kings (Hooke 1998b). Their legal protection was now much harsher and the areas that were covered by forest law were greatly extended, especially under Henry II in the 12th century (Fig 25). The forest core around Feckenham was extended to reach the River Severn in the north-west (to be referred to as the Forest of Ombersley) and the south-west (the Forest of Horewell); northwards it was to include Pyperode extending as far as the Lickey Hills (West 1964a, 81, fig 1). Horewell and Ombersley, however, were to be disafforested in 1229 in the reign of Henry III, leaving Pyperode and land to the south afforested until Feckenham was pushed back to its 'ancient bounds' in 1301. The amount of woodland undoubtedly diminished as the protection offered by forest law was removed and assarting actively encouraged by manorial lords anxious to increase their revenues, as recorded at Alvechurch and Hanbury (Dyer 1980, 63, 91–3, figs 4 and 6). No attempt will be made here to discuss the later evolution of the landscape but it is clear that the region had been of great importance in the Anglo-Saxon Hwiccan kingdom and, through the manufacture of salt, much further afield.

Wicbold – mother church, 'villa regalis', and vill (*by* Lyn Blewitt)

The mother church

Today the church of St Augustine dominates the northern skyline of Droitwich, standing on Dodderhill, at the south end of its parish, and within the Roman fort on top of the hill (Fig 27). The current building was completed in *c* 1220 and has later additions after being heavily damaged during the Civil War in the 17th century; originally it was a cruciform church, cross-shaped in plan and with a central tower, and its current eccentric internal layout is the result of the later damage and the subsequent partial restoration of the medieval building.

Bassett (2008a, 6–17) has discussed the evidence for St Augustine's having been the mother church for a large original parish (Fig 28), noting that this situation might have been

Figure 27 Church of St Augustine viewed from parish boundary of Dodderhill, and looking north across location of Upwich brine well in foreground

of 7th or early 8th century origin but that we can only be certain such mother-church parishes were in existence from the early 11th century. He states that this large original parish covering the upper Salwarpe basin would have included the areas of the later parishes of Droitwich St Nicholas (centred on the medieval church which stood on Friar Street, not the current one which dates from 1870), Droitwich St Andrew, Witton St Mary, Witton St Peter, and of course Dodderhill, including Crutch and Elmbridge. Of the Droitwich parishes, only Witton St Peter (and possibly Witton St Mary) had its own graveyard; burials of residents of the other parishes took place at St Augustine's, a clear indication of mother-church status. The parishes of Hampton Lovett (including Westwood) and Upton Warren are thought to have been part of the larger parish too; and Salwarpe, Martin Hussingtree, and possibly Hadzor are also candidates for inclusion. Corroboration for this comes from considering the areas of the surrounding adjacent mother churches, which abut that proposed for Dodderhill.

In support of the view that the church on Dodderhill goes back to the earlier of the possible date ranges mentioned, it is helpful to consider the history of Christianity in this area. The dedication of the church to St Augustine (assuming this was the original dedication) would suggest that it was part of the Roman Christian tradition, Roman Christianity being officially re-established in Britain following the mission of Bishop Augustine sent in 597 by the pope to Kent initially, and this work being continued by later emissaries from the early 600s onwards. Augustine was later canonised (made a saint). There is a tradition that Augustine met with the British bishops in about 603 at 'St Augustine's Oak', whose location is now unknown but thought to be in the west of the country, and the dedication of Dodderhill's church to St Augustine may reflect a belief that the meeting had been held nearby. Undoubtedly, following Augustine's mission, Roman Christianity spread through the Anglo-Saxon kingdoms, though slowly in many of them. The earliest likely date which can be suggested for the foundation of a church dedicated to St Augustine is, therefore, around 650. However, it should be noted that there is no evidence for the present dedication going back beyond the late 1100s.

There is evidence that the practice of Christianity survived the departure of the Romans, especially in the west of the

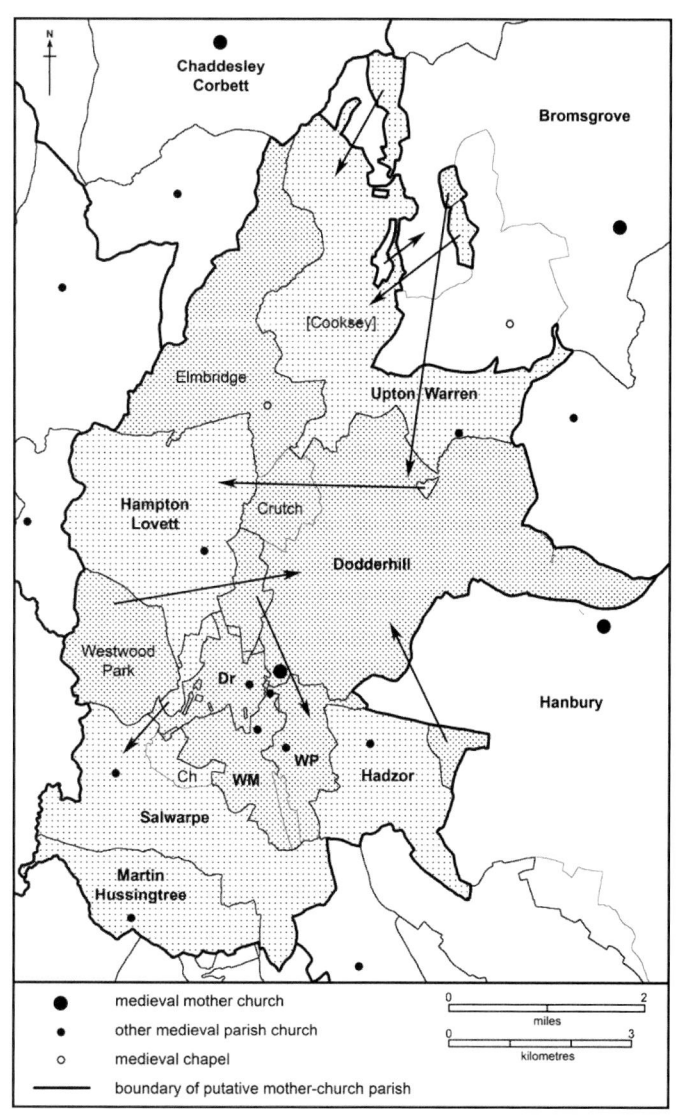

Figure 28 Former parochial affiliations in the vicinity of Droitwich, as alluded to in mainly later medieval sources (Chawson (Ch), Droitwich St Nicholas (Dr), Witton St Mary's (WM), and Witton St Peter's (WP); from Bassett 2008a, fig 2). The distinction shown by heavier and lighter stippling within the putative area of the mother-church parish of St Augustine's, Dodderhill is between former parochial affiliations which are proven and ones which are no more than probable. Copyright of Steven Bassett

province of Britannia, and specifically in this part of the Severn valley. In nearby Worcester, the dedication of the church of St Helen could suggest a very early foundation date (Helena, having converted to Christianity in c AD 310, being the mother of the Roman Emperor Constantine who in 330 had made Christianity the official religion of the Roman empire); the Worcester dedication to St Helen is not recorded until much later but the location of the church, within the late Roman defences, suggests a possible Roman origin. Later it had jurisdiction over eleven rural chapels, indicating that it had a leading role within the region that may have pre-dated the founding of the diocese of Worcester in 679/680 (Bassett 1989, 243–6; Bridges 2000, 233). It may even have been the seat of a post-Roman British bishop (Bassett 1992, 16–19, 39–40).

The church of St Alban in Worcester, not far away from St Helen's, may also be of early date, as St Alban was a Romano-British Christian martyr. It is, therefore, entirely possible that Worcester had a Christian community and Christian churches (perhaps with a bishop) from the 4th century, and that these continued through into the Anglo-Saxon and later periods. Two burials under College Hall, the former monastic refectory at Worcester, could be of 7th century date and might be British Christians linked to a church, or priests of the first minster at Worcester (established c 680); one had fragments of fine spun gold round the neck indicating braid on the garment, fragments similar to which have been found from Roman tunics in 3rd–4th century graves, 6th–7th century graves in Europe, and a 9th century grave at Winchester (Barker & Cubberley 1974; Blair 2005, 31, note 90).

It has been suggested that large mother parishes centred on places which were Roman, such as Worcester, Gloucester, and Wroxeter, began as territories of British churches of a status likely to have housed bishops (Bassett 1989; 1992, 16–19, 39–40). Support for their existence comes from Bede, the Northumbrian monk, who in the early 8th century wrote the first history of the English church. He gives an account of Bishop Chad's consecration in 664: after the former archbishop's death there was not a single canonically ordained bishop in Britain except for Wine of Wessex, who performed Chad's consecration with the assistance of two bishops 'of the British race' (*HE*, III.28).

The Christian church in this area may, therefore, have been well organised, rather than composed of small pockets of believers separated from each other. As Anglo-Saxon incomers did not reach this part of the country until the late 6th century at the earliest, and possibly the early 7th century, the British church may well have continued and flourished as an organised and even influential institution for two centuries and more after the cessation of Roman authority (Sims-Williams 1990, 54–87; Bassett 1992, 13–40). It is worth speculating that this could have been one reason why Worcester was chosen as the centre of the (Roman Christian) diocese of the Hwicce established in about 679 by the archbishop of Canterbury – that there was already a tradition that it was the seat of a bishop, and perhaps it still had a (British) bishop.

The diocese of Worcester was created as the diocese of a folk-group called the Hwicce, and so was identical with the area of their kingdom (Sims-Williams 1990, 87–8). But who were the Hwicce? There is no final answer to that question. They seem to have included Anglian or Saxon kin-groups such as the Weogoran round Worcester, the *Stoppingas*, and the *Husmeræ*, who all presumably moved into the area; and it is said that the names of the Hwiccan royal family are Anglian. But most scholars agree that the majority of the people living in the kingdom must have been native to it (ie the post-Roman British). Equally, the kingdom of the Hwicce may have been an artificial creation by King Penda encompassing the post-Roman indigenous British inhabitants and the Anglo-Saxons who had also settled here. It may be that clear ethnic distinctions are impossible in those times: Penda himself has a name with British/Welsh overtones, and he called one of his sons Merewalh, which means 'famous Welshman'. While 'absence of evidence is not evidence of absence', there is nothing in the written or archaeological record to suggest a violent invasive takeover by incoming Anglo-Saxon people, and however the kingdom of the Hwicce came into being, the scenario of peaceful assimilation of the Anglo-Saxon incomers seems to be most likely.

The Hwicce and their western neighbours the Magonsæte were evidently Christian by 660 and it has been suggested that they 'were converted in an unobtrusive and ultimately unmemorable way by the Britons among them' (Sims-Williams 1990, 77–9). Again, this is supported by Bede who records that in 680 the wife of King Aethelwealh of Sussex was Eaba, a princess of the Hwicce, who had been baptised in her own province and whose father and people were already Christian (*HE*, IV.13), suggesting that the Hwicce were already converted to Christianity in the 7th century and perhaps early in that century.

Place-name evidence combined with the distribution of 'pagan' burials also suggests that the Hwicce (and the Magonsæte) were Christian. Place-names referring to Germanic gods and heathen shrines, thought to be coined in the 7th century when places where heathen religion lingered were considered exceptional, survive only around the north, east and south boundaries of the kingdom of the Hwicce (Sims-Williams 1990, 73–5). The same is true for burials which from the accompanying grave goods are deemed pagan (Sims-Williams 1990, 64–72; Zaluckyj 2001, 14–15). Conversely, ecclesiastical centres recorded before 700 are located more in the centre of the kingdom, and taking these strands of evidence together suggests that Germanic 'heathen' religious beliefs did not penetrate far among the Hwicce, and/or died out quickly (Sims-Williams 1990, 77–9). If there was an active British church flourishing in this area, such a pattern of evidence would be explained (Sims-Williams 1990, 79–81 and 84).

This leads us to a brief consideration of the wider question: what happened in this part of the former Roman province of Britannia after the Roman army and administrators withdrew in the early 400s? Archaeology and some written records show evidence of continuity, 'remarkable resilience' as Myres (1986, 217–8) puts it, with the British retaining their own language and possibly a pre-Roman social structure. As part of this they absorbed Christianity, modified it to fit their cultural needs, and used it as a powerful unifying force and a reminder of links with Gaul, Rome and the Mediterranean. The British population in areas near to Wales, including those of the Hwicce and Mercia, managed for a long time to retain their cultural individuality, social organisation and settlement patterns and even their legal systems, and the language used to express them.

Evidence for this comes from the monk Gildas, writing in the 6th century, who used literary forms which show he was educated in a Roman tradition, and had access to classical Roman texts. He was from the western part of the country and it is likely that he was educated within the British church, which, therefore, had preserved the forms of late Roman secular education. Similarly the Llandaff charters from the 6th and 7th centuries, which record land holdings in south Wales, and even into Herefordshire, used a form of Latin which was not like the vernacular Latin of the early Anglo-Saxon charters, but, instead, revealed a legal structure, concepts and terminology derived from the late Roman period (White 2007, 167).

At Wroxeter, a cantonal capital, the baths basilica complex was rebuilt on a major scale, including a building which could have been a church, during the mid 6th century; the excavators theorised that this indicated the taking of power by a local prominent Romano-British family who could organise such a project, or that a bishopric established in the 4th century by the Romans had continued, with bishops appointing successors from local aristocratic families within their area, the bishop overseeing the construction (White & Barker 1998, 124–5).

It can, therefore, be concluded that there is clear evidence for continuous and structured Christian institutions through the post-Roman period, and, therefore, that an early date for the foundation of the church on Dodderhill is far from improbable. However, there is another question to be addressed: could this same church have been a minster church?

Blair (2005, 3) gives a useful definition of the role of a minster church:

> A complex ecclesiastical settlement which is headed by an abbess, abbot, or man in priest's orders; which contains nuns, monks, priests, or laity in a variety of possible combinations, and is united to a greater or lesser extent by their liturgy and devotions; which may perform or supervise pastoral care to the laity, perhaps receiving dues and exerting parochial authority; and which may sometimes act as a bishop's seat, while not depending for its existence or importance on that function.

A number of factors point to the possibility of St Augustine's being a minster. It is sited in a Roman fort, and at the south of the defences which are likely still to have been visible in the 7th century when such a minster might have been founded. Such a location is a sign of an early/minster church, as their founders wished to site them in a rectangular enclosure to emulate the heavenly Jerusalem of Revelations 21 (Blair 2005, 188–9, 196, 199, 248). It had a cruciform (cross-shaped) plan, again thought to be an indication of a minster (Bassett 2008a, 6, note 18), and has been considered a minster by Bassett (2008a, 14) when wondering if the Cooksey area was originally served by St Augustine's or by the minster at Bromsgrove. All the evidence for its mother-church status may well support equally the idea that it was a minster, as many minsters seem to have evolved into mother churches, and to have had very large territories which later became parishes (Blair 2005, 4) – including that the territory of St Augustine's is surrounded by the territories of other minster and mother churches (Bassett 2008a, 17). Excavation at St Augustine's found a pre-Norman stone structure not aligned with the present church, which suggested 'the case for this being a minster church would seem to be substantially strengthened' (Robson & Hurst 2000, 213).

There is an obvious set of questions which could arise if it is assumed that St Augustine's was a minster: when, how and why was the minster church founded? Who gave the land which would support the minster, and/or paid for the construction of the first buildings? Charter evidence for other minsters and early churches shows that often it was the kings of the Hwicce who set up these institutions, with ratification by their Mercian overlords.

The truth is that we know nothing about the original foundation of St Augustine's, but it can be speculated that the first church would have been built largely of wood, in the cross-shaped plan which was followed by a later stone building on the site (Robson & Hurst 2000, 207–13). What functions the minster carried out are equally a matter of speculation, although it is reasonable to assume that pastoral care (baptism, marriage, burial, instruction in the Christian faith, and more wide-ranging support of the population within the great parish) was included.

One of the objections to St Augustine's as a minster church is the presence of Hanbury minster, now the church of St Mary the Virgin, just a few miles to the east (Fig 29): so why would there be a need for two minsters so close together? However, the survival of British Christianity could explain why there might have been a minster at Dodderhill when there was also one at Hanbury, where the minster was constructed inside a former Iron Age defended hilltop site. A charter of Wulfhere, the first Christian king of Mercia who ruled from 657 to 674/5, recorded the grant of 50 hides there with meadows, woods and 'wells of salt' to Colman who became the first abbot (Sims-Williams 1990, 106; the 'wells of salt' must refer to rights to brine in *Wic*, later

Droitwich). The choice of a location, which is rounded in shape, for this minster church echoes the common form of monastic sites in early Christian Ireland (Blair 2005, 190, 197–8; Sims-Williams 1990, 107). Colman was a common Irish name and he may have come from the Anglo-Saxon kingdom of Northumbria (Sims-Williams 1990, 106 and note 98), where there was a strong Irish element in the church established in 634, and where Irish Celtic Christian customs were observed, including a different way of calculating when Easter fell, up to the Synod of Whitby in 664 (Stenton 1971, 123). It is, therefore, possible that Hanbury was a British or Celtic Christian foundation, which might pre-date or be contemporary with the foundation of St Augustine's. The original charter has not survived except in two 17th century summaries, and, if it represents a grant by King Wulfhere, then it cannot be earlier than 657 and is probably later, towards the end of Wulfhere's reign; though it may also have been, as suggested for many other such charters, a record and confirmation of a grant already made at an earlier date by a Hwiccan king.

It is important to remember that the Hwicce were not a literate people; they relied on declarations (of grants or other matters) made orally in front of witnesses, and, therefore, on memory. No written records seem to have been made within the kingdom of the Hwicce until the takeover by Mercia, so the first charters are around 675, and those which survive are often concerned with grants to churches. Sims-Williams (1990, 85–6, 92) has suggested that many of these charters post-date the time of the original gift, and were 'confirmation' charters requested by the recipient institutions from the new rulers of this area to document their rights to what had been granted perhaps generations before by the kings of the Hwicce. The church had realised the power of having written records of its possessions and how these had come into church hands, and the archive of the church of Worcester shows how carefully these documents would have been preserved; most of the charters relating to the endowments of all churches in the diocese, and elsewhere, are only preserved because the churches came into the possession of the church of Worcester and their documents were kept there (and this was sufficiently far away from Viking raids to avoid being ransacked). After the Norman Conquest, Domesday Book records many estates held by churches before 1066, which by 1086 had been appropriated by incoming Norman lords; so it was even more important to the church to have their previous rights recorded, and indeed it is said to have been Bishop Wulfstan II of Worcester, the only English bishop to remain in his seat after the Norman takeover, who suggested the idea of the Domesday Book to King William at the Christmas court held in Gloucester in 1085.

Figure 29 Site of Hanbury minster (photograph by L Blewitt)

If British Christianity continued as a well organised institution through to at least the beginning of the 7th century, the local population was Christian to a great extent, and the minster at Hanbury could then have been an early British Christian foundation, it follows that St Augustine's minster would not have been founded to convert the local population to Christianity, as there would have been no need for this. Instead, its foundation may be a sign of the arrival of Roman Christianity in the area, and possibly of an incoming Anglo-Saxon ruler, who had been baptised in the Roman Christian tradition, endowing a church in that tradition. There is evidence that later incoming Anglo-Saxons were already Christian but in the Roman tradition, so it is more likely that St Augustine's was founded no earlier than 650, and possibly after the establishment of the diocese of Worcester in 679/80.

Alternatively, as some minsters seem to have been set up to train the bishop's clergy, St Augustine's could have been established for this purpose by the minster/monastery church at Worcester, the centre of the new diocese, rather than by a royal founder. Another possible explanation of its establishment does not seem as likely: that St Augustine's was set up as a 'family minster' (such minsters were created when a landowner turned his/her household into a monastic community, endowed with land from the family estates). Such arrangements could be abused by secular followers, and also by kings, for whom the granting of a charter conferring immunity from taxes due to minster status was a relatively inexpensive way of rewarding supporters.

Economically, minsters had tax-free status as the land and other resources granted to them were given by or with royal assent. The normal renewal of grants on the death of the beneficiary would also not be required, as the minster church was a perpetual institution, independent of the lifespan of its abbots/abbesses and other residents. Minsters were, therefore, in a favourable position regarding financial security and could gradually acquire a standard of living beyond the reach of ordinary people, including luxury goods (for example books, wine, horses for transport). Equally they were drivers in the local economy, able to buy in, and therefore stimulating demand for, food, including meat, fish, butter and cheese, and other commodities such as cloth, hay, straw, candles and even building materials (Maddicott 2005, 31); and there is evidence for their involvement in more wide-reaching trading arrangements, as they might well build up surpluses of agricultural and other commodities which could be sold further afield, and in turn enable them to buy from more distant markets (Blair 2005, 256–9; Maddicott 2005, 14 and 57). It is an obvious speculation that the minster or mother church of St Augustine's might have been endowed with rights to brine from the Upwich brine well, especially as this was within its territory, and so traded surplus salt for its financial benefit. The church in Worcester, under its bishops, seems to have done precisely this, and had trading links to London from the early 8th century (Sims-Williams 1990, 13, 147 (with notes 21 & 22), 328; Maddicott 2005, 45 and 52–3).

Larger minsters were also innovative in land management and the exploitation of other resources, such as organising better ways of farming, building water mills, and making the most of peat, uplands, timber, fish and waterfowl (Blair 2005, 252–60; Maddicott 2005, 13). It is not impossible that St Augustine's contributed to the organisation of the salt industry which was located close by (Blair 2005, 258).

Many of the minsters established in the 7th century and later were 'double houses' of both monks and nuns, but were in the charge of an abbess, often initially chosen from the founding royal family. This seems to have been a Germanic tradition, in which high-status ladies chose (or had the choice made for them by their families) a different path from that of dynastic marriage, but fulfilled an equally important role in maintaining control of the land given to the minster by the royal family to which they belonged. In some cases it appears that every abbess had to be a member of the royal family, so 'brides of Christ could weave networks of influence and cement territorial control like secular brides … a royal abbess could be guardian of her family's history and mortuary cults and wield considerable secular power in its name' (Blair 2005, 85). We do not know whether this applied to St Augustine's, which may have been too small to be such a focus, but there is an account that Abbess Aethelburga, a princess of the

Hwicce whose family had given many endowments to the monastery at Worcester, headed that minster/monastery for seven years in the late 8th century. Furthermore, a charter of King Aethelbald of Mercia dated 743 refers to nuns who were resident at Worcester.

From about 850, minsters were subject to asset-stripping by kings and lords, who saw the minsters' accumulation of land and other holdings as a rich source from which to supplement their own possessions, and/or to assist with the costly fighting which was becoming necessary due to Danish (Viking) raids. Minster sites were also run down, meaning few communities were left in control of autonomous endowments. By the time of Domesday Book, many minsters were associated with secular estates and retained only a modest holding of land, probably surrounded by that estate. No doubt the pressures of fighting the Danish incursions led to the seizure and exchange of minster lands, and by 1066 many estates, which had formerly been minster possessions, were owned by the king and his nobles.

This may be what happened to St Augustine's, as either a minster or a mother church, and certainly it lost its position as the only church in its territory as other churches were set up and assigned land from the original large parish: Salwarpe, Witton St Peter, Hampton Lovett, Witton St Mary, Droitwich St Nicholas, and Droitwich St Andrew. St Augustine's was, therefore, definitely a mother church for the large initial parish area identified, while minster status remains just a possibility. One of the strands of evidence for the former is the continuation of older arrangements relating to church dues. Some church dues, church-scot for example (a payment of grain), were still paid to the mother church by all inhabitants of its original area, and as we have seen St Augustine's was the only church in or near Droitwich, apart from Witton St Peter and possibly Witton St Mary, known to have a burial ground, so it would have received the fees for all burials of the inhabitants of the other Droitwich parishes.

Church dues were generally codified in laws from the 8th century onwards, and from the 10th century, tithes, a render to the parish church of one-tenth of all produce, were introduced. Although by then St Augustine's had almost certainly lost any original endowments, which may have included a share of brine from the Upwich pit, once tithes were in place it would receive, in theory, one-tenth of all salt produced from that pit as Upwich was within the parish of Dodderhill. In practice, as by the 10th century Droitwich seems to have had the status of a borough and the rights to brine were attached to the borough, things may not have been so straightforward, but it seems likely that St Augustine's received some proportion of the salt produced. This would be a coveted asset, the product of a renewable resource (brine) of high value, which could be sold on. In addition, at the east end of the High Street in Droitwich, where travellers would leave the Roman road and enter the main part of the town, there was a gate or 'bar' where it is likely market dues were collected on goods going in or out of the town; this area was also a detached part of the parish of Dodderhill so perhaps the church took a proportion of the market dues collected. Certainly, ownership of St Augustine's was seen as valuable in the 12th century when Westwood Priory and the church of Worcester disputed about which of them was the rightful owner; Worcester was the eventual victor, but assigned to Westwood, in recompense, all land in Clerehall, a meadow, tithes in Westwood, Clerehall and Crutch, and burial dues within those areas. In the 1500s the rectorial income for St Augustine's was worth 40 marks a year, possibly equivalent to over £120,000 in today's value, so it remained a wealthy church long after this period.

As the parish church, St Augustine's would normally have been owned by the lord of the estate of *Wicbold* (this place-name literally meaning 'the great hall at Wic'). In the early part of the 11th century, during the reign of Cnut, it is recorded that this estate was seized from the ownership of the church of Worcester by Edwin, the brother of another of Cnut's earls, Leofric, earl of Mercia and husband of the famous Lady Godiva. Edwin died in 1039, killed by Gruffydd ap Llewellyn of Wales, and the church no doubt pointed to this as an example of what happened to those who seized its possessions. However, there is no surviving charter confirming the grant of *Wicbold* and/or St Augustine's to the church of Worcester, in spite of that church's care over such documents. It is, therefore, legitimate to doubt whether they were ever in the possession of the church of Worcester in the 11th century.

In the mid 11th century, just before the Norman Conquest, the lord of the manor was Earl Godwin of Wessex (Thorn & Thorn 1982, 19, 12 notes), another of King Cnut's earls, and subsequently one of the great magnates of King Edward the Confessor; his daughter Edith became Edward's queen, and his son, Harold, later succeeded Edward as king for a short time in 1066. It is unlikely that he ever came to *Wicbold*, but no doubt the income from the manor, including rights to salt produced from the Upwich brine well, was a significant addition to his holdings.

The vill and the royal residence ('villa regalis')

Dodderhill/Droitwich are among a small group of Anglo-Saxon places where both a mother church and a 'royal vill' are found. Royal vill is a term used by historians in recent years for the territory of a *villa regalis* (Maddicott 2005, 32); vill is also a term used in Domesday Book in many counties including Herefordshire and Gloucestershire (Williams 2002) and is defined as equivalent to the township, 'that unit of community, of social and economic organization that many believe is the oldest territorial unit of the British landscape' (Austin 2002). The supporting territory of a royal vill would have included a complex of timber buildings, almost certainly having a large hall used for many functions including feasting and sleeping, but also 'public facing' functions such as a court, a tax-collecting centre, and an administrative centre for the territory of the vill. Vills were used by the rulers of the area exactly like the castles and manors of the later medieval kings; courts were itinerant, with the king, his family, leading officials and soldiers travelling from one place to another, and probably having no permanent base (although no doubt there was a centre to the kingdom, for instance Lichfield in the case of Mercia). The 'court' would stay for days or even weeks at each vill, using up the accumulated food stocks, collecting income and/or overseeing the accounts of the income collected on the king's behalf, entertaining followers, dispensing justice, and catching up on administrative matters. No doubt the reason for *Wicbold* was the plentiful and renewable resource of brine, which could be so easily converted into salt and, therefore, generated substantial income for the ruling family.

The territory of the vill is assumed to have been identical to that served by the church – the upper basin of the Salwarpe valley, lying mainly to the north of Dodderhill and the settlement at *Wic* (Droitwich): that is extending northwards nearly to Bromsgrove, eastwards towards Hanbury, westwards to the edge of Hampton Lovett, and southwards through the later parish of Salwarpe down to the south boundary of another later parish, Martin Hussingtree.

The interesting question arises whether this land unit was a creation of the Anglo-Saxons? In Roman times, up to the early 5th century, a richly appointed villa on the Bays Meadow site in Droitwich had probably performed a similar function by co-ordinating food and fuel production in the same area, the hinterland for the salt industry. There is evidence for continuity of salt production through from Romano-British to Anglo-Saxon times, as in the 5th to 7th centuries, before the arrival of Anglo-Saxon settlers in any number, a group of new brine-boiling hearths was constructed and used on the Upwich site (Hurst & Hemingway 1997, 17–19 and 23–4). The amount of salt produced must have been much greater than that required for just local consumption, and, of course, a network of Roman roads still radiated out from *Wic*. Salt would still have been in demand, so that the brine springs in the Salwarpe valley would have continued to be used to produce salt which was transported and traded much as before.

Many historians have supported the idea of continuity through from the Roman period, including Stenton (1971) and Myres (1986). More recently White (2007) has argued that in the province of *Britannia Prima* (of which Worcestershire was a part), decisions were made initially at a province-wide level by the ruling elite after the departure of Roman administration, with defence being provided by the people of the province, unlike in the other provinces of Britain where control was handed over to the allies (foreign troops brought in to protect against other incursions). Successful resistance, including the construction of large earthwork dykes (implying a high level of central control) kept the Anglo-Saxons out of the area for another hundred years. While by the end of the 5th century *Britannia Prima* had disintegrated, British kingdoms seemingly centred on former Roman towns emerge, and are later incorporated into the Anglo-Saxon kingdoms in the 6th and 7th centuries, including the Hwicce whose focus appears to have been in the former territory of the Dobunni. From the 5th century onwards there was also increasing evidence of Christianity, involving bishops in the surviving towns (which implies continuity of church hierarchy and its role in local administration; White 2007, 196–206).

Place-name evidence also points to continuity through what should probably be called the post-Roman centuries rather than the 'Dark Ages'. While reference is made to 'Romano-British' people at this time, in fact the majority of the people would have been ethnically identical with their Celtic Iron Age ancestors, the tribe of the *Dobunni* in this area. They may, over time (or even very quickly!) have adopted the benefits of Roman civilisation in so far as they were available in this area, while now paying their Roman taxes. But they would have continued to use their own language for the most part, which like all spoken languages would have evolved and possibly taken in loan-words from the Latin (or Hellenistic Greek) used by the more Romanised officials who administered the area.

Continuity from the Iron Age is, therefore, postulated through the Roman-dominated centuries (when many high-status Dobunni would have become local officials, adopting Roman customs and lifestyle), into the post-Roman and Anglo-Saxon times. A great influx of 'Romans' seems unlikely in that Roman administrators were few, while the army was a transient population in this part of the country, later being based mainly in the North. Similarly there seems no obvious evidence for a massive immigration of Anglo-Saxon settlers driving out the natives, as to some extent does seem to take place in the south-east of Britain. Therefore, the majority of the population of Dodderhill in the 6th century AD, as in the kingdom of the Hwicce and indeed in much of the western part of Britain, was ethnically, if not culturally, indigenous going back many generations.

A British Celtic language (from which Welsh eventually emerged) was spoken here throughout later prehistory until after the coming of the Anglo-Saxons. While Latin had been used for administrative, military and probably commercial purposes in the Roman period, this seems to have left little trace on place-names, and no recorded settlement names in either Latin or the British language have survived in use in Worcestershire (Gelling 1978, 30–62). Indeed, the only more certain Latin or British settlement name known in the county from the Romano-British period is *Salinae* (literally 'the salt-works') for Droitwich, a Roman label presumably replacing an unrecorded British name. Most of the topographical and locative names surviving today in the landscape of Dodderhill appeared from the 7th century onwards using a language now known as Old English, which was of Anglo-Saxon origin. It is likely that, while some of these names represented new settlement sites, others represent the renaming of formerly British sites – archaeological investigation may one day reveal more on this front. At least one older place-name endured locally, *viz* 'crug', as it was known in British (Crutch Hill, as it is now known); this British word denoted a natural hill, small and abrupt in shape (Gelling 1978, 138–9), and so the modern name means literally 'hill hill'.

For the most part today's surviving place-names are those first written down in the dominant language when records began to be kept. Certain elements of such names may have had greater significance, such as the Anglo-Saxon name for Droitwich, *Wic*, from the Latin word *vicus*, meaning village/small administrative unit, possibly with a more precise meaning of 'settlement with a specialised production and commercial purpose' (Bassett 2008a, 25–6 and note 75).

Therefore the territory, which the Anglo-Saxon vill controlled, may have had a continuity going back into later prehistory, when the salt workers would equally have needed food, and fuel, which came from this same hinterland. The Mercian monopoly on salt production may have been directly inherited from the Roman imperial monopoly via (?5th–)6th century organisation, the latter archaeologically evidenced at Upwich (Hurst & Hemingway 1997, 23–4), and possibly from still more distant rights which were exercised by the Celtic rulers of the Dobunni, the Iron Age tribe in this area (Maddicott 2005, 28 note 90). Maddicott (2005, 31 and 49) has pointed out that the surviving charters recording grants by Hwiccan kings related only to land and not to salt, and that it is only with the charters issued by Mercian rulers that grants of brine or salt rights are made, showing that the right to salt had become a Mercian royal monopoly which subordinate rulers, such as kings of the Hwicce, were not then allowed to grant away.

Against this general background the earliest charter which mentions *Wicbold* is dated 692, and usually translated to refer to land here being granted by King Aethelred of Mercia to his former minister Oslaf, then a monk at Worcester, the relevant extract being as follows:

> Est autem prefati agelli particula juxta fluvium quem dicunt saluuerpe in vico quem nobili vocitant nomine Uuicbold.

> '[This] is, moreover, [the] aforesaid little field [of which] a small part [is] next to the river which they call Salwarpe in Wic [or settlement] which the nobles are accustomed to call by the name Wicbold' (author's translation).

The land being granted may not, therefore, have been 'at Wicbold', if the meaning of 'in vico' could be 'in Wic' (ie Droitwich). This might well be the case if the part of the land next to the river Salwarpe is associated with salt-making – the grant, which is effectively to the church at Worcester, would then have been much more valuable. The use in the charter of 692 of 'vico' without any qualifying term indicating royal ownership may be seen as something of an anomaly given later terminology (see below), and so perhaps as supporting the alternative translation 'in Wic'. In the two surviving charters written at *Wicbold* (ie at the royal vill) from 815 and 831, the words 'in vico regis qui dicitur Uuicbold' ('in the estate of the king which is called Wicbold'), and 'in regale villo quae nominatur Wicbold' ('in the royal villa which is named Wicbold') are used of this location.

Maddicott (2005, 32) has described *Wicbold* as follows:

> A royal vill from an early date, probably from a very early date, possibly fortified, and certainly possessing exceptional rights in Droitwich … like its Roman predecessor, [it] may have been intended to provide quarters from which the king's officials could supervise the production of an indispensable resource. If not a regular royal residence (though it may have been), it was indubitably a royal base.

Another charter gives indirect evidence of the existence of the vill at *Wicbold*. Wiglaf, king of Mercia, in 836 granted privileges to the minster at Hanbury, which by then was in the possession of the church of Worcester (where the charter was preserved). Among the privileges was freedom 'ab omni constructione regalis ville' ('from all construction at the residence of the king'), which must surely refer to ongoing maintenance work or new building (presumably by way of extending the facilities) at the vill. It is just possible that this refers to the first construction of the vill complex, but the range of Mercian royal charters of much earlier date suggests very strongly that the Mercian kings would have strengthened their hold over such an important income stream well before 836 by building a local base, from which they could exercise oversight and control, as shown by earlier evidence for the organisation of salt making.

Two other 9th century charters written at *Wicbold* recorded land grants in Kent and Middlesex, and were signed by a number of witnesses who must be assumed to have been present at *Wicbold*, as follows:

> Charter of 815 – Cenwulf, king of Mercia; Ceolwulf, prince and next king of Mercia, then a 'dux' or leader/lord; Wulfred, archbishop of Canterbury; Deneberht, bishop of Worcester; Mucel, and another Wulfred, both 'dux' of Mercia.

> Charter of 831 – Wiglaf, king of Mercia; Cynethryth, queen of Mercia; Wigmund, prince and future king of Mercia; Wulfred, archbishop of Canterbury; six more Mercian lords ('dux') named Tidwulf, Aethelheard, Eadwulf (who was possibly of the Hwicce), Sigered, Aelfstan (who was possibly of the Magonsæte), and Cyneberht; and six further witnesses.

The presence of such a group of notables, the leaders of the kingdom of Mercia, at *Wicbold* shows how important a place it was. Later, King Alfred's son-in-law Aethelred convened two meetings of the Mercian council, the witan, at *Wicbold* in 888 and 903, suggesting that the considerable facilities appropriate for the holding of these gatherings were available.

A glimpse of the scale of entertaining undertaken by the court at such places comes from the laws of King Ine of Wessex which date to the late 7th century: the food and drink needed for one night was '10 vats of honey, 300 loaves, 12 casks of Welsh ale, 30 of clear ale, 2 full-grown cows or 10 wethers (castrated sheep), 10 geese, 20 hens, 10 cheeses, a cask of butter, 5 salmon, 20 pounds of fodder [presumably for the horses] and 100 eels', which was the food rent from 10 hides (a hide, as in Domesday Book, was a way of assessing land or other possessions for tax liability; a hide was often equated to the value/produce of 120 acres of arable land). That such demands might be burdensome on occasion is shown by a further extract from the charter of 836 mentioned above, in which privileges were granted to the minster at Hanbury, where one of them was 'liberabo a pastu regis et principum … et a difficultate illa quam nos saxonice faestingmenn dicimus' ('I will free [the minster] from the feeding of the king and nobles … and from that burden which we in Saxon call *faestingmenn*').

This presumably meant the minster would be excused from providing lavish hospitality for the royal court and for a specific class of officials, the *faestingmenn*, who had the right to claim board and lodging while on royal business.

In post-Roman Britain the dominant structure in society was 'extensive lordship', based on territories not estates, and on exaction of renders from 'free' cultivators rather than imposition of heavy services on tenants, with services and renders in kind extracted by virtue of rule over people rather than ownership of land; and these were first recorded among the early Christian English in the context of rulership and provisioning of royal households, where territories, assessed in hides, owed regular hidage-based quantities of produce to the kings who with their retinues moved round the kingdom living off the food renders (Blair 2005, 154–7). This system is certainly demonstrated by the extent of the provision laid down in King Ine's laws, and although these are later than the situation described by Blair, the extraction of the 'food rents' seems very similar.

A high value commodity, such as salt, had a particular usefulness in an age where loyalty was bought by royal patronage. Anglo-Saxon kings held their lands partly by rewarding their loyal followers who would defend them and fight for them; the followers expected regular gifts of valuable items such as silver bullion, military equipment including expertly produced swords which would cost the same as a medium-sized house today, and/or land. For the Mercian kings, the renewable and highly profitable natural salt resource at *Wic* (Droitwich), was a heaven-sent opportunity which they could use to reward their followers without granting away land, a permanent loss (Maddicott 2005, 31). Giving rights to brine/salt would not reduce their 'capital base' at all; it might slightly reduce their income, but they found other ways to maximise that. Such grants would stimulate the production of salt, and also the use of the woodland necessary for the brine-boiling process, which belonged to a range of owners among their followers.

Charter evidence shows that *Wic* (Droitwich) was usually described as a market (eg 'in vico emptorio'). The majority of the salt-ways, the roads out of Droitwich along which, from place-name and other evidence, it seems salt was transported in Anglo-Saxon times, lead south and east over the Cotswolds towards the headwaters of the Thames at Lechlade (Hooke 1998a, 8, fig 4), which was just inside the boundaries of the kingdom of the Hwicce. The salt-ways do not continue south of the Thames so the salt could have been loaded onto boats at Lechlade for transportation downstream (Maddicott 2005, 44). The bishop of Worcester, who owned salt rights in Droitwich, also had grants of property including moorings on the Thames at London, a customs-house, and exemption from tolls on two ships there (Maddicott 2005, 44–5). London was a growing market from the early 600s, and it too was under the control of Mercia from the later 600s. This could have been part of a deliberate strategy by Mercia, combining the product of Droitwich with the trading networks of London to give an income stream of silver bullion, actual cash, at a time when this was rare. And so Droitwich salt, produced for the kings of Mercia, may well have been exported abroad from the port of London, as well as sold and used locally in a city where large numbers of animals were butchered and processed, the salt being required for preservation of the meat and in the tanneries which turned the hides into leather (Maddicott 2005, 47).

A second method of gaining income from the salt industry was taxes on the salt produced for others apart from the king. A genuine charter of 716/717 shows King Aethelbald of Mercia granting a portion of a salt-house in *Wic* to the monastery of Evesham, free of tax, so the assumption here is that by the early 8th century taxes were levied on all salt production. A dubious charter purporting to be from 884 records Aethelred, King Alfred's son-in-law, granting salt rights and immunity from the associated taxes to an estate in Himbleton (S 219) as interpreted by Maddicott (2005, 39). Later, between 884 and 890, Aethelred and his wife Aethelflaed, King Alfred's daughter, granted to the church of Worcester half their rights within the new burh (defended town) recently created at Worcester for defence against the Danes 'except for the wagon-shilling and the load-penny levied [on salt produced] at Wic which go to the king as they have always done'. This records a royal tax of 1d on every horseload of salt (1 mitt; 102kg), and of 4d on a wagonload (4 mitts; 408kg). At this time a man could be fed for 1d a day, and a sheep cost 5d (Maddicott 2005, 42). The use of 'as they have always done' implies that these taxes had been in place for a long time, conceivably back into the 7th century at least. This dubious charter contains a reference to yet a third way of producing income, which was the imposition of tolls. As well as paying a tax on the salt produced, owners of salt rights would pay a further amount to be allowed to move the salt out of Droitwich (Maddicott 2005, 42–3 and note 145); if they sold it in Droitwich's market, presumably this would have resulted in a proportion being paid as a market fee.

Figure 30 Silver penny of Alfred the Great (diameter 22mm) issued c 875–80 and found next to Upwich brine well (Lentowicz & Seaby 1997) (copyright of Berrow's Newspapers)

Both the taxes and the tolls, therefore, would have given the king a large and reliable continuous income in cash, silver coins (eg Fig 30), which other assets like land did not provide. No wonder they came regularly to the vill at *Wicbold* to keep an eye on the way these taxes and tolls were levied and accounted for, and to ensure the proceeds were being collected. And, according to Maddicott (2005, 56), this elaborate system may have been of some antiquity:

> … it seems not unlikely that the system of double taxation, on brine-shares and, via tolls, on transport and marketing, may have been a legacy from earlier British rulers. If the use of the hide for assessing dues and service on land was an inheritance from the British past, it is at least possible that the taxation of salt was another parallel inheritance. Presumably the unknown men who controlled salt production at Droitwich in the post-Roman and pre-Anglian period expected to make a profit.

Two charters even give a glimpse into the intriguing possibility that brine shares were attached to specific land holdings before the time of the Mercian kings. The first, dating to 675 or earlier, is the lost charter of King Wulfhere (Sims-Williams 1990, 106 and note 77), granting 50 hides to Colman, the first abbot of the minster at Hanbury:

> Cum omnibus pratis, sylvis, puteis salis ad eam pertinentibus
>
> 'with all meadows, woods, [and] wells of salt pertaining to this [the land gifted]' (author's translation; the meadows, woods and brine-wells all seem to be linked to the land).

The second, dated 691, is the lost charter of King Aethelred (Maddicott 2005, 29 and note 94), which grants to Oftfor, Bishop of Worcester, land at Fladbury with associated rights to brine from the Upwich brine well:

> Et in Wic unum casulum cum duobus caminis de magno puteo ad eandem terram pertinentem
>
> 'And in Wic a small building with two furnaces of [linked to?] the great [brine] well, pertaining to that land' (author's translation).

This 'small building' would have been one of the wattle-walled flimsy industrial structures of which remains were found at Upwich (Hemingway & Hurst 1997, 21–2), in which one or more hearths or 'furnaces' were used to boil brine (and presumably ownership of the furnaces included rights to brine). The 'land' mentioned must be that at Fladbury which is gifted by the charter. The phrasing of both these charters suggests strongly that rights to brine, including the use of specific brine-boiling sheds, were linked to particular pieces of land by the mid to late 7th century at the latest; and, if it is accepted that earlier Mercian charters such as these may be confirmations of rights granted by the kings of the Hwicce, then the origins of such grants may be much earlier in date.

How much salt was produced annually from the 7th to the 11th centuries?

The charter of 716/717, which recorded King Aethelbald exchanging land used for salt-making at Droitwich with the bishop of Worcester, mentioned six furnaces in two sheds already there, and that the land given up would be used for the construction of three more sheds with six furnaces. Partial excavation of the likely salt-making area alluded to in these texts revealed hearths of this period, though it was not clear how many were in contemporary use and precisely when (Hurst & Hemingway 1997, 24–7), and so, for this period, it is difficult to estimate the amounts of salt being made.

By the late Saxon period, and so running up to the Norman Conquest, an indication of high productivity of salt is the network of roads radiating out from Droitwich, and a late 9th century reference to wagons being used for the transport of salt. This may also indicate that some major roads were being specially maintained for the transport of salt (and fuel), a provision which required some central control, and was possibly organised from the vill at *Wicelbold* (as it was named by 1086). Such an arrangement could have continued with the collection of tolls on medieval road users both to the north and south of Droitwich (see below). Based on Domesday Book (1086), estimates of annual production of salt from the royal share vary from 1200 tons upwards, and so an estimate of at least 1000 tons should be safe; but there would have been other producers, so the overall figure would have been higher.

Where was the vill?

So far archaeological and documentary research work has been unable to provide any certain location. The following characteristics of such sites have been suggested as helpful in their discovery (M Aston, pers comm):

- on rising ground, not too high but raised above its surroundings;
- close to a water supply;

- close to a (Roman) road;
- away from the minster (if present), and;
- near or in a forest, as the Anglo-Saxons loved hunting (as did the later Norman lords).

Wherever the Anglo-Saxon vill was located, it is possible that it survived as the estate centre long after the Norman Conquest into medieval times. The work carried out by the Dodderhill Parish Survey Project has so far not revealed this site, perhaps suggesting that it remains buried under continuing settlement today. Now called 'Wicelbold' (according to the Domesday Book scribe) the estate continued to be held by great lords whose main family seats lay elsewhere, so they did not live there, and a high-status manor house would not, therefore, have been needed. A steward (probably appointed from the local people) would have managed the collection of dues and made decisions at the local court. The original (now old) royal vill site may well have sufficed for these purposes, perhaps into the 14th century, or even later, by which time other large houses had been built in the area by families who held significant amounts of land in the manor and beyond, and the old centre may finally have faded from the landscape or been supplanted by a new house.

Late Saxon (c 900–1066)

This period saw people much exercised in the defence of the new realm of England from the depredations of the Vikings who threatened to overrun the country from the North. Though Wychbold was a long way from the front line it was, of course, contributing to the effort through paying taxes which were now channelled to the kingdom of Wessex, which led the resistance. The formation of Worcestershire was probably one response to this threat, the new county being tasked with raising resources to provide for the defence of Worcester in the early 10th century. Meanwhile salt production carried on in Droitwich and the main road running through Wychbold presumably continuing as a major artery of this trade. One feature of this period was the long distance movement of essential commodity goods, including salt, and this led to many routes being designated as salt-ways (Hooke 1985a, 125, fig 31), including through Wychbold, apparently en route to Halesowen (Houghton 1929–30, 12–13).

So far archaeological excavation has revealed relatively few late Saxon remains and then these have largely been south of the River Salwarpe and mainly in the Friar Street area of Droitwich (Hughes & Hunt 1992, 139). Occasional finds of artefacts of the period from north of the River Salwarpe, include a single copper alloy pin from the Bays Meadow site (Cool 2006, 193, fig 133, no 36), and a few pottery sherds from Upwich. Finds of individual objects may be the way forward as the Portable Antiquities Scheme has recently reported a copper alloy stirrup terminal from Dodderhill parish (Fig 31) probably dating c 1020–c 1100 (D Williams, pers comm; Williams 1997). Finds such as this may ultimately provide the best evidence for the disposition of settlements in this period, since with the lesser Roman settlements long abandoned the whereabouts of their successors, especially in the countryside, has posed a considerable problem.

Some churches were well established by this date as in the case of the church in Dodderhill, as Hemming records 'Wicbald' among the losses of the church at Worcester, as having been seized by Edwin, brother of Earl Leofric, in the reign of Cnut (1016–35). This place is presumably to be equated with Wychbold and its attraction possibly lay in large salt endowments that may have accompanied its foundation. The disputed possession fortunately proves the existence of the church prior to the late 12th century, which is, otherwise, its earliest date based on architectural considerations (Brooks & Pevsner 2007).

Figure 31 Copper alloy stirrup terminal (length 2in/47mm) found in Dodderhill and dating c 1020–c 1100 (PAS ref WAW-52D216); below the horizontal rib there is a moulded crested animal head. Copyright of the Portable Antiquities Scheme

Domesday Book (1066–1086)

The medieval period is fortunately generally well documented compared with what had gone before. After the Norman Conquest and the removal of English incumbents from high positions (which was almost universal countrywide, the Bishop of Worcester being one of the very few exceptions), the Normans took to firmly installing themselves, often behind the protection of high walls, as castles sprang up across the land. Clearly they only felt really safe when holed up in such great fortifications. These great Norman magnates were generally in control of vast estates, as power was expressed through land ownership and this was now concentrated in very few hands.

Prior to 1066 Earl Godwin (father-in-law of King Edward the Confessor) had held *Wicelbold* (Wychbold), which also had thirteen burgesses based in (Droit)Wich participating in salt making who could be taxed on their profits. This arrangement shows the extent to which Wychbold was still integral to the salt production and the settlement at Droitwich, which was gradually to change as the medieval period unfurled. They participated in the borough of Wich which was, therefore, clearly already in existence by 1066, as the various components constituting the borough can also be largely traced in Domesday Book and a convincing case can be made for the pre-medieval origins of the borough boundary as described in 1456 (Bassett 2008b, 231). It is likely, therefore, that the Upwich area of Wychbold bordering the north edge of Droitwich (now Vines Park) had already been placed within the borough, though originally part of Wychbold (later Dodderhill), which it remained parochially until much later. In 1086 the prominence of Worcestershire salt production and the (by then) scattered ownership of salt rights was readily evident from Domesday Book, where Droitwich is about the most mentioned place in the whole realm.

When Domesday Book was compiled in 1086 the survey listed the resources on which the king levied tax (the geld payment; Round 1901). Wychbold had by then been handed over to Osbern son of Richard, a Norman, but, surprisingly, one from a family that had settled at Richard's Castle (Herefs) before 1066 (see below). The manor was described as comprising eleven hides of land (equivalent to c 1300 acres), with four hides being exempt from tax, and was clearly a large, diversified, and wealthy estate.

Wychbold – the Domesday Book evidence (*by* Lyn Blewitt)

The great survey of assets, and the taxes due from them, which William I ('the Conqueror') caused to be compiled in 1086, may reflect earlier similar records used by the Anglo-Saxons and possibly their predecessors. Certainly, late Roman census accounts of estates exist for other parts of the empire, and these are comparable to those in Domesday Book (Percival 1985; Wood 1986, 50 and 149–56).

As with most entries in Domesday Book, the information for the manor of *Wicelbold* (Fig 32; which, largely, later became Dodderhill parish) is both interesting and frustrating, raising many

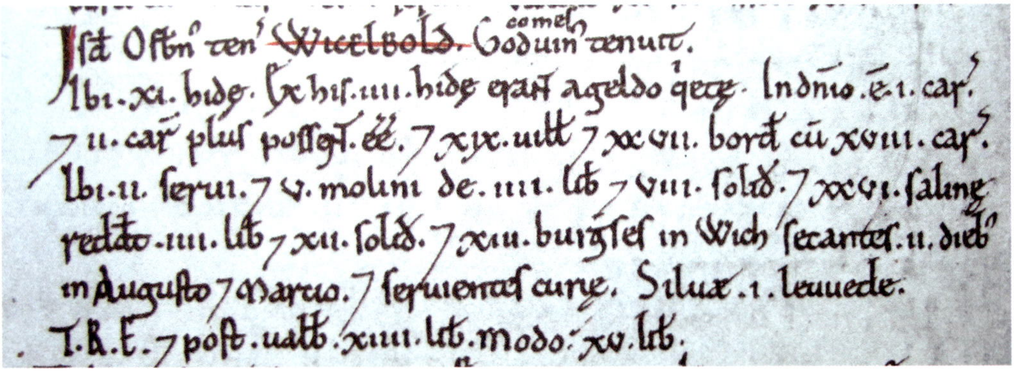

Figure 32 Domesday Book entry for Wychbold in 1086. Reproduced with permission from The Worcestershire Domesday *and copyright of Alecto Historical Editions*

questions as well as answering some. More information was obtained than was written up in the final version, including the numbers of animals held, as this survives for some counties, though unfortunately not for Worcestershire. Below is given a translation of the Domesday Book entry and, following that, some explanatory notes.

LAND OF OSBERN SON OF RICHARD

IN CLENT HUNDRED

The same Osbern holds Wychbold. Earl Godwin held it. [space for more information, left blank]
There are 11 hides. Of these 4 hides were free of tax. In the demesne is 1 plough
and 2 ploughs more would be possible and [there are] 19 villagers and 27 bordars to whom [belong] 18 ploughs.
There are 2 slaves and 5 mills worth £4 and 8 shillings and 26 brine-shares which yield £4 and 12 shillings and 13 burgesses in Droitwich [who are] cutting for 2 days in August and March and serving the court. [There is] woodland [measuring] one league.
In the time of King Edward and afterwards it was worth £14. Now [it is worth] £15.
(*DB Worcestershire* Folio 176d, 19,12; author's translation)

Some explanatory notes

Osbern son of Richard was the 'owner' or chief tenant of the manor in 1086. His father was Richard Scrope, the lord of Richard's Castle (Herefs), who seems to have settled there at the time of King Edward the Confessor, and so before the Norman Conquest. Richard Scrope (the surname being of Anglo-Norse derivation) had probably accompanied Edward on his return to England from Normandy to take the throne, and then been granted land in Herefordshire and elsewhere. Edward had had close ties with Normandy, as his mother was Emma of Normandy, sister to the Duke of Normandy and the second wife of King Aethelred of England. Following the latter's death in 1016, she had sent Edward and her other son, Alfred, back to Normandy, where they then lived, in Edward's case for 25 years before returning to England in 1041 as the likely heir to the throne.

Earl Godwin, who had held Wychbold in 1066, was the father of both Harold (who lost the Battle of Hastings) and of Edith, wife of Edward the Confessor, the last Saxon king of England whose death, childless, earlier in 1066 had initiated the crisis leading to William's invasion of the country. He had earlier, in 1036 during an interregnum after the death of King Cnut, arrested

Edward's younger brother, Alfred, on his return to England. Alfred was blinded and later died of his injuries. Earl Godwin was one of the most powerful people in the kingdom of England, and Wychbold was one of his many estates; it is not known whether he ever visited it. Given the importance of the estate – that is, it included the brine springs of Upwich which generated great income – it is not surprising that it was held from the King by such an important magnate.

The *hide* was a way of assessing the value of a manor for its tax liability, and also notionally a unit of land measurement, indicating both the productivity and the tax liability, and is thought to be the amount of land which could support a family for a year. A standard hide is usually regarded as 120 acres, but in practice its extent varied enormously, and where other resources existed which were more productive than arable land (such as woodland, fishing, fowling, or pasture which was used for sheep), the actual area of the land could be much smaller than the area implied by the number of hides used for its tax assessment. It is, therefore, possible that the value of the salt rights held by the manor (see brine-shares below) has also been taken into account in the valuation of the manor at 11 hides.

4 were free of tax – this indicates that an area of land, and/or other resources, was owned by a person or institution not paying tax. It is probable that this represents the holding of the Anglo-Saxon royal residence and/or of the mother church, St Augustine's.

Demesne was the lord of the manor's own land within the manor, which was worked by the labour of the people who lived on the manor as their 'dues' to their lord; where the lord of the manor was absent, the manor would have been managed on the latter's behalf by a bailiff or local steward.

Plough is a term used to refer to a plough drawn by 8 oxen, which has implications both for the amount and quality of land (ie a team of 8 oxen drawing a plough could plough an acre of good arable land in a morning) and the amount of animal feed needed over the winter, the production of which was dependent on hay-producing meadow land, as at this time no grass was sown and no winter roots were planted. Meadow was both scarce and valuable, as evidenced throughout the whole of Domesday Book.

A villanus (anglicised later as *villein*, and in modern parlance as villager) was an inhabitant who held a larger amount of land in the common fields, perhaps 15–30 acres. He was not free to leave the manor, but some villagers in 1086 could afford to rent whole manors or fisheries. He would have had to do some work on the lord's estate, as well as cultivating his own land.

A bordarius (bordar) was an inhabitant who held a smaller amount of land in the common fields, perhaps 5 acres, and was not free to leave the manor. Bordars were sometimes freed slaves, and they would have had to do more work on the lord's land than a villager. Like a villager the bordar would have had time to cultivate his own land, and to work for pay on the land of other men where the opportunity arose.

A servus (slave) was the lowest level of inhabitant, regarded more as an object rather than a person, who did the majority of the work on the demesne land. Ploughing would have been their main occupation there, with two men required to operate the plough team – so two slaves for the one plough on the demesne land of Wychbold makes good sense. However, a slave had some free time, in which he could work for pay, and he might even save enough money to buy his freedom. He may have had a small amount of land allocated, and did have an annual allowance of food. It is thought that Domesday Book under-records the total number of slaves; the two slaves recorded in Wychbold may have each have been the senior male of a family, any dependents (including those old enough to work) simply not being recorded.

5 mills is an unusually large number of mills in one manor, and is the second largest concentration in the county at this time. The most likely locations for these mills in the 11th century are the sites of Paper Mill (originally a corn mill), the first Wychbold Mill (at the end of Mill Lane, south side), Impney Mill, Briar Mill, and the Droitwich town mill lying to the east of Chapel Bridge (whose site was a detached part of Dodderhill parish into the 19th century), all on the River Salwarpe.

26 salinae (brine-shares) refers to a defined volume of brine (from the Droitwich brine pits), which would be boiled to evaporate the water and produce salt. Each share was 6912 gallons in a year (Rastel 1678, 1061), which at just over 2.5lb of salt from a gallon (Rastel 1678, 1060) produced 8 tons of salt, so Wychbold had 208 tons of salt each year. While some of this would have been used on the manor, and, in earlier times, also at the Saxon royal residence, it is likely that most of this remained in Droitwich to be sold for profit. The amount quoted, £4 12s, was the tax payable on this 'income stream', not the value of the salt itself – that would have been much higher. The term *salina* is often translated as 'salt-house', meaning the small industrial shed in which brine was boiled to make salt. However, as Domesday Book's prime purpose was to list tax assessments, it seems more appropriate to see *salina* here as referring to a measure of the brine which generated the wealth to be taxed.

Burgesses are citizens or freemen of a borough, and often members of the governing body of the town or borough, so the medieval equivalent of a town councillor. In other boroughs they owned property and ran businesses, but in Droitwich we know from later records that to be a burgess meant owning rights to brine shares, and these rights were in the medieval period passed on only by marriage and inheritance. The burgesses mentioned here are Droitwich burgesses who, certainly from 1215 (King John's charter), and probably for some time before, governed the affairs of the town and particularly the regulation of the salt industry. They were probably also salt-makers themselves, processing the brine shares to which the owners of their places of residence were entitled. Domesday Book recorded 89 burgesses in Droitwich itself, together with 4 in Salwarpe, 7 in Witton and these 13 in Wychbold, making a sub-total of 113 in, or very near, Droitwich (the later borough boundary incorporated parts of all these manors/parishes; Bassett 2008a, 6–12). A further three were recorded (one each in Crowle, Cookhill and Morton Underhill), giving a total of 116 burgesses at this time. The Wychbold group is the next largest total after those stated to be in Droitwich, and this may reflect the earlier situation of the main Upwich brine pit being under royal control and administered from the Saxon royal residence. By the time of Domesday Book, and no doubt before that, the existence of burgesses suggests Droitwich is separately established with some self-government as a 'borough' which functioned like other towns, but also gained from the production and marketing of salt by providing labour and supplies and the location for the markets.

Cutting for 2 days in August and March and serving the court is one of the most enigmatic parts of the information given. Instead of 'cutting' (*secantes*) this word is often translated 'reaping', but the literal meaning is 'cutting', and indeed this might make more sense for the days in March when there is not much to 'reap' or harvest. However, hazel withies were cut in March, and we know from archaeological excavation that the baskets used for the collection, drainage, and transportation of salt were made entirely of hazel (Hurst 1997b, 110), so it is possible that the activity referred to is the cutting of hazel withies in order to make these conical baskets (D Hurst, pers comm). Meanwhile the days in August could have been for normal reaping or even mowing, as evidenced elsewhere in Domesday Book; this was during the main six-month salt-making season known from later references. Alternatively, the burgesses could have been engaged in March on *cutting* the 'young pole wood' (straight young growth of either 4 or 8 years age from managed woodland) needed in large quantities as fuel in salt production carried out from June to December. It is strange that only this short time (4 or 8 days at most) is recorded on these activities, when it is likely that most of the inhabitants of the parish, and its neighbours, would have spent a lot of time reaping or mowing, cutting withies, and cutting wood; it is, therefore, possible that the short time period mentioned is connected with the other part of the entry (ie serving the court), so that this is a specific reference to these activities being undertaken for that short time as duties connected with service at the estate centre. The burgesses, like the other inhabitants of the manor, would no doubt have spent a lot more time on some or all of these activities, but did so separately from their 'service to the court'.

There are other examples in Domesday Book of short periods of service on reaping or mowing where these seem to have been specific duties related to an identified person or type of person doing the work, and/or to the work being a customary duty because of holding a particular piece of land, with this situation going back to before the Norman Conquest. Perhaps this is also the case with the Wychbold burgesses who 'served the court' and were, therefore, an identifiably separate type of tenant.

Woodland [measuring] one league is difficult to interpret as the word used, *levvede*, seems to be meant in Worcestershire entries as a measure of area but it is not clear how great that is. League (*leuga, levve*) as a measure of length is thought to be one and a half miles. Using a formula developed in the 1970s to analyse Domesday Book woodland references, which assumes the league to be 1.5 miles and the area to be half as wide as the given length (Rackham 1980, 115), the Wychbold woodland might equate to 504 acres of woodland (approximately 218ha). The area of Dodderhill parish most likely to be wooded is the long triangular piece to the east, leading up to Dodderhill common/Piper's Wood, and this covers 509 acres by modern measurement, so could easily have been the 'one league' mentioned in Domesday Book. The woodland would have been managed or 'farmed', with trees coppiced (cut off near the ground) or pollarded (cut back at about 2 metres above ground) every 4 or 8 years, so that they produced new growth of multiple straight shoots which thickened into 'pole wood' that was easy to cut, transport and use as fuel. It has been estimated that between 4 and 5 acres of managed woodland were needed to produce enough fuel to make one ton of salt per year (Hurst 2004), therefore the woodland within the manor would not have produced sufficient fuel to make the 208 tons of salt that Wychbold's share of brine generated annually, and other sources of wood were needed. The importance of woodland for the salt industry is evidenced by the entry for Droitwich itself in Domesday Book, where the Sheriff of the county states that 'if he does not have the woodland, he cannot pay [the tax due, 65 pounds of silver by weight and 2 measures of salt] in any way'. Though only a rough guide to how much this tax amounted to, the modern value of 65 pounds of silver is nearly £19,000.

In the time of King Edward refers to the pre-Conquest years before 1066. Domesday Book recorded valuations for the tax due from each manor at up to three time periods: the time of King Edward, afterwards (ie between 1066–86), and in 1086, the year of compilation. The value of Wychbold has increased, in contrast to that of other manors or estates, whose value had declined in 1086. From this it can be assumed that salt production continued more or less uninterrupted through the post-Conquest period. The annual value of £15 (1086) was a high value at a time when most manors were worth less than £5 annually, and it follows that this derived from its brine shares and the income which flowed from the sale of its salt.

Medieval (1066–1550)

The Middle Ages had opened with England becoming forcibly re-attached to the Continent, and finally removed from the orbit of Scandinavia which had also been competing for this great prize. The destiny of England was now set to be drawn southwards into continental affairs, which eventually led to famous victories such as at Agincourt, and the emergence of a powerful sense of English nationhood.

But for the moment the English were defeated and English estates were forfeit to the Normans, who now proceeded to put their impress on the wider landscape in various ways. This included the construction of castles symbolising domination of the landscape, and by widening the protection of woodland and creating huge new tracts of forest for the purposes of hunting where they imposed new restrictions and penalties on those living in the countryside. At the outset of the medieval period Worcestershire was 40% woodland (Rackham 1990, 50) with this mainly to the west of the River Severn and north of Worcester. Wychbold, therefore, found itself now largely placed in the Forest of Feckenham, with the boundary cutting through Dodderhill parish following the main road (A38) up to and then along Papermill Lane, thereby placing all land to the north and east of this boundary under forest law with its own courts and special regulations restricting freedom; the local stretch of the boundary of Feckenham Forest was described in 1300 as 'from Gosford [ie Droitwich] by the high road to Leather Bridge … to Wychbold … via the mill belonging to Westwood Priory to Kingsland' (NA C67/6A, mem16).

From the 12th century the manor of Wychbold was held by the Mortimers. Being based in the Welsh Marches their role was, essentially looking westwards, to keep the usual threat of the unruly Welsh at bay, so that Worcestershire was never troubled by raids from this direction. Though not directly involved in this defence, Wychbold taxes will have contributed to maintaining this English peace by contributing to the king's efforts at defence of the realm. Though never resident in Wychbold the Mortimers still asserted their hunting rights locally, as in 1275 when Roger de Mortimer established a warren at Wychbold (Röhrkasten, 2008, 1086).

Despite these momentous political and administrative changes at the top, at peasant level, Wychbold life probably went on much as usual, except that the inhabitants now had to respect forest laws restricting hunting to the elite. Further afield they might have become aware of a new castle and cathedral being constructed at Worcester, the latter being started in 1084 (*VCH Worcestershire* IV, 394). Locally many parish churches were also being rebuilt, which, incidentally, must have created a great deal of employment.

As the new order settled down there was a gathering pace to the economy as fairs and markets began to flourish since landlords sought to increase their incomes. There was a new spirit of commercialism, and families benefited from increasing employment opportunities (Langdon and Masschaele 2006), a trend which lasted until *c* 1300 when the climate seems to have deteriorated with a series of poor harvests, and adverse impacts on prices, after about 200 years of previous amelioration (Fagan 2000, 17). Wychbold inhabitants, though without their own market (probably because it was too close both to Droitwich, where as an early borough a market had long existed, and to Bromsgrove), could have presumably participated in this burgeoning economy by visiting these neighbouring markets instead; new markets were not generally condoned unless the new site was at least 6–7 miles (c 10–11km) from existing ones (Lipson 1949). The increased traffic also generated greater tolls being collected in Wychbold which was an additional way the manor made up for its lack of direct involvement in a market. This period was also accompanied by population growth (Langdon and Masschaele 2006, 60–1), which would again have led to greater traffic, and increased toll revenues. For instance the Priory of Worcester paid a total of 13s 5d in the year 1328–9 on tolls collected north and south of Droitwich, and at ½d per cart this represents a cart nearly every day passing through between its manor at Bromsgrove and Worcester (Dyer 2000, 36–7). Traffic was by no means always that local, as in 1275 a carter heading for Coventry died in an accident at Wychbold, when the large barrel of wine he was carrying crushed him (*ibid* 36).

During the 1200s some towns local to Wychbold grew where cloth making became well established, such as at Kidderminster and Worcester (Hilton 1966), and some inhabitants of Wychbold may well have benefited from the growth in the textile industry since a fulling mill was set up at Impney by the late 13th century where Alice le Walker (ie fuller) worked; this was added to the corn mill so that henceforth there were two mills here. Brewing may have also done well in this period, as the salt manufacture at Droitwich (Fig 33) must have been thirst-making physical work, and so quantities of ale would have been brewed locally for the Droitwich market, as for instance attested at Westwood (Stenton 1934, no 1268), but probably generally roundabouts, including in the Wychbold area. While it is difficult to see where any profit from the salt industry went locally, this industry no doubt remained a source of great employment in the town, and this, in turn, led to a successful and regular market, which again boosted the local economy of the surrounding area. And from the mid 13th century a town also began to develop at Bromsgrove, a market first being mentioned in 1200, and this town concentrated especially on satisfying the appetites of travellers (Dyer 2000, 12–14). Farms and food businesses in the surrounding region, therefore, had the opportunity to benefit through supplying both raw ingredients, and prepared food to these local markets.

Figure 33 Brine extraction at Upwich in c 1300 using the 'rydhoc' that was later replaced by a pump; salt-making workshop ('seal') to rear (illustration by Arthur Davis)

New opportunities also appeared for the king to raise taxes on this booming trade (Langdon and Masschaele 2006, 47), which perhaps served incidentally to free ordinary folk from impositions that might otherwise have happened. By the 13th century English agriculture was being linked to more distant, including foreign, markets, especially where wool was concerned, and even small numbers of sheep per villager could amount to flocks of some considerable value in terms of the wool crop. Though Wychbold was not situated in prime sheep country, and in comparison with south Worcestershire was too far away from the hill grazing of the Cotswolds to really take advantage of this new opportunity, it seems that by the 14th century shepherds (according to personal names; Eld 1895) and, therefore, sheep were becoming a feature of the area (as later; see Townshend, this volume). This was a period when, elsewhere, much woodland was now being cleared usually for arable, and this was also noted in the vicinity, such as in the parish of Hanbury (Dyer 1991, 27–30), and so is likely to have also happened in Wychbold.

The modern extent of Wychbold/Dodderhill now took shape, as Westwood and Crutch were separated off, while Elmbridge found the resources for its own chapel, a sign of eventual parochial independence to come (though not formalised until the 19th century). Detached portions of Dodderhill parish (shown on the 1843 tithe map) seem to show the retention of the most valuable assets (eg the mill in Droitwich). However, sometimes it is difficult to explain these odd pieces of land such as Huntingdrop; though a field-name 'church field' may suggest former church property here, hence its retention, or it may have been that the site of the local gallows was on a green here, and would have been kept hold of as a sign of official authority in the area.

Then the arrival of the terrible Black Death in 1348–9 sent all these positive developments into reverse, and literally, in the case of about half the population, stopped life in its tracks. A second period of plague arrived in 1361–2, and it periodically returned thereafter until the 17th century, putting a continuous drag on the economy, and making health scares a regular companion. Where better evidence is available, for instance for Bromsgrove, of the 39 family names recorded in 1311 only seven remained in 1352–3, a pattern of loss or migration repeated into the 15th century (Dyer 2000, 53). This probably reflects the taking up of vacant urban tenancies by rural inhabitants escaping greater rural unemployment due to an increasing emphasis on pastoral farming – here non-arable land increased from 19% in the late 1300s to 47% in the late 1400s (*ibid* 56). This changing shape of the rural economy with the reduction in arable may well have had a serious impact on local mills by reducing the demand for their services. Monastic incomes relied on such business, such as with Haughmond Abbey's tenure of Wychbold mill held since the later 12th century; here they also came to own other property where the tenants were called upon to attend 'the canons' court of Wychbold' (Rees 1985) from at least the later 14th century.

One advantage of the time was that those who had survived the pestilence were now often much better placed in terms of material wealth (Dyer 2000, 55). Perhaps all this change and ferment during the 14th to early 16th centuries may have contributed to fresh initiatives such as education taking deeper root (see Morris, this volume), and the growth of new ideas which eventually saw much of the old medieval world and its attendant mind-set, cast aside, with the eventual ushering in of a new era.

The medieval landscape of Dodderhill (*by* Derek Hurst)

Most of the 13th century and earlier place-names are all still traceable today in the 21st century landscape of Dodderhill (Fig 34; though not necessarily in the very same places as originally). The earliest version of names only are given here with the explanation of names, where needed, following Mawer & Stenton (1927), unless otherwise indicated: *Dudrenhull* (Dodderhill; for

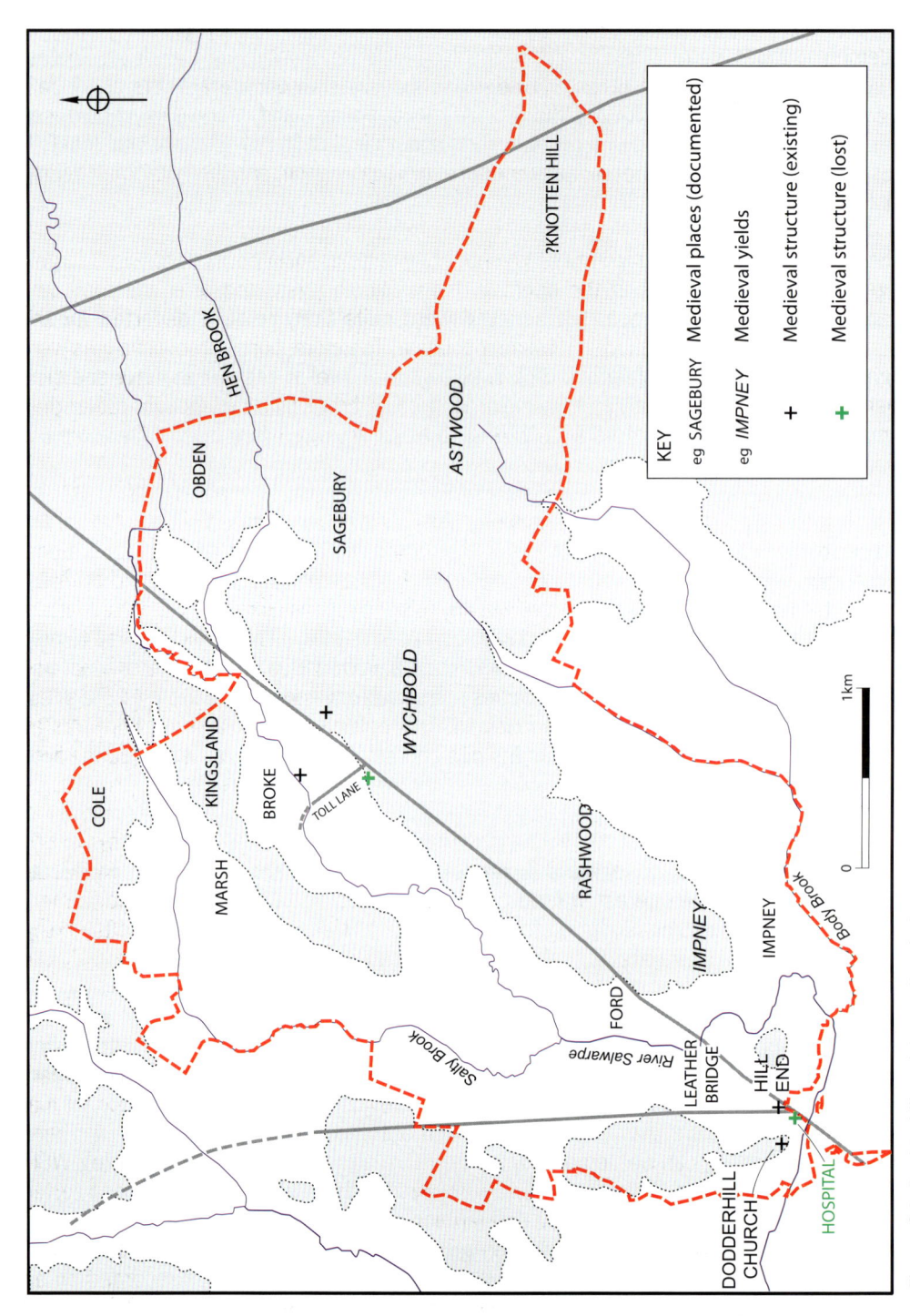

Figure 34 Dodderhill parish: medieval places and structures

explanation see above), *Brok* (Brookhouse Farm), *Colle* (Colley Pit; literally 'pond associated with the [now vanished] Colle stream'), *Forde* (Ford Farm), *Hensbroc* (Henbrook), *Hulle* (Hill Farm), *Obeden* (Hobden; literally 'Ob(b)a's valley'), *Huntingthrop* (Huntingtrap Farm; the name implying a secondary settlement; R Coates, pers comm), *Imeneye* (Impney; probably implying a settlement in a wet area), *Kingeslaunde* (Kingsland Hill Farm; literally 'king's glade'; R Coates, pers comm), *Letherenebruge* (Leather Bridge), *Eshide* (Rashwood; literally 'the ash hide'), *Savagebury* (Sagebury Farm; literally 'the Savage manor house'), and *Wicbold* (Wychbold, see above). Only *Helperic* (Helpridge Farm; derivation uncertain, but literally '[the] helpful [one]'; R Coates, pers comm), and *Knoteshull* present difficulties of location, and the latter may belong to Hanbury.

Members of the medieval community of Wychbold, with its associated manors, were largely engaged in agricultural tasks at the opening of the Middle Ages, and after the trials and tribulations of this period, those that survived were quite likely to have departed for the surrounding towns, during a period of rural depopulation. Therefore, considerable changes were wrought in this period as people gradually gained a greater level of freedom to move and think for themselves, so that change can be measured more by how individuals thought rather than in terms of more obvious indicators of change such as technology, which tend to dominate our consideration of such issues today.

With the institution of the feudal system local authority traditionally resided with the lord of the manor, who will have administered the manorial court, an important part of the national administration system, as it included looking after the maintenance of roads and bridges, appointing the local constable, and dealing with any minor offences. For more personal matters of behaviour there was the church court, known as the Consistory Court, which looked to hold people to account. The family unit was of fundamental importance, and here the head also wielded formidable powers. Social hierarchies were well developed, and there was a great dependence on servants, as part of a household. This political and social framework was as much a part of the medieval landscape as the hills and fields of the land, as it shaped the lives of the inhabitants.

This same period was one when servants travelled long distances to the best markets to buy exotic spices, and when a 2lb loaf and 3 pints of ale per person per meal was regarded as sufficient fare. Clearly the interest in food consumption was as keen as today, and farmers would have been focussed on producing the grains for this, while meat protein was often being provided by fish which was generally eaten at least twice a week (Lucas 1998, 42).

Though Wychbold should not be seen in isolation, as it was also keyed into a larger economic system. In particular its proximity to Droitwich must have presented many marketing opportunities, as, at the outset of the medieval period, arable farming was clearly the primary focus of food production. Here archaeology can help provide some insight into the extent that this occurred in the parish, and, as typical for much of the county where woodland had been cleared, arable farming can be demonstrated by thin scatters of medieval pottery (eg WSM 38360, 38361) and can be shown to be very widespread. This material would have been carted out to fields with the rest of the domestic and farming waste as part of the manuring process. The extent of arable cultivation in the Middle Ages is also well indicated by ridge and furrow earthworks which, in many cases, survived into the mid 20th century to be recorded on air photographs. The 1946 series of air photographs of Dodderhill taken by the RAF (58 Squadron) just after the Second World War do show some ridge and furrow remains throughout the parish, and this was then best preserved particularly around Astwood Manor and Sagebury Farms.

Today only small amounts of medieval ridge and furrow surviving as earthworks still bear testimony to formerly very extensive arable agriculture, for instance the golf course at Ford offering some preservation. Often locally given little attention by archaeologists (eg Cudlip 2009), ridge and furrow in Dodderhill has only been published in detail in fields just south of Church Lane (Hurst 1998), where the lower remnant of cultivated soil was associated with 13th/14th century pottery, and the slightly sinuous character of the earthwork was also indicative of classic medieval ridge and furrow cultivation, while the long thin appearance of these fields (recently developed for housing) was especially reminiscent of enclosed strips of an open field system. Here the ridge and furrow (width *c* 6–8m) was only detected during excavation, and typically this is the case throughout much of Worcestershire, as this type of earthwork is very vulnerable to modern heavy farming machinery.

The survival of such earthworks testifies to the ancient abandonment of arable farming on a large scale, and, though generally it is impossible to say when this occurred, it does seem in Dodderhill to correspond roughly with the period of the Black Death, as the only archaeological evidence to date (see above) suggests it had happened by the end of the 14th century at the latest. For such remains to have survived 600 years means that, once converted to pasture, only minimal cultivation occurred subsequently. Pastoral farming, therefore, clearly remained a key activity over a significant part of Dodderhill until at least 1946 judging from the aerial photographic evidence for the then extent of ridge and furrow. Perhaps similarly in 1300 90% of adjacent Hanbury was arable, whereas until 1937 it was largely grassland (Buchanan 1944, 492).

Other types of medieval land use are much more difficult to locate, but must have included meadow along the Salwarpe and some areas of animal grazing; the 1290–1300 land values in adjacent Hanbury were 2d–3d per acre for arable, 18d–20d for meadow, and 16d for pasture, which was uniformly lower than in the south-east (ie Avon valley; Buchanan 1944, 495), and similar values held for Wychbold (Gaut 1939, 37). This clearly shows that land values were much higher for the non-arable.

Another major element of medieval settlement was that fields were often communally worked. Charting the medieval field system in Wychbold/Dodderhill, and the later conversion to private enclosure, has been difficult given the poor evidence available. Any common fields are only very occasionally mentioned, for instance Rye meadow and perhaps *Rudgeway filde* (in 1576; WRO BA2309/58), or are only very dimly glimpsed (eg *Astodefeld* in *c* 1377; Talbot Pap 73522). Though the project recorded many (now defunct) field-names, the majority of these were 16th century or later when first recorded, including a 1549 reference to the presence of enclosures (BCA ref 505454). Therefore, it has been particularly difficult to establish early agricultural arrangements in any detail.

There seem to be some further clues to agricultural activities in the personal names recorded in the 1327 lay subsidy roll. Though this shows little trace of obvious woodland activity in the *Wychebald* list (including Elmbridge), there seems to be a new interest in sheep farming with *Robertus le shepherde* assessed at 4s, one of the highest payments with most people being rated at 2s or less. There were two shepherds listed assuming their names reflect their occupations. Such developments are more typical of other areas such as the Cotswolds where high quality wool was being produced for export (Hurst 2005). Perhaps the lure of great wealth from wool was enough to generally stimulate sheep farming even in areas not particularly suited; the wool may also have been intended for the home market to supply the advancing textile manufacture of the local towns.

Some place-names in medieval Dodderhill indicate tracts of woodland in the early part of this period, especially on the east side of the parish (Astwood, Rashwood) towards the Forest of Feckenham. Though absorbed into Feckenham Forest Wychbold woodland does not strongly exhibit typical historical woodland landscape features such as '-end' place-names which marked expansion of arable in the 12th/13th centuries, as for instance in Hanley Castle (Toomey 2001, xxiv); though there are occasional exceptions such as Hill End and much later, in 1601, Impney End (WRO Hampton Pap 502). Nor are there any particular indications of woodland crafts at Wychbold to compare with the extensive pottery making, as, for instance, once again in Hanley, a clear sign of access to woodland resources. Though woodland activities can be confirmed, since in 1270 Wychbold was fined for not presenting a venison offence, and in 1274 Robert of Estwode (Astwood in Wychbold), a minor landowner, was removed from his office as verderer (West 1964b). Though the woodland character of Wychbold generally seems somewhat less developed compared to other woodland areas in the county, it still, therefore, exhibited this to a degree, especially where it stretched in the direction of Feckenham Forest.

The local common was at Piper's Hill, where it was contiguous with Hanbury common, and the former Stoke (Prior) common, which was in the southern part of that parish (P Gough, pers comm), and so it is most likely that this area started out as a shared area of common. The Stoke Prior enclosure award refers to the laying out of roads over the common as it was being enclosed here in the later 18th century (P Gough, pers comm). A hedgerow survey during the project identified potentially ancient hedgerows in the vicinity of the common, the oldest hedges noted being along Holmes Lane at the farthest extremity from Dodderhill settlement. Hedges here included field maple, a species noted by Muir (2000, 89) as indicative of a medieval or older date; and now that 'Hooper's Rule' (calculating age from the number of certain species present; Pollard *et al* 1974) is no longer considered generally reliable, it is currently impossible to be any more precise. This field of work is especially difficult in Worcestershire, as there has been surprisingly little comparable data published, and so any more specific interpretation of the landscape, using this type of evidence, lacks a developed research context to take account of localised variation. Elsewhere on Dodderhill common there are ancient trees also showing the comparative antiquity of the natural landscape in this area.

Surprisingly there seems to be no sure example of a moated medieval site in Dodderhill parish, apart from at Huntingdrop. Other possibilities are Sagebury (as observed by Mick Aston in 1969), Astwood Manor where an early 18th century estate plan suggestively shows an elongated area of water on the west side of the house, and at Rashwood (WSM 10977) where an elongated pond suggests one arm of a moat. The presence of such sites would typically have been indicative of farming expansion in about the 12th century where woodland was being cleared, and were broadly typical of woodland areas, where they offered some practical protection for the more isolated farms, as seem to have characterised medieval Wychbold. Further investigation could usefully be carried out to determine the presence/absence of this type of site so characteristic of much of medieval Worcestershire.

The reduction in the population from the Black Death generally led to the phenomenon of shrunken and deserted medieval villages now well established in the annals, and many deserted medieval settlements have been indicated for the adjacent parish of Hanbury (Dyer 1991, 54, fig 13). In Dodderhill the case can mainly only currently be made for shrunken settlement in that most of the smaller settlements, as hinted at the 13th/14th century documents, still survive today, though often now as only single farms. By the 15th century the reduced rural population had impacted in other ways with tenants becoming difficult to find and this resulted in an even greater tendency to conversion to pasture and enclosure of new private fields, including in the woodland areas (eg Arden to the east; Watkins 1998), in order that land could remain productive. The affects in later medieval Wychbold have not been traced, as the historical records for this period are not particularly informative, and so we have to look to adjacent areas to shed some light on developments in this period. New crops may have become more popular as flax was an important crop in Hanbury by the middle of the century (Dyer 1980). The appearance of the countryside was changing greatly and, generally, the potential for employment in rural work was diminishing. This must have led to a general drift to the towns for employment, a trend that gathers pace in the post-medieval period and ensures labour is available for the industrial revolution in that period.

Local organisation was key to protecting livelihoods as tensions between towns and their surrounding countryside were emerging in the 16th century, especially in the leading industry of textile manufacture. Towns then sought to protect their industry by seeking to ban production in the countryside and so in 1533–4 a monopoly of cloth-making was jointly set up by clothiers of Worcester, Evesham, Droitwich, Kidderminster and Bromsgrove (Unwin 1957). This would have put pressure on the livelihoods of country folk who were less able to organise so effectively, though the fulling mills of the area would still have benefited from being able to process the cloth being produced in the local towns.

Manor of Wychbold (*by Jenny Townshend*)

The late Saxon manor of Wychbold had been held by Earl Godwin, one of the most powerful people in England, but was held by Osbern, son of Richard Scrope of Richards Castle (Herefs), by the time of Domesday Book (1086). The landlord himself could either be a tenant of the Crown or hold his land directly of the Crown. In Wychbold the medieval lord of the manor was never resident, his interests being maintained by his steward and the local bailiff. The manor was an economic unit usually consisting of the demesne (property the lord retained for his own use), and the remainder which was tenanted or given over to common or waste. The two main types of tenant were villeins who occupied their lands on condition of rendering services to the lord, such as cultivating his demesne, and freemen who paid a money rent to the lord. The site of the original Wychbold manor house is not known, but in 1474 William Carewe, the then lord of the manor, gave permission for a fulling mill, now known as Walkmill, to be built on demesne land adjacent to the River Salwarpe, showing that the estate extended to land west of the main road (A38; BCA ref 475877).

By the early 13th century the manor of Wychbold was held by Robert de Mortimer of Richards Castle (Herefs), who died in about 1219. It then passed to his widow Margery and then to her new husband William de Stuteville. When he died in 1259 the manor was worth £15 5s (Willis-Bund 1894). In 1275 Margery's son, Hugh Mortimer, died holding the manor of Wychbold, and a survey of property known as an *inquisitio post mortem* (IPM) was carried out. This was an inquest made following the death of a tenant-in-chief of the Crown, and it established the date and cause of death, and the extent of the lands held, as well as the name and age of the heir. In this case the heir was Hugh's son, Robert, who had to pay relief (a tax on a new tenant) to the Crown. The manor was valued at £41 4s, sixteen years after the previous valuation.

The inquest recorded that Hugh had a manor house at Wychbold with grounds attached worth only 2s a year and a dovecote worth a shilling. The demesne, land he had retained for his own use, comprised 240 acres of directly farmed arable and was valued at 5d per acre. His 12 acres of meadow-land was valued at 18s and the pasture at 6s 4d. The woodland was valued according to the quantity of underwood sold each year, which was estimated at 4s.

The lords of the lesser manors within Wychbold had obligations to that lord of the manor. So Peter Corbet held the manor of Impney by a knight's fee worth £30, a knight's fee being the amount of land which could support a knight and his family for a year and was also a feudal tenure which obligated the holder to provide military assistance to the Crown (a system that was commuted to a money payment and finally abolished in 1660); Thomas de Arderne and Henry Peremort held the manors of Astwood and 'Purshull' respectively, both for a fee worth £10; Adam de Elmebrug held Elmbridge manor for a fee of £24; Grimaldi Pauncefott held for half a fee; Joan of Hanewood held the hamlet of Almerigge for a fee of 40s; and Roceline of Kyngeslond (Kingsland) held that hamlet by a fee of 20s.

The villeins of Wychbold manor in 1275 held 6½ virgates (a virgate being 60 acres of land) and 12 acres of meadow, but for every virgate held they owed 4 days' work a week to the lord from Michaelmas (29 September) to the feast of St Peter ad Vincula (1 August). This was valued at ½d a day, resulting in an income to the manor of 44s 5d for work. From the feast of St Peter ad Vincula to Michaelmas each virgate rendered 4s to the lord, raising a total of 26s. This was a busy time on the land when hay was made and the crops harvested. There was no recorded income from pannage (a payment paid by the tenants to the lord for the right to pasture their pigs in the lord's woods), but the villeins did pay tallage, a tax exacted by the lord of the manor, usually at Michaelmas, and this tax raised 60s. The lord in return allowed the tenants the right to graze a fixed number of cattle on the common pasture, and to take a fixed amount of hay from the common meadows.

A toll was taken by the lord from travellers passing through the manor. It was probably used for the repair of the highway and the bridge over the Salwarpe. In 1221 Hugh le Tollnur was accused of levying new toll charges, and of having damaged two carts of books impounded for refusal to pay toll, these belonging to Richard, rural dean of Worcester. In that year the collector had been taking ½d from pilgrims from Worcestershire, and a penny from those from further afield, a woman pilgrim being forced to pay a toll of 2s, an extortionate amount. Hugh had also been taking more than the customary one stick from each cartload of wood that passed on its way to Droitwich. The complaints against the lord, William de Stutville, and his bailiffs were taken to the justices in Westminster (Stenton 1934, 573–4).

Hugh Mortimer's son, Robert, as lord exacted passage (a tax on the passage of goods) and toll from the abbot of Bordesley and his men when they passed by his farm in Wychbold. The abbey had been granted exemption from tolls in cities, boroughs and market towns throughout England by the king, and, as might be expected, the abbot complained about his treatment (*VCH Worcestershire* II, 152). Hugh the toll collector held the toll in fee (ie hereditarily), so it is possible that his son or grandson was responsible for this second clash with the clergy. In 1275 the toll had a value to the lord of 30s a year but by 1308 the value of the toll had reduced to 20s a year. The toll had a long association with the Saunders family from 1558 (and probably before), when William Saunders of The Toll acted as an appraiser to the inventory of William Chadburne, and John Saunders of The Toll was owed money by the deceased.

In 1304 another Hugh Mortimer died leaving a widow, Maud. The manor house was still worth 2s but the dovecote had doubled in value. The demesne land had reduced to 200 acres of arable land valued at 2d per acre, 15 acres of meadow at 16d per acre, several pastures worth 4s, and certain woods valued at 3s 4d. There were 12 free tenants who paid 60s per year, and 14 villeins who paid rent of assize worth 100s per annum, and their services were valued at 40s per annum. The sum of the manor by the year was now £14 14s 8d.

In 1308 the manor of 'Wychebaud' was assessed as worth yearly £32 17s 0¾ (CCR EdII). When Maud died in 1308 there were two orchards worth 4s per year listed with the manor house (valued at 2s). The demesne was now just 25 acres of arable valued at £4, and the underwood was sold at only 2s. In addition to the demesne arable, meadow, pasture and woodland, there was now a water mill, valued at 20s, and the toll was still being collected. The 24 acres of meadow were valued at 3s per acre and the pastures at 5s per acre. A poll penny was being taken at the feast of St Kenelm (July 17) raising 26s 8d, suggesting an adult population of 320, which at this time still included Elmbridge. The lordship passed in 1341/2 to Jane Mortimer, the wife of Richard Talbot of Richards Castle (Herefs), then eventually to the Carewes of Somerset, and finally to John Pakington of Hampton Lovett who bought the manor in 1581.

The lord held a court in the manor by right, and duty of attendance (suit of court) was the chief obligation of the freehold tenants, including the tenants who held the lesser manors. The Court Baron was a 'customary' court, meeting every three weeks. The function of the court was largely administrative, supervising the organisation of the agrarian and social life of the manor. The steward presided over the court and the customs of the manor were stated, relating to land tenure and use. In its judicial capacity the court dealt with offences connected with tenure, services owed to the lord and dues within the manor. The court appointed local men to act as the bailiff (who collected rents), the reeve (who managed the fields and commons), and a jury, also known as the homage. The Court Leet was held every six months, and it had jurisdiction over petty offences and civil affairs of the district. Any offenders could be fined or imprisoned. The lord of the manor also had the right to take the local 'View of Frankpledge'. This was an ancient Saxon presentment by tithings (originally a group of ten households) for the maintenance of law and order. Each tithing elected a spokesman or tithing man who became the constable, who was responsible for law and order (in greater Wychbold manor in 1601 this amounted to six constables, one each in Wychbold, Astwood, Impney, Elmbridge, Purshill and Hill End; WRO Hampton Pap 502). The tithing men were responsible for good behaviour and made presentments at the court as to misbehaviour and infringement of customs of the manor.

The manorial court rolls record the responsibilities of the lord's officials and the services, rents and obligations of the villeins. They also record the payment of relief, heriots (the gifting of the best beast to the lord by the heir of a deceased tenant; subsequently converted into a gift of money), and merchet (paid when the son or daughter of a tenant married). The bailiff was responsible for summoning the court and executing its orders, for returning the jury and levying the fines and heriots. He was elected for the year, along with the reeve, at the Autumn Great Court by 'the most voices'. The reeve had to collect the chief rents for the lord, and he and the bailiff were accountable to the lord. The only non-elected official was the steward, the lord's representative. He was at the court to act as a minister not a judge, and it was the bailiff and tenants who passed judgement in all the actions. There were 12 jurors present at the court but all the tenants who attended, known as suitors of the court, constituted judge, jury, witnesses, and prosecuting council. A year's leave of absence from the duty of attendance (an essoin) could be granted on payment of a fine. The proceedings of the court were written on a roll of parchment under the headings of the tithings or yields, and recorded the enclosure of common land, whether too many animals were on the common, and whether the roads or the river banks in ruin.

The surviving court rolls from the 17th century provide many insights into how the medieval manor functioned and so are still a useful source of information for the earlier period. For instance, in 1661 they recorded that a tenant could keep a sheep on the common for every pound rent he paid or the yearly value of the land or tenement he held, and that he had to forfeit 3s 4d for every sheep over the limit, so that Gilbert Law, having more sheep than was lawful, was fined 6d. Edmund Banner had taken in a stray sheep and had not taken it to the bailiff to be proclaimed as was his duty and so was fined. The bailiff would keep the sheep until it was claimed. If no claim was made then it became the lord's property. Pigs had to be yoked, except in September, October or November, when they were allowed into the lord's woods. This was to stop the pigs pushing through the hedges and breaking them down. Pigs also had to be ringed to stop them doing damage by rooting around in the ground. George Wild and William Walker were presented in 1601 for not ringing their pigs and were fined 3s 4d for each pig. By 1661 a fine of a shilling had to be paid for every four days of non-compliance whether still unringed or unyoked. The lord's waste was opened to the tenants on the 29 September, but, if they entered the waste before that date, they were fined 10s for encroachment.

Parish and church (*by* Helen Peberdy and Derek Hurst)

The parish of Dodderhill goes back well over a thousand years, and for most of that time it included Wychbold and Elmbridge, as well as some small detached areas near Bromsgrove, Huntingdrop near Hadzor, and even an area within the borough of Droitwich known as 'the In Liberties', and so was an enormous parish of over 3500 acres, stretching north from Droitwich, its church standing in a commanding position above the town – but never belonging to it. Its earliest history, both of church and parish, is, however, shrouded in mystery.

Following its forced removal from the hands of the church of Worcester in the early 11th century before the Norman Conquest (see above), contention about ownership of Dodderhill church again emerged early in the medieval period, when it became the subject of a protracted dispute. In the later 11th century the lord of Wychbold, Osbern fitz Richard, placed the advowson with the priory of Worcester (*VCH Worcestershire* III, 67), but then a later lord of Wychbold manor, Osbert, with the bishop's and king's approval, granted the church in *c* 1158 to the nuns of Westwood (CPR Lett II 381), who also benefited from other Dodderhill resources: the tithes of Wychbold mill, and a contribution from the pence of St Peter (formerly received by Dodderhill church); while various other individuals also gave property, including some land in Astwood. But in 1178 Dodderhill church was restored to the monks of Worcester by a decision of the bishop, the nuns being compensated with lands and tithes, including Crutch (*ibid*). The acquisition of Dodderhill church further bolstered the considerable interests which the church of Worcester had in the forest of Feckenham area (eg Stoke Prior, Hanbury). In *c* 1180–5 the bishop was then able to appropriate 100s per annum from Dodderhill church for the prior and convent of Worcester.

With its hold on the church at Dodderhill apparently secure the church of Worcester may then have commenced rebuilding, as in later Norman times a great church of stone (Fig 35) was built to replace the earlier one, and this was finally dedicated in 1220 (*ibid*) to St Augustine of Canterbury – an unusual dedication (and one that could indicate a pre-Conquest date, several instances being cited by Butler 1986) possibly due to the tradition that the bishops of the old Celtic church and St Augustine's mission held a meeting somewhere nearby in 603.

However, disputes continued to occur, as in 1220 the advowson of the church was reclaimed by William de Stutevill, lord of Wychbold manor, and Margery his wife, but was rejected. It was claimed again by Robert de Mortimer in 1274–5 and once more rejected. Of this new Norman building, which attracted such covetous attention, fortunately (despite Victorian 'restorers') quite a lot remains, notably the crossing and the north transept, both being on a very large scale for a parish church, especially one with no village! It would have dominated the early town of Droitwich from its elevated site. It was also during this time that Thomas de Cantilupe was a rector of Dodderhill. He later became Bishop of Hereford in (1275–82), and was the last Englishman to be canonised (in 1320).

Meanwhile the church was extending its work across the area and in 1274–5 there is the earliest mention of Elmbridge chapel, to which the vicar of Dodderhill provided a curate. William de Dover, rector of Dodderhill church, also founded and endowed a hospital in 1285, the master being appointed by the prior and convent of Worcester. In 1291–2 the church was valued at £28 (with a portion worth £5 being held by Worcester Priory) during the ecclesiastical taxation assessment that was carried out across England and Wales on the orders of Pope Nicholas IV.

Figure 35 View looking towards Dodderhill church from the salt-making area of Upwich in c 1300; showing original form of the medieval church (illustration by Arthur Davis)

Other church business included holding its periodic court hearing (the ruridecanal court) to investigate the social misdemeanours of the local inhabitants. In 1300 two cases related to inhabitants of Dodderhill parish (Hamilton 1912, 78): one Henricus de Sawageburi was accused of relations with Alicia filia Johannis, and, after hearing their confessions, 'in the usual fashion they were beaten once around the market-place' presumably in Droitwich ('fustigatur ... semel per forum'). A similar case occurred involving 'Rogerus le pallefray famulus Rectoris' and Julia Wyleket who underwent the same punishment.

Then suddenly in 1301/2 the prior and convent of Worcester were deprived of Dodderhill by the archbishop of Canterbury on the grounds that it had been appropriated without royal licence. In response the prior was urged to encourage the archdeacon of Worcester (Cardinal Neopolitano; clearly an Italian) not just with words but gifts 'as is usual' (CPR Lett II, 381). The prior and convent appealed to Rome against the archbishop's interference in their right of presentation (Haines 1965, 246) and eventually Dodderhill church was restored to them (*VCH Worcestershire* III, 67). About this time a vicarage was now ordained for the support of the local priest.

But soon the king was again questioning the appropriation of Dodderhill church, and in 1332 Worcester monks were insisting that they needed its value (£30) to help support 50 monks in giving hospitality for all the travellers coming to Worcester (*ibid*). However, as he did not have the advowson, he confirmed the licence of Edward I (1272–1307) to appropriate. This seems at last to have been the end of the matter, and the long-running dispute over ownership had finally run its course.

The original Norman chancel of St Augustine's was rebuilt in the early years of the 14th century, when it was enlarged to accommodate the brethren from the adjacent hospital (see Blewitt, this volume), and new altars erected within it. The church from then until the Reformation would have changed little; it would have been full of colour with decorated walls, heraldic glass in the windows, and many statues of saints. In 1536 there was an altar to 'St Kateryn' (*sic*) on the south side, as well as the high altar, because the vicar Nicholas Fownes wished to be buried there. He bequeathed 20s for paving the floor before the statue of 'our ladie of pytie', and money to the chapel of Elmbridge and the church of Upton Warren.

A church house (or parish house; see Blewitt, this volume) is mentioned in later medieval documents; such buildings were often built in the 1500s, sometimes as a brewery and ale house, thereby providing local entertainment which raised rents and funds to support the church (Copeland 1960).

As a result of another dispute Dodderhill Hospital briefly re-appeared in history towards the end of its days. Humphrey Stafford had laid claim to the advowson of the chantry or hospital and to a messuage called the chantry house with its land, and so had presented John Marshall, whereas the prior and convent of Worcester had presented John Sewell at the same time. A jury was appointed but had not decided six months later, so the king, having the bishopric in his hands, presented Richard Cornwall to the hospital (*VCH Worcestershire* III, 68). He turned out to be a somewhat rapacious character, and this was presumably why the appointment was so contentious as it put the successful applicant in control of property that was about to be wrenched from church hands.

As part of the process of eventually suppressing the monasteries, surveyors were sent around church property across the country to ascertain their values, and these were recorded in the 1535 *Valor Ecclesiasticus*, which has the following annual valuation of church property in Dodderhill: *Dudderhull iuxta Wyche* (held by Worcester Priory, £1 7s); rectorial glebe and tithes, £8 3s 4d; rectorial tithe on salt 'at Wyche', £5 6s 8d; tithes due to the vicar, £13 5s; and the Hospital in Dodderhull, £8.

In 1548 the advowson of Dodderhill church was purchased with the rectory by Robert Catlin and Peter Wainwright (*VCH Worcestershire* III, 68), who months later sold it to William and Gilbert Dethick. Thence it passed via the Braces (Philip Brace of Hill Court having purchased it in 1574), after 100 years, to Gilbert Penrice (*ibid*). However, in this way, property of the Church, looted by the State, was transferred into private hands, and then bought and sold speculatively on the open market, much as in the case of any government mismanagement/bankruptcy sale since.

Sometime during the commotion of the Dissolution Dodderhill church acquired a bell from the suppressed friary which had yet to be paid for in August 1552 as listed in an inventory of church goods at £2 16s 8d (Anon 1910). The breaking up of church property at the Dissolution also included the sale of other land originally or still in Wychbold/Dodderhill, sometimes large estates, such as Westwood which eventually fell to the Pakington family, and sometimes smaller, such as the Bordesley Abbey land at 'Rashehede near Wyche' (Rashwood).

Although the church remained Catholic until the reign of Edward VI, Protestantism had been growing throughout the 16th century, and Dodderhill church would have lost some of its wall paintings and statues, the services would have been in English instead of Latin, and would have taken on a simpler form under this influence. However, for the ordinary parishioner, little changed, as they were still all expected to attend divine service regularly and pay their tithes to the rector and the vicar. Cranmer's first Book of Common Prayer was appointed to be used in churches by the First Act of Uniformity in 1549, followed in 1552 by the Second Act which made non-attendance subject to a fine.

Then in 1553 Queen Mary came to the throne, bringing back Catholic forms of worship to England. We do not know how the congregations in Dodderhill coped with all this change-around; there are no records of troubles or vicars being removed. During Mary's reign married clergy were deprived of their livings, and perhaps this happened in Dodderhill. Certainly this area in no way escaped the religious turmoil of this era, as in the neighbouring parish of Hanbury the rector was burnt at the stake for his Protestant beliefs. When Elizabeth became queen in 1558, the Protestant form of worship was re-established, with a Third Act of Uniformity in 1559.

Other religious institutions (*by* Lyn Blewitt)

St Mary's Hospital

St Mary's Hospital was located near Chapel Bridge, on the lower slope of Dodderhill hill below St Augustine's church, to the north of Vines Lane and to the west of the road to Bromsgrove. It was founded by William Dover, rector of St Augustine's, in 1285, and was endowed with a salt share (the salt from 6912 gallons of brine each year, about 8 tons), half a hide of land (notionally 60 acres), and rents worth 26s 4d annually, 50 marks (about £300,000 today) having been paid to the abbot of St Peter's in Gloucester for the land, with King Edward I confirming the grant in the same year, and the prior and convent of Worcester being made its patrons (*VCH Worcestershire* II, 179). The piece of land may have included what was later referred to as 'Spittal Close' (a colloquial version of 'hospital close'), a field to the east side of Crutch Lane at its south end, which kept that name into the mid 20th century. The hospital had a master and a small number of brethren (monks), and would have cared for ill and poor people. Although there is no documentary evidence to support the hypothesis, it is possible that the hospital cared for lepers given its location away from the main settlement.

There are records of some of the masters, but no full list. In 1349 Thomas of Savagebury was appointed, who would have been from Dodderhill, and who was 'presented to the custody of this hospital commonly called the Spittal, with lands, possessions, rents, bullaries and other things belonging thereto'. There is, however, also a record of a different master being appointed that year, William Hull. As the Black Death had arrived in England in September 1348, this may well be an example of how devastating its effects were, as it reached Dodderhill. The last recorded appointment of a master was in 1502 (but see also below).

The hospital seems to have been 'suppressed' in 1535 by its patrons, the prior and convent of Worcester, before the Dissolution. The valuation of church properties made in 1535 recorded 'the hospital or chantry in the parish of Dodderhill' as having an annual value of £8 (about £36,000 today); and in 1536 the prior and convent were accused of having suppressed the hospital 'of Doverhill … without licence of the king', and having 'expelled the poor people to their utter destruction'. They caused the hospital to be pulled down, and the building materials were sold for their own use. They had 'troubled' the clerk and master of the house, Richard Cornewall, putting him 'in jeopardy of his life', and 'held the lands of the same by intrusion'. They had also mowed a meadow which had belonged to the hospital, 'Preast meadow' in Forde in Dodderhill (presumably a later gift to the hospital); the implication here is that the grass or hay produced from the mowing was then taken by the prior and convent to be used or sold for their benefit.

A dispute resulted and in 1538 a complaint was made by the prior of Worcester against 'Syr' Richard Cornwall, during which the property of the chantry and hospital was listed as follows (NA STAC 2/3/84): 'Prestys medow, … Spyttell Close, 2 tenements in Hylleende, a tenement … in Whychbold, a tenement and 2 fields in Elmbryge and a tenement in Saint Mary Wytton … and a seale in Droitwich for salte makyng … The Whyche house …'. In 1542 the property of Worcester Priory, including Dodderhill church, was granted to the Dean and Chapter of Worcester, so that it remained in church hands, but later it was given up to the king. Richard Cornwall then finally seems to have got the hospital property back after complaining to the king (NA STAC 2/35/43).

The Worcestershire historian Treadway Nash recorded in 1781–2 that the hospital 'is still subsisting as a pidgeon house near the bridge', so the remains of some buildings were visible for another 250 years at least. These would have been swept away when the railway line was constructed to the south of St Augustine's graveyard, at the foot of the hill, and so over the hospital's site.

The Augustinian Friary

This friary is thought to have been located to the north of what is now Friar Street in Droitwich. There is no certain archaeological evidence for it, although an evaluation of a site at the far west end of Friar Street (Whitworth *et al* 2001) has produced one fragment of medieval building stone, and a pond (possibly a fishpond associated with the friary). It was founded in 1331, when Thomas Alleyn of Wyche (Droitwich) obtained permission to give a piece of land measuring 300 feet square (about 2 acres) for the building of 'an oratory and habitation' to the Provincial Prior and Austin Friars in England (Austin being an abbreviation of Augustinian). The prior and brethren of the house subsequently in 1343 received from John, son of William Dragoun of Droitwich, another smaller plot of land for the enlargement of their dwelling-place, so that presumably this was next to the first piece of land; in 1351 two chaplains, John Bush and William Mercer, granted plots of land, of five acres in extent adjoining the friary, to the friars for the further enlargement of their house (*VCH Worcestershire* II, 173–5).

July 1388 saw the founding of an anchorite's cell (a dwelling for a hermit, a solitary religious person), paid for by Thomas Beauchamp, Earl of Warwick. It was built on the south side of the church, 'for the inclusion and habitation of brother Henry de Stokebrugge [Stokebridge], where he may lead the life of an anchoret to the honour of God, and pray for the good estate of the founder and his kin …' (*VCH Worcestershire* II, 173–5). The Earl of Warwick would have the right to nominate further occupiers of this cell, but they would have to have been members of the order of friars first.

In early 1531 the bishop of Dover visited the friary, and wrote to Thomas Cromwell (Henry VIII's chancellor who co-ordinated the dissolution of the monasteries) about the poverty of the house.

He records that only one friar could be kept, as the prior appointed the previous Easter had, 'in less than one year that he hath been prior there', felled and sold 140 elm trees, sold a gold chalice weighing 70 ounces (nearly 2kg), a censer, two brass pots each able to hold a whole ox, spits, pans and other items, 'so that in the house is not left one bed, one sheet, one platter or dish' – nor was the prior able to account for what had happened to the money raised by the sale of these possessions. The house itself was not fit for human habitation, needing 'great costs done on it'. Two good bells remained, and a chalice and some vestments, but there was no lead (ie on the roofs) except in two gutters, as the prior had 'conveyed' this into the town. There is a suggestion that the land round the friary had 'tenantries and closes' (ie houses and gardens) which were let out for £5 a year (about £22,000 today).

Several private 'gentlemen of the county' were eager to acquire the site, and the bishop of Dover favoured a Mr Newell, 'servant with my lord of Worcester' (probably the bishop of Worcester). However, in 1538 John Pye of Chippenham (Wilts) said that the king (Henry VIII) had given the property to him, although he did not obtain it until 1543. It was then let out to yearly tenants at an annual value of £3 16s 4d. John Pye, in partnership with Robert Were of Marlborough (Wilts), became joint owners of the Austin Friars in Droitwich and the White Friars in Marlborough, paying a yearly rent to the king of 7s 8d for the Austin Friars. They almost certainly sold on their rights in these lands to others, as did many other speculators in former monastic properties.

The parish house

Recent work across the country has shown that church houses were much more common than has previously been realised, and possibly 'every village south of the river Humber could have had one' (Mattingley 2009, 16). Church houses were built from the mid 1400s onwards, mostly over the following 100 years, but some seem to date from the later 1500s and even into the early 1600s. Their function was that of the later village hall, and they became necessary because pews (ie permanent benches/seats) were put in churches, so that the original open space inside the church was no longer available for the parish's inhabitants to meet in. They were also used for 'church ales' (church fund raising by brewing ale and selling it to the inhabitants), and church feasts. Some church houses, after the change to church rates in the 17th century, became pubs, while others became schools and poor houses. Such buildings were generally passed onto the ownership of the parishioners (*ibid*), and a good local example not too far away from Dodderhill is the Mug House at Claines, north of Worcester, where the plot on which this pub is sited was obviously cut out of the churchyard. That there was a Dodderhill parish house, and that it was in the Hill End area of the parish (ie near the church) is suggested by the following documentary references:

- 'churche howsse of duddurhull' – as mentioned in 1519 by Prior William More in his journal (Fegan 1914);
- 'all that their messuage or tenement with th'appurtenances called the parish house … lying and being in the Hill End in the parish of Dodderhill' to John Attwood and Elizabeth his wife, for a rent of 28s 'of lawfull money of England' – a lease with effect from 16 March 1656, as recorded in the Dodderhill churchwardens' accounts;
- 'Dodderhill p. house' being in good repair – as noted in a survey of the state of the bishopric of Worcester between 1782 and 1808, and;

- mentions in most years of a 'parish house' or 'poors house' in the burials register from 1794 onwards, when the place of origin of the deceased starts to be given, with a specific record in 1823 of the burial of someone from 'the Poors house, Hill End'.

It is possible, therefore, to speculate that there was a building at Hill End that began life as a church house, and that from the mid 17th century at the latest it had passed to the possession of the parish and was, therefore, at the disposal of the churchwardens, hence the lease of 1656. Subsequently, still in the ownership of the parish, it became a poor house, a building set aside for the accommodation of the poor and the sick. There are records from the 18th century of a workhouse which appears to be located in the village of Wychbold, so perhaps that new facility gradually took over the function of the building nearer to St Augustine's, which would then have become available for renting out as housing. So far the precise location of this building has not been pinpointed, but it is presumably on the 1786 plan of Droitwich (WRO BA 7887, s497), though not identifiable as such.

Water mills (*by Cheryl Stewart*)

The earliest evidence for mills in Wychbold dates to 1086, when Domesday Book recorded five mills, assessed at being worth £4 8s (a very high value, nearly 18s each, when many mills only paid 2s, so they were large and busy; F R & C M J Thorn, pers comm). These five mills constituted the second largest concentration of mills anywhere in Worcestershire in the 11th century, and are only outnumbered by Blockley (now in Gloucestershire), which had eleven. Clearly five mills are unlikely to all have been constructed in the twenty years since the Norman Conquest, and so we can be pretty certain that water mills were a feature of late Saxon Wychbold. The function of the mills would typically have been for grinding corn.

Wychbold mill(s)

The earliest recorded mill for which historical evidence, additional to the Domesday Book reference, has been found is 'Wychbold Mill'. Between 1172–86 the then lord of the manor, Osbert (de Say), son of Hugh (Fitz Osbern) and Eustacia (de Say), granted the mill of 'Wichebolde' to the canons of Haughmond Abbey. This mill was located at the end of Mill Lane, most probably in the rear garden of the present Mill House. The mill stayed in the ownership of the abbey, for instance being granted to Nicholas, son of Robert the Miller for 30s rent in 1204–c 1210 (Rees 1985, no 1303), until the dissolution of that monastery by Henry VIII in 1539. In 1553 'a water mill there [Wychbold] and its watercourses, banks and weirs, a parcel of land called The More and a close of land there all in the tenure of John Withbow', was bought from the Crown, along with vast quantities of other properties in counties all over England for £1718 10s 3¼d by two entrepreneurial gentlemen of London, named John Wryght and Thomas Holmes. By this time the mill was probably in a poor state of repair, as the name 'Wychbold Mill' came to be associated with another building altogether, as described below.

At some point in time between 1422 and 1463 the Haughmond Abbey cartulary states that Abbot Richard Burnell leased to Richard and Joan Lawe for 99 years a toft with a curtilage lying between Wal Smith's land and Agnes Lawe's and extending in length along the King's Highway, 2d annual rent to be paid during Richard's lifetime and 4d after his death. Heriots were to be paid when they were due, and Richard, Joan and their heirs were to build an 'insethowse' on the toft at their own cost. This house is believed to be Mill Cottage, which still survives, located about 100 yards upstream from the abbey's mill. It is not known when the second (ie adjacent) corn mill was built, or by whom, but it is likely that it was built by the Lawe family shortly after the Dissolution.

It would appear that by 1600 the original corn mill had become old and no longer viable, and a pair of workers cottages was built on land adjacent to it. Meanwhile the newer (adjacent) Wychbold mill continued to mill corn until about the middle of the 18th century when it became a needle mill, scouring and then polishing the finished needles for the needle makers located in Feckenham and Redditch. This occupation did not last long, as by 1809 it was again listed as a corn mill when sold at auction. Wychbold Mill then remained a corn and malt mill until about 1928, when the river was diverted to allow for a turbine to be installed to generate electricity for Wychbold Court. After electricity came to the village the mill was occasionally used to cut chaff, until its final demise came about in the winter of 1947 when the force of flood-water finally broke the weir. The mill building had a demolition order put on it, and it was finally raised to the ground in 1963, leaving the waterwheel and wheel pit *in situ* as a garden feature.

Paper mill

Upstream from the two Wychbold mills was a mill known later as 'Paper Mill'. This mill was owned by the nuns of Westwood Priory and was already in existence by 1300 when its location helped determine the boundary of Feckenham Forest. This mill also started life as a corn mill grinding the corn of the farming tenants of the priory. After the Dissolution Humphrey Pakington of Hampton Lovett bought Westwood Priory and its estate, of which this mill was a small part, from the Crown in 1541 and at the same time arranged for the mill to become an extra-parochial part of Dodderhill attached to Hampton Lovett.

Papermaking started in this country in 1495 at Hertford, and the expansion of this industry through the country was slow but by 1650 Nicholas Clows was making paper at Beoley (Redditch), and in his will dated 1681 Nicholas leaves the paper mill at Dodderhill to his son William. This mill continued to make paper and pasteboard for a further 170 years, but by 1848 the industry had become so mechanised that the small producers were no longer able to make paper competitively. Later the mill ground corn again, and continued until about 1910 when the building was finally converted into two cottages.

Walkmill

Walkmill was most probably the last of the mills to be built on this stretch of the River Salwarpe. The very long and extensive leat bringing water to the wheel would not have been an engineering feat readily undertaken if the more suitable sites had not already been occupied.

In 1474, the then lord of the manor, William Carewe, made a grant to Rawlyn Walker of Worcester allowing him to construct a purpose-built fulling mill (BCA ref 475877). This grant set out in the greatest of detail the location of the mill building together with the size and depth of the watercourses. The local cloth industry was at its height during the 15th century making the construction of a new fulling mill a sound and economic enterprise.

Reference is made in the will of John Dugard dated 1668 to 'Walkers Field' where the cloth would have been set out on 'tenter hooks' to dry in the sun. The mill stayed within the Dugard family for several generations but by 1766 was sold by decree of the High Court of Chancery, the property then consisting of a dwelling house, four fulling mills, a barn, stables and outhouses, all at the yearly rent of £56. Thomas Roe was then the tenant. Henry Talbot Esq bought the property and in 1770 had a detailed plan drawn up of his latest acquisition.

The property was still owned by the Talbot family in 1785, when it was referred to as 'Rudgway Cloth Mill'. The tenant, Thomas Roe, was at the same time also farming at Ridgeway (Court Farm). In 1798 the mill was known as 'Wharf Mill' and tenanted by John Roe who would appear to have been the last of the fullers. Presumably by 1841 the mills were no more as the dwelling house was divided into two cottages with their inhabitants having occupations totally unrelated to the cloth industry. Detailed in the 1891 Census the building was again one house occupied by a farmer, Thomas Cox.

Impney mill(s)

The earliest record of this mill is during the inquest (*IPM*) detailing the estate of Ada Corbet of Chaddesley Corbet 'made in 1291 on the Saturday before the Feast of St Martin'. Amongst Ada's possessions at Impney, Alice le Walker is listed holding a fulling mill worth yearly 20s, and 'there is there a water-mill that belongs to the ... and is worth yearly 30s'. Perhaps it is not surprising to find mills at 'Imma's low-lying and well-watered place', which is the literal meaning of Impney (Mawer & Stenton 1927), or a fishery which in 1384, in the ownership of Richard Rughale, was poached to the value of £5.

In 1586 George Wylde and John Wheler, gent, (of Astwood) took their dispute concerning two water mills called Impney Mills in the parish of Dodderhill to the courts in London. The manor court records in 1677 report that Benjamine Richards, John Hunt and Edward Wayte, tenants at the mill, 'impounded the water upon the Churchway and also up on the comon highway leading from Droitwich towards Bromsgrove contrary to former paine layd at last court', and were fined 3s 4d each.

A document dated 1695 refers to there being three water corn mills valued at £16 and tenanted by Thomas Atwood. In 1780 the mill was owned by John Pumfrey and tenanted by Job Mears who, until 1794, must have been in partnership with George Webb, as it was then that their partnership was dissolved by mutual consent, although Mears was still at the mill in 1808. In the mid 19th century Thomas Thould, miller, occupied the mill and lived at Impney Lodge (see Blewitt, this volume). The property was bought by John Corbett, who had the mill buildings (Fig 79) pulled down in 1879, and the land was then incorporated into his grounds and garden at Impney.

Droitwich town mill

Though located on the eastern edge of Droitwich this mill was situated within a detached part of Dodderhill parish. By the mid 17th century the association of this mill with Dodderhill was already a matter of local dispute, and a hearing was held to determine whether the mill was really attached to Dodderhill. The evidence of local witnesses described the vicar of St Augustine's, while doing his perambulation of the parish of Dodderhill, as standing by the hopper of the mill, thereby indicating that by rights it was part of Dodderhill parish. It was finally burnt down in 1909.

Other possible mill sites in Dodderhill

There are two locations where other mills may have been sited in the past. The first is underneath the present motorway bridge, where it crosses Crown Lane. On the Henry Talbot plan of 1770 referred to above, a quite large pond is marked which might have been an early mill pond and in the area adjacent to it there have been several archaeological finds of a medieval date. The other site is at Ford where the River Salwarpe, north of the Ford Lane bridge, has obviously been straightened.

Yet another mill may have existed, as the nuns of Westwood Priory also owned a mill at Astwood (Kerr 1999). Dressed stones have been discovered along the River Salwarpe, fairly close to Hobden Farm, and could have formed the walls of a waterwheel pit or mill race. Unfortunately there were no other building remains and this mill did not form a part of the possessions of Westwood Nunnery at the Dissolution in 1536, intimating that it had ceased operation at an early date (see below; Stewart, this volume).

Meet the locals (*by* Derek Hurst)

The following is a chance to see some of the locals at work and play in the local community, though obviously it probably gives a very lopsided view of Dodderhill folk, as it tends to concentrate on the higher levels of society, on bad behaviour, and occasional out-of-the-ordinary events (for more insights into the medieval community see also Townshend, this volume).

In 1221 Hugh the toll collector was accused of abusing the toll collection on road passage through Wychbold implicating both the toll collector and the bailiff of the manor (Stenton 1934). Unusually the lord of Wychbold was able to levy tolls from travellers towards the maintenance of the road, at a time when passage was normally expected to be free of any encumbrance. Usefully the description of the toll system reveals that it was located on the main road 'through [the] middle of the settlement (villa)', and the toll was supposed to only be levied on carts carrying merchandise or for sale, though with the exemption of any goods carried for higher ranking churchmen or aristocracy in the area; each county cart was supposed to pay ½d and out of county 1d (ie toll was aimed at commerce rather like our VAT and the local toll raising was rigged to favour local business). By custom each carter of firewood was supposed to hand over one stick but in 1221 the bailiff was accused of selecting a 'greater piece of wood' (*maius lignum*). Heavy wear and tear on roads in the area is also reflected by the many pavage grants received by Droitwich in order to keep the salt trade moving (Hilton 1985, 12). The focus on firewood is suggestive of this being the chief cargo being moved in the direction of (Droit)Wich, such as the brushwood ready for carrying to Wich which was stolen at Romsley in 1294 (West 1962). In order to ensure that the toll could not be easily avoided there must have been some attention paid to ensure there were no suitable routes so it could be easily by-passed.

Occasionally there were horrific events such as the killing of Osbert the son of Hilary in 1221, or really strange reports such as that of a pig eating a boy named Walter le Palmere of Wychbold in 1275 (Röhrkasten 2008, 1164).

The 1275 lay subsidy list for Wychbold also covered Westwood, and Crutch as well (Willis-Bund & Amphlett 1893), and since the numbers omitted are unknown, it is difficult to use this to estimate population numbers, but it does allow us to explore where people lived and their relative status in society. Usefully it does have many locative personal names which are recognisably identifiable to places today (Elmbridge and Impney are already being listed separately, showing that these were places with sufficient weight of numbers to have their own identity). The relative levels of taxation make it possible to suggest those who would have been classed as knights, as this social rank was very much equated to individual wealth. The valuation of a knight was usually at least 10s in this tax list (Hilton 1966), in which case only one person in Wychbold would have qualified, *viz* Robertus de Mortuomari (20s); though it could be also as low as at least 6s 8d (*ibid*), in which case others would just have qualified as well: Willielmus Gylofre, Robertus de Estwode, Willielmus de Wichebald (also called 'the clerk'; BCA ref 474382, 475197; see also below), Henricus de Peremort, Johanna de Herewinton, and Adam de Sockeleye, suggesting there were in fact quite a few minor gentry in the area. Knights were members of medieval society who were expected to be equal to certain administrative and military roles when called upon, and so formed part of an elite serving the king.

The Willelmus of Wychebaud, who was the 'ballivus' (bailiff) in 1275 (Röhrkasten 2008, 1330), was presumably the same person as Willielmus de Wichebald in the 1275 lay subsidy roll, where he was assessed at 10s indicating that he was the wealthiest person in Wychbold after the lord of the manor, the latter assessed at twice this sum. If we only knew where he lived we would be able to identify the manor house of Wychbold. The term 'court' is often found today attached to the site of the main medieval house in a manor reflecting its local use for holding manorial court meetings, but it is usually quite unclear when this term was first applied and so its historical significance can be uncertain. In the light of this it remains presently unclear whether the present-day Wychbold Court was the local manor house from sometime in the 16th century, though such an impressive large house would certainly have been entirely appropriate to this function.

Clues as to types of employment at this time are infrequent, as only more exceptional skills, such as reading, would have led to special recognition, as in the case of the clerk above. Otherwise the only other occupations that seem to be recorded (mainly based on the lay subsidies) are: (in the late 13th century) cap-maker, merchant, and miller (2); and (in the early 14th century) shepherd (2), when there was also a blacksmith. The latter was granted a place and twelve acres next to the main road (BCA ref 474387), where he would presumably have been in a good position to take advantage of passing travellers, especially when they were stopped to pay tolls and he could spot that horses needed reshoeing.

In the 15th century some of the families that were to play a big part in Wychbold life seem to have appeared on the scene, for instance in 1445/6 there is the first mention of a Saundres taking on land here (BCA ref 475875). When Leland rode through Wychbold in *c* 1540 (Smith 1964) he saw a rich and diversified countryside, where farmers seem to have been taking the initiative, and had already decided on enclosure as the way forward, which would allow greater specialisation and experimentation, including the breeding of animals to higher standards. And it also reveals that farming was at last going with the grain of the land in that its true productive character included being more suited to dairying than the blanket arable cropping that typicalised so much medieval agriculture in the English Midlands and beyond.

Post-medieval (*c* 1550–1800)

The upper echelons of society were now rapidly enriched with the disposal of suppressed church property into private hands; an increasing interest in farming improvements; the growth of population in towns and, therefore, of consumption; and the making of large fortunes from exploitation of the New World. The new wealth became evident through the building of new and bigger houses than before, which were now designed for privacy rather than communal living (see Price, this volume). New foreign, especially Dutch, influences also took hold on fashion which permeated many aspects of life from cooking pots to frilly lace on clothing, and there was a new spirit of English thought and expression that gained strength from military success, though the dark period of the English Civil War (1642–51) was soon to stem this tide of success and well-being. This was also a period when the climate was far from favourable and was associated with many hard winters up to *c* 1800, with rivers like the Thames (and presumably the Severn) completely freezing over; as a result it has been labelled the 'Little Ice Age' (Fagan 2000).

Dodderhill lay well away from that part of Worcestershire where the enclosure of fields occurred late and required an act of parliament, typically in the 18th century. Where the process of enclosure has been tracked from the later 16th century in neighbouring parishes (eg Yelling 1977, 65–9) there are signs that it was already advanced by this early date. These new enclosures were particularly used for grazing and dairying, as elsewhere, though even in woodland areas some corn growing would occur for local consumption (*ibid*, 175–6). Dodderhill, therefore, by this period may have had a pastoral economy, perhaps initiated in the later Middle Ages when lowered population favoured farming with lower labour inputs, and market trends encouraged wool and meat production (*ibid*). A general survey of east Worcestershire shows that by the 16th century Dodderhill fell well within an area where most farming wealth was based on livestock in contrast with the situation in south-east Worcestershire, and, therefore, had a similar farming profile to that of the neighbouring Forest of Arden (Warwickshire; *ibid*, 178, fig 9.1). However, livestock were also quite common in arable areas as they provided motive power and manure, and farms were by necessity, therefore, mixed, with oxen remaining useful for this purpose. Cattle were numerous across east Worcestershire in this period, and in Dodderhill there seems to have been a greater tendency to be grazing cattle instead of sheep than elsewhere in the county (*ibid*, fig 9.3), suggesting that it had emerged as an integral part of the premier dairying and possibly beef raising area of the county. Crops were still being grown in Dodderhill and the 16th century crop profile has more in keeping with south-east of the county, with pulses, wheat, barley and oats/rye/muncorn being sown in that order of precedence; whereas just a little further to the north both the more exposed terrain and the topography favoured rye and oats as the chief crops in this period (*ibid*, fig 9.4).

Land deals were prolific from the mid 16th century; in 1563 Thomas Carewe of the City of Coventry was selling land to Bowky (Fig 36). 'Frances Bulkye of Hadsor' had purchased other land in Wychbold from Dethicke in 1562 (5 acres of arable 'in a certeyne felde there called Kafull felde' costing £5 6s 8d; Hampton Pap 468). This family (the Bookeys) was destined to play a large part in Dodderhill history for the next few hundred years, and briefly held the lordship of the manor before this was purchased by the Pakingtons in 1580 (Hampton Pap 443). We had already met the Saunders in the 15th century, and by 1571 John Saunders was ensconced at Rashwood; in 1599 the Toll Field (3 parts comprising 20 acres) was sold by Perkes (probably of Ridgeway Farm at this time) to Saunders. Seemingly the local land market was very active, as the most ambitious families were busy consolidating their holdings.

In the late 16th century/early 17th century the southern part of Dodderhill parish within the borough of Droitwich is depicted for the first time on a map (WRO BA 8060; Fig 37). However, much in keeping with maps of the period the execution is generally sketchy (Bassett 2010), except for the Upwich brine well area which has been demonstrated to have some good correspondence with archaeological remains (cf Hurst & Hemingway 1997, fig 50). Since tithes were later a bone

Figure 36 Detail of indenture of Thomas Carewe, lord of the manor of Wychbold, dated 20 January 1584 (CRO DIC/SU9/2/54). Copyright of Cheshire Record Office (photograph by D Hurst)

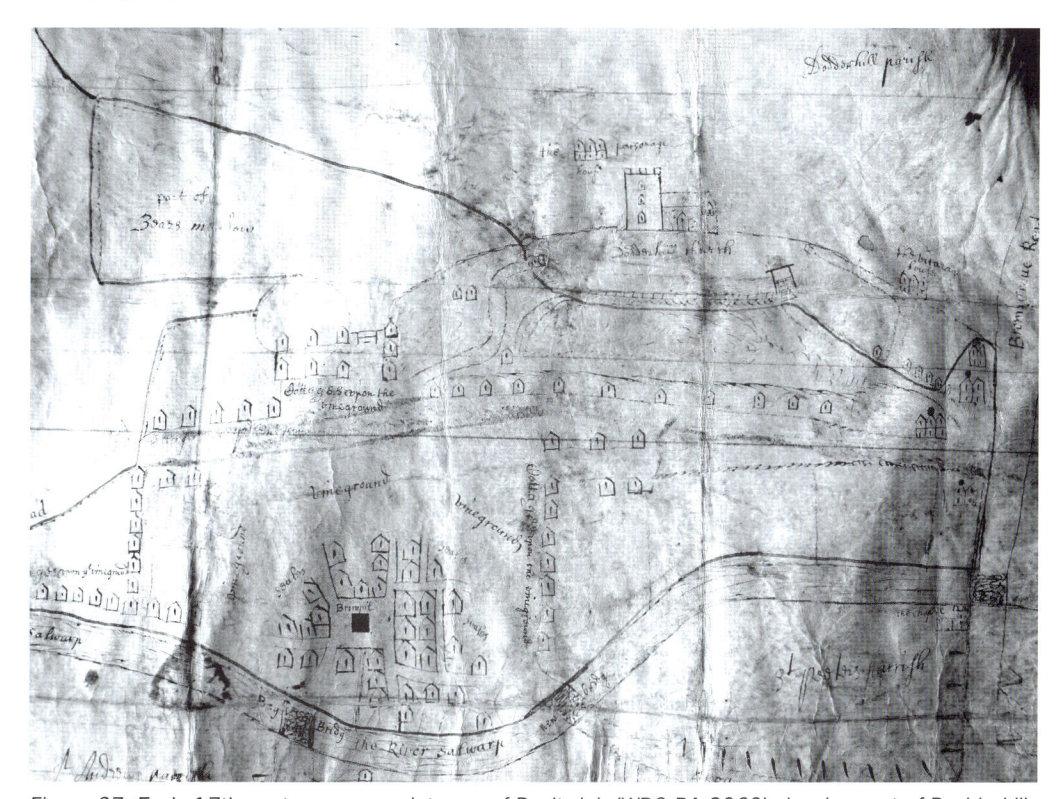

Figure 37 Early 17th century manuscript map of Droitwich (WRO BA 8060) showing part of Dodderhill parish. Reproduced with kind permission of Droitwich Spa Town Council and Worcestershire Record Office

of contention (1658; NA E134/1659 Easter/11), it is possible that the map was drawn in the main to put on record parish boundaries.

In the 17th century the detailed evidence of life in Dodderhill finally emerges in surviving records of the Wychbold manor court, which covered Wychbold, Impney, Purshill, Elmbridge, and Hill End; the number of entries suggest that Wychbold was by far the most populous area. The jury in September 1601 seemed to be packed by those recruited from certain well established local families (Perkes (2) and Saunders (4)), who also figured prominently in the 1603 lay subsidy roll indicating their rising status (Amphlett 1901). Though, when it came to the charges, some of these same families were in the dock. Various misdemeanours were listed: William Saunders junior 'de Towle' had made affray, apparently with a member of own family (12d fine); encroachment on the waste in Wychbold attracted a 2d fine (Saunders again); another encroachment had been made into woodland at Rashwood (12d); the Bowkyes had diverted the road at 'helprighe'; waste at Tolle Greene had been encroached on (2d); the [archery] butts had not been made, as they ought to be by law, and village was fined 12d; and the road had not been repaired 'in the vicinity of Leatherne bridge ... and at hill end' by 'John Wheeler of Wich'. Even the local Wychbold constable, Thomas Lawe (!), had been assaulted by an Edward Barret of Droitwich. Apart from the occasional fight it was clearly an era where any open space was under threat of being seized for private use, and where public duty was perhaps in short supply.

A leech pit was mentioned in 1623 (with the Kidderminster road on its north side; Hampton Pap 494) and was presumably the source of leeches used by the local doctor. In 1635 both Spyttle causeway from Dodderhill to Bromsgrove and 'Leathorne bridge' were in a poor state; and 'a miskyn of muck' left by Gilbert Glover alias Penrice was causing 'great damage to the inhabitants of Dodderhill' (*QS*, no 159). In the same year the local supervisor of ways was William Saunders who noted problems with the 'Hutt bridge in the way leading from Wichbould to Kidderminster' (*ibid*, no 161; otherwise 'Tunbridge', *ibid*, no 152).

Locals were called upon to maintain the church and in 1637, in settlement of a long-standing controversy, Elmbridge inhabitants were ordered to pay one-third of the repair costs of Dodderhill church (*VCH Worcestershire* III, 68). Sadly the newly refurbished church was not to remain in a good state for long, as it suffered much damage during the Civil War. In 1647 repair of Dodderhill church was being ordered using lead from Worcester cathedral (CPR Lett II, 381) revealing that lead had been stripped from the church

Figure 38 View looking north across Wychbold in c 1600 (illustration by Arthur Davis). Left: the Toll. Centre back: the mills. Right: Wychbold Court with the south wing in course of construction

presumably to make musket shot, and this must have been a common fate for the churches of places where soldiers were billeted.

Meanwhile the agricultural round continued. Sheep were now apparently kept in some numbers as a sheep-cote was noted at Sagebury in 1648 (NA Crown lease 24C1 1648, 709; see Townshend, this volume); the sheep-cote was a specialised sheep-house designed for over-wintering the sheep and the collection of copious amounts of rich manure as a useful by-product. There seems also to have been an increasing trend towards dairying (see Townshend, this volume), which may echo similar developments in Cheshire where it came to be understood that the soil has much to do with cheese making, lime-rich ground being judged the best as the resultant milk had a high percentage of lime which held back the acidity of the milk. In Cheshire the pasture was carefully managed and manuring salt was used, large quantities of salt also being used in cheese manufacture (ie 6oz to 20lb of curd; Driver 1909, 71). Though not specifically commented on in Worcestershire sources it seems likely that farmers of Dodderhill were also aware of these possibilities. Arable production also continued, and many of the fields walked (Fig 4) produced lots of 17th/18th century pottery, this being indicative of the intensification of production through increased manuring. Another feature of this period was the frequent reorganisation and renaming of fields (Fig 39), indicating an era of agrarian experimentation.

Houses were in short supply and sometimes desperate attempts were made at securing a home. For instance Susanne Woodward erected a cottage on the lord's waste called Piper's Hill, but was ordered in 1677 to pull it down (Hampton Pap 503). In contrast with this tiny cottage there was one large house in Dodderhill rated at 12 hearths falling well within the band of house size (8–19 hearths) representing very wealthy families indeed; in Warwickshire, for instance, about 40% of parishes lacked such a house, and in Cambridgeshire and Kent there were virtually none (Alcock 2006). Surprisingly the identity of this house has not been firmly established.

Greater tolerance seems to have followed the Civil War. Dissenters were now accepted into ordinary English society, though they were being carefully monitored by the State, and in 1676 a religious census recorded only one non-conformist in Dodderhill against 3 papists and 500 conformists, though nearby Bromsgrove seems to have been a hot-bed of dissent with its 300 non-conformists or one in seven of the population of the town (Anon 1910). The house of William Dugard of Dodderhill was included in a 1696 list of protestant dissenters' meeting houses, the dissenters avoiding penalties as long as the authorities under an Act passed in 1689/90 were notified of their presence (Noake 1856, 124–5; C Stewart, pers comm). The large wall-plaque found by R Butler in Crown Cottages on Crown Lane in 2000 must mark the site of this meeting house; it was inscribed 'SWD 1695'.

With the coming of the 18th century there were many new trends in evidence: greater access to education and free thinking leading to the Enlightenment when science opened many doors; new crops and methods bringing about higher farming productivity; and new technologies fuelling an industrial revolution. In the countryside improvement was the watch-word and landlords tightened their hold on the land with an eye to maximising profits, as capitalism also took hold. Enclosure was now generally pursued with vigour where it had not already occurred, and any remaining waste was commandeered by the lords of manors as of right and converted to enclosed grazing. Further depopulation of the countryside often resulted, but the newly industrialised towns of the Midlands and the North were able to absorb new labour. Money from

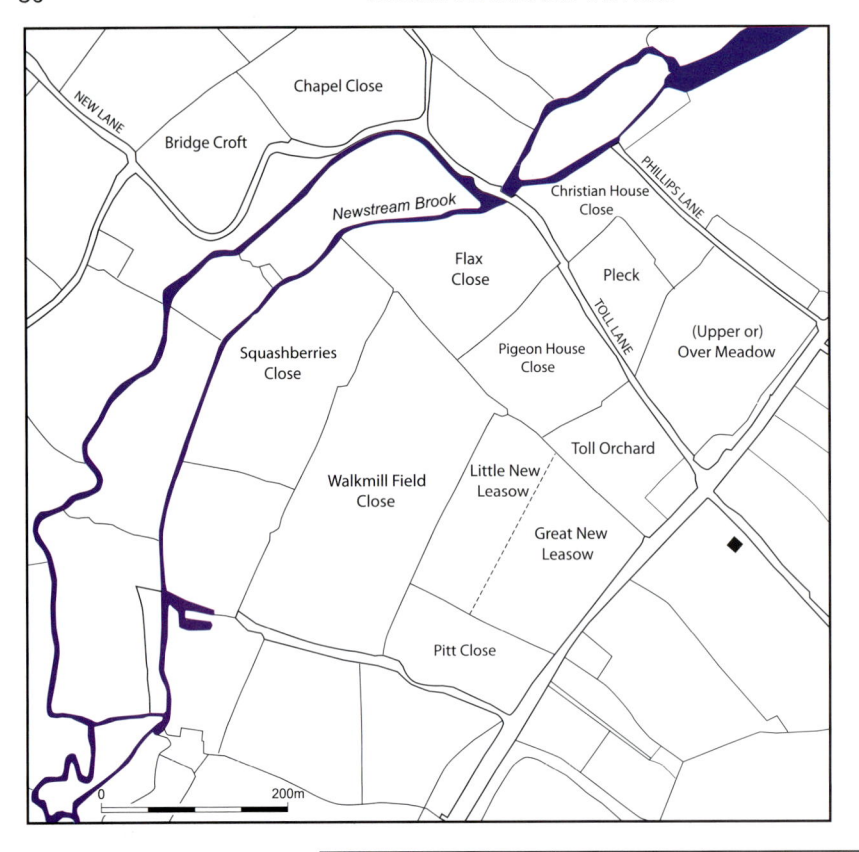

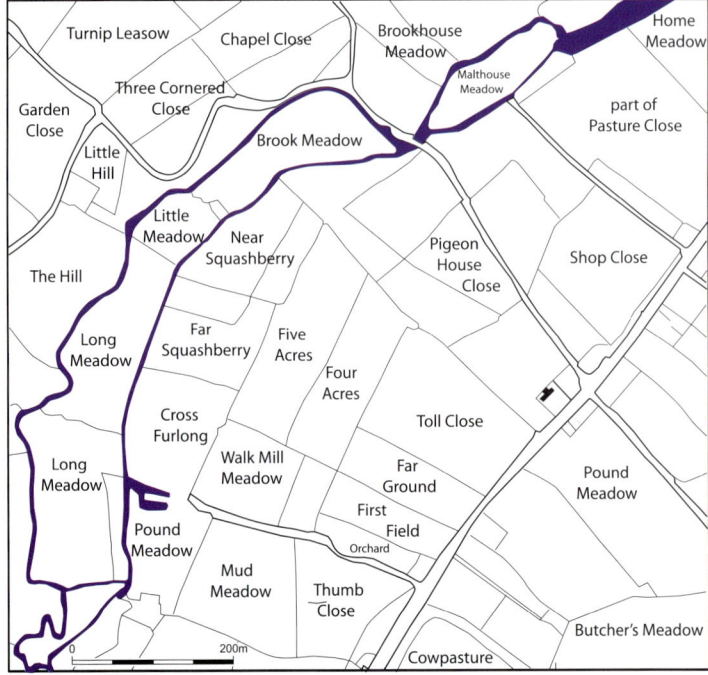

Figure 39 Reorganisation of fields in Wychbold based on 1671 documentation (BCA 431440, Hampton Pap 584; above) compared with 1843 tithe map (below)

slaves and sugar in from the New World also continued to flow and led to new building of aristocratic residences both in the country and the town, in the former often accompanied by newly landscaped parks. This was a new era of confident control of nature and of elegant style displaying wealth.

Locally, in the salt-making industry at Droitwich there was also a new spirit abroad as the industry appeared to have a bright new future with the overthrow in 1695 of the old borough monopoly, and many independent salt makers were now digging deeper shafts to get at greater quantities of brine. Overseeing this new impetus a massive new tower for Dodderhill church was built in 1708.

Much earlier traditions, however, also survived. Church tithes continued to be paid and fortunately the complexity of Dodderhill parish, due to its size and claims of tithe-free areas, caused documents to be drawn up to settle disputes. One description of tithes, dated 21 October 1728, recorded the three tything units in Wychbold as Impney, Wychbold, and Astwood yields, and mentions a 'farm called Feckenham Tree [Thickenapple], alias the Park, late held by Richard Postins, part of which farm lies in Dodderhill tything of Impney ... two farms called Crutch Farms which are said to be abbey lands ... Brine pit has tithe-free land (re great tithes) where it is in Wychbold yeald and tithed where in Impney yeald ... except one piece called Chapell Close in possession of Richard Pitts have paid great tithes in Wychbold yeald. ... Rents and profits of the Park Farm are applied to a charity in Droitwich to clothing 24 poor men and women and 24 boys for schooling setting up apprentices at £4 ...' (paraphrased from NA E134/2Geo2/Mich8). This document provides evidence of a surviving medieval system that was to continue into the mid 19th century. Incidentally the reference to a park in the farm name may recall the former existence of a medieval park here, as the 1275 lay subsidy (Willis-Bund & Amphlett 1893) listed Henry del Park in the Impney entry; the main house (site now lost) with its dovehouses ('the Corbett place of Impney' and *IPM* evidence respectively) was somewhere on the borough boundary with Droitwich, as described in 1456.

In 1786 the first detailed and accurately surveyed map of Droitwich was made showing parts of Dodderhill parish, but only that part within the borough (published 1794; WRO BA 7887 s497; Bassett 2008b, plates 1–2). This shows the new canal which had been completed by James Brindley in 1771 (Nash 1781–2, 306), and presently ended in the town. Part of the medieval Dodderhill Hospital seems to have survived into the late 1700s as an 'edifice is still subsisting as a pigeon house near the bridge' (*ibid*), and presumably this is shown on the 1786 map if only we could spot which building.

We leave the 18th century with news of a horse stolen from the stable of William Haynes, farmer of Dodderhill. Mary Holme, mistress of the Air Balloon public house on 'Crichley Hill, is mentioned as a witness on the same day as the theft, indicating both the felon's rapid progress and route. Having sold the horse in Stroud, the thief was caught on the Bristol to Bath road just three days later, an impressive feat of policing. In the dock at Gloucester assizes he claimed to be from Scotland, where relatives would vouch for him being of good character. The initial sentence at Gloucester on 17 March 1797 was death, respited for one week (HO 47/21/16). No evidence of a reprieve was found in the records, which is a reminder of the extreme justice that was being meted out for what might be regarded as a relatively minor offence, in the sense that the horse was presumably returned to its owner, and no lasting harm done.

Astwood (*by Cheryl Stewart*)

Astwood, literally meaning the 'east wood', was not a name exclusive to Wychbold. Many hamlets, especially in north-east Worcestershire, had their own 'east wood' (eg Worcester, Inkberrow, Hanbury), and in the large parish of Feckenham the east wood was divided into at least three separate areas: Astwood Musard, Stretcheastwood and Astwood (Bank). All of these 'Astwoods' were within the Forest of Feckenham during the early Middle Ages showing that this part of the county was well wooded, just as place-names, such as Elmbridge, Woodgate and Rashwood, also signify. The original authors of documents in the 13th to 16th centuries knew which Astwood they meant, but later historians now have to establish which Astwood was intended, and sometimes this can be mistaken. In the course of the research reported here on the history of Astwood in Dodderhill, all instances of the name have been collected, and this has led to the recognition of where connections can be made between the various surviving references.

In the 11th century the entirety of the parish of Dodderhill was within the boundary of the Forest of Feckenham, which at that time covered the majority of Worcestershire and a part of west Warwickshire. In 1229 Ombersley and the area to the south-east of Worcester were disafforested (ie taken out of the control of forest law; *CCR 1227–31*, 220; *CChR 1226–57*, 102), however Astwood was to remain within the forest. Later, King Edward I was finally forced to accept the claims of his powerful barons and in 1300 a series of perambulations were made in many forested counties, including Worcestershire (*CPR*, 1298). The outcome was the disafforestation of the greater part of the Forest of Feckenham including Astwood and the manor of Wychbold in 1301. It was not until 1608 that the entire forest was finally legally disafforested, but even then it took until shortly after 1627 for Sir Miles Fleetwood to action the statute (*CSPD 1627–8*), and by that time what remained was little more than a park.

The earliest written reference to Astwood was recorded in the Domesday survey of 1086. This Astwood is not included in the entry for Wychbold but is recorded within the entry for Hanbury where it states that 'Urse (D'Abitot) holds ½ a hide (approximately 60 acres) in Estw[o]de' (Thorn & Thorn 1982, fn 2,79). The same source also tells us that there was a *radman* or 'riding man' at Hanbury, and Dyer (1991) has suggested that Ralf the *radman* was in possession of this small manor.

At this time there is no mention of anyone actually living at Astwood within Wychbold manor. During the late 12th century Henry de Arden gave Astwood in Dodderhill to his daughter Leticia on her marriage to Geoffrey Savage who lived at Newton (Warks; *SLB* 8). In 1230 this estate, which came to be known originally as Astwood Savage, then later as Astwood Meynill, passed to Geoffrey's son, another Geoffrey. He died in 1248 without issue so the estate passed to his uncle William Savage, rector of Newton (*ibid*). It is highly probable that it was this William who built the original manor house at 'Savagebury' during the mid 13th century. He died in 1259 and according to the inquest (*IPM*) of 'William Savage of Astwood', his associates, including his neighbours Robert de Astwode and William son of Henry de Astwode, made the oath that William le Savage held '2 carucates of land in Estwode of Sir Thomas de Arderne by the service of the fourth part of a knight's fee worth by the year £8, and Phillipa the wife of Hugh de Meinyl, sister of William, was his next heir'.

In the 11th century Astwood was a large wooded area which straddled the boundary between Hanbury and Dodderhill (Dyer 1991), which is borne out by a judgement of the Worcester Eyre (forest court) of 1275 when William of Wychbold (bailiff of Wychbold) and others filled in a certain ditch in Astwood to the nuisance of the free tenement of Robert of Astwood. It was judged that the ditch was to be repaired at William's cost, and he was also fined 12d. From this account it can be deduced that there was a small detached manor called Astwood Robert in the north-west part of Hanbury parish. The free tenants who lived in the manor also held lands further to the north, in the wooded area which was within Wychbold manor. Roberto de Estwode paid half a mark (6s 8d) as recorded in the lay subsidy roll of Wychbold in 1275.

The site of a 12th/13th century Astwood habitation has been located archaeologically at a cross-roads on Astwood Lane (Morris 1994). Unfortunately a 30m long ditch aligned on the road was not even sampled; this was possibly enclosing a medieval homestead. The presence of the 12th century ceramics is particularly significant, as this is its only occurrence so far known in the parish. Medieval pottery and a stone hone were also recovered from an area of ridge and furrow just to the west of this Astwood site (Farwell and Barnes 1994).

In the Worcester Eyre of 1275 Phillipa was referred to as 'Phillipa, the lady of Astwood'. In the same year Phillipa de Sagebury (in Astwood) paid 20s (as recorded in the lay subsidy roll) for her lands at Elmbridge, while in 1327 'Hugone de Memel' (great-grandson of Phillipa) paid the second highest tax in Wychbold manor at 5s; his contemporary 'Willelmo Corbet' paid 6s for lands at Impney, with the majority of the inhabitants paying between 12d and 18d. These figures might suggest a rapid clearing of the trees and scrub, or 'waste', (viz 'assarting') at Astwood, thereby allowing more and more land to be brought into cultivation, and so increase the value of their estate.

In 1349 'Thomas Sanugebury (sic) chaplain was presented to the custody of the hospital commonly called the Spittal, with lands, possessions, rents, bullaries and other things belonging thereto' (Nash 1781–2). A year later, Sir Hugh Meynell received a grant of free warren at Astwood with similar grants on his estates at Kingswood and Stonydelph, Warks (*CChR 44 Edw III*, m 4, no 8; *DBR* 420, m 147). In the early part of the 15th century Astwood Meynill eventually passed to John Dethick of Newhall in Derbyshire, through his marriage to Margaret Meynill (*Feudal Aids* v, 331). The Dethickes became a very prominent and wealthy family, forming the nucleus of the local gentry in the Wychbold area and owning many of the local large farms, for nearly 150 years. It is very probable that there was a high status timber-framed manor house with barns and out-buildings, as well as its own chapel, close to the site of today's Sagebury Farm. What this house looked like we will unfortunately never know because a document dated 20 November 1599 refers to 'the scite and demeanes of the saide manor of Sagebury' (WRO BA 1307/18), suggesting that the original house had already been demolished.

Astwood was, therefore, made up of two distinct hamlets, Astwood Robert, with the main dwelling house being within the manor of Hanbury but with a large proportion of its attached lands extending into the manor of Wychbold, and Astwood Savage/Meynill, with its manor house and chapel located very close to the current site of Sagebury Farm house. From fragments of detail gathered from deeds, wills, inventories and tax lists, the 'yield' (a unit for taxation purposes) of Astwood stretched from Dodderhill common and the boundary with Hanbury parish, through the Astwood of today, and continued in a north-westerly direction to include the farms of Old Astwood (Hanbury), Sagebury, Hobden, Moors, Wychbold Court, Elm Court, Astwood Court, Astwood Manor, Causeway Meadows, Rashwood and Yew Tree, with a probable westward boundary being the River Salwarpe.

Over time, the centre of the manor which was sited around Sagebury was split up again and again to form small estates or farms as the 'waste' became cleared and more land could be brought into cultivation. The clearing operations appear to have commenced somewhere around where Shaw Lane is today and worked progressively northwards, enabling the estate to be split roughly in half with the creation of 'Obden' or Hobden. Clearing the woodland and scrub to the south of Shaw Lane most probably began in the late 15th century or early 16th century, culminating in the construction of Astwood Court Farm c 1600.

Clearing land for agriculture was also in progress around the nearby hamlets so that they eventually all joined up. These newly cleared lands were held in a piecemeal fashion of small lots or large common fields, but this pattern of possession only lasted until the late 17th century when much buying and selling and even exchange of land took place to create consolidated holdings. Whereas many parishes, especially throughout the English Midlands, required an Act of Parliament to enforce the consolidation and enclosure of lands within their parish, this was not required in Dodderhill as it had already happened at least 150 years earlier by mutual co-operation.

Figure 40 Late medieval ceramic drinking cup (rim missing; height c 3in/80mm) manufactured in the Hanley Castle area; found at the base of an uprooted tree at Astwood Manor Farm (photograph by C Bowers)

Astwood Savage

Sagebury

The farm known today as Sagebury (Fig 41) was once the site of a prestigious, if not the most prestigious, estate within the parish of Dodderhill, taking its name from the Savage family who owned it during the 12th and 13th centuries. The estate and manor of 'Savagebure' was owned by William Savage, who, when he died in 1259, was recorded as being 'of Astwood', suggesting that this was where he was then living (writ dated 20 May, 1259; *IPM*, 1259, no 23, VIII). Prior to this date 'Sagebury' had been owned by his nephew Geoffrey who died young without issue when William had been rector of Newton (Warks). Upon gaining his inheritance, William set about starting to build what was later to become a high status manor house and chapel. Phillipa, William's sister, and the wife of Hugh Meynell, inherited the estate and on her death the property remained within the Meynell family for many generations, finally passing to John Dethick through his marriage to Margaret Meynell (*Feudal Aids*, v, 331). It is unlikely that they lived here as they already held extensive properties in Derbyshire, but their son John and his wife did make their home here in about 1460. Sagebury was to be inherited by a further four generations of the Dethick(e) family.

In 1599 George Dethicke mortgaged 'the mansion house capital messuage and farm of Obden together with the site and demeanes of the manor of Sagebury', which implies that the manor house of Sagebury, if still existing at all, was in ruins (WRO BA 1307/18). George Dethick no longer had any use for his properties in Dodderhill as he was living in London, so he sold the entire estate of the manor of Sagebury together with Obden, Moors and Greenes in 1605 to Edward Smyth Esq, of Stoke Prior, for the sum of £3400 (*FF* Mich 2 Jas I). Later, Sir Anthony Smythes mortgaged both Obden and Sagebury to Thomas Nott of London, who eventually bought both properties in 1637 (*FF* Mich 13 Chas I). They remained the property of the Nott family for

Figure 41 Sagebury farmhouse

a further 100 years. In 1662 the hearth tax return records Edmund Daunce and his wife Alice as paying for one hearth, suggesting that there was at least one habitable cottage on the estate. In 1725 William Olives was the tenant of Sagebury (WRO BA 1307/19). In November 1753 John Baylis signed a 21-year lease for the farm (WRO BA 1307/20), and he also signed another lease for the farm at £200 per annum many years later in April 1797, but for one year only (*ibid*). In the May of that year his wife Ann died, and by April 1798 a new tenant had taken over. The owner, Robert Wilmot, subsequently leased Sagebury together with a cottage called 'The Blue Boy', in which John Baylis was living, for a term of 21 years at £275 per annum to John Wheeler of Stoke Prior (WRO BA 5589/69). John Baylis 'of Sagebury' was buried at Dodderhill in April 1804, being the last of the three generations of that family to have farmed Sagebury for a period of over 60 years.

Prior to taking the lease of Sagebury in 1798, John Wheeler had been farming as an under-tenant to Jacob Wilson at Obden. Taking on Sagebury it meant that he could farm both lands collectively. He and his family moved into Sagebury. In 1822 John Wheeler, the younger, of Sagebury, married Mary Wilson of Obden, and they went on to have a large family of eleven children, but sadly not all survived to adulthood (Dodderhill parish registers). Of those who did, Richard Wheeler, the eldest, took on the farming of Obden. The 1851 census tell us that, at the age of 24, he was farming 120 acres assisted by his sister, Sarah, acting as housekeeper for him, and employing 2 men, 2 boys and 2 women. In 1861 another son, Jacob Wilson Wheeler, then aged 32, was farming the 247 acres of Sagebury, employing 6 men and 3 boys, and was being assisted by his sisters Susan and Mary (1861 census). Also in 1861 John Corbett bought the lordship of Sagebury together with the capital messuage (the farmhouse) and farm for £16,472. In 1921 the farm, consisting of 242 acres, was sold again together with 2 cottages, when it only realised £10,674 8s 5d (WRO BA 8851/5).

Wychbold Court

Wychbold Court is a magnificent timber-framed house (Figs 42 and 65) set back from, and to the east of, the main road (A38). To the untutored eye it would appear to have all been built at the same time, but extensive historic building research has now proved that this is not the case (Price 2010a; see Price, this volume).

The land on which the house was built belonged to the Dethick family of Sagebury and Obden. Richard Dethick (1490–1546) is known to have had eight children, of whom four were boys. His eldest son, also a Richard, inherited Sagebury; his second son, Gylbert, inherited Obden; his third son, William, inherited Hill Court (the site of Dodderhill and Whitford School); and his fourth son, 'John gentleman of Dodderhill', is believed to have inherited Wychbold Court, but it is not known whether the house was already built at the time of his inheritance, or whether he built it himself later. Recent survey has shown that the earliest part of the house is the main range, but, unfortunately, it has not been possible to date this building phase dendrochronologically, as the timbers are almost wholly elm and much old timber was reused in its construction, though, stylistically, a late 16th century date has been proposed (Price 2010a, 9). The apparently earlier north wing now, constructionally, appears later (*ibid*), and so further investigation is needed to try and resolve this conundrum. If John Dethick was the builder of Wychbold Court, he did not enjoy it for many years, as he died in February 1559. His only son, also named John, was at the time a motherless baby and financial provision was made for him should he survive to adulthood (will dated 1558; WRO BA 3585, 1558:60). The dwelling house or tenement had been leased from his father, Richard, and this lease was transferred to John's nephew Simon Croswell/Cresswell, the son of his sister, Joyce.

Figure 42 Wychbold Court as shown on a postcard dated 1903 (John Brettell Collection)

By 1630 Wychbold Court had come into the ownership of Nicholas Lilly of Bromsgrove whose wife was Dorothy Perks from Ridgeway. Nicholas and Dorothy had no children and the estate passed to Nicholas' nephew, another Nicholas who came to live at Dodderhill in 1640, aged 19 (Consistory Court Rolls; WRO BA 2102). In February 1643 he married Elizabeth Kimberley at Upton Warren and they had three children, two of whom survived to adulthood. The 1662 hearth tax return records Nicholas Lilly, 'gent', as paying for six hearths. In 1687 Nicholas had a very elaborate document drawn up providing for his wife (Elizabeth), son (William) and grandson (John), in the event of his death (WRO BA 5524). The estate consisted of:

> … all that capital messuage or mansion house in Wichbould together with Great Millway Close (then in 4 parts) 14 acres; Little Mill Way 3 acres; Phelphers Close 6 acres; Sanders Close 3 acres; The Butts 7 acres; a cottage called Hemings tenement, then in the occupation of William Jesse, 2 acres; Howells Close 2 rods; Yates tenement in the occupation of Elizabeth Arden, widow; Bounds tenement (now called Mill House) in the occupation of Thomas Tipson; Christian Close and Laurymers Close (in one parcel) 4 acres; Andrews Pieces (4 pieces); Lane End Close 2 acres; Overmeeres and Nethermeeres 2 acres; Heathes Close 12 acres; Orchard Croft, and a little tenement thereon lately erected in the occupation of John Evans 6 acres.

Nicholas Lilly died in 1690 and his inventory (9 March 1691; WRO BA 3585) records the following rooms at Wychbold Court: kitchen, buttery, parlour, kitchen at the great house, pantry, hall, parlour, parlour chamber, pantry chamber, painted chamber (perhaps implying wall paintings), cheese chamber, and the kiln house. After Nicholas' death the entailed estate was inherited by his son, William, and partly by his grandson, John. In 1693 John Lilly conveyed his inheritance ('Over Moores, Nether Moores, Little Millway and Andrews Pieces') to Thomas Bearcroft of Worcester, a clothier, and John Cheetle of Worcester, gentleman, upon trusts for barring the entail, in order to facilitate possible sale.

In 1697 both William and his son, John, attended as jurors at the manor court. William died, and in 1723 John inherited the entailed estate from his father. Six years later John and his wife, Eleanor, brought a court action to bar the entail of a 'mansion house and 4 closes, Great Milway, Phelp's Close, Saunders Close, The Butts, Hemings Tenement, Howells Close, Yates' Tenement, Orchard Croft and Little Tenement' (WRO BA 5524). This action would usually indicate an intention to sell or otherwise dispose of the property, but it was not sold and remained within the family. In 1741 John's son, William Lilly, appeared on the freeholders list for that year and in 1754 he was referred to as 'late of Wychbold but now innkeeper of Bromsgrove', and his son William was born there in 1756. However, he must have returned to Wychbold, as he is listed as a juror at the manor court in 1764, and again in 1775. The younger William died about 1808 and his estate was inherited by his four children as 'tenants in common'. His eldest son, another William, would appear to have taken on the mill which had become part of the estate, as in 1815 he is referred to as 'miller', but by 1840 he has regained the whole estate and is referred to as 'farmer, miller & maltster'. The 1841 census shows this William as a prosperous farmer with his wife, Sarah, and five children, their governess, a further two female servants, and a male servant, all living in the house.

In the 1830s the house is described as 'a quaint gabled farmhouse, with black oak timbers, standing back from the road' by Edward Benson whose father took the tenancy of 'Ivy Cottage' (the property next door to Wychbold Court) for a short while before moving to Brook House. According to the 1851 census William Lilly, his wife (Sarah), and children (Mary aged 25, Harriet aged 24, Susan aged 22 and Louisa aged 19) were all in residence at Wychbold Court. Living next door in the newly built Elm Court (1850) was their eldest son William Mence Lilley, and his wife, Sarah Ann, née Garner. The Lilleys were enjoying affluence and good fortune, yet within a few years their estates were sold, they had left Wychbold for good. It is possible that this was because William Mence Lilley was not a keen farmer like his father and had no desire to take the estate on. There is, however, another possibility. In 1850 the Bromsgrove bank of Rufford Biggs & Co suspended payments and went into liquidation, precipitating the bankruptcy of a great many farmers and small investors in the locality. Francis Rufford, a partner in the bank had for some 20 years been providing capital to one of the two ill-fated salt companies at Stoke Prior, the British Alkali Company. Domestic and overseas competition together with an expensive rock-salt mine which had to be abandoned due to impurities in the salt, and finally increasing seepage of surface water into the brine shafts, resulted in Rufford Biggs & Co's collapse. In 1852 Francis Rufford was himself declared bankrupt. Both of the companies at Stoke Prior went under financially, and in 1854 John Corbett acquired part of the British Alkali's works, starting his progress to becoming a salt magnate.

It is highly likely that the Lilleys were among the many local investors who, having banked with Rufford Biggs & Co, lost everything, and had no choice but to sell up, and, out of pride if nothing else, move elsewhere. The Lilleys were bound to pay back the money borrowed in order to build Elm Court, making it even more imperative for them to cash in their assets – their land and houses. In March 1853 William senior, then aged 66, had the main estate valued at £9933 10s and, in addition, the water corn mill was valued in October 1854 at £2461 10s, out of which the £5000 loan to build Elm Court had to be repaid to Thomas Harris of Tardebigge. After 200 years and seven generations of Lilleys the family not only left Wychbold Court but the village too. William senior, his wife and daughters moved to Birmingham, and his son William Mence and wife Sarah Ann, to Broadway. It is difficult to imagine that they would have chosen to change their lives and social status so completely, unless they were compelled to do so by a major catastrophe.

The entire estate was eventually sold, prior to April 1861, to Sir Richard Paul Amphlett of Wychbold Hall. John Gibbs became the tenant and it may well be that he was already the miller at Wychbold Mill, as he had previously worked at the New Union Mill, Edgbaston. He was certainly living in the village in October 1849 when he married a local girl, Sarah Baylis. The 1871 census shows John Gibbs as a farmer and miller of 114 acres, employing 4 men and 2 boys, a house-maid and a dairy-maid. Prior to 1881 John Gibbs left Wychbold Court and moved to Heath Farm, Bromsgrove. The 1881 census shows that Thomas B Jackson aged 32 was now the tenant farmer, and he was still there in 1891, although the ownership had changed in 1885 from Sir Richard Paul Amphlett to his nephew, the Rt Hon Richard Holmden Amphlett.

On Monday 28th October 1912 at 4.30 pm to the minute 'Elm Court, Wychbold Court Farm, a pair of cottages, Wychbold Mill on the river Salwarpe which affords good fishing, 84 acres of excellent arable and pasture land having long frontages on both sides of the main road, several eligible building sites, a 21 acre arable field suitable for one or more small holdings, the Wychbold Post and Telegraph Office, other well-built houses and several lots of cottage property, all well situated in Wychbold, the whole comprising an area of about 115 acres', were auctioned by Edwards, Son & Bigwood in 14 lots. At the time of the auction William Pritchard was the tenant farmer and miller, at a yearly rent of £183 10s, and Wychbold Court and the mill were bought by Sidney Wilkinson.

George Jackson farmed the land throughout the mid 20th century and passed it to his daughter Yvonne and her husband Kenneth Baillie-Hill. After Mrs Baillie-Hill's death in the mid 1990s the estate was split up, the land was added to that of Sagebury Farm where their daughter Georgina was already farming, and the house was sold to new owners who renovated it, and the once working barns were converted into new dwellings.

Elm Court

Elm Court lies adjacent to Wychbold Court on the main road, and was once part of the lands owned by the Dethick family. Originally a timber-framed house stood on this site together with a range of barns forming a small farm of about 35 acres (1831 estate map; WRO BA 3760), and through the 18th and early 19th centuries it was a part of the Hanbury estate owned by the Vernons. During the early 19th century John Baylis, whose father had farmed at Sagebury for many years, was the tenant.

In the 1830s the property was bought by the William Lilley of Wychbold Court who farmed the land and leased out the house. The first tenant who came to live at Ivy Cottage, as the house was then known, was Edward White Benson and his family from Birmingham, who had been appointed manager of the large alkali works at nearby Stoke. In 1894 Mr Benson's grandson,

Arthur, recalls his father's recollections of the house: '… while I had been away they had removed to Wychbold, to an old rambling little house right well deserving its name of Ivy Cottage … a low irregular timbered house … [it] has a large garden and was overshadowed by tall trees; at the end of the garden stood a building, formerly a stable, used by my grandfather as a laboratory for chemical experiments'.

Ivy Cottage soon proved too small for the growing Benson family, and they moved to Brook House in Colley Pits Lane (Benson 1894). George Laughton, a clerk, and his family were the next tenants, followed in 1840/1 by John Whittaker, a farm labourer and his wife. The Whittakers were Ivy Cottage's last occupants, as it later caught fire and burned down.

William Lilley demolished the old house and by 1851 had 'erected a new messuage' which he leased for 50 years to his son, William Mence Lilley, at a yearly rent of £20 10s. Unfortunately William and his family were not to live long at Elm Court, as the house was sold along with the rest of the Wychbold Court estate. Both properties were bought by Paul Amphlett of Wychbold Hall, with the prestigious Elm Court then being leased out to a succession of well-to-do families.

Obden (now Hobden)

Obden is probably a settled place of considerable antiquity, the place-name *Obeden* possibly being derived from an Old English personal name, Obba, and so meaning 'Obba's valley' (Mawer & Stenton 1927, 282–3). In 1375 'John of Obynden' was the parson of Upton Warren (as recorded by Habington; Amphlett 1895–9). Gylbert Dethick, when writing his will on 21 January 1558/9, stated that he lived at 'Abdon'. Created out of the Sagebury estate, the farm has more recently become known as Hobden Hall.

The earliest description we have of Obden is that by Thomas Habington who, in the early 1600s said that 'Obden exceedethe nowe all Wychbaud in buylding' and that it was 'so fayre a house' (WRO BA 1307/20 & 1307/18). The present house is made of stone on older stone foundations, so it is possible that this first house was stone-built, as were many of the prestigious buildings in the area. The importance of Obden estate is reflected in the lay subsidy roll of 1603, where Sir Samuel Sandys and John Harris, the then owners, paid 16s, the largest amount collected in Dodderhill.

In 1605 the whole estate was sold to Edward Smith of Stoke Court, Stoke Prior, Worcestershire, for £3400, but he sold one half of the estate in 1613 to George Smithies (Smythes), Alderman and Sheriff of London, for £1900. He died in 1613/4 and his son Arthur appears to have inherited the property in its entirety. Twenty-one years later Sir Arthur Smythes raised a loan of £2000 from Mr Roger Nott, citizen of London, using the property as surety.

In 1637 Sir Thomas Nott (Fig 43), eldest son of Mr Roger Nott of London, bought the estates of Obden and Sagebury for the enormous sum of £11,000. He was born in 1606 and attended the Merchant Taylor's School, London and later Pembroke College, Cambridge. In 1640 he acquired the lands of Twickenham Park, Middlesex, and became a royalist army officer serving Charles I during the Civil War. As Lieutenant-Colonel Nott, he was mistakenly reported killed by the New Model Army during the capture of Highworth (Wilts) in June 1645. Later, he became one of the Gentleman Ushers in Ordinary of the Honourable Privy Chamber to Charles II. He was also an original fellow of the Royal Society. In 1649 he led an attempt, which failed, to declare Charles II as king. When he died in 1681 he was living at Richmond in Surrey, having sold Twickenham Park in 1659. and it is doubtful that he had ever visited his property in Dodderhill. He left Obden and Sagebury to his son, also named Thomas. Another of his sons, Edward, emigrated to America and was appointed Govenor of Virginia by Queen Anne on 15 August 1705.

Obden in c 1664 was being rented from Sir Thomas Nott by George Sheldon Esq and his wife, Frances, and tax was paid on nine hearths. They did not stay long at Obden due to Frances' death, and George's second marriage being to Elizabeth Hales of Snitterfield (Warks), who inherited a manor in Canterbury, where they went to live.

The will of Richard Edwards dated 1676 states that he was 'of Obden' but it is not clear whether he, and his wife, Susanna, were living in a part of the main house, or whether they rented land together with one of several houses and cottages which belonged to the estate.

Figure 43 Sir Thomas Nott 1606–81

The details in the will reveal that the hall was furnished with a large table, forms, stools and chairs (ie where the family ate their meals). The draught from the door was excluded by a screen, making this the warmest room in the house. Cellars are mentioned being used for storing the drinking vessels and a powdering tub (used to soak pork in brine when bacon was being made). The pantry, near the cellar, was used as a store and housed the cheese press, and some spinning wheels. There were three other chambers, including one known as the 'matted chamber'. This room probably had woven rush matting on the floor. It held a table which was covered with a carpet (at this date carpets were not put on the floor), chairs, chests of linen and yarn, a trunk, and a cupboard. This was a storeroom which also held cheese, malt, and wool, as well as some French beans. One of the other chambers was also a storeroom, and held threshed wheat and muncorn (a mixture of grains) and a 'cratch' (cheese rack). The remaining room was the bedchamber. The inventory valuation of Richard's possessions at the time of his death amounted to the substantial sum of over £221. His wife remained at Obden until her death in 1685.

There were some changes made after her husband's death, as it seems that Susanna moved into the 'matted chamber', as she bequeathed a bed there to her grand-daughter, Susanna Chellingworth. Susanna had fallen out with her son, whom she accused of being 'undutiful' and showing 'great unkindness' to her, and she made her daughter, Susanna Green, her executrix. She claimed that her son had £52 in cattle and money from her and part of this was to pay his children's legacy left to them by their grandfather. Susanna wanted Richard to pay back the money he owed 'peaceably' and then she would give him an extra £10 'if she could spare it', but if he caused 'disturbance' or a lawsuit, then he would receive only 12d.

John Green died suddenly after his mother-in-law, Susanna, in 1685, leaving £274 1s. The rooms are not described in his inventory but the manner in which his possessions were listed intimates that the hall was still being used as a kitchen, suggesting that the house was still divided. His brother-in-law, Richard Edwards, was the appraiser of his goods, and it is possible that he carried on running the farm at Obden.

If the main house was divided at this time, it is possible that Edward Howel, who died at Obden in 1681, was living in the other half, as Susanna Edwards and her son-in-law, John Green, and his wife, Susanna, were witnesses to his will. He had a kitchen and possibly two other chambers, one of which was a bed chamber, as listed on the inventory of his goods and chattels. In his will he refers to the 'Great Chest' in the parlour 'which is mine' implying that there was other furniture in the parlour which was not his. He had no wife, but clothes belonging to a Mrs Saunders had been left at his house and were valued in his inventory at 15s; perhaps she was his housekeeper. He owned 12 sheep and lambs, and 4 beehives, but does not seem to have been farming so was possibly an old man.

Thomas Nott, son of Sir Thomas Nott, was 'late of Obden' according to the inventory of his goods and chattels dated 12th April 1704. The inventory lists all the rooms in the house: the kitchen, the parlour, the pantry, the brew house with two furnaces, the cellar, the chamber over the parlour, the chamber over the pantry and closet, and the garret. Amongst his possessions were a 'silk crimson bed', and fashionable cane chairs, a couch, a clock, and £16 worth of silver plate. He left a total of £155 17s 2d. Because he owned property in more than one county, Thomas' will had to be proved in the Prerogative Court of Canterbury; he also owned property, called Queen's Stables, at Richmond in Surrey, and a property called Berringtons in Gloucestershire.

By 1728 the house is described as having a kitchen, hall, buttery and cellar with chambers over the kitchen, hall and buttery and a 'toploft' which held two old beds. There was also a cheese chamber, 'day house' (dairy), malt house, and an area called 'The Space'. The latter was where the cheese press and churn were stored. Mathew Wilson left over £837 when he died in 1728, and would seem to have been living in the whole house.

The farmhouse, as it appears today, was built sometime after 1734, when Lazarus Wilson, who was already in occupation of the property, signed a 21-year lease with the owner Daniel Nott. Lazarus was to have the existing farm buildings, plant flax and hemp, maintain the grazing, and erect a new messuage (farmhouse), cart house, 'pigcote' and sty, at a rent of £105 per annum (WRO BA 1307/20 & 1307/18). The house that Lazarus built was most probably erected on the same foundations as an earlier house on this site. The front elevation of the current building is built entirely of dressed stone, but the sides

Figure 44 Steps leading up from the cellar of Hobden Hall

and rear of the property have stone walls to about 8 feet (2.4m) high, with the remainder of the walls to roof height built in brick. It is possible that the earlier house on the site was made entirely from stone which was reused in the c 1733/4 rebuild, until it ran out, brick then being used for the remainder of the build.

The walls of the cellars are made of large rectangular blocks of dressed sandstone (Fig 44). One of the blocks has a crude carving which could be considered 'ecclesiastical'. A very large rectangular block, which has moulded detailing, today forms a lintel across an opening between two parts of the cellar, and was obviously never originally intended for its present location.

Figure 45 Drawing of Hobden Hall by A Aldham in c 1870, which shows the early 19th century extension to the north (left) of the house

In 1802 the owner of Hobden, Miss Ann Wilmot, married Thomas H Bund, and it is at about this time that the north wing of the house was greatly extended, increasing its size by about a third (Fig 45); this addition became unstable and had to be demolished in the late 1980s.

In 1818 a visitor could approach the farm in one of two ways. There was a driveway from Stoke Prior direction which continued in a

Figure 46 Hobden Hall farmhouse as it is today

westerly direction until it reached the Droitwich to Bromsgrove road (A38), with Hobden Hall being situated approximately halfway along the carriageway, from either end. A gravel quarry (now the pools of Upton Warren Sailing Club) has now completely obliterated all trace of the driveway from the A38, but it is still possible to walk along the footpath in the other direction to Stoke Prior.

By 1874 the ownership of Hobden Farm, consisting of a 'capital messuage' together with just over 141 acres of land, had descended to the Revd Thomas Hill, who agreed to sell it to the local salt magnate, John Corbett, for £10,800. In 1920 the trustees of the Corbett estate then sold the farmhouse, buildings, with just over 138 acres and 2 cottages, to the existing tenant farmer, William Wilson, for the far lesser price of £6435 15s 5d (WRO BA 1307).

Moors Farm

Although not entirely in the parish of Dodderhill today, this farm once formed part of the original Sagebury estate, with its ownership descending similarly through the Savage, Meynill and Dethick families. In the early 16th century the Sagebury estate was effectively split into two when Obden was formed. This most probably came about when Richard Dethick made provision for his son Richard to inherit Sagebury, and for his younger son, Gylbert, to be established at Obden. Later in that century Gylbert's son, William Dethicke of Obden, granted a lease to John

POST-MEDIEVAL (C 1550–1800)

and Parnell More, which was confirmed in 1599, and again, in 1605, when it is referred to as 'all that messuage, tenement or farm known as Mors with 6 closes of meadow or pasture' at a yearly rent of 50s.

After several different owners the farm was eventually bought, prior to 1655, by the Earl of Shrewsbury (Grafton estate records, WRO, BA 705/100). In the June of that year he granted a lease for 99 years to Robert Woolmer (WRO BA 1120), and Moors Farm remained part of the Grafton estate until 1941.

The current house most probably dates from the early part of the 19th century (Fig 47), when after more than 200 years the existing house on the site was probably in a poor state of repair. In 1811 the Earl of Shrewsbury granted a lease of 20 years for Moors Farm to Francis Bagnall at a yearly rent of £309 per annum. In 1840 he signed a new lease for another 20 years, this time for a rent of £322 per annum, and was helped out by his nephew Francis Symcox. However, by 1851 there was a new tenant, and Francis stayed on to help another of his relations, Michael Lovatt, with the farm. William Boulton in 1872, aged 66, took on the tenancy for Moors Farm (208 acres; WRO BA 1307/20), and continued until 1886, with his wife Elizabeth continuing on her own until 1892, when it was taken on by another 'William Boulton', who was presumably a close relative.

Figure 47 Moors farmhouse in July 1968

A news item in the August 1893 edition of the 'Advertiser and Messenger' reported 'Fire ruined a 20 ton hay rick belonging to William Boulton of the Moors Farm, Upton Warren. It was spotted by Mr Boulton who immediately rode to Bromsgrove to raise the alarm. The brigade, under Lt Perks, was soon on the spot and had the blaze under control in about four hours. Fortunately the rick was insured'.

William and his wife, Florence Maud (Fanny), left Moors Farm in 1913, and moved to a much smaller and more manageable farm called Helpridge (known today as Wyken), at Wychbold, which they had bought from the Corbett Trustees for £1450. In 1918 the Moors Farm with 143 acres of land and a yearly rental value of £203 10s was put up for sale by auction as part of the Earl of Shrewsbury's estate, but it failed to reach the reserve price of £5000. The whole of the Grafton estate was auctioned in 1941, and now with only 147 acres, it was finally sold.

Greenes (later known as Lower Henbrook; now site of Sagebury Cottages)

Situated on the main road (A38), there was another small tenement owned by the Nott family, known as 'Grenes' in 1599 (WRO BA 1307/16) presumably after the occupier at that time, who was William Grene. Nicholas

Figure 48 Sagebury Cottages in 2010

Cloves, a paper maker from Beoley near Redditch lived here from 1681, whilst he converted the mill on the opposite side of the road to make brown paper, possibly for the packing of salt. By 1690 the property, a house and 12 acres known as 'Lower Henbrook', was leased for 100 years to Moses Everton, a tailor of Worcester, following John Page, a previous occupant. However, Moses did not live there long, as he died in 1696 and his wife, Ann, passed away in 1698. Thomas Palmer bought the property from the Revd Pinson Wilmot in 1759, and this family association was remembered for years in the local field-name 'Palmers Meadow'. Today it is the site of a pair of houses built by John Corbett called Sagebury Cottages.

Astwood Court Farm

In c 1604/5 George Dethick, the last in the line of this family, sold to John Wheeler the land on which this magnificent timber-framed house was built (Figs 50 and 66). There were many families named Wheeler living in and around Astwood in the past, the earliest reference in Astwood being to a William Wheler listed in the 1524 lay subsidy roll as paying £5 (Faraday 2003, 140), when a John Wheler in nearby Stoke Prior was paying £4. They were probably related, as there were family connections between the Astwood and Stoke Prior Whelers in the following century. There is also a possibility that the John Wheeler who built Astwood Court came from Droitwich, as there is a 1601 reference to his failing to make up the King's highway around 'Leathorne Bridge' and 'Hill End … as he should according to the law'. Wherever he came from, this local gentleman married Elizabeth Bearcroft of Mere Hall at Hanbury church in 1579, and, according to the *Visitations of the Heralds* in 1634, he was the son of John Wheeler and his wife, Alice Wylde, of Astwood.

John Wheeler of Astwood was buried in the chancel of St Augustine's church on 16 December 1635 having written his will just a few days before he died, on the 7 December. He left the majority of his estate, which included 'lands and tenements in Dodderhill, Stoke Prior and elsewhere in the realm of England' together with 'three phates or bullaryes of salt water in Droytwich', to his son, John, a gentleman, then living in Stoke Prior. He was also to have all the best 'standards' (the tablebords, frames and forms, the best bed and bedsteads with all the bed hangings), which were in the wainscoted chamber over the parlour. To his well-beloved wife be bequeathed 'the bed whereon I usually lye and all the appurtenances thereunto appertayninge'. John's brother-in-law, Edmund Bearcroft, and his wife's cousin, Philip Berecroft of Mere Hall in Hanbury, were appointed to carry out his wishes. His wife, Elizabeth, died in 1639, and was buried in Dodderhill church with her husband.

Figure 49 Cheese rack with shelf supports still in position at Astwood Court Farm c 1985 (photograph by N Molyneux)

An inventory of John's goods and chattels was taken by his neighbours on 28 December 1635 (WRO BA3585 1635/233), and this document lists all the rooms and contents of his three-storeyed house and his outbuildings (for description of the house, see Price, this volume). In the main house there was a hall, containing, amongst other things, a long pike (a weapon that may have shortly seen service in the forthcoming Civil War); a parlour, with a carpet (for a table, not the floor); a pantry which contained two silver bowls, a gilt salt, a dozen silver spoons, 'threescore' (60) pewter dishes, and some glasses; 'chambers' including beds were over the parlour, pantry, and hall, and a gallery at this end of the house above the parlour and pantry, which was used for storage of oats and peas at the top of the house. Returning to the ground floor and at the other end of the house there was a kitchen, and buttery, the former including plenty of iron and brass equipment, and 'chaffing dishes'; upstairs again, and over these rooms, there were three bedrooms and a study containing a coffer and books, and then presumably up to the top floor, we enter the 'great gallerie over the hall and kitchen', where there was more storage (ie apples, cheese (with a 'cratche'; Fig 49), flax and wool). After mention of two cellars, a 'mens chamber' (possibly quarters for the male servants) is listed (more beds). The 'boulting howse' and 'backhouse' (a ?brewhouse) were presumably nearby, but separate, buildings. There was a total of 21 rooms, and the overall inventory, including stock, was valued at £452 10s, so John Wheeler had been a very wealthy man.

John's son, John, married Anne the second daughter of Richard Vernon, rector of Hanbury, and they had six children, all baptised at Stoke Prior church. After his father's death, John moved into Astwood Court, and this is where he died in 1656. He too was buried in the chancel of Dodderhill church and, like his father, he wanted his 'joined' bed and the cupboard in the chamber over the parlour, a great 'joined' chair in the parlour, the long table in the hall, and the long table in the kitchen, to remain in the house as 'standards'. They were to be for the use of his wife, and son, John, but after his son's death he wanted them to go to his grandson, yet another John. John made sure that his 'beloved' wife Anne had all the necessaries she needed after his death. She could choose six of his pewter dishes, a chest, and two beds for her own use, and he bequeathed a silver bowl and all the silver spoons to her. John's father had owned two silver bowls, a silver-gilt salt and a dozen silver spoons, and it is possible that the bowl and spoons bequeathed were these same items. The witnesses to John's will were his relations John Bearcroft and Richard Vernon, but, unusually, he made two of his daughters, Sarah and Susanna, his executrices, rather than his sons, John and Richard. It would seem that John was appreciative of the abilities of women, as he also left his bible to his daughter-in-law, Elizabeth, wife of his son, John.

In 1692 Thomas Lowe of Chadwick in Bromsgrove, and Thomas Bayley of Coventry bought the property. By 1735 Thomas Lowe owned the whole property, and he willed it to his daughter, Frances, who firstly married Thomas Vernon of Stourbridge and, after her widowhood, married George Draper of Hartlebury. In 1785 George Draper, gentleman, was 'of Astwood' when he made his will leaving the property to his sister's son, Bonham Caldwell. In 1792 Bonham sold the estate to Thomas Ingram Esq, of Birmingham for £2000. It is likely that either George Draper or Thomas Ingram, both of whom went to live in the house at Astwood, added the brick facade to the front elevation of the house, giving it a Georgian appearance, in total contrast to the back and side elevations of the house, which remained timber-framed. Ralph Carpenter was the tenant farmer in 1735, a busy as well as a prosperous yeoman farmer because at the same time he was also the tenant of one of the farms at Ford, today's Ford Farm. When he retired his son William took on the tenancy. In 1797 William Tolley of Astwood, husbandman, took on the tenancy for 25 years at a rent of £260 per annum. He too was a very busy man, as in 1791

Figure 50 Astwood Court Farm (as illustrated in VCH Worcestershire III)

he had bought another of the farms at Ford, now the home of the Droitwich Golf Club, for £3600 and farmed them together. When William died in 1807, his son John, who was not yet 21 years old, continued with the lease of Astwood, as well as farming his own farm at West Ford which he inherited from his father. After a few years John gave up the Astwood lease to concentrate his endeavours on his own property, and by 1818 a Mathew Wilson was in residence.

It was also in 1818 that Thomas Ingram sold the estate to the Revd James Volant Vashon, rector of Salwarpe, and only son of Admiral Vashon, who bequeathed the property to his daughter in his will dated 1842. Mary Anne married Edward Wheeler, and they remained the owners until the trustees to Mrs Marianne Wheeler, of Kyrewood House near Tenbury, sold the estate in 1887. John Corbett, who had already bought many of the farms and other properties in and around Dodderhill, purchased the estate consisting of a dwelling house and just over 160 acres for £9750. With Mathew Wilson being tenant in 1828, the Wilson family probably continued in this role throughout the rest of the century, since in 1900 Mrs Emma Wilson signed the leasing agreement for the dwelling house, farm buildings and yard, four cottages and just over 244 acres at a yearly rent of £333 per annum. Her son, John Pardoe Wilson in 1921 bought the farm and buildings, together with just over 161 acres of land for £6190 2s 11d. By 1940 Mathew, the son of John P Wilson, was farming on adjoining land at Causeway Meadows (WRO BA 8851).

Astwood Mill

In the 12th century Hugh de Arden granted rents from the mill at Astwood to the nuns of Westwood Priory which had been founded *c* 1153 (Kerr 1999). Unfortunately there are no surviving documentary records to indicate where this mill was sited, but it might possibly have been on the River Salwarpe fairly close to Hobden Hall where dressed stones can be seen on both banks of the river (SO 940673), and, from their position, could have channelled the water into a more restricted space to drive a water-wheel.

The mill disappeared from surviving priory records and does not appear in the *Valor Ecclesiasticus* of 1535, which valued all monastic assets just prior to the Dissolution in 1536. It may well be that this mill was allowed to fall into disrepair after the nuns had acquired a mill at Wychbold further downstream on the River Salwarpe, which was surrendered to them by the monks of Worcester. The nuns had also received gifts of mills at Briar Mill, Droitwich and Martley (*Valor*).

In documents belonging to the Obden and Sagebury estates dated 20 November 1599 and 20 May 1613 reference is made to 'all that scyte or place where one mill did stand in Sagebury with waters, streams, dams and other commodities …', which might perhaps indicate that a mill once stood on the bank of the nearby Hen Brook. With so many changes having been made to the course and flow of the Hen Brook over the last 50 years, it is not surprising that its site is not yet confirmed, though a possible site has recently come to light (Fig 51).

Figure 51 Possible site of Astwood mill near Hobden Hall (photograph by C Stewart)

Astwood Robert

Astwood Robert was probably named after 'Robert de Astwood' who lived there in the 13th century. The main dwelling house was within the bounds of Hanbury parish, but some of the lands attached to it reached north into Dodderhill. It is likely that the majority of the land to the south of Stoke and Shaw Lanes remained densely wooded until the late 15th century, with just one or two small farmsteads in the clearings. The Wylde family appear to have owned a great many acres of land in the area, having sold land at Astwood (Hanbury parish) to Robert Vernon prior to 1587 (WRO BA 7335/70 iv). The Wyldes would seem to have been in Astwood since at least 1558, and there were well-established branches of the family at both Ford (Dodderhill) and at Hanbury.

Astwood Manor Farm

Astwood Manor estate was located at the top of a hill having commanding all-round views of the surrounding countryside. An exact date for the building of this beautiful timber-framed farmhouse is not known but the oldest parts are very likely to have been built by John Wylde in about the 1560s or 1570s, with later generations adding to it over the years. A possible moat to the south-west of the main building suggests that there may have been a much older building on the site. Alternatively this feature may be a ha-ha (sunken boundary ditch) suggesting that in the 18th century the house could have looked out onto a parkland landscape.

There is a good description of the rooms at Astwood (Manor) Farm in 1683 from an inventory taken of the 'goods and chattels of John Wylde of Astwood, gent'. The dwelling house comprised: a hall with 1 clock and 3 carpets; a pantry; a cellar; a brewing house; a day house (dairy); a wash house; a kitchen containing, amongst other things, 5 flichens of bacon, 2 pistols and 1 gun; a parlour chamber; pantry chamber; hall chamber; matted chamber; kitchen chamber; chamber over the buttery, containing 1 silver tankard, 1 silver plate, 1 silver cup and 12 silver spoons; chamber over the day house; servant maids' chamber; cheese chamber; servant man's chamber; and a brew house (WRO BA 5589/106). At the time the inventory was taken there was £283 in money in the house, and the whole inventory was valued at £774 13s, a very large sum at the time.

Figure 52 Astwood Manor Farm in 1947 as drawn by William Albert Green (1907–83). Copyright of and reproduced by courtesy of www.ewgreen.org.uk

During the early 1700s the Vernon, Wylde and Wheeler families sold and exchanged land with each other, so that their scattered acres throughout Astwood, in both Hanbury and Dodderhill, formed a consolidated estate around each of their respective houses. Obviously satisfied with the result of the land transfers, in 1722 John Wild engaged the services of Joseph Dougharty of Worcester to survey his estate, which amounted to just over 206 acres, then in the occupation of Thomas Guise (Fig 53).

In 1786 the farm was in the ownership of the Revd John Wylde, and the occupier, John Guise, signed a new lease for 21 years at a yearly rent of £200, together with '2 couple of fat pullets on Christmas Day' every year. The Revd John

Figure 53 Survey and map dated 1722 of Astwood estate of John Wild, as drawn by Joseph Dougharty (WRO BA5589/106). Copyright of Worcestershire Record Office

Wylde sold the farm in the late 1790s to Josiah Lea of Kidderminster, who paid land tax on the property of £17 16s 2d in 1799 (WRO BA 8851/22). However, the Guise family remained in occupation, and in 1832 Sarah Guise, widowed, signed a new lease for the manor of Astwood, 'capital messuage or mansion house', and farm with 204 acres, at a yearly rent of £315. Sarah was ably assisted by a close relative, John Roe, who had taken over the running of the farm by 1836. Many generations of the Roe family continued to farm Astwood Manor for another 75 years, until Martin Roe died in 1911, aged 72 years (Dodderhill parish register). In 1886 Lydia Wodehouse had sold the lordship and manor of Astwood together with the farmhouse and land amounting to just over 199 acres to John Corbett. When the trustees of the Corbett estate came to sell the farm, they gave the then occupier, Charles Verney, notice to quit by 29 September 1920. Astwood Manor was sold for £6939 10s 7d to Alfred Hill of Rednal House Farm, Rednal, Birmingham (WRO BA 8851/4).

Causeway Meadows Farm

An indenture dated 10 December 1563 is the earliest known document relating to 'Corsey Meadow Farm'. This was a lease by the lord of the manor of Wychbold, Thomas Carewe Esq, to William Hill for the messuage, outbuildings, farm lands and hereditaments thereon, for 3000 years at the yearly rent of one penny, payable on the Feast of St Michael, 'if demanded'. By this indenture William was, in effect, buying the freehold of the property (WRO BA 8851/28).

Prior to 1615 George Hill of Bentley, yeoman, had inherited the estate from his father. George himself died in that year leaving his estate 'in the yield of Astwood with a house newly erected', to his son William when he attained the age of 20 years, and at the age of 18 years George, his youngest son, was to have his house, barns etc at Bentley, which he had newly purchased (CRO DIC/SU9/2/50). A descendent, also named William Hill, was still in possession in 1634, but Thomas Nash attended the manor court in 1635 representing the property. In 1664, Sir Thomas Nash paid hearth tax on 12 hearths, suggesting that this house was the largest in the parish of Dodderhill at that time. The house with 12 hearths is likely, therefore, to have been Causeway Meadows, as the Nash family were not associated with any other residence in Dodderhill at the time judging from other hearth tax evidence.

In 1699 John Hill, 'clerke of Upton Warren' wrote his will, and in it he left his wife Sarah £15 from the estate called Astwood. His son William was already in debt to George Martyn of St Giles in the Fields, Middlesex, so he relinquished ownership of 'the estate called Astwood or Causeway Meadows' for the remainder of the 3000 year lease in settlement of the debt. This is the first documented evidence of the estate being referred to as 'Causeway Meadows'. The Revd Edward Talbot, archdeacon of Berkshire, became the next owner of the estate, courtesy of his wife Mary, the daughter of George Martyn. Edward died at the age of 27 in 1720, his young wife never remarrying, and on her death in 1784 she bequeathed the property to George Berkeley who had been an unsuccessful suitor to Mary's daughter, Catherine, who had died in 1770. Born in 1734 George was also a man of the church, as he was a son of the bishop of Cloyne (Ireland), a celebrated philosopher. The family moved to Oxford where George had been educated, and, when he died in 1795, he was entitled 'The Revd George Berkeley LLD, Prebendary of Canterbury'. Again, the estate became his wife's, who, when she died in 1800, left the property to Mrs Dorothy Monck. The identity of this lady has not been established, but it is likely that she was a close member of the family. George and Elizabeth Berkeley had had only one son, George Monck Berkeley, who had died prior to his mother in 1793.

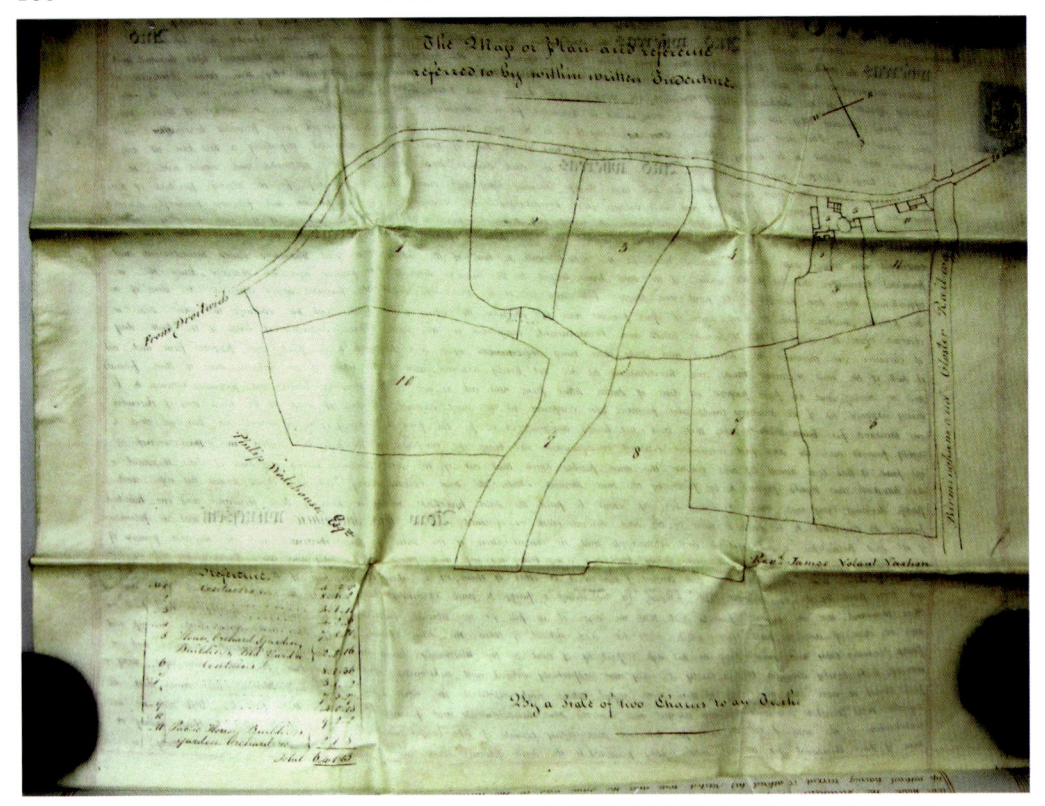

Figure 54 Causeway Meadows Farm: plan dated 1845 (CRO DIC/SU9/2/50). Copyright of Cheshire Record Office

During the Berkeley ownership Joseph Nash was the tenant. He died in 1808 leaving a wife, Sarah and ten surviving children, nine of whom were under the age of 21. The eldest son, Joseph, emigrated to Waterford in Ireland before 1815 where he remained for the rest of his life; Humphrey, the second son, travelled to the West Indies and was buried there, so it was Joseph's third son, Samuel, who eventually took on the tenancy of the farm. By 1817 he was a married man, having married Ann Preston at Inkberrow in the October of that year. Children followed, thick and fast. Samuel and Ann had seventeen children born to them between August 1818 and October 1841. It would appear that the farm was a success, as he was able to buy the lease for both Causeway Meadows and Redhouse farms for £600 in 1832.

The majority of Samuel and Ann's children went globe-trotting: the eldest four children and two younger siblings all emigrating to Chicago; two children to Denver, Colorado; two to Victoria, Australia; one to Cleveland, Ohio; and one to Baltimore (buried, aged 42, in 1866 at Bradley Green, Worcs). Only three of their surviving children, all daughters, stayed in England.

There is a brine stream which runs close to Causeway Meadows Farm and it is possible that Samuel may have speculated on possible

Figure 55 Causeway Meadows Farm: view of a now demolished timber-framed part of the house

profits from the brine under his land. This was, unfortunately for him, not to be, and in order to pay his debts Samuel transferred Causeway Meadows Farm in 1845 to his son, Thomas, and leased Hasler House just outside Cropthorne, Worcestershire, where died in 1850, aged 58, and was buried.

The farm remained in the Nash family until 1880, when it was bought by Mathew Wilson, the owner of neighbouring Astwood Court Farm, and, seven years later, he sold it, together with Redhouse Farm at just over 35 acres, the Bowling Green public house, and two cottages to John Corbett for £13,000. On the same day John Corbett bought the freehold of Causeway Meadows Farm, finally making the original 3000-year lease of 1563 obsolete. By 1910 Thomas Mathew Wilson was in occupation, and in 1920 he bought the farm (Fig 56), amounting to just over 101 acres from the trustees of the Corbett estate for £5644 7s 8d.

Figure 56 Causeway Meadows Farm: as pictured in the 1920 sale catalogue

Red House Farm

Red House Farm (Fig 70) was probably named as such due to its wholly brick construction, in an area where buildings had been largely either timber-framed or stone-built. In 1779 the farm, owned by Anne Purshall, was in the occupation of 'Widow Nash'. Anne left it in her will to Elizabeth Lechmere, her niece (WRO BA 3847/13). The property remained in the ownership of the Lechmere family until 7 August 1862, when it was sold at auction at the George Hotel in Droitwich at 5 o'clock. The farm, comprising a farmhouse and agricultural outbuildings together with 'about 70 acres of highly productive land in the tenure and occupation of Mr Thomas Nash' was sold to John Corbett (WRO BA 3762). Shortly afterwards Thomas Nash gave up the tenancy, and by 1871 the house was no longer occupied.

From the latter part of the 19th century the house was successively let to: John Pinches, blacksmith; Frederick Pincher, foreman pansmith; William Solven, coal merchant; William Colley (formerly of 22 Sagebury Terrace), who paid a rent of £14 per annum; Revd Dan Wrigley; and finally, in 1920, William Reeves of Stoke Works, rate collector, who was tenant at the time of its sale by auction. He bought the farmhouse together with over three acres for £164 from the trustees of the Corbett estate.

Rashwood Farm

In 1138 the Queen Maud gave lands at Rashwood, then in Astwood, to the Cistercian monastery at Bordesley, near Redditch, and it formed part of their original endowment (Mawer & Stenton 1927). Very little is known about the land in their ownership or who was farming it, but in 1522 the abbey was required to contribute to the military tax and was judged to hold lands worth 5s, one of the smallest amounts listed. A John Perkes of 'Rashehyll', who had goods valued at 20s in the same survey, may have been their tenant. In 1538, like all monastic houses in Britain, the abbey was dissolved and its lands sold. In new ownership this small estate was no longer considered to be a part of Astwood, and became associated with Impney.

Hill Court (*by* **Helen Peberdy**)

Hill Court, a Georgian house lying just to the north of Dodderhill church, has much earlier origins than its present appearance might suggest. On an early undated map (probably 17th century; WRO BA 8060), a house occupying the site is named as 'The Parsonage House', while a terrier listing the possessions of the church in 1585 (when Robert Glover was vicar and Philip Brace was patron) tells us that 'there belongs to the vicarage one close whereon the Mansion House now standeth ... which was till of late in the tenure or occupation of the vicars'. A 1616 terrier also records this, so Hill Court, in some form or other, must date back to the 16th century. The house can then be traced in an indenture of 1611 where John Brace, son of Philip, was described as 'of Hill Court' (the first mention of this name), and his will of 1630 confirmed this, though the main Brace family home was at nearby Doverdale. The Brace family had eventually come to own the rectory and patronage of Dodderhill parish after the Dissolution. The Brace family remained patrons of the living until 1674, John's second son, Edwin, being vicar from 1644–6, while also being rector of Doverdale. The family association with Dodderhill ended after 1674 with the death of Philip Brace, followed within three years by the deaths of his three sons.

Early in the 18th century the patronage, and the house at Hill Court, were purchased by Gilbert Penrice, and he lived there with his wife, Mary (daughter of Thomas Watkins of The Ford, a nearby farm). After his death in 1726 the house passed to his eldest son, also Gilbert (his brother, Humphrey, was the vicar of Dodderhill in 1717, remaining so until his death in 1771!). He may have lived at Hill Court, but did not own it. His daughter, Dorothy, married Thomas Holbeche thus passing the patronage to him, and they certainly lived there. They had four daughters, three of whom died in infancy, and the other only lived until she was sixteen. Dorothy herself died at Hill Court in 1771, and Thomas married again the next year, this time Christian, widow of William Amphlett of Hadzor, having a daughter and a son, whilst they lived at Hill Court. Meanwhile the house was sold to John Holmden of Crowle, who had two daughters, Lydia inheriting Hill Court when her father died in 1775. She married Richard Amphlett, son of Christian and her first husband William, and they lived at Hadzor whilst the Holbeche family continued at Hill Court. Their children, Lydia and Richard Holmden Amphlett, were both baptised at Hadzor before Richard senior died in 1785. Thomas and Christian Holbeche both died in 1807, she only a matter of days before him, and they were buried in the same burial at Hadzor. After that, Lydia Amphlett moved into Hill Court, and she lived there until she died in 1831.

After Lydia's death there was a sale of the contents of her home lasting three days with a catalogue running to 24 pages! This catalogue gives an invaluable picture of life in a gentleman's residence at the time and, in addition, tells us who bought each lot, and for how much. Hill Court itself was left to Lydia's son, Richard Holmden Amphlett, who lived at Hadzor where he was rector, and he sold it to William Ricketts of Droitwich, surgeon, and part-owner of the asylum there. He is shown on the Dodderhill tithe award of 1843 as the owner and occupier of Hill Court. The house stayed with the Ricketts family until it was bought by John Corbett of Impney in 1883 for £2500, the Misses Elizabeth and Susan Ricketts continuing to live there as his tenants. The house remained part of the Corbett estate into the 20th century until after the deaths of John and his brother.

During the First World War, when under the ownership of the Hollyers, it was opened to two war casualties of officer rank, for whom they arranged free treatment at the brine baths, and the numbers were increased until, in June 1917, the house was officially recognised by the War

Office as an Auxiliary Hospital for twenty officers, for each of which 6s per day was sanctioned with a trained nurse and two visiting doctors being provided (Anon 1921). Mrs Hollyer, after her husband's death, lived on at Hill Court, keeping it as a boarding house for patients visiting the brine baths in Droitwich, until she died in 1949. The town guides of the 1920s (Fig 57) and 1930s feature pictures of this fine house described as 'standing in its own park-like grounds of nearly twenty acres', and with excellent facilities which in the 1930s developed to include 'central heating, electric light and hot and cold water in all bedrooms'.

Eventually the house became used as a school, firstly as Glenhyng, a pre-preparatory establishment under the ownership of Mrs Price, then in the 1970s as Dodderhill School for girls 11–18, a senior school for Whitford Hall at Bromsgrove. Later the two schools combined on the Dodderhill site, and it now takes children from a much wider age range, and the school has been much expanded to cater for the increase in numbers. Despite the additions and alterations, the Georgian house – or at least its external appearance and some interior features – remains as a fine example of that architectural style.

What has been particularly elusive in this history of the building is any firm evidence for rebuilding and alterations between about 1600 and 1831. Perhaps either before or after Lydia Amphlett lived there, is the most likely time for a major rebuild, but, in many cases, previously half-timbered houses were just refaced and rendered over in the late 18th century. Some of the roof timbers of the present Hill Court show signs of antiquity, and the foundations are of large sandstone blocks. It would be good to discover more about when changes were made, and whether anything still remains of the 16th century house, still there, hidden and unrecognised, inside the present school building.

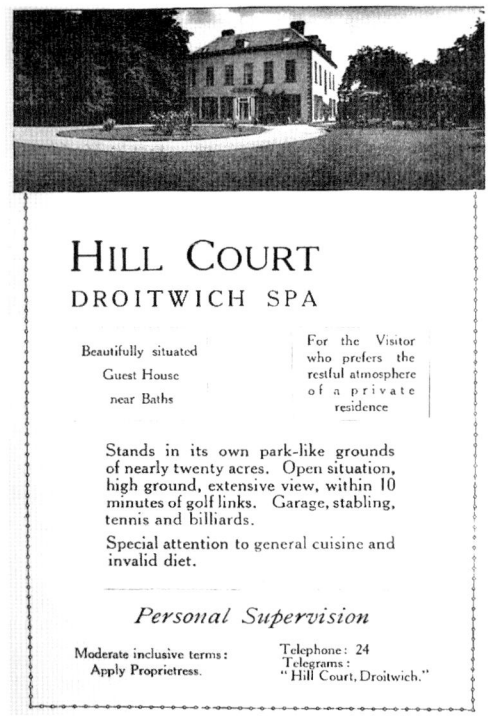

Figure 57 Hill Court as featured in 1928 Droitwich town guide

Local administration through the manor court (*by* Jenny Townshend)

The long established manor court continued to function beyond the medieval period, and now for the first time surviving court rolls allow us to see it in action. For instance, in September 1601 the Court Baron and View of Frankpledge of Sir John Pakington was held at Wychbold (unfortunately we do not know exactly where; BCA ref 473131:502). The steward was Roger Moore, and the homage (the tenants who were to act as jury) comprised fifteen men, four of them named Saunders, and two named Perkes. There were 34 people listed as present in the court roll, though widow Yardley and Dorothy Dallye made excuses for not being there. Those who were absent without excuse (defaulters) were fined: George Littleton, knight, from Woodcote 3s 4d; Robert Winter, knight, for Goures Farm at Huntingdrop, the heirs of John

Littleton for Timberhonger; Thomas Fownes, gentleman, for Dodford Priory 1s; William Fownes 4d; Richard Saunders 6d; and Thomas Ison 2d.

The first cases looked into were for breach of the peace. The men (and they were all men) were fined for affray, most being fined 1s, but when blood was drawn the fine was heavier at 3s 4d. Young Edward Barrett, shockingly, assaulted the constable, Thomas Lawe, and was fined 6s 8d. The court then passed a fine of 5s for trespass in the lord's park, and then moved onto the encroachments onto the lord's land, at the foot of the lord's wood at Rashwood, on the lord's waste at Toll Green, on the common at Satten Green, and for diverting the king's highway at Helpridge. The roads which passed through the manor had to be kept in good repair, and John Wheler was fined for not making up the king's highway around Leather Bridge and Hill End, as he should have done. Richard Saunders of Wyche was directed to scour the ditches from Kingsland Lake to Thomas Saunder's meadow.

The jury agreed that Mathew Lawe should allow Simon Perkes and others a road and passage from Coleway Pit to Wattleton with carts, horses and carriages, or be fined 40s, and Henry Sherrife was to make up his hedge between Chapel Close and his flax land or pay 20s fine. The rate of the fines was laid down by the court, 5s for a broken down hedge, 20s for cutting wood in Cleve Wood, and 20s for cutting furze on Piper's Hill. The village of Wychbold was then fined 1s for not keeping the [archery] butts in good order, at a time when all men were required to keep a bow and four arrows and to practice by law, though towards the end of Queen Elizabeth's reign the practice was in decline.

Huntingdrop was included in the presentments of Wychbold, and John Walters was instructed to maintain his hedges and gates into its Middle Field each year. When sown with wheat or rye, it was to be done before the Feast of St Luke (October 18), and when sown with peas and beans it was to be done before the Feast of St Mathias (February 24). He also had to cut the grass in the field or pay 5s. He had to make up the hedges of the meadows before Candlemas (2 February). These entries show to what extent the farming year could be laid down and enforced communally, which must have been a great incentive to the more ambitious farmers to embrace enclosure.

Since the last court six tenants had also died, and so heriots had to be paid and the heir recorded. The final part of the Wychbold proceedings of the court was the election of the new constable, William Saunders. The court then moved on to look at the events elsewhere in its jurisdiction. Richard Cox, gent, who had land at Obden and Sagebury, was fined 2d for non-attendance, along with ten others. There had been four deaths in the yield including that of William Dethicke, gent, who held his land by a quarter of a knight's fee. John Wheler, gent, had encroached onto the lord's waste with his hedges, but in Impney yield Thomas Parker had gone further and built a house on the waste. There was also a breach of ordinance in Impney made by William Yate and William Bromley, for which they were fined 6s 8d. An ordinance had been made for Rashwood and Holloway for the enclosure of Walmore meadow, showing the process of early enclosure in progress. Elsewhere in greater Wychbold, in Hill End, the stocks were in a bad state of repair, and the 'village' (sic) was fined a shilling.

By 1677 the number of encroachments upon the lord's waste had increased in Astwood, an area which had previously been wooded. There were eleven encroachments in Piper's Hill, as opposed to just five in Wychbold and three in Huntingdrop. The five in Wychbold were to be pulled down by 29 September and all were fined 4d. Susanna Westwood had erected a cottage in Piper's Hill and enclosed part of the waste, and she too had to pull it down or forfeit a penny. It is possible that by paying the small charge of a penny the cottage could remain and the fine was seen as a rent.

The number of alienations was also increasing in the second half of the 17th century as men began to consolidate their land holdings into more workable blocks of land, and wealthy land owners began to acquire land outside their own parishes. And so John Perkes 'aliened' (ie transferred the ownership of) his land in Rudgeway to Thomas Berkley, gent, and John Saunders 'aliened' a house and lands to Richard Cox, gent, of Clent.

Parish and church (*by* Helen Peberdy)

Most parish priests in the diocese just carried on with their jobs throughout all the religious changes, despite the fact that Worcestershire had many important families who remained Roman Catholic, some of whom were involved in the plotting which culminated in Guy Fawkes' attempt to blow up the Houses of Parliament in 1605. Dodderhill people had connections with several of these families, but managed to avoid direct involvement, and hence any retribution. It is worth mentioning Thomas Habington of Hindlip Hall, as his home was a regular haunt of Catholic priests and although not directly concerned with the 'Gunpowder Plot', he was arrested and tried with the conspirators. When the others were condemned to death, his sentence was that for the rest of his life he must not leave Worcestershire. He was then 46, and until his death at the age of 87 he spent his time in collecting material for a history of the county, and for this all subsequent historians of the county have been much indebted to him.

Whilst the state authorities were troubled by the Catholics at one end of the scale, at the other end a strong Puritan element was developing, which wished to forbid dancing and games on a Sunday, but contrary to this, in 1618, the 'Declaration of Sports' was issued, officially authorising the historic Sunday games. There is no direct evidence of approval or disapproval for these in Dodderhill, so presumably the tenor of local parish life carried on in the middle of the ecclesiastical road! But during this period at least one Puritan decided there was too much fun being had in the area and left Droitwich – Edward Winslow, baptised at St Peter's in 1595, eventually sailed on the *Mayflower* to America with the 'Pilgrim Fathers', and became the first governor of Massachusetts.

At Dodderhill church, almost in response to the drastic change of recent times, Robert Glover had become vicar in 1575 and remained so until his death in 1636, an incumbency of 61 years! Marriage was once again acceptable for clergy; Glover was indeed married, and his son succeeded him in the living.

Towards the middle of the century Worcestershire was central to momentous national events. The English Civil War started here with a skirmish at Powick Bridge in 1642, when Prince Rupert's Cavaliers were victorious. The Parliamentary Army occupied the City of Worcester and caused great havoc and desecration of the cathedral before abandoning it, after which Worcester was held for the king until his surrender in 1646. During these years, the bailiff's accounts for the town of Droitwich show frequent references to monies paid out when 'the soldiers' had been in the town. Dodderhill church was garrisoned by the Parliamentarians and attacked by the Royalists causing the destruction of the nave which accounts for the unusual shape of the church still evident to this day, even with the proceeds from the sale of lead from the bell tower of Worcester Cathedral being allocated to 'the repair of the Church of Dodderhill burnt by the King's men' (Fig 58).

Robert Glover the younger was vicar until his death in 1644, then for two years Edwin Brace, who was also Rector of Doverdale, followed by William Jones. The latter was deprived of the living in the time of the Commonwealth, and one Thomas Francis was substituted, presumably being of a more Puritan turn of mind. During the Commonwealth, records are difficult to find as parish registers were not always kept up, nor were churchwardens' or overseers' accounts. Wills are often missing too although there is an inventory of the goods of William Jones when he died in 1669. His goods were of very little worth but were in a ten-roomed house. He had been reinstated as vicar after the restoration of the monarchy in 1660, and the parish was glad to have him back judging by the churchwardens' presentments in 1664 when he was described as a 'Person without exception'. In 1668 Thomas Hanbury, 'Gent', in his will left his black cloak to Will Jones, vicar, so he was clearly seen to be in need of charity.

Figure 58 Dodderhill church at the end of the 18th century as illustrated by Nash (1781–2) showing Civil War damage still much in evidence

By the time the next vicar, Edward Phillips, was installed, a Fourth Act of Uniformity in 1662 had decreed the use of the revised Book of Common Prayer and this remained in use for all services in Anglican churches with very little change until 1980, when alternative forms were introduced (traditional services are still used occasionally in Dodderhill church). Until then one could visit any parish church and find the same service being read – rather as it had been before the Reformation, except that the service then would have been in Latin, not English.

During the reigns of Charles II and James II Roman Catholics were excluded from corporate office, and not until 1829, with the Catholic Emancipation Act, did it become legal for them to take an active part in local or national affairs. Dodderhill parish has revealed nothing to reflect this religious tension, though as indicated earlier, there were many notable Catholic families in the area and certainly some in the parish – sometimes only the wife appears in the presentments as a Catholic, so perhaps the husband preferred to conform, at least outwardly, so that he was not excluded from local politics.

The central tower of the church had been unsafe since the Civil War and, at the beginning of the 18th century, it was finally demolished and a new tower, a massive structure with walls eight feet (2.4m) thick, built at the end of the south transept. However, subsidence became a problem and tie-rods have had to be used to strengthen even this massive tower. There had certainly been bells in the original tower, and in 1551 an inventory taken of the church goods included five bells, while wills c 1600 included bequests for repairs to the bell frame and bells.

One had been bought from the suppressed friary in the town; there is no record of where the others came from – or indeed where they went when the tower was removed. For the new tower, Richard Sanders, bell-founder of Bromsgrove, either re-cast or cast four bells. In 1754 a fifth was added, then a sixth in 1756, both of these cast by Abram Rudhall of Gloucester. Although the ring was recast and augmented to eight in 1928, the old treble made by Richard Sanders in 1708 still hangs in the belfry.

After the restoration of the monarchy in 1660, it seems there was a period of stability in Dodderhill, with only three vicars in the next hundred years: Edward Phillips, his son, also Edward, and Humphrey Penrice, the last-named holding the post for 54 years! At this time the advowson was in the hands of his father Gilbert, who had purchased it from the Braces. The first, Edward Phillips who died in 1685, left goods worth over £300, including musical instruments and a study full of books (value £30). His vicarage was obviously a good-sized house, well appointed but he does not tell us where it was. His son left less in 1718 and may or may not have lived in the same vicarage. Humphrey Penrice left his property in Dodderhill, with the dovehouse, to succeeding vicars 'for ever'. However, it is by no means clear where any of these vicarages were but there were successive buildings in the area to the east of the churchyard which were probably used at times by the incumbents. It may be that Humphrey occupied Hill Court, the house immediately north of the church which is referred to as 'The Parsonage House' on some early maps (the parsonage being where either a rector or a vicar lived); his father, Gilbert, the patron of the living, certainly lived there but he was never vicar. This house later passed to Thomas Holbeche who married Humphrey Penrice's daughter, Dorothy.

During the 17th century the number of non-conformists grew, the early ones being Baptists and Quakers. There was much persecution particularly of Quakers and it was 1689 before the passing of the Toleration Act enabled non-conformists to have their own places of worship and preachers. In the Dodderhill parish registers, burials of Quakers are listed during the incumbency of Edward Phillips Junior. These were mostly from St Andrew's parish in Droitwich, but the Quaker Burial Ground was within Dodderhill parish (see Peberdy, this volume). Records of burials as being of Quakers, however, disappear from the parish registers early in the 18th century.

The early Dodderhill church would have looked very different inside from its present-day appearance. The church of St Swithun in Worcester retains the sort of church interior of that time – plastered and painted throughout, with high box pews and a gallery under the tower. Preaching being then the most important part of regular worship, there would have been an imposing pulpit. The outside of the new tower was blackened by the smoke from the brine evaporation pans and this still remains visible today, as a lasting testimony to the salt industry.

Quaker burial ground (*by* **Helen Peberdy**)

The Quaker movement began in the middle of the 17th century, when the 'seekers' after a more simple form of worship, were united by George Fox, and Quakerism quickly spread from the north-west of England, despite the 'Friends' (as they were otherwise known) suffering for their beliefs, as did other dissenters at the time. The first recorded meeting of the Friends in Worcester took place in 1655, and by 1670 the churchwardens' presentments for St Andrew's listed nine Quakers in Droitwich. Only one Dodderhill Quaker has so far come to light, a William Tombs in 1690.

But where were these local Quakers meeting? The answer, so far, remains elusive. In 1674 John Roberts was keeping a 'house of conventicles' (ie his house was licensed for Quaker meetings), but it is not known where he lived. A Beatrice Roberts, widow, lived in St Andrew's parish and kept an inn 'The Hen and Chickens', and this was probably the house referred to. She was definitely a Quaker, and her burial in 1696 was in the Quaker burial ground 'called a Graveyard which is in the parish of Dodderhill'. Edward Phillips, the vicar, entered it in the Dodderhill church register. Also in this register for that year were the burials of the following Quakers: John Watts Junior, and Francis Watts, 'Gent', both of the parish of St Mary Witton; John Tyler of St Andrew's (who had been left 5s in the will of Beatrice Roberts); and, in 1697, William Sale of St Andrew's. The burial of Widow Tiler (sic) in 'ye graveyard' in 1701 appears in the St Andrew's register, when James Tinker was the rector.

Some of the Quakers left wills which leave no doubt as to their religion. Beatrice Roberts and John Tombs both specified bequests to the 'Poor Friends', and Anne Hiatt in 1711 wished to be buried after the manner of the Quakers. She was the widow of a blacksmith in St Andrew's parish. In 1735 John Haydon, currier, died, and his son, Joseph, being the sole executor 'appeared personally ... and being of the sect called Quakers made a Solemn Affirmation according to the statute' (ie Quakers refused to swear an oath).

And where were these local Quakers being buried? A map of Droitwich made in 1786 shows a 'Graveyard' towards the western end of the Vines area of the town. This can be identified as the piece of land called the 'Quakers' Graveyard' which was described in a 19th century deed as being 'in the Vines area of the Parish of Dodderhill in the Borough of Droitwich' (WRO BA 4963/2), and located (according to 1846 and 1898 deeds; WRO BA 4963/28) as lying between the River Salwarpe and the lane from Bromsgrove Turnpike to Berry Hill Gate (now known as Vines Lane). The site still remains there today as an undeveloped plot. Perhaps some descendants of those early Quakers would like to search out their ancestors' resting place within the ancient bounds of Dodderhill parish?

Lives revealed – some insights based on wills (*by* Jenny Townshend)

Probate documents were left by 451 Dodderhill folk between 1527 and 1857, excluding Elmbridge. These documents are, in the main, wills and accompanying inventories, but where no will had been made, then an administration accompanies the inventory. The administrators were usually the next of kin, and it was their duty to see that the estate was valued. Duty could be levied on the value of the estate and paid to the church. As the executors and appraisers were friends and neighbours there is doubt that the total quoted was a true value, and in the case of one Edward Davies, gent (1616 and 1617) there were two inventories taken with a substantial difference between the two. The first was valued at £19 11s 8d and the second at £318 5s 10d (WRO ref 1616:182 and 261q).

Wills were usually made shortly before death when the testator was ill, but always of sound mind 'thanks be to Almighty God'. The first part of the will is concerned with the disposal of the body and the care of the soul. After this the personal estate (worldly goods) is disposed of, including any leasehold land and houses. Real estate, that is land and property the testator owned, was often not mentioned in the will as the eldest son and heir automatically inherited this.

The probate documents from Dodderhill have been transcribed and indexed. Most of the early documents were written in secretary hand, a common form of writing used in the late 16th and early 17th centuries. Often the only address given for the testator is Dodderhill, apart from as follows: the yield or district of Wychbold (46 cases); Astwood yield (10); Hill End (3); and Impney (2). Farms are named as follows: Obden (1558–1704; 7 examples), Sagebury (1668), Helpridge (1557, 1576), Ridgeway (1609, 1610, 1703), Rashill (1565), Rashwood (1614, 1615, 1643, 1695), Brine Pits (1654, 1670, 1708), and The Ford (1560–1730; 12 examples). Henbrook was where John More lived in 1591, which may be the origin of the name of Moors Farm.

As would be expected in a rural area there are a few trades recorded amongst the inhabitants: weavers, blacksmiths, tailors, carpenters, a mercer, a mason, a locksmith, a shoemaker, and a hatter. The hatter, Thomas Lawe of Wychbold, had been pressed into the king's army in 'South Handfield' in Essex. Not knowing what was to become of him, he made his will in May 1625, in the house of Thomas and Elizabeth Francklinge in 'Haires streete' in Hornchurch. He left £10 to his brother, George, and another brother, John, was to have the rest of his goods and cattle if he should 'retorn not againe'. He died in January of the next year. His estate consisted of the lease of Christian Close worth £12, £3 owed by Simon Perkes of Wychbold, and £20 owed by Raphe Finch of Little Coxall, in Essex, a chest with his cloths, a drum and his hat bands.

The mercer (general merchant), Nicholas Rose, who died in 1570, lived comfortably in Dodderhill, probably near to Droitwich. His personal goods were valued at £8 10s 4d. The wares in his shop were mostly cloth: cottons, kersey (coarse, narrow, ribbed, woollen cloth), canvas, Holland (fine linen fabric), chamblet (camlet, a fine fabric of a combination of wool, silk, hair or linen), fustian (coarse cloth of flax or cotton), worsted, dowlass (strong coarse linen), sowtwich (possibly cloth from Southwick), mockadowne (a piled cloth of wool and silk or linen and silk, imitation velvet), and silks. He also stocked thread of all sorts and colours, inkle tape (linen tape), crewel (thin worsted yarn) and lacing, and had pins, thimbles, combs, buttons, men's and women's hose, clasps, gloves and purses, and sold books and paper, soap, tar, pitch and raddle (both the latter used by sheep farmers; the last being red ochre to mark sheep), nails, graters, sealing wax, matches for guns, bow strings and arrows. Mercers also often sold food-stuffs, and Nicholas sold pepper, saffron, raisins, and other unnamed grocery. The gentry of Dodderhill and Droitwich probably depended on his services. It must have been quite shop to visit!

Edward Davies (1616) had books worth 20s, two new needlework cushions, five arras hangings, and one of coloured and gilded leather. He bequeathed four silver spoons and a *vat* or bullary of salt water in Upwich (a *vat* comprised 6912 gallons of brine; D Hurst, pers comm). George Wilde of The Ford (1629) had five silver spoons worth £1 5s, and 3 venice glasses, and 10 green glasses which were kept in a little cupboard. John Perkes of Ridgeway (1609) had the only musical instruments listed in Dodderhill, a lute and a pair of virginals (a keyboard instrument set in a box and, like trousers, referred to as a pair).

John Wheeler of Astwood (1635) lived in great style in his house of nineteen rooms. Servants and family lived in the house, which held fifteen beds. A sign of his wealth was the silver-gilt salt, two silver bowls and twelve silver spoons, which he had in the pantry. He also had the right to three bullaries of salt-water in Droitwich.

There was a walk or fulling mill in Wychbold, which belonged to Johane Stynton in 1635, who, as a widow, had married George Stynton. She had brought goods worth over £78 to her new husband, and, when she married him, her goods became her husband's, including books, twelve silver spoons, two flower cups, a silver bound 'cruse' (a drinking cup), three silver wine cups, and two silver wine bowls, and a double silver and gilt salt. By the time she died she had been widowed again, so she once more owned the items she had brought with her to her second marriage, including now being owed £33 for three-quarters of the annual rent for the mill and lands by Henry Pigeon. She also had two gold rings, which were probably her wedding rings, but no other jewellery. Wealthy widows were often reluctant to remarry, as they then gave up their financial security.

The inhabitants of Dodderhill grew their own food, baked their own bread and brewed their own ale. In the absence of banks they borrowed money from the more affluent members of their immediate society, as in the case of William Saunders of The Toll in 1586 who owed money to 24 people, including 6s 8d to the Church and 10s to the parish overseers. They were self-sufficient lives in the main, and, though few had any luxury in their lives, they lived comfortably by the standards of the day. The occasional luxury item sometimes got a mention, so, for instance, the Lawe family had silver spoons, a bible and glasses. Silver spoons in particular were regarded as an heirloom signifying some status, and were often bequeathed to younger members of the family, and so gave rise to our expression 'being born with a silver spoon in your mouth'.

Farming (*by Jenny Townshend*)

The geology of a district has an affect on its landscape, soil character and water supply, which in turn affects the agriculture. The heavy, red clay soil in Dodderhill is predominantly Mercia Mudstone (formerly known as Keuper Marl; Triassic period), which, when drained and combined with a favourable climate, produces good crops of grain. There are also islands of naturally better drained gravels, laid down over the clay by ancient rivers (Fig 2). Most of the land is below 200ft (61m). To the east of the detached part of the parish, on Huntingdrop Common, the ground is covered by widespread marsh and peaty alluvium. The salt beds of Droitwich, to the south, and Stoke Prior to the north, are known to be connected, the brine flowing below the marl in Dodderhill, and the name of Brine Pits Farm suggests that the brine was once brought to the surface here, but otherwise local farmers today make no reference to the surface soils being affected by this deep brine run. The River Salwarpe, as it flows through Wychbold in a south-westerly direction, is joined from north to south by the Hen Brook, Capel Ditch/Salty Brook, and Body Brook (Fig 3). Water loving vegetation, including osier beds, were once a notable local feature on the banks of the Capel Ditch and the Salwarpe (Buchanan 1944).

Dodderhill has long been an agricultural community, and the system of agriculture in the Middle Ages was communal in that tenants had strips of land in shared, arable fields, and in smaller closed fields. However, there is no evidence of land strips in Dodderhill by the early 16th century, when wills and inventories first become a useful source of evidence. There are some references to common fields being divided into closes in early deeds and wills, such as an indenture dated 16 June 1576, which refers to 'Rudgeway' Field (tithe map field 354), where one 'leasowe' was held by Richard Saunders in the south part of the field (WRO BA 2309/58). 'Cavoll filde' was another common field, and Walkmill Field (tithe map field 218) was referred to in 1625 as being 'nowe into six parcels'. Tenants had a share in the hay from the meadows, and pasturage on the common lands. The common meadows that have been identified are Rye Meadow (tithe map field 225; WRO BA 2309/58) and 'Cavall Meadow' (?Capel Meadow), where William

Saunders had 'a meadow pleck, called a dole containing ½ a days math' (ie work; WRO BA 2309/58). A tenant on the manor was restricted as to the number of animals allowed to graze on the common according to the size of holding (1661; BCA 473134, Hampton Pap 506). The largest area of common or waste was in Astwood and stretched to Sharpway Gate, which joined up with the common lands of Stoke Prior and Hanbury. Today the remaining wooded area is called Piper's Hill, but is still known locally as Dodderhill common. Astwood and the part of Impney to the east of the main road (A38) had been in the Forest of Feckenham, but by the 16th century had been cleared when closes began to dominate the landscape of the parish.

As the feudal system declined and monastic land was sold from the 1530s, the independent, land owning yeoman farmer emerged as a potent force. The increased prosperity of the yeoman is indicated today by the number of fine houses, with barns nearby, which still survive, such as Astwood Manor and Astwood Court farmhouses. Landowners hoped to take a share of the increased profits of farming, taking an interest in change, introducing new crops and new ideas of crop rotation. Permanent grassland and permanent tillage was converted to temporary tillage, typically seven years of cereals followed by grass leys of 6 to 12 years. In this livestock area, as much as three-quarters of the land could be grass at any one time (Wade Martin 2004, 2). In Dodderhill just over 75% of forty-two 16th century inventories revealed arable interests, whereas 100% listed animals.

Corn growing

The grain most often recorded in the inventories was 'corn' and in the 16th century 66.7% of the inventories listed corn, but it is difficult to know which grain this actually was. It was described variously as 'brush corn' (1694), 'fallow corn' (1694), 'hard corn' and 'malt corn'. Brush corn was wheat or barley planted in the stubble fields after the summer crop had been harvested. In the case of malt corn it was probably barley, although corn is generally thought of as wheat today. Richard Wylde of The Ford (1585) had hard corn (wheat or rye) and barley worth £24, a considerable sum. In the last half of the 16th century three farmers grew muncorn, which was a mixture of grain, usually wheat and rye, grown together; in other areas this mixture was known as maslin. The percentage of farmers growing this mixed grain remained the same at the end of the 17th century. However, in the 18th century there is no mention of muncorn in any of the inventories studied suggesting that this long established practice had ceased.

Between 1550 and 1600 rye appears on 16.3%, and barley on 18.6%, of the inventories made (Fig 59), both growing on poorer soils. Barley could be used to make bread, as well as malt for brewing, and also winter feed for stock. In March 1720 Grace Selvester had barley described as 'fallow barley' and valued at £1 per acre. Fallow barley was grown on the fallow field as part of the rotation of the crops. In 1730, Joseph Ireland of Impney had 13 acres of 'fallow for barley' valued at £13.

There are only a few inventories that list acreage and value for crops, which means that it is difficult to compare prices. Walter Saunders had 5 acres of lent corn 'upon the ground' in April 1564, worth £2 (at 8s per acre). Corn growing in February 1575 was worth 6s 8d per acre, and the price had increased to 13s 4d per acre in December 1593 (based on the inventories of Richard Crompe and John Richards respectively). In April 1609, Thomas Lawe of Wychbold had 6 acres of hard corn valued at £8 showing that the value was continuing to rise. The most comprehensive inventory is that of William Geeves (1624) of Wychbold. He had 2½ acres of wheat and muncorn at £3, 11 acres of barley valued at £14 3s 4d, and 3½ acres of oats and

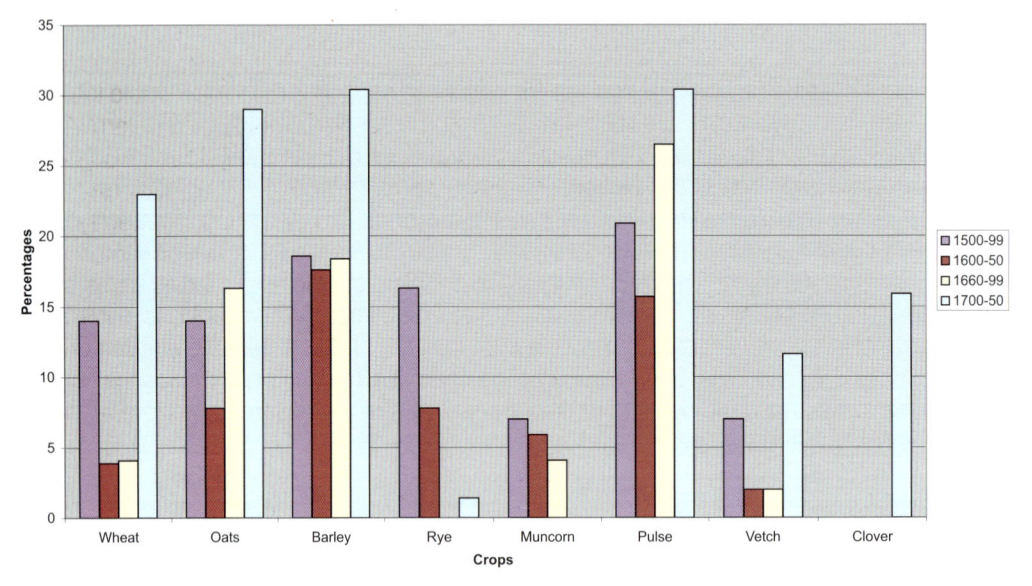

Figure 59 Percentages of inventories showing crops

peas valued at £2 6s 4d. In May 1640, George Hill had 2 acres of winter corn worth £3 10s. In the 17th century the number of inventories listing corn fell to 23.5%, a great reduction on the preceding century.

Wheat and oats both appear on 14% of the inventories in the 16th century. Wheat was used to make a superior bread (and biscuits), and was much preferred to rye bread. Oats, like rye and barley, would grow on poorer ground, and it produced a grain which could be eaten as gruel, porridge or cakes, or used to feed livestock. Thomas Pearkes of Helpridge (1576) had a winter sowing of rye, and rye with oats in his barn, indicating that the poorer soils were on the higher ground of the parish.

By the 1600s, in Worcestershire as elsewhere, there was a change in the pattern of crops being grown, with wheat being sown alongside rye as a winter crop, and oats and pulses being grown in the spring. Manorial custom in 1601 required that wheat or rye, alternating with peas and beans, should be sown in a field in Huntingdrop (WRO Hampton Pap 502). By the middle of the 17th century there was less rye being grown in Dodderhill (7.8% rye, 3.9% wheat) although it continued to be grown in preference to wheat, as on the much lighter soils of Chaddesley Corbett and Bromsgrove (13% rye, 3% wheat). Rye was grown as a crop in Bewdley until 1741, although in Dodderhill it is only recorded once between 1650 and 1725, when Humphrey Tomes of Piper's Hill left 2 bushels of rye. This was worth 2s 6d per bushel compared with wheat at 3s, and oats at 1s 6d per bushel. Rye and oats were being grown half as frequently as in the previous century, which suggests that conditions for cultivation were improving dramatically as the century wore on, although clover, the main soil improver of the period, was not recorded in the inventories of Dodderhill until August 1714, when two loads of late mowed clover were valued at £1. However, from 1670, grain prices were falling, and so farmers then began to diversify more into livestock.

Soil Fertility

During their exile, following the Civil War, the Royalists had seen the advantages of the intensive farming practiced in the Low Countries. On their return after 1660 they were determined to improve their land by introducing the agricultural practices they had seen on the Continent. Land improvement was encouraged locally by Andrew Yarranton of Astley, near Stourport, who introduced clover into Worcestershire. He published a book in 1663 giving his views on the uses of clover and its value as feed for cattle and sheep. Clover seed was sold in Bromsgrove, Kidderminster and Ombersley at 7d per pound (Gaut 1939), but the use of clover came slowly to Dodderhill. By 1724 a bag of clover was valued at 30s, although the quantity is unknown. In spite of his book and his offers of help, it was not until 1673 that it appears in inventories in Chaddesley Corbett, and 1680 in Bromsgrove. The change in farming practice was the concern of the farmer himself and the benefits of clover seem to have been spread by word of mouth, reaching Telford in Shropshire in the 1720s (Trinder & Cox 1980).

Before clover was grown the soil was also improved by growing other leguminous plants, mainly beans, peas and vetches. They were grown as a food crop and as cattle fodder, but also improved fertility by fixing nitrogen in the soil. In the 16th century peas and beans are listed on 20.9% of the inventories but vetches were on only 7%. In 1669 John Dugard had 22 acres of peas growing, worth £65. The numbers of farmers growing peas and beans remained about the same in the 17th century, increasing to 30.4% by 1750. The numbers growing vetches fell but then increased to 12.7% in the 18th century.

The main soil improver used historically was dung. As the animals wandered over the stubble and the fallow fields they manured the land, which would eventually be ploughed and planted with seed. Most farmers must have had dung or midden heaps, and evidence for this being spread in the fields is where medieval and later items are found in the plough-soil today, but only 5% of the inventories in the last half of the 1500s listed dung. It is not recorded at all in the second half of the 17th century. This is possibly because the appraisers did not consider it as a commodity worth recording. However, in 1729 Richard Humphries had a sizeable amount in the form of 6 loads of muck valued at £3. The Quarter Sessions recorded that in 1635 James Parker, the constable of Wychbold, presented Gilbert Glover alias Penrice of 'the Hill parish for not carrying away a dunghill from before his door to the great annoyance of the neighbours thereby' (*QS*). This was an offence, for which he could be fined, as dung was only appreciated in the right place. Dung heaps seem to have been a preoccupation of the Glover family as the vicar, Robert Penrice alias Glover, objected to the alterations made to the church grounds and the position of his dung heap.

Cattle

The cattle listed in inventories included bullocks and steers, which were castrated animals that were then fattened for food or kept as work animals, like oxen to till the land. Hay seems to have been the mainstay feed for cattle and horses, being found on 50% of the inventories, in varying amounts in the earlier period under review here. The amount had fallen to 45% later on but was still obviously an important winter animal feed. It was found in stacks, ricks, bottoms and parcels, as well as in barns.

In the 15th century 40.5% of farmers owned ox teams to plough their land. Four oxen were considered to be the minimum number required to pull a plough, but William Perkes of Rashhill

(1564) had 11 oxen, the largest holding. Nicholas Saunders (1557) had an ox harrow and yokes for 10 oxen, which may suggest that they farmed on heavy soils, as the heavier the soil the greater the number of oxen needed to plough. By the first half of the 17th century the number of people owning oxen had fallen to 9.8%. Four men had teams of six but William Bromley (1602) of The Ford had 10 oxen. The improvement of the soil and the breeding of bigger horses led to the decline of the ox as a work animal, and after 1650, John Jewe was the only farmer who had any oxen. The numbers of oxen were very similar in Chaddesley Corbet, but Bewdley by contrast had 26 inventories listing oxen between 1660 and 1707. In 1553 oxen were valued at £1 each, and this gradually increased over the century to between £2 and £3. In 1576 William Wylde of The Ford had his best ox, which was leased as a heriot, valued at £3 16s 8d, a heriot being a feudal due paid to the lord of the manor at the death of a tenant. By the 1630s the value of oxen had risen to between £4 and £5.

At the end of the Middle Ages the ox had been central to farming economy. So common was the use of oxen that English land measurements derive from the distance and area achieved when ploughing with an ox team, a furlong (⅛ mile) being the distance ploughed by an ox team before the animals needed to rest. With the bull's natural aggressive tendencies removed, it became docile and reliable. Hardy and healthy, able to pull steadily and cheaper to keep and shoe than a horse, they were the ideal work animal. The working life of an ox was six to eight years (Urquhart 1983), after which they could be fattened for slaughter. Oxen continued as draught animals until eventually displaced by the new breeds of heavy horses, which could do the job more quickly and needed only one man to work them. Nicholas Saunders (1557) had both a horse harrow and an ox harrow which indicates that his gelding was a work animal, but he also owned 9 oxen worth £20, so it would seem that they were the preferred animal for ploughing. Apart from the three 'load' horses of Johane Stynton, together worth £4 in 1636, and the cart-horse of Daniel Hawkswood, a miller, there is no indication in the inventories studied of other work horses, although horses are listed on 56% of inventories throughout the period reviewed here.

In the 16th century all the inventories listed animals, of which 80.9% listed cows (often referred to as 'kine'), ranging from one old cow, valued at 18s in 1579, to the largest herd of 10 cows belonging to John More of Henbrook, valued at £16 13s 4d in 1591. William Wylde of The Ford (1576) had a large herd of nine cows, ten two-year-old, and six one-year-old cattle, and five calves. It would seem that Dodderhill parish in Tudor times was dairying country, as all but eight, out of forty-two inventories, listed cows.

In the first half of the following century the number of inventories increased but the percentage listing cows fell from 83.3% to 47%, although the herd size was increasing (Fig 60). This was also noticed in Bromsgrove and suggests that specialisation was starting to take place, as farmers with the most productive and improved grazing could increase the size of their stock holding, especially on their new enclosures. For instance, William Geeves of Wychbold in June 1624 had 17 cows, three one-year-old beasts and a bull. However, the Civil War had an effect on the numbers of livestock held, as both armies requisitioned animals as they made their way through north Worcestershire. This may have been a great set-back for farming in the area, as prized animals were presumably lost. In the 17th century cows were valued at between £2 and £3, but it is difficult to value livestock, as the age of the animal and the time of the year can affect the value. John Wheeler of Astwood Court had a large holding of cattle that were valued as follows in December 1635: 6 oxen at £24, 6 six-year-olds at £6, 6 three-year-olds at £15, 8 kine at £23, 7 two-year-olds at £14, and 3 feeding beasts at £12.

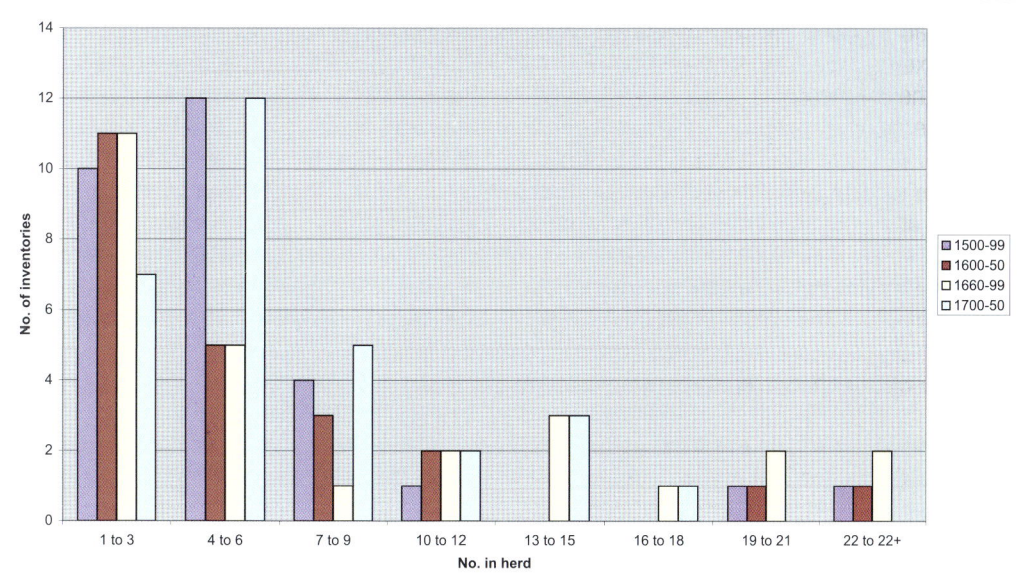

Figure 60 Size of herd

The breed of cow kept is unknown but they are described as black, 'bryndyd' and 'tagged'. Cows, then as now, were named and from the will of John Perkes of Ridgeway (1608) we know that he had a cow called 'Damsel'. Bulls seem to have been owned by a few farmers who shared the bull's services with their neighbours, as with John Boulkey of The Ford, who owed 7s (when he died in 1560) for half a bull he had bought with John Bruer of Worcester.

In the second half of the 17th century the number of farmers with cows increased to 63.2%. The largest herd of 20 cows belonged to the widow Alice Daunce of Sagebury (January 1686), who had doubled the size of the herd left by her husband in the summer of 1668. John Saunders of Rashwood had 11 cows and heifers valued at £25, and John Wylde of Astwood Manor (June 1683) had 10 feeding cows valued at £39 5s, as well as 10 store cattle at £23 13s 4d, and three steers at £9. The only known farmers with bulls in the second half of the century were Edmund Daunce (June 1668) of Sagebury and Richard Edwards of Obden (March 1676).

Overall in the 17th century there were fewer farmers in Dodderhill with cattle (55%) than in Chaddesley Corbett (65%), where the cows were also valued at £2 to £3. These animals were predominately dairy cattle, as opposed to a similar number in Bromsgrove, which were beef cattle. The skins from these animals probably supplied the thriving leather trade in Bromsgrove, on which the shoemakers and saddlers depended. The percentage of inventories listing cattle remained the same in the 18th century at 55%. Now the largest herd was that of Thomas Guise (January 1728) of Astwood Court, who had 24 cows valued at £96. John Hemming of Brine Pits Farm had 21 cows in February 1757, described as: 5 cows with calves, 2 milking cows, 3 cows 'in straw', 2 calving cows, 5 cows, a bull in 'the Brumhills', and 4 calving cows in 'Collits Ground'. Most people had 4 or 5 cows, but there were also herds of 12, 14 and 17 animals in the parish by 1724, suggesting an increasing reliance on dairy farming, with the larger estates being farmed by wealthy owners who were interested in the new methods of farming.

Dairying

The number of cows mentioned in the inventories of Dodderhill, compared to the few mentions of beef cattle, means that the references to cheese and butter may be of local economic significance. Inventories only record the goods which were of a more permanent nature, and perishables were not listed. This means that milk and, to a certain extent, butter is not mentioned, though because of the keeping quality of cheese it appears in varying amounts, from the modest amount for household consumption to quantities which must have been intended for sale in local markets.

Milk was not drunk much in the 16th and 17th centuries, except by invalids or children, so most of the milk production would have gone into cheese making. No quantities of cheese are given in the 16th century but John More had a herd of 10 cows at Henbrook and had produced cheese worth £2 6s 8d. Richard Wilde (1585) of The Ford, who owned 6 cows, had cheese worth £3 6s, and his son, George, had 75 cheese valued at £2 14s when he died in 1629, made from the milk of his 10 cows. An indication of the scale of milk production was the 18 milk pans he had in his dairy. At this time the price of cheeses seemed to vary from 4d to 8½d each which seems to indicate a variation in size. Cheese in Bromsgrove at this time was similarly valued at between 4d and 8d.

The number of people producing cheeses in Dodderhill increased slowly in the 17th century to 41%, and then dropped slightly to 37.7% of the total number of 18th century inventories. The amount of cheese being produced increased during this period, with between 100 and 500 cheeses recorded on each of eight inventories. The largest number of cheeses recorded were those of Edmund Daunce of Sagebury in 1667, made from the milk of his 10 cows and valued at £4 10s. By the 18th century Richard Cox (1718), a wealthy nailer, had 400 cheeses, Nicholas Lilly (1730), otherwise a cooper, had 300 cheeses valued at £2 14s, and Thomas Guise of Astwood Manor (1729) had £30 worth of cheese. In 1727 the 49 cheeses of Richard Humphreys of The Holloway were valued at 12d each, and Sarah Humpfries had 266 pounds of cheese valued at 2d per pound. By comparison the large parish of Bromsgrove to the north of Dodderhill listed cheese on only 24% of its inventories in the 17th century. Extensive cheese production is further corroborated by quite a number of the houses in the parish having a room called the cheese chamber where cheese, along with other items, could be stored securely and matured. Where evidence survives today, as at Astwood Court Farm (Fig 49), such rooms were at the top of the house. Humphrey Tomes of Astwood had 17 cheese shelves in his cheese chamber where his cheese was worth £4 18s, and 25% of the inventories which list rooms, dating from the second half of the 17th century, list cheese chambers. This number rises to nearly 36% in the following 50 years. Cheese chambers and dairies were exempt from the window tax by a statute of William III.

The dairy, or day house, was usually a stone- or brick-paved room on the coolest side of the house. A cool temperature is essential for butter making, although cheese making requires some warmth. The women made cheese from Spring through to Autumn, the summer milk being the richest and producing the best cheese. The equipment needed for cheese and butter making appears in some of the inventories. Warm milk was put into a milk pan or cowl, and then rennet was added to the milk. Rennet was made from the stomach lining of a calf, and this, when added to milk, made it curdle into curds and whey. Some inventories specifically mention whey skeels (a skeel being a wooden bucket with some of the staves projecting to make handles), rendling cowls and cheese cowls or vats. The curds were then salted, cut into small pieces and then packed into cloths in cheese vats. These were left to drip and then squeezed to remove the liquid. Cheese presses or wrings were the item of equipment most often mentioned in inventories. In 1691 the press and stone of Nicholas Lilly of Wychbold Court was valued at 2s 6d. Giles Lumbard (1615) had a cheese ladder (a wooden frame placed over a cheese tub or skeel to support the cheese vat, while the whey was pressed out, so dripping into the whey skeel below). Stones were superseded by wooden screw presses, which were easier to use. Making the cheese took about three days, and then the green cheeses were left to mature on shelves or a cheese cratch (rack) for at least three months. John Dugard (1669) had 40 mature and 42 green cheeses stored on his three cheese shelves and cheese rack. The cheeses were turned every day for the first week, and then twice a week until they were thought to be ready. Edward Daunce of Sagebury (1667) had a frame with 13 shelves on which to store his cheeses. Soft curd cheese was also eaten fresh, and used in cooking to make deserts such as curd tarts, which were similar to our cheesecakes.

The second most mentioned piece of equipment was the churn. Churning butter was hard physical work, also done by the women (Fig 61). The cream was skimmed off the milk, using a slotted spoon called a skimmer, and then churned in a wooden churn until the butter 'came'. The butter was then salted by hand and packed into butter pots (tall straight-sided ceramic jars of this period are still referred to as butter pots), and such pots could have made the longer distance transporting and then sale of butter feasible, most especially in the cooler times of the year (D Hurst, pers comm). The buttermilk left in the churn was used in cooking, while the butter was either used at home or taken to market to be sold.

Figure 61 Traditional churning of butter

From Tudor times the more affluent farmers had a dairy. It was recognised that cleanliness was crucially important when making cheese and butter to avoid any tainting. Hours were spent by the women of the household, scrubbing the floors and scouring the vessels used to make cheese and butter. In 1615, Gervais Markham, who wrote a number of practical manuals, recommended that this was to be done daily. Robert Herrick, the 17th century Devonshire poet, wrote:

> Wash your pails and cleanse your Dairies,
> Sluts are loathsome to the Fairies.

From the 17th century there was a general trend in farming to raise soil fertility with the introduction of clover, and this eventually seems evident in Dodderhill (see above). The close proximity to Droitwich and Bromsgrove meant that Wychbold farmers could shift their attention to dairy cattle to cash in on an increased demand for dairy products, as these urban populations grew. Relatively small farms could produce quick and frequent returns from dairying. Dodderhill's red clayey soils were suited to rich pasture, and parallels can be drawn with Cheshire which was also developed as a dairying region, the latter often claiming that underlying salt beds improved the quality of the cheese (Driver 1909). Whether this is true or not for Dodderhill, salt was certainly readily available in both cases for use in production, as were ready markets for the end-product. Strangely, Worcestershire cheese, unlike Cheshire, did not survive as a recognised local delicacy, despite its obvious reputation in the past reflected by the cheese fairs of north Worcestershire in the 18th century (Gaut 1939, 127–8), and it had to be reinvented in the late 20th century by the likes of Ansteys, farmhouse cheese makers of Worcester, with their Double Worcester cheese.

Sheep and the cloth trade (*by* Jenny Townshend)

Sheep were important stock in Worcestershire in medieval times as producers of wool. The woollen industry in the county was said to provide work for 8000 people, as the numbers of sheep increased (Gaut 1939, 64), so that corn growing began to decline with the labourers switching to working in textile manufacture. The government became so concerned by the growth of sheep farming that in 1517 it commissioned an inquisition in Hereford, Worcester and Gloucester to find out how many buildings had been destroyed, and how much land had been converted into pasture. This had little effect but in 1534 restrictions were also made on the number of sheep which could be kept by any one man, to check the change-over from arable cultivation to pastoral farming. Again in 1533–4 acts were passed restricting cloth production to certain towns (Worcester, Evesham, Droitwich, Kidderminster and Bromsgrove), in order to combat this movement away from arable farming (*VCH Worcestershire* II, 286). However, by the end of the 16th century the wool trade began to decline and then parliament reversed its previous policy and instead enacted legislation to try to sustain the industry, in 1570 passing a law to compel the wearing of woollen caps on Sundays and holidays.

Sheep were thought of as the most profitable of livestock in the 16th century, as they produced wool, meat, and milk. They also manured the land as they wandered over it, so improving its fertility. However, they do not do well on wet, lush ground, which is better suited to cattle, so it is probable that Dodderhill sheep largely roamed the higher, grassy hills of the parish, thereby avoiding the dampness that results in foot problems and infestation by liver fluke. Land enclosure seems to have come early in the parish of Dodderhill, the enclosing of land favouring the advance of pastoral farming. The rise and fall in numbers of inventories listing sheep is similar to that of cattle over the same period. The 16th century incidence of sheep on inventories is approximately half that of cattle at 46.5%, the largest flock belonging to Thomas Yeate of Holloway, his 70 sheep being worth £10 in January 1576. Thomas Perkes, also living in Holloway, had 56 sheep in December 1567, and Richard Wylde of The Ford had 50 sheep in October 1585. It would seem that the land in the south of the parish was best suited to rearing sheep.

In the first half of the next century the number of inventories with sheep fell to 27.7%, from 1640 the number of inventories listing sheep falling to just two. This may have been due to the requisitioning of food by the armies of the king and parliament in the Civil War, so as to feed their soldiers as they marched through the area. After 1650 the numbers rose again to 41.1%, and this was maintained in the first half of the next century (after which inventories were no longer taken). To further encourage the wool trade the Burial in Woollen Acts were passed by parliament, between 1666 and 1680, levying a fine of £5 on those not complying and burying bodies in other fabrics.

By far the largest flock in Dodderhill was now that of Edmund Daunce of Sagebury, who had 207 sheep. These were valued at £44 in June 1668 and would have been both sheep and lambs. When his wife, Alice, died in January 1686 she still had a sizeable flock of 87 sheep, worth £25. Sagebury, together with adjoining Obden, was a productive estate in cattle and sheep in the second half of the 17th century, and probably benefited from the better land management that was being advocated by Andrew Yarranton and others.

The sheep of John Wylde of Astwood (June 1683) are described in some detail in his inventory. He had two feeding sheep valued at £14, 29 ewes and lambs valued at £22, 9 yearlings valued at £15, and hog sheep (yearlings which have not yet been sheared). There were no references to rams (tups) in any of the inventories studied, but there were undoubtedly some in a parish the size of Dodderhill. Sarah Humphries had 17 wether sheep (castrated males), couples (ewes and lambs), and 6 hog sheep in August 1714. John Penrice had 8 sheep worth 10s each and 16 'twarholds' (two-year-olds) worth 6s each, in January 1729. By this period sheep were mainly being farmed for meat; wethers were butchered at four- or five-years old, when they were at their fattest, after a summer on grass or a winter on peas, beans and hay.

The sheep were put in a fold made of hurdles at night and would have been moved over the common land during the day. Some sheep (known as bell wethers) wore bells to help the shepherd locate them, as can be seen in rural Spain today. Giles Lumbard, in 1615, had such a bell, together with 9 'slips' (a slip being 720 yards; 658.35m) of woollen yarn worth 4s 6d, and 5lb of course woollen yarn worth 4s, although at the time of his death he had no sheep.

In the winter sheep were housed in folds and began lambing from January to March, and by spring the lambs were able to follow the ewes over the common land, the meadows being closed to livestock at this time to ensure a good crop of hay. Hay was important as winter-feed and a poor crop resulted in animals being culled at Michaelmas. Sheep were sheared in the early summer (June) when the fleece naturally began to come away from the skin. Wool was recorded on 7 inventories in the 16th century, 20 in the 17th century and 7 again in the first half of the 18th century. The largest quantity of wool found was the three stone (42lb; 19kg) of Walter Crumpe (1643). The wool waste removed from the fleece after shearing was known as 'flocks', of which John Richardson had a stone (14lb; 6.4kg) worth 2s 6d in 1665, although he had no sheep of his own.

Fleeces are only found in three inventories, that of George Watkins (1663) who had 6, Richard Baker of Wychbold (1682) who had fleeces worth 5s, and Elizabeth Yate of Astwood (1730) who had 22 worth £1 2s 6d. Thomas Davis (1595) had wool scales, which suggests that he was collecting the wool produced by his neighbours which they did not need for their own use, and was, therefore, possibly a local dealer in contact with travelling buyers, who supplied the textile industry. William Wylde of The Ford had 2½ tods of wool (70lb; 31.8kg) and 30 sheep in May 1576. Thomas Yeate in January 1575 had a stone (14lb) of black and 'colly' wool worth 10s. This was of lower value than white wool, as its uses were limited by the difficulty in dyeing it. In 1615 the tod (28lb) of wool of Walter Hill was worth 28s, but by 1639 the 15lb of wool of Robert Penrice was only worth 10s. By 1679 two stone of wool (12.7kg) owned by John Jewe was worth only 16s, suggesting the declining value of wool during the 17th century.

Once the fleece had been washed the wool was carded to smooth and align the fibres so that it was ready for spinning. William Wylde (1576) and Giles Lumbard (1608) had cards which were made from leather set with iron teeth. The carded wool was then spun using a spinning wheel or a distaff. Women, who were known as spinsters, usually did this work. In the 16th century the wheels were described as turns. They are found in six inventories, the word being spelled in five different ways (tourne, tworn, toorne, turn, torne). The turn was not the same as a great wheel, and William Saunders (1582) had both. The turn was moved by hand to wind the thread onto a spindle. The invention of a treadle mechanised the process, leaving both hands free to manipulate the wool and thread. A little wheel was developed which was used particularly for spinning flaxen and hempen thread. The thread was then wound into a ball using yarn blades, of which Charles Stewart (1728) had a pair. William Saunders (1629) owned 4 pairs of yarn blades and 3 reels, the latter probably being another name for a turn.

In Dodderhill, flax and hemp, both annual plants with fibrous stems, were grown to also produce yarn. The processing of the stems required them to be soaked in pits of water to 'ret' them, that is to break down the cohesion between the fibres. The fibres were then dried and scutched with tools known as tewtaws or breaks, and then combed or heckled with a hatchel to separate the more flexible fibres from the shorter, more brittle fibres. William Hill (1577) had both a tewtaw and a hatchel, and John Wheeler (1635) had a tewtaw and a brake. The flax and hemp were known as dressed at this stage. William Saunders (1564) had hemp and flax, both dressed and undressed, and George Hide (1729) had 14lb dressed flax worth 6s.

The flaxen and hempen fibres were spun into a yarn. The shorter, coarse fibres produced hurden or noggen yarn which, when woven, made a much cheaper, coarse cloth, the shortest fibres from wool, linen and hemp being called tow. Thomas Lawe (1610) had 40 lea (a lea being 300 yards; 274.31m) of hurden and hempen yarn worth 13s 4d, and 15 yards of hair cloth. Haircloth was a stiff cloth made from horsehair, or sometimes linen. It was used to make sieves, used in brewing. One lea of hempen yarn was valued at 4d in 1604, and a slip of linen yarn was valued at 10d in 1582, and at 12d in 1650. However, a slip of woollen yarn was only valued at 6d in 1615. Leas and slips could vary in length in different parts of the country.

The yarn was sent to the weavers, of which there were two in Dodderhill who left inventories: William Taylor of Hill End (1559), and George Snape (1616). Neither man was wealthy, the old loom and gears of George Snape being worth 50s which amounted to a third of his total wealth. In the 17th century broad cloth was produced on looms 88 inches (2.24m) wide and narrow cloth on 54-inch (1.37m) looms. William Taylor had one broad loom and two narrow looms. The smaller parish of Elmbridge, which was once part of Dodderhill parish, was home to six weavers during the same period, the last one dying in 1726. Thomas Lawe (1609) had 8 yards (7.32m) of woollen cloth at the weavers worth 2s. Thomas Perkes (1576) had 15 ells (an ell being 45 inches; 1.14m) of noggen yarn at the weavers worth 8s.

Once the cloth was woven it was subjected to various finishing processes, including, dyeing, fulling and shearing. The cloth could be dyed either before or after fulling. There do not appear to be any dyers in Dodderhill, and it is probable that the cloth was taken to Droitwich or Bromsgrove for this purpose, whereas any fulling could have been done more locally, for instance at Walkmill. The cloth was treated with fuller's earth to cleanse and degrease it, and then it was beaten to tighten the weave and thicken it. In the past it was trodden by the fuller, who was also known as a walker, but by the 16th century the process had been mechanised, water driving a wheel with wooden hammers attached for beating the cloth as it rotated.

John Richardson (1665) was a cloth worker and was probably resident at Walkmill. He had four mill feet (the hammers needed to beat the cloth) listed in his inventory, together with five loads of clay worth 7s, and a strike of earth worth a shilling (a strike was a variable measure). A local clay found in Timberhonger was used for fulling in Bromsgrove (Lacy 1774), and would probably have been used in Wychbold too. After the cloth was fulled it was dried on his racks, which were worth 6s 8d. He then stroked the surface of the cloth with teasels set into handles, to raise the nap. He would have stretched the cloth onto his shearboard, trimmed the nap and cut off the knots with his shears, of which he had two pairs. Therefore, he had all the equipment appropriate to a finisher of cloth and might have covered a large rural area.

The finished cloth was returned to the owner, who could then make it into household items or clothes. Walter Saunders of Wychbold (1564) and Moses Everton (1696) of Dodderhill were tailors. Walter Saunders had animals and crops growing, hemp and flax dressed and undressed and yarn, as well as 18 ells of new noggen cloth and 18 yards of woollen cloth 'of all sorts'. Moses Everton had no cloth or implements listed in his inventory, and so he might have been fully retired.

Some of the wool produced was felted and was then made into hats. Thomas Lawe was a hatter who came from Wychbold; although in 1626, when he died, he was living in South Hadfield in Essex, having been pressed into the king's army. A possible relation, John Law, who died in 1687, was described as a felt maker, although there were no tools of his trade on his inventory. The manufacture of linen cloth and hats continued into the 18th century with three fairs being held annually in Droitwich, which were specifically for the sale of linen cloth and hats (Owen 1756).

The growing of hemp and flax was encouraged by the government which, by enactments in 1532 and 1563, required for every 60 acres of land under tillage, one rood (¼ acre) should be sown of either hemp or flax, a ratio of 1:240. This was to encourage the manufacture of cloth for domestic use and reduce the need to import foreign cloth. In the 17th century the cultivation of hemp and flax was again encouraged by lease of land. In the 18th century bounties were being given to promote the growing of flax. Flax growing was not popular with farmers, as it was thought to impoverish the land, but must have been grown in spite of this, as fairs were held in Worcester, Kidderminster, Holy Cross, Bromsgrove, and Bewdley, as well as Droitwich as already mentioned, for the sale of linen cloth.

From the 14th to the 16th century the way in which land was farmed gradually changed in Worcestershire from arable to pastoral. Sheep had been an important class of stock, requiring less labour than in the case of cultivation of the land, which was an important consideration with the reduction in rural population following the Black Death. This resulted in enclosure coming early to the county, much of the north-east and north-west being enclosed before 1540. John Leland described passing by enclosed land hereabouts, and he described Worcester as follows: 'The wealth of the Towne of Worcester standeth most by Drapering and noe Towne in England at this present tyme, maketh soe many Cloathes yearly, as this Towne doth'. With cloth making restricted to five Worcestershire towns, much of the wool came from adjoining countryside and was worked by its rural population who no longer tilled the land (Gaut 1939, 64). These land enclosures were not only made by the yeoman farmer but by the gentry, who acquired land at the Dissolution. The land of the nuns of Westwood, which included part of Wychbold, became part of the extensive land holding of Thomas Pakington, and a similar acquisition was made by Henry Windsor at Hewell Grange, near Redditch. Enclosures favoured animal husbandry, but it would appear from similar studies done in the north of the county that sheep farming was in a steady decline from its heyday in the Middle Ages, and that farmers were now increasingly rearing cattle, supported by arable farming. Sheep were instead now more farmed for meat and less for wool, as the centuries progressed, so as to supply the needs of the growing urban populations. By 1756 Worcester, Kidderminster and Dudley were the only towns with wool fairs, and sheep fairs were only held in towns to the west of the county, where there would also be sheep from Wales for sale (Owen 1756). An advert for a fair in Belbroughton in 1742 illustrates how far sheep were driven to be sold, as they were expecting 2000 Welsh sheep at the sale, along with cattle and horses of all sorts (Gaut 1939), which demonstrates how extensive the farming networks were in pursuit of the best quality and highest prices for those fortunate to have the land and money to participate.

Food in probate inventories (*by Jenny Townshend*)

It is possible to glimpse the way in which the people of Dodderhill lived in the past from the inventories that were made of their goods and chattels, after their decease. The surviving 217 inventories, dating from 1539 to 1775, provide evidence in the most cases for the 'middling' sort of people of the parish. However, there are also examples of the possessions of the less well off, and of those who had considerable wealth. As inventories were made in the several weeks after death, perishable foods were not mentioned. Because of these shortcomings the picture drawn from inventories cannot be complete, but an indication of the diet and domestic arrangements does emerge from their scrutiny.

Before the invention of the kitchen-range at the end of the 18th century cooking was done over an open fire. Originally wood was the fuel used, being placed on the floor of the hearth in the centre of the hall. The logs were raised up on andirons, metal frames which stood in the hearth, that allowed air to circulate under the wood to assist in combustion. However, in the 16th century, eight inventories listed grates, the first being in 1564 (Walter Sanders), two of which also list coal. These grates were baskets made of wrought iron, which raised the coal up from the floor to allow the ash to fall away and the air to pass through. At this time cooking was still being done in the hall, the largest room of the house. Very few houses had kitchens, and these were generally used as store rooms rather than places where food was prepared. With the introduction of the chimney, the hearth moved from the centre of the room to a side wall. In larger properties that had more than one hearth, cooking was restricted to another room, the kitchen, and the hall instead became a reception room.

Coal had been used in Droitwich since the 14th century where a ready supply of fuel was needed for the salt industry, although wood was the most commonly used fuel at this early date (Hurst & Hemingway 1997, 40). By the 17th century the vicar, Robert Penrice, had a coalhouse containing 5s worth of coal and wood 'in the backside'. There are twenty references to grates during this century, which demonstrates the increase in the use of coal. Phillip Wylde of Brine Pits (1670) had 3 grates, 3 small grates and a 'grate with brass knobs', in his house. Thomas Geeves, a yeoman living in Wychbold (1686), had 4 tons of coal worth £2 on his inventory, and may have been dealing in coal. The cost of coal does not seem to have risen much over the next century as John Hemming had a ton worth 10s in 1757. By the middle of the 18th century the number of houses with grates listed in inventories had risen to 27. As wood became a scarcer commodity, coal was preferred, especially as it burns longer than wood and requires less attention.

The metal utensils associated with cooking over an open fire are nearly always listed on inventories, even when the fireplace, a fixture, is not mentioned. Meat and poultry were roasted on spits, known as broaches. These were held by hooks attached to a pair of long bars called cobbards or cobirons, which were propped in front of the fire at an angle of 45-degrees. A dripping pan was placed under the spits to catch the meat juices and fat. Later in the 17th century these were often made of tinplate, as this made them resistant to the corrosion caused by meat juices. A basting spoon, usually made from brass, and a flesh fork were the utensils needed by the cook, who had to turn the meat as it cooked to prevent it burning. A jack, with chains and weights, was developed in the early 17th century, to turn the spit automatically. This was replaced by a jack placed in the chimney, which was worked by the rising hot air and smoke, or by clockwork turning the spit.

Cooking was also done in a kettle or cauldron, suspended over the open fire from hooks on chains, hanging from a gale or crane. Meat and puddings were wrapped in cloth and boiled in the cauldron. Posnets, dabnets and skillets, all found in Dodderhill inventories, were smaller pots, designed to stand in the hot ashes, or on a trivet in the hearth. Frying pans were long-handled to distance the cook from the heat. Frying was a good way to cook small quantities of food quickly; so many people had frying pans. William Wylde of The Ford (1576) had four, which may suggest that a good fry-up was provided for his servants and workers. Pots, pans and kettles were often made from brass, an alloy of copper and zinc, which was used for cooking vessels as it has a high melting point and can withstand the high temperatures of an open fire. Those who could not afford brass had iron pots but these were prone to rusting. The brass pots and pans were highly valued by the housewife, and were often bequeathed to members of the family in her will. As for drinks, mulled ale and possets were popular in the 16th and 17th centuries, and iron plates were often used in the hearth to stand beer on to warm, as possessed by Nicholas Lilly (1690).

Small quantities of food could be heated at the table in a chafing dish, heated by charcoal. In the 15th century these were made of maslin, an alloy like brass, though unusually, Edmund Daunce of Sagebury (1668) had a pewter example (ceramic ones were generally not listed; D Hurst, pers comm). The last chafing dish recorded was in John Wylde's house at Astwood, in 1683. Pewter has a lower melting point than brass and was usually used to make platters, jugs, bowls and dishes. Where cutting food at table was involved most people ate off wooden trenchers, since pewter, an alloy of lead and tin, is relatively soft and easily marked by a knife. By the end of the 17th century earthenware plates were beginning to replace pewter, and start to appear on inventories, and treen (wooden) ware appears less and less, perhaps because of the latter's low value, but also due to the increasing availability of ceramic alternatives (D Hurst, pers comm). Though everyday earthenware was also little mentioned, again because of its low value, together with its relative fragility, making it not worth recording.

Many of the utensils used in the kitchen would be familiar to us today: chopping knives, skimmers (perforated spoons), colanders, pie plates, patty pans, sauce pans, pasty pans, stew pans and pudding pans are all mentioned. In 1670 Phillip Wylde of Brine Pits had a jack, two pairs of racks, six spits, three pairs of pot hangers, two pairs of pot hooks, tin pans, two pie plates, a pasty plate, four brass kettles, a brass pot, a posnet, two skillets, an iron pot, a skimmer, a cleaver, a chopping knife, and an iron plate in his kitchen. Pies were cooked over an open fire but the pastry had to be browned using an iron plate on a long handle, which was heated in the fire. Henry Saunders (1621) had a wafering iron, two iron plates between which dough was cooked to make crisp cakes or wafers. When the food came to the table, spoons and knives were the only utensils used until the end of the 17th century, when forks were introduced from the Continent. Because of the lack of forks to manipulate food, napkins were essential and hands were always washed before a meal. In more gentrified households a ewer of water and a basin were used to wash hands at the table.

Condiments were mentioned on inventories, in particular salt, which was also needed in cheese making, and generally for preserving food. Thomas Bassett (1558) had white (the best quality) and black salt, and Thomas Davies (1595) had four mitts (a mitt was equivalent to a pack-horse load) of 'Barrowes', all of which would have come from Droitwich. Barrows were the conical wickerwork baskets which were packed with salt. Thomas was a wealthy yeoman who left his son and heir, Thomas, 1½ *vats* in 'the lower seal and greate vine' (a *seal* was a salt-making house). This would suggest that Thomas was producing his own salt. In the 17th and 18th centuries salt for cooking was kept in boxes, or in the side of the chimney where it could be kept dry. For everyday use salt was put into a shallow dish, often made of pewter, called a salt. Johanne Stynton of the Walkmill (1636), a wealthy widow, had a silver-gilt double salt, as a symbol of her wealth, which would have taken pride of place upon her table. Another condiment used was verjuice, a vinegar made from sour fruit, such as crab apples. It was used in cooking, as a preservative and as a medicine, much as cider vinegar is used today. Thomas Geeves (1686) had 3 hogsheads of 'verges' worth £4.

From medieval times spices had been used in cooking meat to add flavour, but also to disguise the strong taste of meat, which was difficult to keep fresh. Pestles and mortars for grinding spices, mustard mills and pots, and pepperboxes appear on inventories. Spices, sugar and peppers for flavouring meat and sweet dishes were bought from the mercers in Droitwich, and Nicholas Rose, a mercer lived in Dodderhill parish in 1570. He had, amongst the many things in his shop, pepper, raisins and saffron, none of which could be produced locally. The main sweetener in the 16th century was still honey, as sugar was expensive and had to be brought from Bristol or London. Although hives are listed on household inventories, honey and sugar are never mentioned, except that Thomas Saunders (1706) had a pewter sugar box. William Saunders, of The Toll in Wychbold, had six hives of bees worth 6s in August 1582, and may have sold his honey to supplement his income. In August 1681 the four hives of Edward Howell of Obden were worth 10s.

Bread, long the main staple of the English diet, could not be cooked over an open hearth, so bread ovens were built outside the house. When chimneys were built against the wall of the house a bread oven could be built into the side of the hearth. It is not clear how many people had an oven and so could bake their own bread, and it is possible that some baked for neighbours who had no oven. In 1595 Thomas Davies, a yeoman, had a set of brass bread weights, three peals (long-handled wooden shovels with paddle-shaped ends for loading bread into the oven), and an oven fire shelf. This would suggest that he was baking bread and selling it to his neighbours. He had no grain in his house but he did have an oatmeal tub. Many people had small quantities of grain in their houses, a kneading trough and a bolting, the latter being a tub in which flour was sifted to separate it from the bran or the husks from the grain. The grain was often stored in the cop loft or attic, but George Wylde (1629) had a room specifically called a corn chamber. Oats were made into porridge and porringers were listed on some inventories. These were small bowls with horizontal, ear-like handles, sometimes made from pewter, and used for eating soup and other semi-liquid foods. John Wylde of Astwood had four porridge dishes in 1683.

When looking at inventories to learn more about diet, we can get only an incomplete picture, as perishable items and crops which were harvested by breaking the ground were not recorded. There is no evidence from inventories that sheep and poultry were eaten although they must have been. However, both pigs and cattle produce meat which can be preserved by salting and so stores well, and this was listed on inventories.

Pigs were thought of as the ideal animal to keep, as they will eat most things, are easy to house and popularly it was said that every part of the animal can be eaten, except its squeal. They were an important source of meat during the winter, in the form of bacon and salt pork. In Dodderhill, however, not everyone kept a pig. In the 16th century only three-quarters of the inventories listed pigs, with William Wylde of The Ford (May 1576) having the greatest number: 27 swine, young and old. No-one had only one pig, most people had four, and this number persisted into the 17th century. However, in the 17th century some farmers seemed to specialise in pig breeding with larger holdings of 12 to14 pigs. In the 18th century fewer people had large numbers of swine, the exception being Joseph Ireland, who had 23 pigs valued at £9 in January 1731.

Pigs kept for fattening were called stores or store pigs; these could also be castrated males, which were known as hogs. The hog of William Hill of Astwood was valued at 13s 4d in 1612, and must have been a good size. John Clinton had two fat hogs worth £3, and eight store pigs worth £2 16s in December 1732. Individual prices for the animals are not given on many inventories but the fat pig of John Penrice (January 1729) must have been a record breaker, being valued at £2 2s. In 1616 a sow and 9 pigs were valued at 24s. The word 'pigs' was used for what we would call piglets. Boars are not mentioned very often, but Thomas Yeates (January 1576) had 13 swine, a boar, and 6 sucking pigs.

Although it has probably been overstated in the past, Martinmass (11 November) was traditionally the time when beasts were slaughtered before the winter. This was so that they would be as fat as possible before it became difficult to feed them, although killing went on throughout the winter and early spring. John Wheeler (1635) had lard in his kitchen in December and Thomas Lawe had a pot of hog's liquor in April 1609, probably indicating that a pig had recently been killed. Both beef and pork were butchered, and the larger joints were salted by soaking in brine in powdering tubs or the salt was rubbed into the meat to preserve it. Thomas Davies (1595) unusually had two lead powdering tubs. John Penrice of The Ridgeway (1730) had a brine cask. Bacon that was being prepared was said to be 'in the ruff'. The meat was then hung on cratches (racks) suspended from the kitchen ceiling, or, in earlier times, in the smoky roof space of the open hall. The open fire in the centre of the hall created smoke, which rose into the roof space and out of the louvres in the roof. With the introduction of chimneys, a smoke bay was sometimes created in the chimney space in which meat could be hung to cure (eg Wychbold Court; see Price, this volume). In April 1677 John Attwood had four flitchens of bacon in the chimney. A flitch was a side of pork or beef that had been salted and smoked. There were only nine mentions of beef in all the inventories looked at, which suggests that salt beef was not much eaten in Dodderhill. The greatest number of flitchens was those of William Wylde of The Ford (May 1576), who had 15 flitchens of bacon and 3 flitchens of beef. He also had 27 swine at the time of his death and so may have been producing pork and bacon for sale in Droitwich, rather than for just home consumption. It is generally considered that meat consumption, even by the lowly peasant, increased significantly in the late medieval period (Dyer 1989, 159), and there seems no reason to consider that this appetite for meat would have been reduced in the post-medieval period.

Poultry and cheese were referred to as white meat in the 16th to 17th centuries, and cheese making and poultry were said to be the responsibility of the housewife. We know that cheese was made in quantities in Dodderhill and was certainly eaten by all (see Townshend, this volume). Poultry provided meat, eggs and feathers, all of which were used or sold. Feathers were used in pillows, mattresses and cushions, and as pens, and goose wings were used as dusters.

Thomas Davies (1595) had a goose pen. As would be expected hens were the most common fowl, occurring on 23 inventories in the 16th century, and 10 in the 17th century. After 1650 poultry were not recorded in inventories in any numbers (4 poultry, 1 geese), and, after 1700, they are not mentioned at all. This was also the case in Bromsgrove, and was probably due to their lack of value. In the 15th century capons were recorded on five inventories, a capon being a castrated cockerel, which will then fatten like a hen, but with later more intensive poultry production capons seem to have declined.

The second most common fowl kept was the goose (17 mentions in the 16th century). Goose feathers and down are superior to those of hens, and were used to fill mattresses and cushions. Once a year the mattress fillings were changed by the housewife and new feathers added. Phillip Salmon (1611) had 10lb (4.5kg) of feathers worth 3s 4d. As well as providing feathers the roast goose provided large amounts of fat, which was used in cooking, but also medicinally. According to the 16th century poet, Thomas Tusser, goose was the traditional dish eaten at the harvest-home supper, and in later centuries it became associated with Christmas. Geese also make admirable 'watchdogs', making a great noise as they chase off intruders. In 1586 William Saunders of The Toll had 2 geese and a gander valued at 2s, 6 hens and a cock also valued at 2s, and 4 ducks valued at 1s 4d. Ducks were not popular fowl but in a parish well supplied with streams, wild ducks must have been a regular sight. In the early 18th century several yeomen had fowling pieces, presumably for shooting wild ducks and geese.

The most unusual birds kept in Dodderhill were the turkeys and peacocks kept by Simon Saunders in 1606. He had a peacock and two peahens, which must have been something of a novelty. The peacocks may have been destined to grace the table at nearby Grafton Manor, where John Talbot lived. Turkeys eventually replaced peacocks as a meat for a special occasion, such as Christmas. Turkeys had been introduced from America in about 1530, but they were expensive birds and difficult to keep, not liking draughts or loud noises. They were certainly being eaten by the 16th century when Tusser (1580, 65) referred to them being served in his instructional poem *Five hundred points of Good Husbandry*. Hart (1633) in his *Klinike or diet of the diseased* recommended that 'Turkeys of a middle age and reasonably fat are a good and wholesome nourishing food and a little inferior to the best capon'.

Fish were very much part of the diet in the past, particularly on Wednesdays and Fridays, but do not appear on inventories as they do not keep well. Thomas Payn (1606) was a carrier who, at the time of his death, was owed money for carrying fish, probably from Worcester. Barrels of salt fish, and red and white herrings, were brought up the River Seven to Worcester and Bewdley, and from there they were distributed around the county (Bewdley Historical Research Group 1999, 14). Payn also carried salt from Droitwich to Pillerton (Warks), and a butt (108 to 140 gallons) of sack (a dry white wine from Spain) to Stratford-on-Avon. This had probably come up the River Severn from Bristol with the fish. Fishing must have been a pastime and a way of supplementing the diet, although the only reference to fishing was the two fishing nets of Phillip Wylde of Brine Pits (1670).

The inventories only give a limited view of the varieties of fruit and vegetables grown in Dodderhill. The more delicate and perishable produce were not recorded, but apples, pears, beans and peas were found stored in houses and growing on the ground. Onions, garlic and carrots are recorded as growing in Bromsgrove and Chaddesley Corbett in the 17th century (Townshend 2000, and Chaddesley Corbett Local History Group 1988 respectively), so it would seem likely that they grew in Dodderhill too. It has been suggested that they were not grown in sufficient quantity to appear on inventories, although they may have been considered as perishables. There was no mention of the new crop of potatoes at Dodderhill, but in January 1728, Thomas Guise had French beans, presumably ready for planting. Peas and beans were grown as soil improvers, as fodder for livestock, as well as for human consumption.

Worcestershire has always been recognised as an apple and pear growing area, and as one of the counties that produces cider and perry. John Wylde (1683) had a perry mill; this was probably an edge runner mill, with a stone which was turned by a horse, in a circular trough, like the cider mill of Thomas Saunders (1706); while Richard Postins (1724) was leasing his cider mill. The fruit was crushed and then pressed to extract the juice, which was then fermented. Thomas Watkins (1691) had a 'great cider vessel' which may have been used for the fermenting process. William Tomes (1701) had two and a half hogsheads of cider and perry, and a half hogshead of verjuice. Francis Beck (1732) had two and a half hogsheads of perry. Humphrey Tomes (1725) had a hogshead of cider worth £1, and a hogshead of wine (63 gallons). William Bookey (1714) was also producing cider in some quantity as he had a cider house, as did Richard Price (1737). The contents of his cider house were worth £18 18s, and he also had a cider chamber in his house. Wine was an expensive luxury and only found in two houses, the other being that of Joseph Ireland (1731), who had six wine casks.

There was no mention of spirits, aqua vitas or hot waters in Dodderhill, but three inventories listed stills, the first being owned by the wealthy widow, Johanne Stynton in 1636. The distilling of spirit from fermented fruit was considered to be one of the housewife's duties. The resulting liquor was known as aqua vita or hot water. These fruit spirits are still very popular on the Continent and are often produced by small family concerns. Glass was a luxury item and drinking glasses were only owned by the wealthy. George Wylde (1629) had three venice glasses, which were fine glasses from Murano, near Venice, in Italy and ten green glasses. Similarly glass bottles were expensive and not used much until the late 17th century. Aaron Westwood (1725) had 10 glass bottles, which may have held beer or cider, or even medicines.

In common with the rest of the country, ale, brewed from barley and without hops, was the drink of the people and many had brewing vessels, and furnaces or kilns. An essential ingredient of ale is malt, and there is evidence in many homes of malt, malt mills, and malt sieves. Malt was made from sprouting barley or dredge, a mixed grain, usually barley and oats. The sprouted grain was then roasted in a kiln on a haircloth or sieve. William Wylde of The Ford (1576) had a kiln chamber, and 2 weys and 20 quarters (645 gallons) of malt in his house. John Wheeler (1635) of Astwood had a beer cellar in which to store his brew, and, like William Wylde, he needed to provide beer or ale for his family and also for the men and women who worked for him. The first Dodderhill mention of hops, an essential in beer, was in 1663, when George Watkins had 20lb (9kg) of hops. William Jones, the vicar, was brewing in his brew house in 1669 where he had six brewing tubs and eight little beer vessels. Perhaps he was providing the beer for the parish meetings held in the church house (see Blewitt, this volume). John Attwood, a miller at Impney, had 15 brewing vessels and some mashing vessels along with two hogsheads of strong beer worth £2 (1677). The mashing vessels were where the malt and warm water were mixed to make wort, the first stage in the brewing process. The large number of brewing vessels seems to indicate brewing on a commercial scale. Clearly there was plenty of alcoholic drink about and, judging from the inventories, in Dodderhill it was mostly very locally produced at this period.

Tea and coffee were introduced into Dodderhill, as elsewhere, at some time during the 18th century, and were probably first sold locally by the grocers in Droitwich. By 1775 the ritual related to tea was well established when Phillip Pumphrey, a schoolmaster, died, and his tea-drinking paraphernalia were described in some detail. As tea was a pricey commodity he kept it in canisters in a tea chest, which could probably be locked. He also had a tea-kettle valued at 7s, and his china tea-pot was described as 'blue and white'. His red and white china also included six teacups, seven tea saucers and a painted earthenware sugar cup. He had a tea-pot stand, to protect his table, a silver tea tray valued at £1 10s and silver teaspoons. Mary Wilson of Obden (1797) had a pair of 'tea tongs' and by the 19th century John Amphlett, a wealthy man, owned a silver tea caddy, a silver tea-pot and a silver coffee-pot, and he also owned a Worcester china desert service. The use of porcelain, commonly called china, started in the 18th century with the setting up of factories in England, particularly in Worcester from about the middle of the century. Phillip Pumphrey was also the owner of delftware butter boats and lemon strainers, a type of ceramic unsuitable for tea wares and so, by the later 18th century, no longer much in demand.

Vernacular buildings (*by* Stephen Price)

Dodderhill parish contains a fascinating collection of vernacular buildings, ranging in date from the late medieval period to the 19th century. A few have long attracted the interest of artists, antiquaries and architectural historians, but there are many others which help to tell the story of traditional building and domestic planning over the centuries. Like historical documents the buildings can be read and interpreted to tell their stories.

Over the last decade the Dodderhill Parish Survey Project has commissioned appraisals of historic buildings in the parish, followed by more detailed examinations and dendrochronology of selected sites. This account attempts to set the results of this work in the wider context of other historic buildings in the parish and draw attention to some of the emerging themes, as well as some of the issues which need further research in the future.

Source material

A useful starting point for any study of Dodderhill's historic buildings is English Heritage's website where *Images of England* (http://www.imagesofengland.org.uk) has 28 entries and *Listed Buildings Online* (http://lbonline.english-heritage.org.uk) has 24 entries. But many other non-listed buildings, perhaps considerably altered or of only local importance, are still of interest. An extremely useful resource is the Worcestershire Photographic Survey of Dodderhill carried out on behalf of Worcestershire Record Office by members of the Birmingham Photographic Society in June 1985, when almost every building in the parish was recorded by black and white photography. The records of the former Hereford & Worcester Architecture Record Group (HWARG) are also a major source, and, thanks to the contributions made by Andrew and Richard Harris, provide detailed records of a number of local buildings in the 1970s prior to alteration.

In the 1980s the present writer, with Nicholas Molyneux, investigated the attic cheese room at Astwood Court Farm and in 1997 undertook a preliminary examination of Wychbold Court. In 2005 Derek Hurst and the late Paul Williams undertook rescue recording at Impney Farm in advance of redevelopment (Williams *et al* 2005). Further recording of individual buildings has been commissioned as part of the Dodderhill Parish Survey Project since 2005. These comprise

Mill Cottage (Robson-Glyde 2005), Ridgeway Court Farm (Robson-Glyde 2006a), Wychbold Court (Robson-Glyde 2006b; Price 2010a), The Old Cottage (Williams & Price 2008a), Redhouse Farm (Williams & Price 2008b), Crown Cottage (Williams & Price 2008c), Astwood Court Farm (Price 2010b), and Tudor Cottage (Price 2010c). Thus taken together a corpus of field records exists, varying from brief accounts of small changes to full surveys.

Documentary evidence can often throw light on a building's development and the social context of the people who lived and worked in the houses. From time to time documents point to rebuilding in describing a house as 'newly erected', while wills and probate inventories can greatly enhance our understanding of the interiors and how they were furnished. Documentary and physical evidence should be seen as complementary, but the first priority is to establish whether the house mentioned in the document is the one surviving today. Map evidence too can be used, with the usual *caveat* of caution about a mapmaker's reliability, where a block plan of a particular house is shown at one point in time. The work of the celebrated Dougharty family of mapmakers includes views of a number of Dodderhill buildings in the early 18th century.

Late medieval

The earliest of the houses so far identified is **Mill Cottage** – a T-plan timber-framed house. The stem of the T was built as a cruck hall and the bar, a storeyed crosswing of box-framed construction. The apex of the cruck blades in the former open hall is heavily smoke-blackened (Fig 62) and there are signs of a louvre or ventilator which allowed an escape route for smoke drifting upwards from the open fire. The house was built of elm and, therefore, cannot be dated by dendrochronology. However, analogy with similar cruck houses elsewhere in the West Midlands which have been firmly dated, indicates a date in the 15th century. Crucks are also to be found at **Fownes Cottage** in Colley Pits Lane but, most interestingly, were re-used as curved tiebeams in a 17th-century rebuilding. As such they may not necessarily have originated from that site and, perhaps, were brought in from elsewhere to serve their new function.

Figure 62 Mill Cottage: apex of cruck truss (photograph by N Molyneux)

Tudor and Stuart

The appropriately named **Tudor Cottage** (27 Bromsgrove Road, Hill End, Droitwich) is a remarkably complete timber-framed building of L-plan and is of considerable interest in the story of the development of domestic planning in the 16th–17th centuries (Fig 63). The main range started as a two-bay building comprising a single bay open hall with a brick fireplace, and a second bay to the south which may have had an upper floor from the outset. A date in the middle of the 16th century is proposed for this primary phase. A second phase, probably late

16th century, involved the insertion of a floor and staircase in the hall together with the cutting of a doorway through the central truss to give access between the first floor rooms. An extra bay was added to the north end of the original house, perhaps in the early 17th century, and this was followed by the addition of a two-storey wing to its west.

The house retains a fragment of a wall painting depicting King David (Fig 64), which may have been part of a larger scheme once showing all of the Nine Worthies. The surviving element depicts part of the crowned head of King David, one of the Nine Worthies. The Worthies were a popular subject and widely distributed as continental prints in the 16th and 17th centuries, and those produced by the Dutch designer and print maker, Philips Galle (1537–1612), were especially popular. His publications enjoyed wide currency, and were bought, as Galle intended, by patrons for their workmen, but they were also bought by the workmen themselves (Wells-Cole 1997, 119). In 1585 a Shrewsbury bookseller, Roger Ward, had no less than forty sets in his shop (Moran 2003, 347).

Figure 63 Tudor Cottage: view from the south-west showing the rear elevation of the main range (right) and the later wing at the far end (photograph by S Price)

Figure 64 Tudor Cottage: fragment of wall painting depicting King David with the king's crown to the lower right (photograph by P Walker)

No wonder the Worthies appeared as decorative schemes in various forms derived from these prints in contemporary English homes. Whether the painting at Tudor Cottage represents a primary decorative feature, or is part of a later redecoration scheme, is not known. At Great Binnall in Astley Abbots in Shropshire the Worthies were painted in decorative ovals on the late 15th-century coved dais canopy in the hall but appear to have been part of a redecoration scheme dating from 1611 (Newman & Pevsner 2006, 120). Another, rather cruder, set is to be seen in a 17th-century timber-framed house at Amersham (Bucks; Wells-Cole 1997, 119).

During the 16th–17th centuries the open hall went out of use; many former open halls had floors inserted to create an upper chamber and a chimney was inserted through the house (the so-called axial stack), or built against the back wall (the lateral stack). Alternatively, a new house was built from the outset with upper chambers. One stage of this process included the retention of a narrow smoke bay, which was, in effect, a very much compressed version of the open hall;

the fire was confined to a narrow space between two closely set trusses which acted as a flue for a fireplace at ground floor level. Some years ago Eric Mercer (then of the Royal Commission on Historical Monuments) showed how the emergence of the smoke bay was part of a long drawn-out process attempting 'to obtain more accommodation at the expense of the hall and to find an alternative to the open hearth and the resulting smoke-encrusted walls and roof' (Mercer 1975, 20). That process seems to have begun in the 15th century by flooring over one bay of an open hall-house and turning the second into a smoke bay. New houses might also be built with just one bay of the hall open to the roof. The next stage was the contraction of that bay to a narrow opening at one end of the hall and confining the open hearth to the ground floor of the smoke bay.

The first phase of **Wychbold Court** (Fig 65) is a good example of this last type. Originally comprising the long north-south range parallel to the main road, it has a heavily blackened smoke bay which is just 1.3m long, with evidence for a louvre. Either side of this the house was fully floored. Because so much of the Court is built of elm and re-used timber, it is not suitable for tree-ring dating. Sixteen houses across England and Wales containing a primary smoke bay have, however, been dated by dendrochronology in results reported annually in the journal *Vernacular Architecture*. The earliest two have been dated to the 1470s but the majority belong to the mid to late 16th century with a handful continuing into the 17th century, the last being dated 1641/2. We can begin, therefore, to close in on the dating of this first phase at Wychbold Court by the fact that the main range pre-dates the construction of the south wing. Both the main range and the wing exhibit a distinctive combination of close studding with a mid-rail to the ground floor with square panels above. This style of framing can be found across the county in the third quarter of the 16th century through to the 1630s and 1640s. This evidence suggests that the two elements – main range and south wing – are probably not far apart chronologically. The use of straight downward and upward braces seen in the main range would be unlikely earlier than the second half of the 16th century. Bringing this evidence together a late 16th century date is proposed for the main range followed in the early 17th century by the addition of the south wing (and this corresponded well with the date of archaeological finds in the immediate vicinity of the house; D Hurst, pers comm). The fact that the infill of the side wall frame of the main range was completed, and its external face is slightly weathered, suggests that there was a break in the building programme, rather than the wing following on immediately.

Figure 65 Wychbold Court (west elevation): the smoke bay lies within the space occupied by the later small chimney of the main range (photograph by S Price)

Only a handful of smoke bays have, so far, been identified in Worcestershire. This is partly because they are difficult to recognise without a thorough investigation of roof spaces. The examples found are divided into three main groups: first, is a so far single example at Ankerdine Farm, Knightwick, where a smoke bay was created within what had been an open hall (Mercer's type I); this space was later filled by a stone chimney. The second type is where the smoke bay is part of the primary build of a large two-storeyed house. Sugarbrook Manor at Stoke Prior was built like this and has a smoke bay in the stem or hall range of a T-plan house next to the junction with the wing; a brick stack was later built within the bay. Wychbold Court belongs to the second type and provides a good example of a long storeyed range in which a narrow smoke bay existed from the outset. The third type is found as the end bay of more modest 1½-storey cottages: Maypole Cottage at Wythall, and Orchard Croft, Callow End, are examples which retain evidence for the mantel beam of the fire opening; at Wythall there was a stair to one side of the hearth as part of the primary build.

The 16th century also saw the development of the brick and stone chimney, built either as part of newly floored former open halls, or in completely new buildings which were floored from the outset. The most spectacular of these new houses is **Astwood Court Farm**, which has been dated by dendrochronology to 1599. Astwood Court Farm represents an entirely new H-plan house, although the origins of the plan echo the tripartite division of medieval houses with a cross-passage and hall, a solar or parlour at the upper end, and service rooms beyond the screen at the lower end. The new house built at Astwood was, however, built from the outset with three storeys.

The framing at Astwood Court Farm is now best seen at the rear due to a re-fronting of the main elevation in the late 1840s (Fig 66). It is mostly close studded with a mid-rail to each storey and long downward braces. To demarcate the parlour wing more decorative framing (struts making herringbone patterns and cross-bracing) was used in the attic gable. Further decoration was applied externally below the jettied trusses of the wings, which have richly carved brackets carrying the overhang. While

Figure 66 Astwood Court Farm: rear (north) elevation (photograph by S Price)

the framing of the front has been either largely obscured by brick or removed altogether, there is evidence to suggest that originally there were probably multiple gables lighting the attic floor, and a storeyed porch in the angle between the kitchen or service wing, and the eastern end of the main range (the present entrance being formed at the west end when the brick was added and blocked the old entry). The porch once led into a cross passage which had a screen protecting the occupiers of the hall from draughts. Three stone chimneys with multiple star-shaped stacks were built against outside walls heating the hall, parlour, kitchen and upstairs rooms. Internally three of them retain impressive stone fireplaces which were once enhanced by richly carved wooden overmantels and surrounds (Fig 67), all of which were removed after the 1920 sale of the Corbett estate.

There are several parallels for the framing to be found in the immediate neighbourhood. The distinctive elements of close studding with a mid-rail and downward braces were used extensively on local farmhouses in the first half of the 17th century, and good examples are to be seen at Tanhouse Farm, Stoke Prior (1631), Foster's Green Farm, Bentley Pauncefoot, and The Old House in Alvechurch. These three houses have a jetty at first floor level, whereas the only evidence for a jetty at Astwood is at attic level. Even closer is Mere Hall at Hanbury (Fig 68), another H-plan house where, like Astwood, the jetty is confined to attic level. The similarities in the framing between Mere Hall and Astwood Court Farm are so close one must wonder whether both buildings are the work of the same carpenter.

Figure 67 Astwood Court Farm: panelled parlour with 17th century overmantel (from the auction sale particulars of the Corbett estate, 1920 – WRO BA 8851/24)

Mere Hall has been the subject of a detailed recent study by Meeson and Alcock (2005). It was built in 1611, and in its early form had two symmetrical wings with downward braces, close studding and mid-rails (one of the wings was later raised at the front). The overall frontage of Mere Hall is 22m, that of Astwood 17.8m and the length of wings at Mere is 16.5m, and 10.9m at Astwood. Astwood was in effect a smaller version of Mere Hall. Mere is grander, not only because it is larger with more rooms in the wings and a longer hall, but also because of its most distinctive feature – the row of five conjoined gables lighting the attic at the front. We have already noted that there is evidence for at least two attic gables along the middle of the front of Astwood. Whether they were multiple gables, as at Mere, we cannot be sure, but it seems highly likely. Gables in this position were clear architectural statements of social position, and are to be found in gentry houses in the locality in the early 17th century. Close to Astwood there are examples at The Moorlands, Hanbury (1615), and Middle Beanhall Farm, Feckenham (1635), where they were added to a pre-existing house.

Figure 68 Mere Hall, Hanbury (rear elevation): the painted brick gables between the two wings and the sloping extension against the right-hand wing are part of the 19th century alterations (B Meeson & N Alcock)

Most interestingly there were family ties between Mere Hall and Astwood Court Farm. John Wheeler of Astwood had married a sister of John Bearcroft, who owned and rebuilt Mere in 1611. When Wheeler died in 1635, one of the appraisers who compiled the inventory was his brother-in-law, Edmund Bearcroft, who would have known the house well. Both Astwood and Mere were built at the beginning of the 17th century as gentry houses. The sequence of building has recently been established at both houses through dendrochronology, and has shown that Astwood Court Farm pre-dates the present Mere Hall by a decade. The timbers for Astwood were felled in 1599, and building would have followed later that year, or immediately afterwards; tree-ring dating shows that Mere Hall was erected in 1611. Until the tree-ring date was secured for Astwood, it had been assumed that Mere Hall was 'the oldest of a number of highly distinctive multi-gabled gentry houses in the vicinity, with an H-plan, including a storeyed hall range and wings with jettied gables' (Meeson & Alcock 2005, 1). It now appears that Astwood is the oldest of the group, and, as such, therefore, has a special place in the history and development of the gentry house in late 16th–early 17th-century Worcestershire.

A house, which appears to follow a similar H-plan, is **Astwood Manor Farm** (Fig 52), but may be slightly later, perhaps early 17th century. One wing has been rebuilt in later brick, but the other wing exhibits square panels with downward braces and some decoration at the rear, while there is an impressive stone chimneystack against the wall of the middle range facing the farmyard. A house displaying more decorative framing, albeit just over the parish border (ie in Hanbury), is **Old Astwood Farm**. What was probably the parlour wing shows close-studding, quadrant and cross-bracing together with herringbone framing, and has been dated by dendrochronology to the date range 1572–87.

Another distinctive plan form of the post-medieval farmhouse was the lobby-entry type. Here the visitor entered a narrow space between the front door and the axial stack, thus having to turn either left or right into the main rooms. The equivalent space on the far side of the stack was often occupied by a staircase. In Dodderhill parish evidence has come to light for at least five examples. Tomlins, formerly Rectory Farm at Dodderhill common, is a timber-framed version, and has an L-plan comprising a main range and a cross-wing. Back-to-back fireplaces in the chimneystack heated rooms in the main range and the wing. The entrance door has long been blocked. Sometimes later brick walls conceal buildings of this type. The terrace of three cottages (**Christmas**, **Rosemary** and **Laburnum Cottages**) on the Worcester Road near to

Figure 69 Christmas, Rosemary, and Laburnum Cottages, Wychbold: the position of the porch and star-shaped stack suggests that a 17th century lobby-entry house is embedded within much later outer walls (photograph by S Price)

Figure 70 Redhouse Farm: originally a lobby-entry plan house with an axial stack (photograph by S Price)

Crown Lane clearly has a much older history than their current outward appearance of brick (Fig 69). An elaborate star-shaped stack rises through the centre point of the roof of Christmas Cottage and is in line with the storeyed entrance porch, hinting at the building's origins as a further example of the lobby-entry type. Another hidden example is at **Redhouse Farm** (Fig 70). Embedded within an early 18th-century exterior the large rectangular stack separates the front range into two rooms and provides a small lobby between the entrance door and the base of the stack. Because of so many alterations it is not possible to be sure whether Redhouse Farm was built as a relatively late example of this type, or whether it incorporates an earlier house. Other examples are the first phase of **Impney Farm** (demolished in 2005), and a secondary phase of **Tudor Cottage** when the northern bay was added to the earlier house, both probably dated to the early 17th century.

Constructional detail

The framed houses of Dodderhill provide much evidence for the process of construction. At **Wychbold Court** the roof timbers of the south wing retain red lines which were used by carpenters in the yard to mark out the timbers. Across the parish there are many excellent examples of scribed and chisel-cut carpenters' numbers denoting mortice and tenon joints. Those at **Astwood Court Farm** provide some of the clearest evidence for sequences of assembly. Not all pegholes seen in a frame are associated with mortice and tenon joints; some of the larger ones were used to hold shelf supports. At **Tudor Cottage**, as well as these larger holes, a few centimetres below are cut-off angled pegs which acted as props to the shelves above. Quite remarkable is the evidence for cheese racks at **Astwood Court Farm**. Several of the shelf supports survive in the vertical studs in one of the attics, the only missing feature being the shelves themselves, although their position can be deduced from the supports (Fig 49). Together, they are a physical reminder of the importance of the local cheese trade (see Townshend, this volume).

Local houses also prove that recycling of building materials was very well developed in the past. At **Wychbold Court** most of the roof trusses in the main range have been re-used from an earlier open hall house. The timbers are partly smoke-blackened and the mortices have been re-cut to suit their new role in the 16th-century house. Similarly at **The Old Cottage**, **Sharpway Gate** (Fig 71), the framing shows such extensive re-use that it suggests that the whole building may have been moved. Recycled timbers such as these have given rise to stories of ship's timbers, an apocryphal but persistent myth, which may be a misunderstanding of the authenticated reservation of naval timber growing in local woodlands.

Figure 71 The Old Cottage, Sharpway Gate (from the auction sale particulars of the Corbett estate, 1920 – WRO BA 8851/24)

There is a long tradition of using stone for building in Dodderhill, first as the plinths for timber-framed buildings, and, later, for chimney stacks. But it was also used more extensively, as in the earliest surviving phase of **Ridgeway Court Farm** where the cellar and ground floor are built in ashlar with two- and three-light mullion windows (Fig 72). A moulded stone stringcourse demarcates the level of the first floor above which there is timber-framing and later brick replacement or cladding. It has been suggested that the first floor framing is contemporary with the stonework and a late 16th-century date has been proposed. Yet the stonework is hard to date, and much of the timber used is of slight scantling with straight downward braces which suggests a relatively late date. Is it just possible that the combination of materials points to a late 17th-century date? Not far away there is a group of houses in the Bromsgrove area which can be dated to the 1670s and were using both stone and timber. At that time the cost of timber had risen steeply and alternatives, including such combinations of materials, were being sought.

Brick was used increasingly in the second half of the 17th century for whole buildings, but so far only **Crown Cottage**, with a re-set datestone of 1695, represents the new medium. Its most distinctive feature is the gabled end brick wall where the brickwork, albeit largely covered by render, is carried up as a parapet above the tiles, and is a reminder of what is to be seen elsewhere in the county at this date and into the early 18th century.

Figure 72 Ridgeway Court Farm (copyright of Worcestershire County Council)

Georgian

Timber-framing continued to be used until the early 19th century, but this later work is usually detectable by the slighter scantling of the timbers, and the fact that the panels were designed to be filled by brick nogging from the outset. A good example of this later framing is the stable from **Ridgeway Court Farm**, now re-erected at Avoncroft Museum of Buildings, and which dates from the second half of the 18th century.

During the 18th century brick became the dominant building material. Somewhat surprisingly, the study and dating of 18th and early 19th century vernacular brick houses in Worcestershire is not well advanced, partly because the houses themselves have received less attention than their earlier timber-framed counterparts, and bricks are still notoriously difficult to date. Pattern books demonstrated to owners and builders how classicism could be incorporated in new building. Most of these publications were concerned with grand or urban houses, model farms or estate cottages. It was not until the end of the 18th century that there were the first published designs for ordinary farmhouses in the West Midlands. In 1796 William Pitt of Wolverhampton published his *General View of the Agriculture of the County of Stafford*, and in 1813 produced the equivalent for Worcestershire. In his Staffordshire volume he published three designs for farmhouses (Fig 73), and recommended their adoption by proprietors, either for their own use

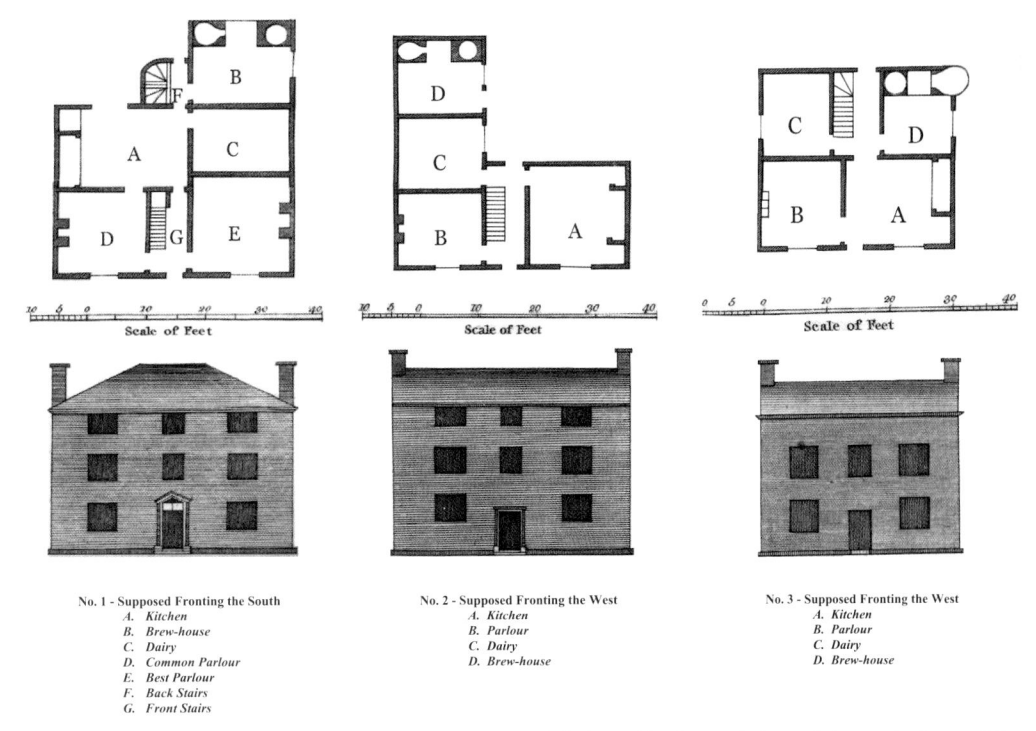

Figure 73 Designs for farmhouses by William Pitt (1796) from his General view of the agriculture of the County of Stafford *(photograph by P Walker)*

or that of 'a respectable tenant'. In his Worcestershire volume Pitt does not include designs for farmhouses, but he does acknowledge the need for improvement. He had found the majority of farmhouses 'of ancient construction, badly designed, and placed off the farm in villages, and often with walls of timber and mortar or plaster; when these shall be decayed, more attention will probably be paid to their future construction'.

In his advocacy of these designs Pitt explained that a farm's acreage determined the size and layout of the outbuildings, as well as the expenditure thought appropriate for the farmhouse itself. The designs show houses suitable for small farms between 50–100 acres, medium-sized at 100–200 acres and the largest between 200–500 acres. All his designs included a symmetrical façaded frontage with single or multiple wings behind. The variations were concerned with the height – the largest has three full storeys, a hipped roof to the front and end stacks. The middle-sized farmhouse, still had three storeys with a pitched roof and end stacks, while the smallest was of two storeys with an attic lit by windows in the gable ends.

Despite Pitt's claim that his designs were original, it is clear that farmhouses of very similar plan and appearance had been built in Worcestershire for some time before. The frontages of Worcestershire's Georgian farmhouses give the initial impression of pure symmetry but there are often subtle differences which reflect their internal functions. Where there are two end gable stacks, one is usually wider than the other, because at ground floor level it is part of a deep kitchen fireplace (internally the kitchen is identifiable by the wider fireplace opening with a large mantel beam). The kitchen, with a solid floor, is invariably wider than the other main room, the parlour, which has a boarded floor over a cellar. The centrally placed entrance between the two rooms usually led into a hall and stairway, but in some of the smaller houses it led directly into the larger room. A rear wing housed additional service rooms, such as a brewhouse, back kitchen, or dairy. In Dodderhill surviving wings are usually of one or two storeys; elsewhere single-storeyed examples have been found which were later raised.

Some of the earliest farmhouses have end gabled walls which extend above the roof line. **Hobden Hall** (Fig 74) is perhaps the best example. In 1737 it was described as a 'new erected tenement or messuage called Obden', and this date would be entirely consistent on stylistic grounds. At the rear the early 18th century brickwork sits on a contemporary stone base and forms a blind wall to the main range which is of single room depth. There are end stacks and a gabled parapet. Hobden was substantially changed in 1984 when one end bay was reduced to single storey height, thus giving an initial impression of a symmetrical house with a centrally placed porch.

Figure 74 Hobden Hall: the stone entrance elevation with its decorative and storeyed porch (from the auction sale particulars of the Corbett estate, 1920 – WRO BA 8851/24)

Also of the early 18th century is **Piper's Hill Farm** (Fig 75), perhaps the prettiest of Dodderhill's Georgian houses. Its main elevation is of three bays and 2½ storeys with dentilated brick eaves, and gabled dormers lighting the attic bedrooms. There are segmental arched sash windows to the ground and first floor, and a central entrance under an elegant shaped canopy, which extends over small fixed light casements set either side the front door. A particularly charming feature of Piper's Hill is the later forecourt with its Gothick iron railings. Closely related is **Yew Tree Farm** at Rashwood, which has gable end stacks, and displays many of the features seen at Piper's Hill. Here the catslide roof at the rear is an addition to the original build.

Figure 75 Piper's Hill Farm

Nearby, **Rashwood Farm** (Fig 76) probably dates to the late 18th century. It still has the single depth front range as seen at Hobden, this time with a hipped roof and is of three full storeys.

Much of the rear elevation is thus a blind wall and there are blind windows in the side elevation. At the rear is a two-storey wing. **Sharpway Gate Farm** probably dates to c 1840 (Fig 77), and, as such, is a late example of the Georgian farmhouses described above, with a three-storey symmetrical façade, gable end stack, and much lower rear wing. Its distinguishing feature is the use of heavy stone lintels to the windows, of a pattern found in suburban houses in Birmingham in the 1830s.

Consistent features of these Georgian brick farmhouses are dentilated eaves, and segmental brick heads above windows and doorways. Gradually elements of 'polite' architecture were introduced. These included multi-paned sash windows, in place of two- or three-light opening casements, and a classical doorcase in which the open pediment above a fanlight and six-panel wooden front door was widely adopted. Inside, the houses have elegant chimneypieces with cast-iron hobgrates, cornicing and staircases with moulded handrails and turned balusters;

Figure 76 Rashwood Farm: a symmetrical three-storeyed brick farmhouse of the 18th century (photograph by S Price)

Figure 77 Sharpway Gate Farm: early 19th century front elevation (photograph by S Price)

a style which lasted until the third quarter of the 18th century. Detailing at upper levels was less elaborate so here we find more modest fireplaces, and very often the stairs have splat or simple stick balusters.

From the pattern books and published design drawings it would be easy to assume that all Georgian farmhouses were entirely new buildings, where landlords followed the exhortations of writers to replace their unsuitable ancient buildings on cleared or new sites. The reality is somewhat different, and occasionally an earlier wing remains behind a classically inspired frontage. At **Impney Farm** detailed recording by Paul Williams prior to demolition revealed remains of an early 17th-century brick and timber house embedded within a major rebuild carried out in 1757. This latter date was declared in large numbers formed by blue/grey brick headers in an orange brick end gable wall which returned along the front and back elevations with the usual dentilated eaves giving no hint of the earlier building represented by the axial stack embedded in the rebuilt main range. The Georgian builders also kept the south wing of an earlier brick house. Similarly at **Ridgeway Court Farm** a large part of the earlier stone and timber farmhouse was incorporated within an early 19th-century re-fronting, which turned the orientation of the main elevation away from the farm-yard to a garden.

Even less well studied are cottages. Many buildings now known as cottages started as small farmhouses, but a number of timber-framed examples of genuinely humbler dwellings have been studied by Andrew and Richard Harris. Those around Dodderhill common may have started as encroachments on the waste. Photographs taken in 1985 of a timber-framed example, **Lumbarde Cottage**, show what was originally a modest 1½-storey dwelling, whose roof had been raised in the 19th century to provide more space upstairs. Nearby **Warren House** appears to have started as a 1½-storey brick cottage, but was extended at one end with an additional room on each floor.

In his book on Worcestershire agriculture William Pitt in 1813 deplored the general state of labourers' cottages in the county:

> ... the cottages ... are of different ages of construction, and ... have, in general nothing particular to recommend them; in the ancient villages and common field parishes, they often consist of timber and plaster walls covered with thatch, and are merely a shelter from the weather, without any particular attention having been paid to comfort and convenience; but with the addition of a garden for potatoes and other vegetables.

Pitt, however, provided a plan and elevation of a terrace of three brick cottages, which had been built recently at Lickey, and which he considered 'the most comfortable cottages I had an opportunity of observing in the county'. At ground floor level they contained a kitchen heated by an inglenook fireplace with a pantry beyond. At either end was a single storey room, one containing a brewhouse for washing and baking, and the other a workshop for a nailer. Many examples of these plain brick cottages with end stacks, dentilated eaves, and segmental headed ground floor windows were once to be seen across the county, but the late 20th-century desire for modernisation and extensions means that unrestored examples are becoming quite rare. Although having many modern changes to doors and windows, **Crutch Cottages** still show some of the characteristics noted by Pitt, while a two-cell detached brick cottage built c 1800 in Astwood Lane was recorded by Andrew Harris prior to change. It is against this background that the late Victorian improvements in local housing carried out in the 1870s by John Corbett should be seen, when he erected 'numerous comfortable dwellings for the workmen in his employ' (Littlebury 1879).

Conclusion

This overview of Dodderhill's traditional domestic buildings has attempted to define the main building types found in the parish from the late medieval period to the time of the tithe map of 1843. Critical to such a study is the ability to provide close dating of particular buildings. The Dodderhill Parish Survey Project has been able to advance our knowledge considerably in this respect for some of Dodderhill's timber-framed buildings by commissioning dendrochronology. However, since many local buildings were built of elm rather than oak this technique was not suitable for every building. Then reliance has to be placed on recognising similarities with buildings elsewhere which have been securely dated. The paucity of oak used in construction raises questions about the local management of timber resources and whether oak supplies were exhausted earlier here than in other parts of the county. Much woodland in the area must have been managed largely with a view to supplying firewood for salt making rather than timber for building; elms have been regarded as being companions to hedging (Edlin 1966, 209) and, therefore, the local prevalence of elm in buildings might be a good indicator of how early on field enclosure was well established in Dodderhill (D Hurst, pers comm).

Equally, the study of the dating and development of Georgian farmhouses is still in its infancy, but a number of elements can now be distinguished which link to plans of West Midland farmhouses published by the agricultural writer William Pitt at the end of the 18th century. Parallel studies of Worcestershire's post-medieval farmhouses are in place and are already bringing together data about securely dated examples which have the potential to help refine the chronology of their development.

This study has been primarily concerned with the physical evidence of the buildings themselves. Documentary research into the history of Astwood Court Farm has shown how the written record can remarkably supplement and enhance understanding of the structural evidence. In the case of this gentry house it has been possible to correlate the rooms listed in the 1635 inventory (WRO BA3585 1635/233) with those in the standing building (see also Stewart, this volume). There are close architectural similarities between the first phases of Astwood Court Farm and Mere Hall at nearby Hanbury. These can be explained more fully by knowing that their gentry owners, the Wheelers at Astwood and the Bearcrofts at Mere, were closely related. Dendrochronology has added immense precision to the sequence of building here – Astwood Court Farm in 1599 or very soon after, and Mere Hall in 1611. This raises questions about how their owners financed their building programmes, and hence what were the sources of their wealth.

As well as structural history, the study has demonstrated that evidence for fixtures and fittings can also enhance our understanding of interiors. At Tudor Cottage the hall had fitted shelving along one wall opposite the fireplace, and in the adjoining parlour the walls were covered by a decorative paint scheme which included images of the Nine Worthies. Photographic evidence reminds us what we have lost and the few images of the interior of Astwood Court Farm reveal the quality of the panelled parlour with its richly carved overmantel which was stripped out sometime after 1920 (WRO BA 8851).

Not every building mentioned in this chapter has been examined internally. Therefore it is likely that some of these preliminary findings will need to be revisited. Only by an examination of both the exterior and interior, including attics and cellars – areas which have usually seen least change – can a building be properly understood. It is hoped that this excursion into Dodderhill's vernacular architecture will stimulate more research on the lesser known and so far uninvestigated historic buildings of the parish, so that these too can contribute to the overall story of the local development of the house and home, and thereby provide an intimate back-drop to social history of the past inhabitants this parish.

Education (*by* Carolyn Morris)

From medieval times there was considerable provision for the education of clerks (or clerics) in reading, writing and Latin, with 300 to 400 grammar schools being scattered throughout England. These establishments were usually small, and in the medieval period had generally been under the control of monasteries, cathedrals, hospitals, guilds, or chantries, the appointed masters being secular clergy. Familiarity with Latin was essential to any professional career, and diplomats, lawyers, civil servants, physicians, merchants' accountants, and town clerks all required a knowledge of Latin for the many documents connected with their daily work.

The sons of the nobility and gentry were sometimes educated by being taught their letters by the local chaplain, but more usually they were sent away to be educated. Some went to the grammar schools, some to smaller private schools, and others boarded at the monasteries. Most ladies learned from their mothers to read, write, sew, and manage the household. In contrast, no attempt was made to teach the mass of the population to read or write, until in the 18th century this was brought about by the charity schools (see below). The historical evidence for even major schools at this period can be slim. In the Droitwich area the earliest mention of a school is in 14th century presentments (court rolls), where an accusation was made of carrying off doors and windows 'from the schools' (*VCH Worcestershire* III, 76). Further evidence is that an Evesham Abbey monk wrote a letter seeking advice on Latin prose style from a schoolmaster in Droitwich named 'Sir John', his title indicating that he was a secular priest (Orme 1978, 46), as typically the case with schoolmasters of the time.

Clever boys from humble origins had the opportunity through the grammar schools to rise to be clerks or priests, for the church was the career of ambition most easily open to the lower classes. Here in the Elizabethan grammar school the most able pupils from all social strata were brought together 'sharing benches and floggings' (Trevelyan 1944, 181), which was in complete contrast to the schools of the 18th and 19th centuries, when the charity schools, village schools, and great public schools operated a system of rigorous social segregation.

A 'Fre Scole' at Droitwich was the first recorded school to generally offer children in Dodderhill parish an education. In 1555 William Dawkes, the son-in-law of a London mercer (John Rayse), left £40 in his will to build a free school at Droitwich, with an additional £10 per annum presumably to pay the master (NA PROB 11/37; as cited by Sutton 2005, 366); though its income was often deficient, even when supplemented by a charitable legacy (worth £7 per annum) from a Feckenham yeoman (*VCH Worcestershire* IV, 529). Later the Droitwich Free School was endowed by the Right Honourable Henry Coventry in his will dated 1686, and existed as part of the Coventry Hospital workhouse (now the Coventry Almshouses in The Holloway). This provided for the education of children from the age of 8 to 14.

Eventually the charity school movement introduced the principle of community co-operation into the field of educational endowment, and this policy was to excite the local interest of a parish in setting up its own school, citizens being encouraged to make and collect subscriptions. By the end of Queen Anne's reign in 1714 there were said to be some 5000 boys and girls in charity schools in London and 20,000 nationwide. This was an age of great philanthropy, and an essential part of the plan was to clothe the children decently while at school, and to apprentice them to good trades afterwards.

The charity schools (sometimes called 'ragged schools') and the Sunday school movement, which took on such large proportions after 1780 (these were an alternative to full-time education for children who were already part of the workforce, were organised and run by the local clergy, and concentrated solely on reading and reciting the Bible), were the first systematic attempts to provide an education for the working people. However, in the 18th and 19th centuries it was expected that workmen and labourers would remain in the social class into which they had been born, and that youngsters would keep to their appointed position in society. The higher echelons had no interest in advocating the cultural development of the working classes. On the contrary, the effects of the revolutionary spirit in Europe had reinforced the prevailing conservative attitudes. The aim was largely, therefore, to train up a submissive generation, and, accordingly, members of parliament were generally against any proposals for the state to finance education for the poor, and so, for example, Davies Giddy, Tory MP for Helston in Cornwall, is quoted in Hansard as saying in 1807: 'Giving education to the labouring classes of the poor … could teach them to despise their lot in life, instead of making them good servants in agriculture and other laborious employments to which their rank in society has destined them' (Byard-Jones 2007, 37).

19th century

Only in 1801 do we finally have an official count of the population of Dodderhill, and this totalled 472 living within the borough and 677 in the rural part of the parish, a total of 1149. Based on parish registers, earlier population levels have also been estimated in Dodderhill parish as follows: 324 in 1620–30, 465 in 1666–75, and 837 in 1750–9; and so it seems that since the 17th century the local population had been increasing, with perhaps the greatest rate of increase being into the 18th century. This may have coincided with a period when farmers were building cottages for renting to labourers, and there were attempts to throw up cottages by encroaching on waste and verges, signifying a shortage of homes. The latter was most evident along the main road where encroachments were noted in the early 19th century on the waste land beside the Droitwich to Bromsgrove turnpike road, in effect a linear common where sand and gravel could also be dug, and other parts used for dung or wood storage (Hampton Pap 443). Occasionally this type of gravel pit was recorded on the 1843 tithe map (eg Hemming's Pit; WSM 6604). It was only the centre of the road which was being kept in repair by the turnpike trust as the summer road. One of these encroachments became a public house at Rashwood called the Robin Hood which had been built on the waste c 1770, and still admirably serves the same purpose under the same name today.

The 19th century saw the end of the long established tradition of giving one-tenth of produce to the local church, and, instead, all dues were converted to money payments. The resulting tithe map remains an important source of information about the earlier landscape. The State now had the means to produce detailed modern maps of great accuracy and embarked on a programme of national mapping. As a result, in the early 1880s, a solitary military man (E G Oldham, sapper, Royal Engineers) arrived in the parish to draw up the first large-scale map of the area for the Ordnance Survey. His note-books still survive, including much crossing out suggesting how confusing he found the overlapping parish and borough boundaries of Dodderhill and Droitwich (NA OS 26/11398; eg Fig 78). He had some local assistance, as he could call on the local 'meresman' (literally the keeper of boundaries), and in the case of Dodderhill this was John Wall, who carefully advised that in Dodderhill parish the owners of hedges and banks generally claimed 4 feet into adjoining land for a ditch, but that walls were built to the edge of the property.

The religious landscape was also changing. In 1836 a congregational chapel was established at Wychbold (*VCH Worcestershire* III, 68), and finally, in 1877, Elmbridge formally became a parish in its own right. Then in 1888 a new ecclesiastical parish of Wychbold was formed from Dodderhill (*ibid*).

Meanwhile the scattered character of settlement in Dodderhill, despite the increasing gravitation of new settlement towards the main road (now A38) at Wychbold village, presumably meant that it was never thought to merit its own railway station and, instead, it shared one with Stoke Prior after the construction of a link line in 1847; the same link incidentally leading to the discovery of the Bays Meadow Roman villa. About the same time the Droitwich Junction Canal was built to link the Droitwich canal to the Worcester & Birmingham Canal which had been

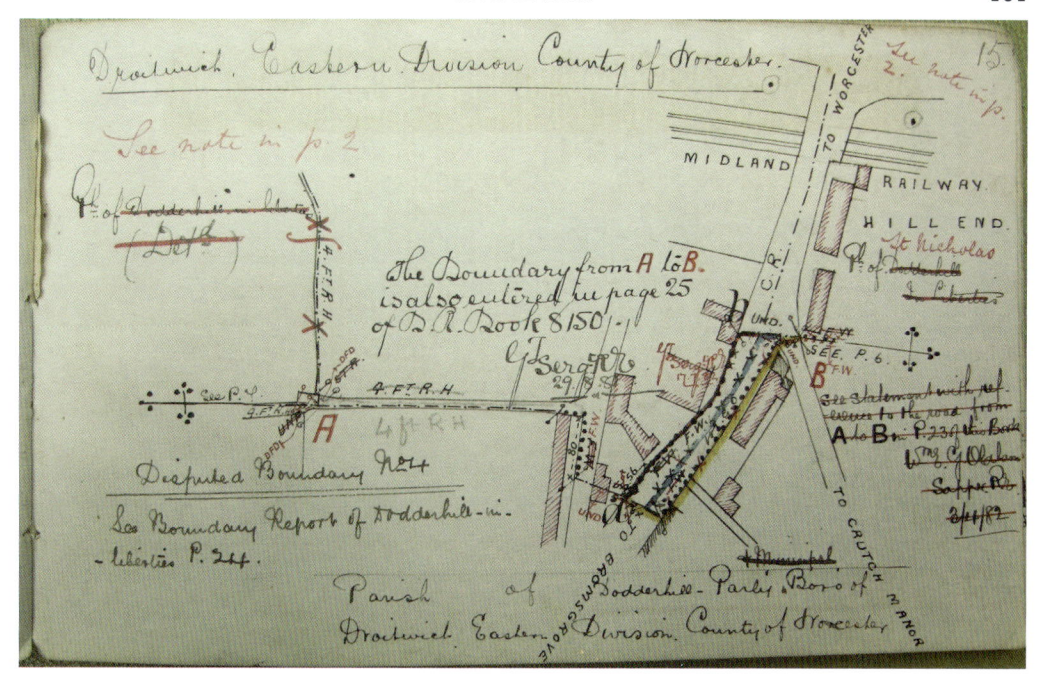

Figure 78 Sapper Oldham of the Ordnance Survey trying to make sense of the overlapping boundaries of borough and parish in 1881 (NA OS 26/11398) (photograph by D Hurst)

finished in 1815, but had by-passed the town. Such developments in transport will have significantly boosted the local salt industry, and hence the local economy.

This was also the great age of industry when England was the workshop of the world, and the local example to Dodderhill was John Corbett who came to build the incongruous but magnificent house at Chateau Impney (see Blewitt, this volume). Corbett showed remarkable vision, as he oversaw the transformation of Droitwich from being largely a scene of industrial grime and toil, where many small companies now competed for small profits (thereby keeping prices low), to a fashionable spa town with a new future based on the health-giving properties of the brine. In the course of this he set up his salt production facility at Stoke Prior, just north-east of Wychbold, where modern production methods were used, combined with improved transport links on the canal and railway, to create a modern efficient factory.

Though the later 19th century saw the character of Droitwich being drastically changed through the efforts of John Corbett, this probably had little effect on the rural population of Dodderhill, as the town presumably still remained a useful market centre, where local products were made available to those attracted to the new brine baths and entertainment facilities. Salt brought Corbett immense wealth which he wisely invested in property and land, as the banks of the period, as it turned out (and as in later times), were not to be trusted with other people's money.

Parish and church (*by* Helen Peberdy)

Around 1836 an Act of Parliament had been passed altering the way in which the clergy were paid, and reforming the ancient system of tithes where one-tenth of income from produce of the land, stock or labour went to support the incumbent, and was paid to the rector who might then pay a stipend to a vicar or curate to work in the parish. After the Dissolution, the tithes which the rectors had received had fallen into lay hands; hence the value in being patron, holding the advowson to a living, and being able to claim the tithes. The Act of 1836 was intended to commute tithes to a rent charge which was fair to the landholders. The most valuable result of this for future historians was that large-scale maps were produced with detailed schedules of who owned which land, and who occupied it as tenant at this time.

One of the most momentous events of the time was the arrival of the railway, and in Droitwich this impacted severely on the foot of the hill just beneath Dodderhill church. A large retaining wall had to be built along the south side of the churchyard in 1852, and this slightly altered the route of the old 'Burial Lane', which led up to the churchyard from the Vines at Chapel Bridge.

In the 19th century the 'restoration' of medieval churches was all the rage, and at St Augustine's, Dodderhill, this was begun by the Revd John Jackson (vicar 1843–54), and only finally completed in 1890 under the patronage of John Corbett. It saw the plaster being removed from the interior of the church, together with the box pews and galleries, but fortunately it stopped there, leaving the original stonework undamaged, so that today we can still admire the massive Norman pillars of the central crossing, and the Early English arches and window tracery of the east end. By the end of the 19th century much of the restoration work, notably the stained glass in the windows, was due to the generosity of John Corbett, the 'Salt King', who was then the patron of the living.

Meanwhile Elmbridge, which as part of Dodderhill, had had a chapel of its own since 1274, was finally made a separate parish in 1877, and, to the north, a new church (dedicated to St Mary de Wyche) was built to serve the new parish of Wychbold, which was created in 1888 and included much of the rural area formerly in Dodderhill parish. At that time Dodderhill had a large population in the south, around the Vines and Hill End (on the north side of Droitwich town), mostly composed of salt workers, so had quite sufficient congregation to justify maintaining the old church of St Augustine.

At the beginning of the 20th century a new parsonage was built further up Crutch Lane, the gift of Dr Thomas Corbett, brother of John; this was later converted to a nursing home, and at present it is called, rather confusingly, The Priory. Dodderhill remained as a separate parish until 1987 when it was subsumed into Droitwich, and a new parish of Droitwich Spa formed to include it together with the parishes of St Andrew, St Nicholas and St Peter de Witton. Since then changes to the interior of the church have been made, the altar moved to the west wall, where the demolished nave would have been, and a new meeting room built above a kitchen in the north-east corner. When this was done, earlier foundations were exposed, showing possibly Saxon masonry. There have been suggestions that Dodderhill's early foundation was as a minster church, like Kidderminster and Hanbury nearby, sending priests out to surrounding areas (see Blewitt, this volume). Maybe with the shortage of priests nowadays, this function is being reborn, though Dodderhill has lost much of its important individual status in the current parish organisation.

Whatever its future as a place of worship, Dodderhill church remains a landmark, and a witness to the faith which built it, throughout its long, and sometimes, turbulent history.

From manor to mansion: the ownership of Impney (*by* Lyn Blewitt)

By 1875 the manor at Impney, for much of its existence an agricultural estate with its main components being a manor house, cottages, and a varying number of mills, had been transformed into a showpiece stately home complete with deer park, landscaped gardens, and ornamental watercourses. But how was the land assembled for this transformation?

Two different accounts have been published of who owned the land at Impney before John Corbett and of how he acquired it, *viz*:

   a) the *Victoria County History* stating that John Corbett purchased all the land from Edward Charles Somers, son of Lord Somers, whose ancestors had acquired Impney manor through the marriage of Margaret Nash to John, Lord Somers, in 1785, and;
   b) Holyoake (1977, 17) stating that his great-grandfather sold the land 'with its plain square white house' to John Corbett, though possibly only as the selling agent (Middlemass & Hunt 1985, 46).

The following is a fresh attempt to throw light on this apparent confusion over the ownership of Impney before its acquisition by John Corbett, and it is based on having had access to new documentary evidence in the form of two privately owned original conveyances, as well as on a fresh appraisal of documents available in the local record office (WRO).

Late 18th century–1869

Land tax returns recorded Thomas Holbeche at Impney Mill (Fig 79) in 1793 as its owner and occupier, and 'buildings, land and Impney Mill owned by John Wood, occupied by Thomas Thould' in 1799. The Impney land that John Corbett purchased in 1869 (see below) was almost identical to land owned and occupied in 1843 by Thomas Thould on comparison with the Dodderhill tithe map and schedule, apart from one field ('Edward's Leasow'; parcel 462 on the tithe map) then owned by Earl Somers. The national censuses for 1841, 1851, and 1861 record that Thomas Thould, born at Severn Stoke or Kempsey, lived at Impney Lodge, and was a miller. This house must have been the 'plain square white house' alluded to by Holyoake (1977; see below). This land was sold on the death of Thomas Thould in 1868, and in his will (WRO BA 3689/5) he had included 'John Holyoake of Droitwich, Solicitor' as a beneficiary, but also as one of his executors. John Corbett's property register shows his purchase on 15 January 1869 from 'Thos Thould's Executors' of 'Impney Lodge estate: freehold land, Lodge and mill', in area 63 acres and 14 perches, for £10,513, with repairs and expenses of £299 15s 2d making the total cost £10,812 15s 2d.

Figure 79 Impney Mill as copied in pencil in 1825 from an original sketch by Miss P Amphlett (Prattinton Collection; copyright of The Society of Antiquaries)

An interesting detail of this sale was that there was an 'impropriate yearly tithe rent charge of £1 12s 8d issuing out of part of the premises known as Edwards or Haford's Leasow ... subject nevertheless to the payment of an annual Crown rent of £2 3s 2d'. This was in contrast to the rest of the Thould property which had been tithe-free, incidentally an indication of its special status in the more distant past.

If there was any doubt about the location of this land this is finally removed by a reference in the 1872 conveyance (see below) to the land then being described as 'lying to the North and South of the land conveyed by the hereinbefore recited [*viz* 1869] Indenture'.

Conveyance by the Somers family to John Corbett (April 1872)

John Corbett purchased more land at Impney from two trustees of Charles, Earl Somers, by direction of Earl Somers who also signed the document (WRO BA 10398/977), in a conveyance dated 25 April 1872. These lands were among those settled by Earl Somers on his wife Virginia, Countess Somers, by an earlier indenture dated 26 March 1862; the trustees, Thomas Somers Cocks and Reginald Thistlethwayte Cocks, both of Charing Cross in Middlesex, had the duty to ensure that Countess Somers would receive £1200 yearly if she survived her husband, as her jointure and in lieu of dower (ie to stop her having any further claim on her husband's estate). These trustees had power, with Earl Somers' consent during his life, to sell any part of the lands designated to provide the jointure (except Eastnor Castle and its lands – the main seat of the family), and they were exercising this power by selling the Impney land to John Corbett.

The special value of the 1872 conveyance, for the purpose of clarifying which lands were sold by Earl Somers and his trustees to John Corbett, is that it includes a map of the lands sold, together with a detailed list of the fields which were numbered in accordance with the 1843 tithe map and schedule. The map shows clearly that the Impney lands being conveyed were located to the north and the south of the 'central' area of the later Corbett Impney estate, and in the middle is an area shown as belonging to 'John Corbett Esq' – so by the time this conveyance was made in 1872, Corbett had already acquired about one-third of the land, and specifically the site of his new house, or rather 'mansion' as it was described by the late 19th century census. The map of what was conveyed in 1872, and which later became Corbett's Impney estate, shows fields and Impney Farm, but no other buildings. It is clear the Somers property did not include any 'plain square white house' (see above).

The conveyance listed the following (summarised here):

> Firstly, all that Manor or Lordship or reputed Manor or Lordship of Impney, otherwise Impney Court;
> Secondly, an annual payment of £2 2s payable in half-yearly instalments on 2 February and 1 August each year by the Rt Hon Sir John Somerset Pakington 'to the Lord of the Manor of Impney otherwise Imney' [an interesting mention of a much earlier spelling of the name] which arose out of ownership of Boycott Farm (described in a marginal note as extending into the parishes of Salwarpe, Hampton Lovett, St Andrews and St Nicholas);
> Thirdly, Impney Farm in the parishes of Dodderhill and St Peter's Droitwich, with lands specified in the schedule to the conveyance (these are the majority of the fields conveyed);
> Fourthly, a piece of land in Dodderhill parish with 15 cottages on it, leased in 1859 for 99 years to William Causier, Coal Merchant (this land and its cottages lie in Hill End in Dodderhill parish);

Fifthly, two pieces of land in Dodderhill, St Peter's, and the In Liberties area of Droitwich 'or some or one of them' [ie, the writer of the conveyance was not sure which parish(es) the land lay in] with saltworks and other buildings, leased in 1864 for 21 years to a group of individuals presumed to be members of the Droitwich Salt Company (they are listed and include Sir Charles Hastings of Worcester, founder of the British Medical Association, and John Wheilly (*sic*) Lea of Worcester who was the 'Lea' in Lea & Perrins);

Sixthly, 5 cottages and gardens next to the above land and in the same parishes 'or some or one of them' (*sic*), and;

Seventhly, a meadow now divided by the railway and again described as in Dodderhill and St Peter's parishes 'or one of them' (for a detailed list, including the tenants in 1872 with cross-referencing to the Dodderhill tithe map and schedule, see Blewitt 2006)

John Corbett's character and motivation in building at Impney could have made the first and second items purchased (ie the lordship of the manor of Impney, and the annual payment by the Pakington family to whoever held that lordship) almost as important as the land itself (Middlemass & Hunt 1985). John Corbett turned most of his new land into the park of his new stately home, and the land left available to Impney Farm was much reduced.

John Corbett ensured a full register of his properties was kept (WRO BA 8851/41), and for 25 April 1872 he recorded the purchase from 'Lord Somers' Trustees' of Impney Estate (304 acres, 17 perches); cottages (32 perches); meadow (5 acres, 3 roods, 31 perches); 'Woodfield Terrace' with 15 cottages [in Hill End] (1 acre and 19 perches); and a 'Salt Works, Droitwich' (2 roods, 21 perches). Only the land is listed, not the other items. Tenants were recorded: John Wilson Snr paying £410 half-yearly for Impney Farm, Wm Horton paying £25 half-yearly for the meadow, and the Droitwich Salt Co paying £100 half-yearly for the salt-works, the lease to the latter ending on 25 March 1885. The purchase price was £27,200. To summarise, the 1872 conveyance shows John Corbett purchasing the lordship of the manor of Impney, Impney Farm which included some of the land he used for his Impney estate, and some other pieces of land in Hill End and elsewhere; but the central part of the later Impney estate already belonged to him.

Sale of land by John Corbett to Harry Foley Vernon (April 1872)

Two days before John Corbett signed the indenture by which the Somers land transferred to his ownership, he had formally agreed to sell on part of the land of Impney Farm which he was about to acquire, to Harry Foley Vernon of Hanbury, the owner of neighbouring land. The plan attached to the list of parcels of land concerned shows that they were around the south-east and south of the later Impney Park, and included both whole fields and parts of fields. The net effect was to tidy up the edge of the future Impney Park, giving straighter lines for its borders, and change field boundaries which may have been of some antiquity.

This 'Particulars of a Portion of the Impney Estate situate in the parishes of Dodderhill and Saint Peter', dated 23 April 1872, also included a valuation of the land at £5813 (for a total of just over 85 acres, including timber; WRO BA 5589/53). This included parts in St Peter's parish valued at £1010. Vernon was to be responsible for making and maintaining the fences; but the fee farm rent of £4 19s 4d chargeable on the whole Impney estate was to remain Corbett's responsibility. In order to make the purchase, Vernon took a mortgage for £3000 from William Hunt of Aire House, Castleford, near Normanton (Yorks) at 4% per annum interest, and this commitment was recorded over his signature on the document.

Although the document conveying this land to Harry Foley Vernon has not yet been located, the transaction is recorded in the property register of John Corbett, under the purchase by Corbett of the Somers lands two days later. The two transactions were obviously linked – the £27,200 paid by Corbett for the land obtained from 'Lord Somers' Trustees', plus expenses of £460 3s 1d, is shown with the £5813 paid by Harry Foley Vernon deducted to give a net cost of £21,847 3s 1d. Similarly, the area of the land purchased from Earl Somers is also reduced by that of the land sold to Vernon, giving a net area of 226 acres, 3 roods and 25 perches. As an aside, the property register also shows that in July 1886 Corbett purchased from 'Sir H F Vernon Bart' land described as 'part of Impney estate' for £2500; however no area or location was given, so it is not possible from this record alone to tell whether this represents the re-acquisition of any of the Somers land previously sold on to Vernon in 1872.

Conveyance of land from Harry Foley Vernon to John Corbett (July 1872)

Two further pieces of land 'being the northern part of the land' (as sold in the 1925 sale of the Impney estate), originally purchased in July 1872 were described in Corbett's property register as 'Rough Bank and part of Hawthorn Hill at Rashwood' (parcel 497 on the 1843 tithe map and schedule where named 'The Eight Acres'). These were purchased for £589 14s and added to Impney Park, the tenant, G Baylis, paying £12 12s each half-year.

Further purchases in 1892

The Corbett property register also recorded in October 1892 the purchases from 'Samuel Smith and Chas John Rowley' of the fee farm rents of Impney Manor for a total of £250. These rents, apportioned, represent the annual rentals for 'part of Impney Manor Estate' (£5 5s 5d), Impney Lodge (£1 15s 6d) and Ford Farm (12s 8d), a total of £7 13s 7d. The register says 'This extinguishes annual payments by Mr Corbett of the amounts set forth', so John Corbett bought out the entitlements of these two persons to annual payments of a relatively small fee farm rent. Impney manor and estate were now free of any encumbrances, even those of a minor nature.

Conveyance of Impney Mansion and Park from Corbett estate to James Ward (1925)

Following the deaths of John Corbett in 1901, and of his brother, Dr Thomas Corbett, in 1906, the Impney estate was leased to various individuals, mortgaged with permission from the courts, and eventually sold by the Corbett trustees in December 1925 to James Ward JP of Barbourne Terrace, Worcester, for the incredibly low sum of £15,000.

This review of the evidence, therefore, points to both the earlier accounts of how John Corbett acquired his Impney estate as being partially correct.

Education (*by* Carolyn Morris)

Droitwich Free School

The Droitwich Free School, first founded in the 16th century, continued into the 19th century (Fig 80), and in 1852 it was described as follows:

There are two schools, in one of which forty girls, and in the other forty boys, receive an excellent education. The school rooms are spacious and well ventilated, and the master and mistress appear to pay great attention to their duties. A master tailor and a master shoemaker attend to give instructions, in their respective trades, to a certain number of the boys; and, by the adoption of this plan, together with the employment of the girls in sewing, the trustees have been able to save a considerable expense in the supply of clothing.

And the salaries of the different persons connected with the institution were as follows (Griffith 1852, 128):

	£	s	d
The governor, who is also schoolmaster, in addition to house, coals and candles	70	0	0
The schoolmistress, with house, coals and candles, and £5 for reading to the poor people in the hospital	40	0	0
The surgeon, for medicine as well as attendance	10	0	0
The nurse, 7s. per week	18	4	0
The master tailor	12	18	6
The master shoemaker	12	18	6
	164	1	6

The Coventry Hospital was admitting children from all the parishes in Droitwich, including 8 boys and 8 girls from the In Liberties (that part of Dodderhill within the borough). The aim of the charity was to teach 'reading, writing, and the common rules of arithmetic, and such works of industry as may be deemed proper', and in the report on the Free Schools of Worcestershire dated 1852 there were said to be 50 boys and 48 girls enjoying 'a plain and useful education' and receiving a 'system of apprenticeship [which] is a valuable addition to their advantages' (*ibid*, 131).

Figure 80 Engraving of the Coventry Hospital in 1833. Copyright and reproduced by permission from Blewitt & Field (1994)

National and British Schools

Education in the 18th century had been at the centre of religious squabbling between the established Church of England and the dissenters (non-conformists who rejected the accepted religious doctrines of the day). In Queen Anne's reign the dissenters were excluded by law from the universities of Oxford and Cambridge, and, by law and custom, from many schools, so they set about establishing their own system of education. From 1808 onwards they began to set up British Schools, where scripture and general Christian principles were taught in a non-conformist manner. In 1827 they founded the new University of London to specialise in the teaching of science and modern studies rather than the Classics.

In 1811 the Church of England took up the challenge and set up the National Society for Promoting the Education of the Poor in the Principles of the Established Church. Their main interest in the provision of literacy was to ensure that the Bible and hymns could be read by the masses, and their stated aim was 'that the national religion should be made the foundation of national education, and should be the first and chief thing taught the poor, according to the excellent liturgy and catechism of our church'. The National Society became active in many areas of education, publishing books, providing equipment, and training teachers, and they built many schools, mainly in rural areas.

Both British and National Schools raised their own funds in order to begin educating the poor, since at this stage there was no state provision. It was thought that, as the voluntary school system was being quite successful, it was better not to encourage government intervention. The dominant laissez-faire philosophy of the day meant that any direct intervention by the state in the field of education was to be discouraged. But eventually money was made available by the government, and in 1837 £20,000 was given to the two societies if they would raise an equivalent amount. This grant was increased in 1839 to £30,000, and in 1857 to £540,000. British Schools were more prevalent in the increasingly industrialised towns, while National Schools became the most usual vehicle of popular education in the English village. In some areas they existed side by side. The first purpose-built school located in Dodderhill was a National School (see below).

Eventually the 1870 Education Act set up a Board of Education, and local areas were allowed to build Board Schools (see below) which were paid for out of the local rates, although initially these were only to be built where a National or British School did not already serve the area.

National School in Dodderhill

Plans for the National School survive (WRO BA 4173/2) which are entitled 'Building School House and Master's Dwelling in the Parish of Dodderhill', with the date 1846 shown in the roundel above the door (Fig 81). This building is described variously as Upper Street School (1881 census), Wychbold School (school log 1885) and Overstreet School (1891 census), and it was sited at what is now the corner of Astwood Lane and Stoke Road. The field-name of the site on the 1843 tithe map is given as Upper Coal Hill, and the land belonged to the Woodhouse family at Astwood Manor Farm. Two local residents (Audrey Hackett, née Sutton, and Joan Moore, née Serrell; Fig 82) have confirmed that the plans relate to the buildings in which they spent part of their childhood in the 1940s and 1950s, which were then known as Overstreet Cottages, having been converted for residential use when the school closed (see below). The school building was to be 60ft 4in (18.4m) long and 20ft (6.1m) wide with a classroom measuring 20ft by 19ft and 11ft 6in high.

At this time there were already two schools within the boundaries of Dodderhill parish. The first of these was at Stoke Works, and this had begun life as a Wesleyan chapel. It was situated on the works site next to British Row and near the Shaw Lane canal bridge, just beyond the chemical works with its tall chimney. In the 1851 census there were two schoolteachers living at the Chapel House: John Wood, schoolmaster, and Jane Wood, schoolmistress. The second establishment was a ladies' boarding school at West Ford House in Ford Lane (now the clubhouse of Droitwich Golf Club). This is first mentioned in the 1861 census, and in 1881 had fourteen pupils aged from 11 to 17 years, though all were from outside the parish, with two lady principals and two language teachers.

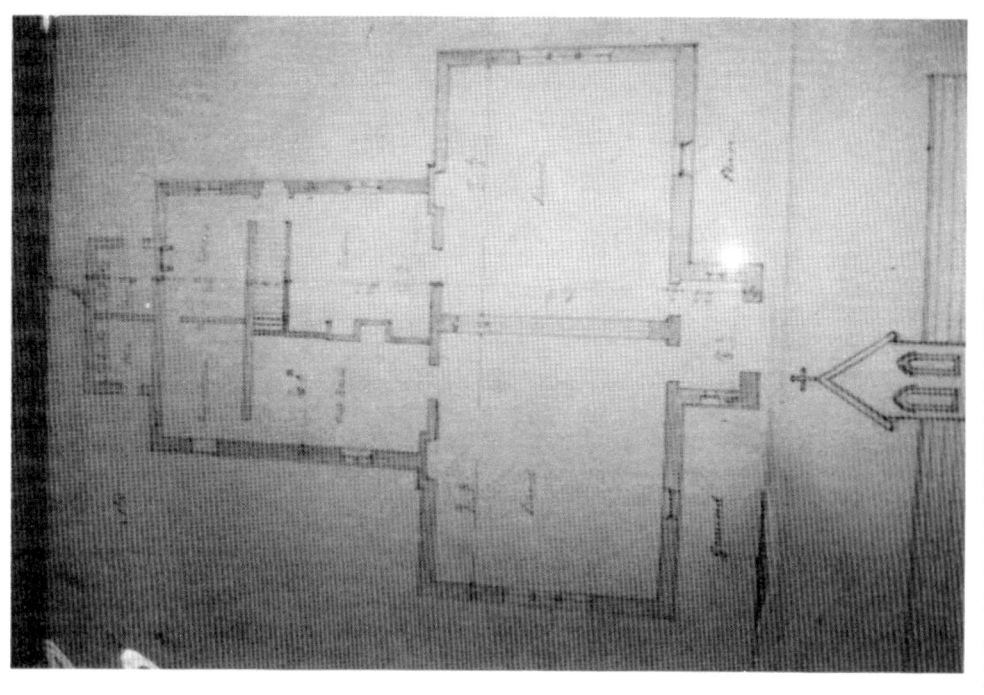

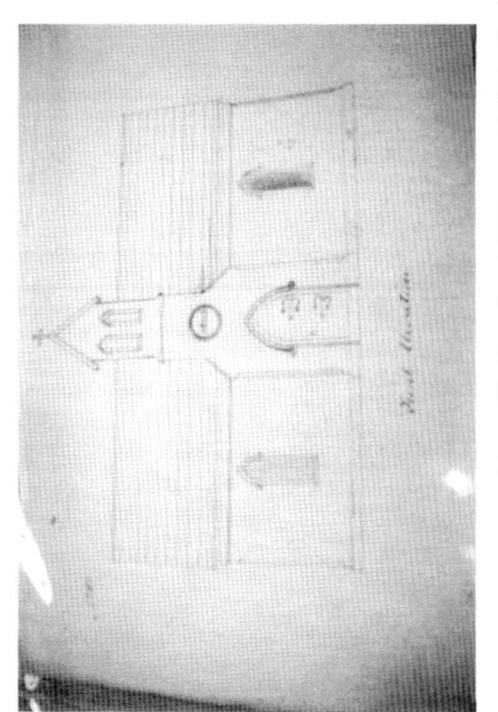

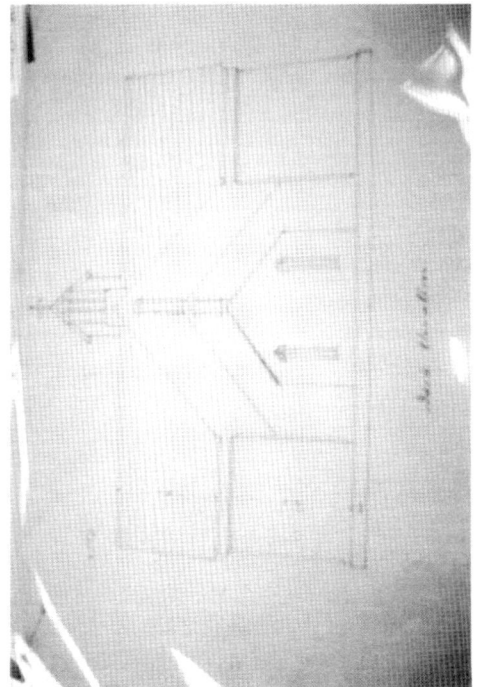

Figure 81 Plan dated 23 August 1845 for National School in Dodderhill (WRO BA 4473/2)

Figure 82 Mrs Sutton in 1930s (left) and Joan Serrell in 1950s (right) outside Overstreet Cottages

The first entry in a log book of the National School at Overstreet is dated 5 April 1869 and states that 'School re-opens after 3 month's closure. 26 children. Prior to this it has not been customary to keep a log book'. Even after this date the entries are spasmodic, unlike those of the later school where entries record absolutely the minutiae of school life. It appears from the log that staffing was an ongoing problem since the school closed again in June 1871 because 'The Committee have not advertised for a master', only reopening in January 1872 with Henry Jolliffe (a 'Certified Master') and 53 scholars. However, he did not stay for long, stating in September of the same year that he 'Resigned charge of school, my engagement as to transfer to Stoke new school having fallen through and numbers here being but small'. The school remained closed this time until 10 March 1873, when a Mrs Hyatt was appointed 'Mistress of this school', with 19 children attending in the morning and 18 in the afternoon. She was still there at the school-house at the time of the census in 1881.

Records in the form of log books, registers and punishment records allow an insight into school and village life, and show that the early school could be a pretty grim place with its persistent truancy, bad behaviour, and severe corporal punishment. The log book for 24 May 1869 states that 'school was very noisy in the morning – many of the new scholars have been taught by a woman whom I should judge they easily mastered'. Prior to the opening of the endowed schools many rural children had been educated in the homes of local women in exchange for a small fee. These 'Dame Schools' were often little more than child-minding facilities where the woman of the house who was literate (and possibly numerate) started by teaching her own children and then took in a few other pupils who could afford to pay a few pence for the privilege. Entries in the later logs of Rashwood School identify two of these dames as Miss Dance and Mrs Mainwaring, suggesting that they still existed side-by-side with state-sponsored schools.

Education for all was still a novelty and had to be paid for to some extent, and parents often kept their children at home to help with childcare and household chores, or sent them out on casual work when it was available. At a time when the wages of an agricultural labourer could be as low as £1 a week it cannot have been easy to find even the few pence required to pay for schooling. Indeed all the early log books show a constant battle against unauthorised absences. In August 1869 school was delayed until 9:30 each morning 'To give the children a chance to assist the parents in the fields which many of them do before coming to school', but even so the log book reports 'Few children present – many absentees are at work'.

On 4 November 1870 the log records 'Many children away acorn getting – it will be impossible to get a good school together until the acorns are off the trees as a good price is given for them owing to the scarcity of cattle food'. The normal pay for acorns was apparently 1 shilling (5p) per bushel (an 8 gallon container; Boynton 1990, 19). In April 1873 the comment was made that 'This working in the fields and gardens is a great drawback to regular attendance'. There are constant references to absences for getting blackberries, gleaning beans, cider-making, fruit getting, bird-scaring, stone getting, picking dandelions, picking cowslips, and pea picking. Gleaning was a popular occupation, where whole families would go round the fields after the main harvest had been gathered, and collect and keep any of the crop that had been left by the reapers.

Until education became compulsory from 1870 onwards, children often started and left school when it was convenient for the parents. Child labour was still common practice in the 19th century, and working-class families were reluctant to give up the earnings of their children, which helped to supplement the meagre family income, for the benefit of education. The various Factory Acts of 1833, 1844 and 1867 gradually focused on improving working conditions and imposed restrictions on child labour, which in turn favoured the opportunity of an alternative, the education of the child.

In the 1851 census for Dodderhill there were 41 boys and 41 girls noted as scholars out of a population of 1190, with 12 children, aged 15 and under, shown as agricultural labourers, 15 as servants, 12 as labourers and a further 8 in the trades of pansmith, tailor, blacksmith, salt boiler, bricklayer, carpenter, and gardener. This means that over one-third of children in the parish were in paid employment rather than going to school, the youngest being only 8 years old.

John Corbett School, Stoke Works

The 1881 census shows that out of an increased population of 1616 there were 197 boys and 216 girls described as scholars in Dodderhill. It is likely that most of these children would have been attending the new school at Stoke Works, which was built by John Corbett and opened in 1872 for the education of children of his employees at the salt-works. This school cost £2000 and was built by Corbett's own workmen to cater for up to 500 children. It was completed in under a year, and the Gothic-style building incorporated a lecture hall measuring 90ft (27.4m) by 36ft (11.0m) which could be partitioned into two rooms, a classroom 12ft by 36ft, and an infants' school 22ft by 30ft. There was a large playground and a school-house attached, and the building was licensed for divine service, and furnished with an American organ. No wonder Mr Jolliffe from Overstreet School had applied for a teaching post there!

In 1996 local residents recounted their memories of Stoke Works School to the Revd Alan White (1996, 2–4). Edith Healey, born in 1901, recalled being told by her mother Elizabeth Harper that she had attended the school on it's opening in 1872 and that her parents had paid 1d towards the cost of her schooling. Joe Harrison, born in 1907, remembered there being about 100 pupils in classes of 15 to 20 and that the head teacher was Thomas Williams. Interestingly, in the 1881 census Thomas K Williams was registered at the school house at Stoke as a

Certified Teacher aged 44 years, from Hakin in Pembroke, but in 1891 the name registered is Thomas C Williams, Elementary Certificated Teacher, aged 38 from Briston, Norfolk, presumably two different people with virtually the same names.

Stoke Works School continued to serve the village for over 100 years until its closure in 1986. After that it was still used for educational purposes as the John Corbett Centre, until it was sold by the Local Education Authority in c 2000. It has now been converted into dwellings and is part of a small modern housing estate.

School Life

The National School at Overstreet continued its struggle against absenteeism and offered a seemingly poor standard of education to those who did attend. The main focus was on the 3Rs of reading, writing and arithmetic, with the 4th R of religious instruction very close behind. Since the declared aim of the National Society in providing mass education had been to increase knowledge and understanding of the teachings of the Church of England, it is perhaps unsurprising that the influence of the clergy was very strong. The firm grip of the Church on the curriculum required mutual understanding between the teacher and the clergymen, and most clergy saw themselves as the superior partner here, since they not only hired and fired the teachers, and decided who should be free scholars, but had also had the school built. The intense involvement of the Church in the schoolroom continued even after the introduction of the first truly national system of education in 1870.

The Dodderhill National School received regular visits from the local clergy and their 'ladies'. They taught the children their catechism and read the Bible and prayer book to them. On 3 June 1869 'The first division read the 23rd of Genesis … but as they were unable to answer the questions upon it they were obliged to read it again'! On 23 July 'The vicar and his lady called – the latter instructed the needlework'. In November 'The vicar came to the school door but being on horseback he did not come in'. As well as overseeing the needlework Mrs Nicholson started a clothing club in March 1873, presumably in an attempt to alleviate the stress of poverty. The churchmen and their wives, daughters, and other female relatives seem to have taken a genuine interest in the welfare of the children and were very much involved in the day-to-day running of the school.

However, the standard of education which the children received at Overstreet was consistently poor, and results were constantly deemed unsatisfactory. In 1872 when Henry Jolliffe took over he had stated that 'In consequence of the irregularity of attendance at school by the children the attainments are lamentably deficient; after classification not a single child placed in the first class could work a sum in simple subtraction and only one or two had any idea of notation'.

The inspection report for the year ending 1876 stated that:

> The order is good and I wish I could add that the instruction is also, but it is not satisfactory; especially in spelling and arithmetic. The reading and writing are fair. The infants are pretty well taught; their classroom should have a fire in it on a cold day especially as the floor is of brick. The boys' office [lavatory] needs cleaning. My lords have allowed an unreduced grant with some hesitation – much better results in spelling and arithmetic will be expected next year.

But in 1878 once again 'The class subjects are less satisfactory and it is only by the passes in needlework that I am able to recommend the grant'. Well done Mrs Nicholson! Standards obviously did not improve, for in the final inspection report, dated 1885, the comments were as follows:

> Infants' School ... but the elementary instruction is not satisfactory. In reading the children are very inattentive and therefore dull and backward ... the writing is very unequal; a few write very well, many poorly or not at all. The idea of number is vague and slight in the extreme.

It seems that the school was paying the penalty suffered by so many small country schools in having the same incompetent teacher in charge for such a long time. But the report does go on to say that 'Allowances should also be made for the small unhealthy room in which the infants were obliged to be kept. The teacher could not be kept there even all day so that the teachers were changed morning and afternoon'. The first entry in the 1885 log book of the new school at Rashwood to which the pupils were transferred later that year tells us that 'These schools (ie mixed and infants) have been recently erected by Stoke Prior United District School Board – the education Department having condemned Wychbold School as being unfit for educational purposes', even though it had only been built 40 years previously. At last Wychbold had its own decent premises for a school, which would benefit the educational process.

The National School building at Overstreet was then converted into living accommodation, and the 1891 census shows Charles Cuff to be living there, with his wife and two young children. The property was sold by the Corbett estate in 1920, together with Astwood Manor Farm, to Alfred Hill, and by the 1940s had been converted into four dwellings. It was demolished in 1958 to make way for the pair of semi-detached houses which stand on the site today.

The emergence of the Board Schools

Political change

The closure of Overstreet School and transfer of the children to the new school at Rashwood mirrored a much larger reorganisation of education throughout the country. The standard of English education had been lagging behind the rest of the developed world during the 19th century, with a sparse network of voluntary schools spread over the land. These were paid for by private subscriptions as a result of religious and sectarian zeal. At the beginning of the century only a third of the population could read, and in 1839 one-third of men and half of all women had been unable to sign their names on the marriage registers.

When the majority of the working classes were employed in manual labour on farms or factories there was little need for literacy, but as Britain became a more industrialised nation more men and women were needed who could read, write, and use basic arithmetic. The industrial revolution of the 18th and 19th centuries produced a new elite of skilled engineers and mechanics, who were better paid than their fellow workers and who took the lead in educational progress and invention. A doctrine of self-help also began to emerge.

As wealth and manufacturing power increased through Queen Victoria's reign it was seen that there was a corresponding need for an increase in both the scope and quality of the education system in order to improve the quality of the industrial workforce. International affairs also influenced the need for improvements, as it was commonly believed that the Prussian military and economic successes were due to the soldiers and workpeople having received a thorough elementary education. There was a growing need for leadership both at home and overseas, as the British Empire expanded and became more powerful, and this period saw a rapid flowering in the popularity of the great (but thoroughly elitist) public schools of Eton, Winchester, Harrow and Rugby. School life in these institutions placed the emphasis on religion, chapel services, and the monitorial system, and suppressed the traditional problems of bullying, ill-discipline, and profligacy with which public schools were often besmirched. Education became fashionable for the rich and would-be-rich, and offered the middle classes an entrance for their sons into the governing class. This was strictly a boys' only opportunity and the old landed gentry, professional men and the new industrialists were welded together in the Public Schools, and were further divided from the rest of the nation brought up under a separate educational system.

Education Act of 1870

It was only after the 1867 Reform Act, which enfranchised the male urban working classes, that politicians decided to provide for state education. Gladstone's Education Act of 1870 was the turning point in English educational and, therefore, social history, and gave rise to a national system of state education which continues to this day. It ensured the existence of a dual system of voluntary denominational and non-denominational state schools. The 1870 Act required the establishment of elementary schools nationwide, but these were not intended to replace or duplicate what already existed, but rather to supplement those already run by churches, private individuals, or guilds. The great majority of the voluntary schools, by which the primary education of the people was supplied, were conducted on Church of England principles by the National Schools. The new Education Act doubled the state grant to the existing Church Schools (including the less common Roman Catholic Schools), so as to enable them to become a permanent part of the new system. New publicly controlled schools were then introduced in order to fill the large gaps in the educational map of the country.

These new schools were to be paid for out of local rates and governed by popularly elected school boards, and so were known as Board Schools. The school boards had to guarantee attendance for all children in their respective districts, and could appoint officers to enforce attendance. They could also charge a weekly fee of up to 9d (about 4p), or pay the fees themselves if parents were unable to do so. The voluntary schools could also receive such payment of fees from the school boards. Education became compulsory for children aged 5 to 10 in 1880, but did not finally become free in all state schools until 1891. The school leaving age was raised to 11 in 1893 and to 12 in 1899. In 1895 the concept of state secondary education was introduced for the over 11s, and was to take place in separate institutions. The new Board Schools were to be non-denominational. While religious instruction was to remain an integral part of the curriculum, it was not to be compulsory, and the use of catechism or formulary distinctive of any particular denomination, was absolutely prohibited.

A further Education Act in 1902 abolished the school boards and transferred their powers to elected county councils who would set up education committees. The improvements, due to larger areas and broader views, was of great benefit to primary education and still greater for the secondary sector. Without the Education Acts of 1870 and 1902 England could not have competed in the forthcoming industrial age, and between 1870 and 1890 average school attendance increased from one and a half million to four and a half millions.

Rashwood Board School

Although conditions in the new school at Rashwood (Fig 83) were a great improvement on those at the old National School at Overstreet, life continued to be extremely harsh by today's standards. The new school opened on Monday 29 June 1885, when 23 children were admitted into the infants' department under the care of Miss Jessie Andrews (formerly a pupil teacher in the Droitwich National Girls' School) as a 'Provisionally Certified Teacher'. She was assisted by Norah Hyatt (possibly the daughter of Mrs Hyatt from the old school at Overstreet) who was appointed as 'Monitress'. There is no contemporary record for the school, but in the 1891 census there is a Thomas Jones and his wife, Alice, in residence at the school-house, and they are both school-teachers. Thomas was from Penmore, Anglesey, and Alice was from Stoke Prior, and they were still there in 1918. The school was to provide education for children living between Droitwich, the village of Wychbold and Stoke Prior, hence it was erected at the meeting place of roads from these directions on top of Rashwood Hill, opposite the end of Stoke Lane. The building was to accommodate 149 boys and girls, and 80 infants, with pupils moving up from the infants' department into the mixed school at 6 years of age.

Figure 83 Rashwood School 1905 (Robin Skerratt Collection)

The Board Schools were much better regulated than the voluntary schools with compulsory records being kept and annual visits and reports from school inspectors. The code at the front of the 1887 admissions register for the new school states that:

> The Code requires that before any grant is made to a school the Education Department must be satisfied that suitable registers are provided, accurately kept, and periodically verified by the managers and … the grant may be reduced upon the Inspector's report for faults of registration. In every school there should be 1) a register of admission, progress and withdrawal 2) registers of daily attendance for all schools 3) a book of summaries.

The admissions registers show that, while most pupils in the mixed school had moved up from the infants' department, many had come from schools outside the local area, so there must have been a considerable amount of family movement, presumably for employment. The log dated 2 October 1896 tells us that 'At Michaelmas there are always great changes amongst the farm labourers – 3 families left the district'. Children had previously attended schools in, for example, Epsom (Surrey), Hampton-in-Arden, Bidford, Kidderminster, Malvern, Bolton (Lancs), Hereford, Worcester, Stirchley, Erdington, Stourport, Chesterfield (Derbys), Wolverhampton, Northfield, Walsall, Brecon, and Edinburgh.

Since the amount of money granted to the school by the local authorities depended largely on the number of pupils, it is perhaps not surprising that there was a strong focus on regular attendance. James Nosworthy was the local Attendance Officer, and he paid regular monthly visits to take the names of absentees. He appeared in the 1891 census as a 'School Board Officer', but in the 1881 census he had been classified as a 'Pensioner – Sergeant Major –

Rifles'. Born in Widdecombe, Devon, he had obviously led a very adventurous life, since his first son is recorded as having been born in Trinidad, West Indies, his first daughter was born at sea aboard *HMS Orontes*, his second daughter in Dublin, and his third in Worcester. Then he settled down on leaving the army, and the rest of his family were born in either Droitwich or Dodderhill.

School attendance continued to be a problem even after education became compulsory and free, and the Attendance Officer must have been kept busy. On 24 May 1895 it was reported that 'The small 7th standard attends very irregularly, consequently little progress is made, especially in arithmetic', and eventually effective prosecutions were made. On 18 October 1895 'Attendance has greatly improved, no doubt owing to Mr Jones of Crutch being fined for the irregular attendance of his son. All the parents have also been warned that in future proceedings will be taken against them unless their children make full attendances'. Yet ten years later the problem still persisted for, on 14 December 1906, the Head Master wrote that he had attended court where two parents were fined 6d (2½p) with 5s 6d (28p) costs for not sending their children to school. On 11 January 1907 it was stated that 'The prosecution of 2 parents for the irregularity of their children has had a most beneficial effect, and the percentage of attendance this week has reached 98.8%'. Serious action, therefore, continued to remain necessary on occasion in order to guarantee school attendance.

In July 1886 a prize scheme for attendance was introduced as follows:

> Children making 400 attendances were awarded   1s prize;
> Children making 420 attendances were awarded   1s 6d prize;
> Children not absent at all were awarded   2s prize.

In 1894 the prize for full attendance was raised to 3s for the mixed school – a not inconsiderable sum at the time. Children also received a bronze medal to mark their achievement, and an example has been discovered in the garden at Mill Cottage in Wychbold. It is dated 1904–5 and had been awarded to Elsie Hughes. Unfortunately, Elsie does not appear in the Rashwood registers of the period, and so must have attended a different local school, but she does appear in the 1911 census aged 15, and had been born in Stoke Prior.

Gradually the numbers on roll increased and truancy decreased as full-time education for all children became the norm, and by 1911 there were 111 children on the roll. However, absenteeism due to bad weather and disease continued to pervade the log books for many years, until improved social conditions and medical advances occurred during the course of the 20th century. Vagaries of the weather affected attendance considerably in the early years, and harsh winters reduced numbers for weeks at a time. Although pupils lived within walking distance, the flooding of streams (which are now culverted) onto dirt roads (which are now surfaced) meant that children often had grave problems getting to school. On 26 November 1885 'The children from Crutch [were] taken home in a farmer's cart as the roads are unfit to walk on', and a week later 'The children from Crutch [are] still unable to come to school owing to the state of the roads'. In the winter of 1895 'The severity of the weather keeps the younger children from commencing school', and on 1 February 'Another heavy snowstorm during the night … Today only 7 children presented themselves at school'. Later that same year, as the snows thawed, it is commented that 'Those possessed of good boots or shoes ought to have come to school, but the poor ones, so ill shod, could hardly be expected in their places'.

People in the developed world of the 21st century have an expectation of continuing good health, but factual records from earlier times show how all-pervasive ill-health and disease used to be, and how it regularly affected life to a degree we find difficult to comprehend today. Illness and death are recorded without comment or elaboration because of the ordinariness of it all, and it was taken for granted during the 19th century that school would be closed at least once virtually every year while epidemics raged in the locality. Living conditions for the rural poor were generally appalling, with labourers residing in tied cottages which were small, cold, and damp, and without running water or indoor sanitation, making it difficult for mothers to keep their children clean and healthy, and infestations of fleas and lice were part of country life. Children usually shared beds, and so infectious diseases spread very quickly, and the schoolroom provided a new opportunity for the spread of contagion, as well as knowledge! When outbreaks of disease became rampant the Ministry of Health (through the action of the attractively named 'Nuisance Officer') sometimes closed the school for weeks at a time, while the infection burnt itself out.

There are constant references in the log books to local epidemics, and to school closures due to the incidence of diseases which are virtually eradicated in our modern society, and even those diseases which we still recognise caused far greater disruption than they would today. For example, measles was not the minor nuisance that it is now, thanks to modern vaccinations, but was frequently accompanied by high fever, carrying the threat of hearing loss and mental incapacity, especially in the younger child. And scarlet fever lasted several weeks, often ending in death. The following is a small sample of such entries from the school log:

9 March 1886	'Notice received from the Nuisance Officer not to receive 2 children named Gilbert at school as the mother is suffering from scarlet fever.'
12 April 1890	'School closed owing to the measles epidemic.'
February 1891	'Influenza prevails greatly.'
25 May 1891	'Whooping cough very prevalent.'
24 September 1892	'School closed for measles epidemic.'
6 October 1892	'Earling Vine, a little scholar, five years old, died during the night.'
13 October 1893	'Poor attendance for the week – influenza and bronchitis are again beginning to spread among the children. Scarlet fever has attacked an inmate of the Master's house.'
27 October 1893	'School closed for scarlet fever.'
14 January 1894	'Attendance exceedingly poor – only 30 children present today. A great deal of sickness prevails both in Droitwich and Wychbold.'
25 September 1894	'Cholera at Hill End – 3 family members of pupil died.'
16 October 1894	'2 cases of Typhoid at Hill End.'
January 1898	'School closed for measles epidemic.'
May 1898	'Whooping cough seems to be spreading rapidly.'
May 1899	'Many children suffering from mumps.'

School managers often took the opportunity to extend the harvest holiday (a 4-week period during the main grain harvest, and the main holiday of the school year in recognition of the fact that prevention of truancy would be impossible at this crucial time of the agricultural year), when a closure was forced on them by an epidemic. On 18 July 1900 school had to close before the end of term, after notification of a case of diphtheria in the neighbourhood. On 3 September there was a note that 'School reopened today after a prolonged holiday during which the schools have been thoroughly cleansed, whitewashed and disinfected. It is earnestly hoped that the epidemic has now ceased'. But on 13 September 'School closed again due to diphtheria', and on 19 November the school had been 'Now closed for 4 months overall apart from 9 days'. The disease surfaced again in May 1908 when 'School closed for a fortnight plus one week', until on 7 July 'Acting on the recommendation of the Medical Officer of Health the school will be closed until after the Summer Holiday'. Diphtheria, a bacterial disease born of poverty, poor sanitation and poor water supply, is a very contagious disease, which attacks the throat and nose, where the bacterium produces a poison which is carried in the bloodstream. It spreads very quickly when an infected person sneezes or coughs, and sometimes a child can carry the infection without appearing ill. It was once one of the most common causes of infant death and, while still common in some parts of the world, in England there has been an effective vaccine programme against infection since 1940.

Primary sources used

Census returns 1841–1911
Dodderhill National School maps/plans – WRO BA 4473/2
Log books Dodderhill School 1869–94 – WRO BA 1618/16
Infants log book 1885–1912 – WRO BA 1618/14
Log books Rashwood School 1894–1906 – WRO BA 1618/15
Admissions registers Rashwood School 1889–1935 – WRO BA 1618/20
Punishment book Rashwood School 1901–53 – WRO BA 6331/2

20th century

By the first quarter of the 20th century some of the many great houses that John Corbett had bought with his salt profits were coming back on the market after his death, such as Hill Court sold in 1909 (see Peberdy, this volume), and sometimes other industrialists can be seen buying rural property, such as Sydney Wilkinson of Brickhouse Works in West Bromwich, ironmaster, who bought Wychbold Court in 1912 (see Stewart, this volume). The prices reached were usually much less than John Corbett had bought them for, suggesting that his policy of buying so much local property had led to the localised inflation of prices.

Between the world wars improved transport enabled city dwellers to escape briefly to the countryside. Dodderhill common was popularly used for such outings from Birmingham, and sometimes a visitor was accused of stealing 'seedlings' (Smith 2010); suggesting that the visitors were being closely watched!

Wychbold was very much put on the map during the Second World War with its landmark transmitter when, under the guise of Droitwich, it broadcast the BBC *Home Service*, the main British Station (Carpenter 1995), and much activity must have been seen at this important communications site. It can also be revealed that the transmissions from here often had a military purpose as well (see Jones & Wilks, this volume). With the war in progress official focus was directed at the productive use of the land resulting in a national farm survey of all agricultural land holdings above five acres during Spring 1941–2 (see Allan, this volume). This survey captures a picture of a busy and intricate farming life that was shared by many in the parish, as well revealing the still largely agricultural context of most of the inhabitants' lives.

Parish at war (*by* Colin Jones and Mick Wilks)

To date only one defence site relating to the First World War, and none for earlier periods, has been recorded for Dodderhill parish, and so the following account of Dodderhill at war is primarily concerned with the Second World War and its impact on the locality.

World War I

Red Cross Hospital at West Ford House

During the First World War West Ford House (now the clubhouse for the Droitwich Golf Club) was used by the Red Cross as a hospital for the treatment of wounded soldiers (Bromhead 1996; Jones *et al* 2008; WSM 28674), and Hill Court also opened its doors (for the latter see Peberdy, this volume). The demand for bed-spaces for the treatment of service casualties in that conflict far exceeded the provision in pre-existing military and requisitioned civilian hospitals and, as a consequence, the Red Cross established large numbers of auxiliary hospitals in large houses and other suitable buildings throughout Britain. Over 130 auxiliary hospitals were established in the West Midlands alone, with local voluntary organisations, including Voluntary

Aid Detachments trained by the Red Cross, providing the additional nursing and ambulance capacity required.

World War II

BBC at Wychbold

This BBC transmitting facility was opened in 1934 (Skerratt 2001; Jones *et al* 2008), and was probably the most important of the defence-related sites in the parish. The site was chosen because Wychbold provided a location from where good transmissions could be made to the whole of the United Kingdom, due, it is said, to the presence of a brine stream which gave good earthing qualities for the power supply used in the transmitter. No radio programmes were actually made at Wychbold, and these were created primarily in the BBC's London studios and, using the GPO telephone land-line system, were transferred to Wychbold for broadcasting. The main transmitter at Wychbold broadcast on 1500 metres Long Wave. A second transmitter station, to the south of the main transmitter hall, was built subsequently for broadcasting the *Forces Programme*, including *Voice of America*, on Medium Wave.

A blast-proof store-room, and associated staff huts for engineers and draughtsmen, were constructed in the north-east corner of the site to house site and installation drawings for all of the BBC facilities in Britain. The drawings were moved here from London in 1939, probably at the same time as the emergency broadcasting facility at Woodnorton, near Evesham, was established, and as part of a wider government scheme to evacuate to Worcestershire the departments vulnerable to air attacks on London.

During the Second World War the main Wychbold transmitter came under the partial control of the Ministry of Information, and was consequently used for transmitting propaganda and other information to occupied Europe, including coded messages to resistance workers (Jones *et al* 2008). A former engineer there recalls that these were transmitted in Morse, and so all engineers had to be proficient in this skill. Although obviously meaning something to the resistance organisations, the messages were apparently a little strange and might be, for example: 'There are fairies at the bottom of the garden'!

During the war the transmitter site was also designated as a Priority 1 Vulnerable Point, and as such was given a high level of defence against enemy ground or air attack (NA WO 166/1226). Apart from recording a number of small air raid shelters on the site (Fig 84), rather surprisingly, so far, no information has come to light, either documentary or oral, of any ground defence works such as pillboxes or other weapons' positions, or even trenches being constructed there. However, it is known that the BBC raised its own Home Guard Platoon (see below) in May 1940, and shared the task of defending the site with, initially, a contingent of the 11th (Home Defence) Battalion, The Royal Warwickshire Regiment (WO 166/4617), from July 1940 to June 1941, followed by a contingent of Military Police, who had been specifically trained at Norton Barracks for guarding vulnerable points (NA WO 166/14558). In addition, there is some evidence of Royal Artillery light anti-aircraft batteries having sited Bofors 40mm light anti-aircraft guns on, or near the site, at different times, but for apparently relatively short periods. There seems to have been regular movements of these guns to and from the various designated Vulnerable Points in Worcestershire, possibly in response to perceived changes in Luftwaffe target priorities (NA WO 166/2715 and 2817). In addition, a light anti-aircraft gun, and apparently two searchlights, were mounted on the roof of the main transmitter hall (Skerratt 2001, 58). In this

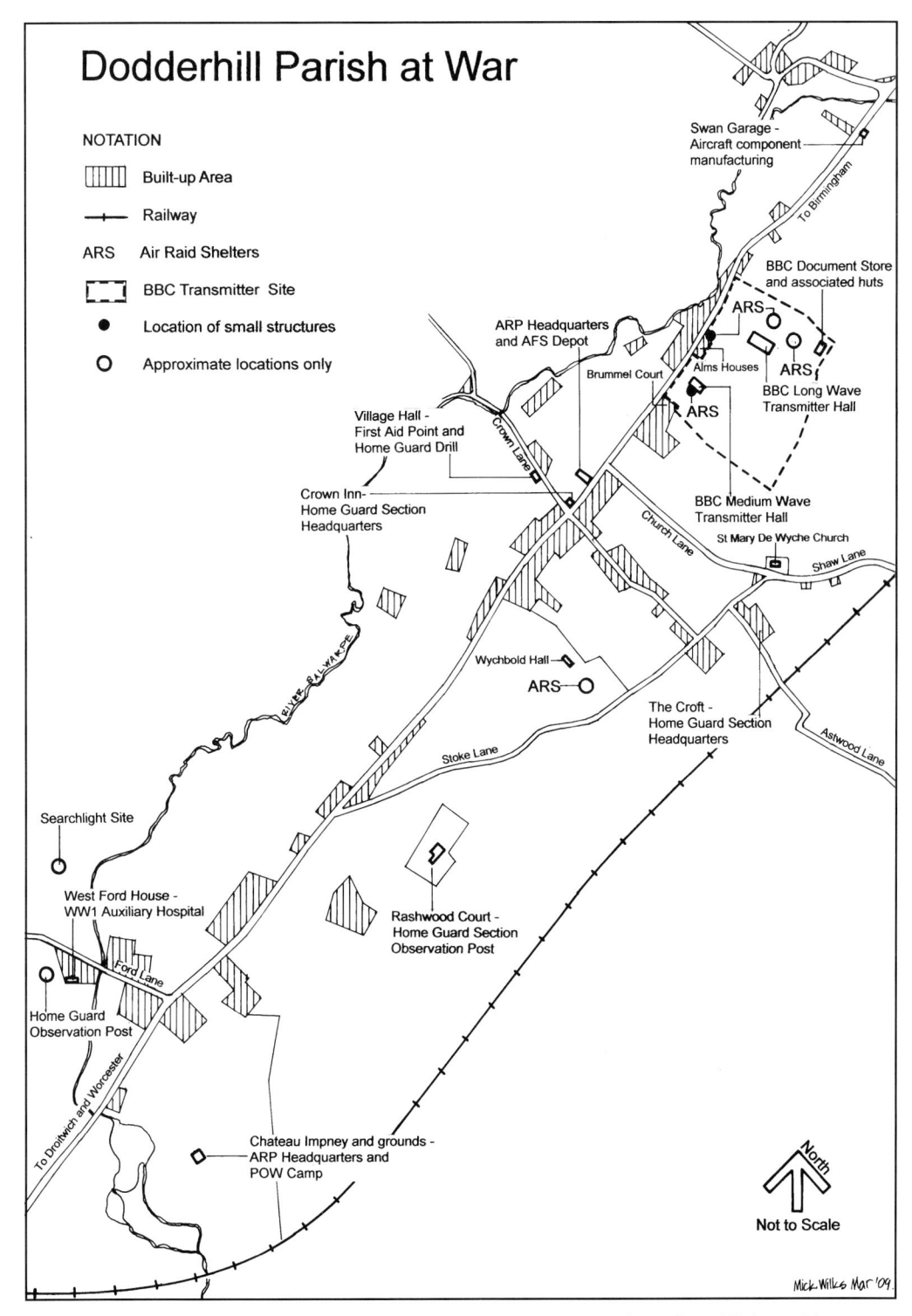

Figure 84 *Location of known sites and buildings with wartime associations. Searchlight positions are approximate*

case, and based on the evidence gleaned for other vulnerable sites, the gun was probably a Lewis gun and operated by the Warwicks, and the lights were probably small and more to do with site security at night, rather than for anti-aircraft use. Searchlights were heavy items of equipment and were regularly the target of Luftwaffe aircraft. It seems, therefore, unlikely that they would be sited on top of a transmitting facility which was already vulnerable to air attack.

Although the site had been reconnoitred by air in advance of war in mid 1938, and was often over-flown by the Luftwaffe on their way to and from targets in the Birmingham area, and further north, and the enemy aircraft were evidently fired at by the Bofors guns sited in the vicinity, no aerial attack was ever made on the transmitter site. There are a number of theories for this, one being that possibly any German forces successfully invading the UK from 1940 onwards would have wanted to use the transmitter for their own propaganda purposes. This had certainly occurred during their attack on Norway, when Vidkun Quisling, a collaborator, had used the Norwegian radio station for making a broadcast to try to stop the mobilisation of Norwegian forces. Another theory was that Luftwaffe aircraft used the powerful signal from the transmitter as a homing device and so wanted to keep it in being. Whenever air-raid sirens were heard, staff working in the main transmitter hall would remain at their posts, since the building had no windows, was strongly built to withstand blast, and was considered to be one big air-raid shelter. The on-duty BBC staff also came to know when offensive British bombing raids were on because the transmitters were always tuned to 200 kilocycles for two hours at specific times (R Curtiss, pers comm).

During wartime many of the staff were bussed to the BBC site from the surrounding areas, including Droitwich, although a number were billeted locally in Brummel Court, in the Alms Houses alongside the main road and at The Croft in Astwood Lane. In September 1944 the Home Guard, and other guards, ceased operational responsibilities for, and were withdrawn from, vulnerable points in Worcestershire, including the BBC site (NA WO 166/1226).

The Home Guard

Two units of Home Guard have been identified which had responsibilities for defence in Dodderhill parish: part of No 11 Platoon, one section being based for most of the war at The Croft in Astwood Lane, and a second section being based in the function room at the Crown Inn, on the main road in Wychbold; and No 13 Platoon formed by the male staff at the BBC Station. However, before going on to discuss its activities, it would be as well to briefly sketch in the background to the formation of the Home Guard. The force was formed from volunteers who responded to a request broadcast on 14 May 1940 by Anthony Eden, the newly appointed Minister for War, and was initially to be called the Local Defence Volunteers (LDV). The name was intended to describe their function, but it was quickly changed to Home Guard, at the behest of Winston Churchill. Their initial role was to watch for enemy parachutists and agents, report their presence to the nearest regular troops, man road blocks, and place a guard on vulnerable facilities that could be sabotaged by the enemy, such as electricity and gas supplies, telephone exchanges, water supply and, in the case of Wychbold, the BBC Station. Later, when the Home Guard was better trained and equipped, the force was expected to take on the enemy forces in battle (Wilks 2007).

Both No 11 Platoon, commanded by Lieutenant Bidwell, and No 13 Platoon (BBC), commanded by Lieutenant Sellen (one of the senior engineers there), were part of C Company, which in turn was part of the 2nd Worcestershire (Bromsgrove) Battalion Home Guard, whose headquarters were in the drill hall at Bromsgrove. The C Company Commander was Captain Ryland, and the Battalion Commander was initially Colonel E F Du Sautoy, and, later, Lieutenant Colonel J T James.

No evidence has come forward for any road blocks in Wychbold village, although being located on one of the main roads through Worcestershire, heading towards the West Midlands conurbation, there almost certainly would have been one or more; to the south at Chapel Bridge anti-tank cylinders can still be seen by the side of the road (Wilks 2007, 67). The role of the Home Guard section based in the Crown Inn is also not known, but manning road blocks on the main road in the village would have been a strong possibility. More is known about the Home Guard section based latterly at The Croft. Their first base and observation post (OP) was at Rashwood Court, now a nursing home, but then the home of Hugh Sumner. The junior NCO of the section at that time was Corporal Bill Allington, who was farming locally. He recalls that the Section Sergeant was Major Edward Kay, a former cavalry officer in the Great War, and a member of the Worcester-based mail order company family. Major Kay apparently did not take kindly to his Home Guard rank of sergeant and insisted on being referred to by his former army rank, and wearing his tailored officer's uniform! The role of his section was to carry out night patrols, in pairs, around the extremities of the gardens of the court and to observe the area to the east of the court, where there were extensive views over the countryside. For this role the section was based in the gardener's cottage.

Major Kay lived at Rashwood Lodge, and whatever other faults he may have had, he was a stickler for discipline. He, therefore, had but a short distance to go to make surprise visits to the section at night so that he could check that they were actually carrying out their duties properly. He was incorrectly challenged on one occasion, and as the NCO in charge of the detail that night, Bill Allington was taken to task by the Major. Later, when Bill asked the offending volunteer why he had not challenged the Major correctly, the reason given was that he "part knowed the Old B****r!"

Major Kay arranged for the LDV volunteers to be given drill training. This was undertaken at the former village hall in Crown Lane, a building which has now gone. The instructor was RSM Smith of the Coldstream Guards, who was at the time attached to an officer training unit based at the War Office buildings (latterly occupied by the Army Medal Office) at Witton, in Droitwich. Major Kay also paid labourers to dig defence trenches in various parts of the parish in readiness for the expected invasion by German forces. Bill Allington could not recall where these were, except for one trench being located on the north side of the road from Wychbold Church, going towards Stoke Prior. This was probably to cover the railway bridge over the lane, a good location for a road block, although there is no other evidence for this.

As a result of the Home Guards disturbing the sleep of Mrs Sumner, while they patrolled the gardens of Rashwood Court, their base for night patrolling duties was moved to the upper floor of the stables at the back of The Croft, a large house in Astwood Lane. This was used by the Home Guard until they were stood down in November 1944. In addition to the aircraft crash described below, another incident at The Croft that Bill recalled, almost resulted in tragedy for the Home Guard. It was the regular practice of men returning from their patrolling to clear the magazines of their rifles, and then ease the springs of the breech mechanisms, by shuffling the bolt back and forth. On one occasion, a single cartridge was left in a rifle resulting in an accidental discharge. The bullet passed through the floor into the stables below, narrowly missing Bill, who was resting on the floor. The bullet was never found, but the men were initially concerned that it may have harmed one of the cows kept in the stable below.

Tragedy did visit the local Home Guard when, in May 1944, No 11 Platoon was part of an attacking force in an exercise with regular troops near Redditch. Bill Allington, by this time a 2nd Lieutenant, was accompanying one of the umpires. During the exercise, the umpire, Lieutenant F Chaplin (a BBC Engineer and member of No 13 Platoon), suffered a heart attack and died almost immediately. He was buried in Wychbold Churchyard, has a Commonwealth War Graves Commission (CWGC) headstone, and is one of ten or so (the precise number has yet to be established) Home Guards who died in the course of their duty in Worcestershire (as listed by the CWGC).

No 13 Platoon was formed entirely from the male members of staff at the BBC transmitter site, all of whom were expected by the management to join the force. However, there was apparently little time for Home Guard activities, since there were seven separate shifts managing the transmitter station. Nevertheless, with a platoon of 70 men, there could be ten men on Home Guard duty at any one time, and their role was to patrol the inside of the perimeter fence looking for enemy agents or saboteurs. It has not been established for certain what the regular troops on the site were doing, but presumably they were supplying the gate guards, and in 1940 and 1941, when the invasion scare was at its height, manning any weapons positions on the site. Training for the BBC Home Guard was generally conducted on the open areas within the site, although use was also made of the Whitford Rifle Range at Bromsgrove. One unusual feature of Home Guard duty at the BBC was the possibility of being 'stung' by a charge of static electricity jumping from the edge of a steel helmet down to a man's shoulder, if the helmet was not worn squarely on the head! The shock would occur when the main transmitter was operating.

In the early part of the war, while men of No 13 Platoon were patrolling the inside of the perimeter fence, men of No 11 Platoon would be patrolling the surrounding roads and fields. Bill Allington recalled that men from No 11 Platoon later joined the BBC Home Guard in patrolling on the inside of the security fence, after the Warwicks had left.

There is evidence of the Home Guard establishing an OP near the first tee to the west of the golf clubhouse, adjoining Ford Lane, but this does not appear to have been for No 11 Platoon. It was quite possibly something to do with one of the platoons of D Company of the Bromsgrove Battalion, based in the drill hall at Droitwich. A hut was constructed for use as a shelter by the Home Guards patrolling the golf course, which would have made a potential landing ground for enemy parachutists (Bromhead 1996).

One event that is remembered by many Home Guards in the north of Worcestershire, including the men of No 11 Platoon, was the appearance of empty German parachutes over a wide area between Redditch and Kidderminster, one night in early August 1940. At the same time German radio had broadcast that parachutists had been landed in Britain, and many hours were spent by the Home Guard searching for the enemy troops or agents. This event coincided with a serious fire at the Britannia Batteries factory in Redditch, and it was widely assumed at the time to have been the work of enemy saboteurs. Similar thoughts may well have been entertained that enemy agents would try to enter the BBC site. In the darkness, some of Bill Allington's section saw figures crossing one of the nearby canal bridges and thought that they might be some of the enemy. They were thankfully recognised as other Home Guards before the firing started! It was expected by the authorities that the parachutes found as a result of the search would be handed in to the nearest regular troops, but in fact some were not and were quickly converted into ladies underwear by local seamstresses. It later became obvious that the empty parachutes had been dropped by German bombers on their way to bombing raids further north, and that this was an attempt to ratchet up the anxiety and fear in the British population about the expected invasion (NA WO 166/94).

A supplementary task for the Home Guard was to place a guard on any aircraft that landed within their area, enemy or friendly. Two British aircraft landed in the vicinity for which the local Home Guard provided the guard; the first was a Fairy Swordfish which landed in a field to the north of Shaw Lane after suffering engine trouble, and was flown out by a bearded Fleet Air Arm pilot two or three days later, when the problem had been fixed; the second involved a small training aircraft that landed in the Hanbury area when it became too dark to reach its base, and this was flown out the next day by its young sergeant pilot.

German aircraft crash at The Croft, Wychbold

On 12 March 1941, a crewless German Junkers Ju 88 aircraft crashed close to The Croft, just before midnight, in circumstances that, but for sheer luck, could have brought death to the local Home Guards on duty that night, or destroyed The Croft and its occupants. Piloted by Feldwebel Gunther Unger, the twin-engined aircraft (with the codes F1+BT) took off from an airfield just to the south of Paris for a raid on the docks at Birkenhead. On the approach to the target area, the aircraft was attacked by a Boulton Paul Defiant night-fighter and one engine set on fire. After setting the apparently crippled aircraft to fly westwards out to sea, the crew of five men successfully baled out and subsequently became prisoners of war. The crew had expected the aircraft to crash out to sea soon afterwards, but, instead, it reversed course and flew itself about a hundred miles overland to Wychbold where, after clipping the trees in nearby Church Lane, it went between the house and the stables at the back of The Croft (its wings touching both stables and house), demolished a close-boarded fence around the swimming pool, and finally crashed in the adjoining field (Warren 1991).

Bill Allington was a member of the Home Guard detail using the stables that night as their base for patrolling the local roads on their dusk-to-dawn watch around the BBC. Their duty entailed two hours on, and four hours off, throughout the night and so, while some would be patrolling in pairs, others would be resting or playing pontoon. Bill was playing cards with some of his colleagues, when the noise of the aircraft crashing caused them to dash outside, but not before someone, who was never identified, had the presence of mind to pocket the gambling money from the table! Outside, the burning aircraft had disintegrated and amongst the wreckage could be seen cylinder-shaped objects, thought to be unexploded bombs. It later transpired that these were oxygen cylinders, but their appearance certainly added to the excitement that night! In the cold light of day, the Home Guards realised what a fortunate escape from death they, and the occupants of the house, had had. The damage caused by the aircraft passing between the two buildings was apparent, with part of one wing being left in front of the stables.

Air defences

Anti-aircraft guns were generally sited at, or around, the primary vulnerable points, like the BBC Station at Wychbold, or gun-defended areas, such as the Birmingham/Coventry/Black Country conurbation. However, from 1941, the searchlights, which had provided the illumination for the guns, were moved away from main expected target areas and arranged in a specific pattern in the countryside surrounding the target areas. This would both avoid conveniently marking the target areas for the Luftwaffe, and help patrolling night-fighters to detect and attack enemy aircraft on their way to their targets. Consequently, the whole of Worcestershire formed part of a so-called 'Night Fighter Killer Zone' that surrounded the West Midlands conurbation, and the searchlights within this zone were sited in a grid pattern, with a spacing of approximately 6000 yards (5486m; Wilks 2007).

One of the searchlights in that pattern was sited in a large field on the north side of Ford Lane, across from the Droitwich golf course (Bromhead 1996). Precise locations for the light and its ancillary facilities have yet to be established, the latter usually consisting of a group of three circular defence earthworks to protect the searchlight, its generator and a light anti-aircraft gun, together with a number of infantry trenches to protect the site from ground attack, and one or more accommodation huts. Although the searchlight site here, as elsewhere, has long since been restored to agriculture, the former earthworks do sometimes show as crop marks (Wilks 2007), sometimes being mistaken for Bronze Age burial sites!

Civil defence

A few civil defence related items have been recorded in Dodderhill parish, although there will certainly be others still awaiting discovery. The main civil defence interest in the parish is the use of Chateau Impney and its grounds as the local Air Raid Precautions headquarters from 1939, when a number of huts were constructed behind the chateau, and the grottoes were used as practice gas chambers. This use ceased in 1943, and the house and grounds then became a prisoner of war (POW) camp (Grundy 1994).

Wychbold village hall, then sited in Crown Lane, was requisitioned as a First Aid Point in October 1939 (WRO BA 1392). As such, somewhere in the building, a stock of medical supplies, bandaging, and blankets would have been stored ready for any emergency caused by enemy attack. It had been expected that enemy bombing attacks on Britain could occur almost anywhere, and so preparations were made throughout the country to treat the civilian casualties. The First Aid Point should not be confused with a First Aid Post, where a doctor and nurses were present and beds provided. The latter were manned 24 hours each day, and were usually established in the towns and larger population centres (Jones et al 2008).

The Chief Air Raid Warden for the parish was Sidney Gittins, and the Wardens' Post was established in the former blacksmith's shop, just to the north of the Crown Inn. Here two men would man the post each night, with others patrolling the village. The adjoining garage, owned by Mr Gittins was also requisitioned for the Auxiliary Fire Service in August 1940, probably to accommodate a trailer pump (WRO BA 1392). In addition two volunteer fire watchers from the BBC staff would have been posted on the roof of the BBC transmitter hall every night (Skerratt 2001).

Five air raid shelters have been recorded in the parish (Fig 84): three within the BBC site; one on the north side and behind the row of Alms Houses fronting the BBC site (earth-covered this is visible from the road); and an almost perfectly preserved Anderson Shelter recently discovered in the former grounds of Wychbold Hall.

Prisoners of war

While a POW camp, Chateau Impney was used to accommodate German officers from 1943, and was associated with the camp at Hampton Lovett, where other ranks of German prisoners were housed (Grundy 1994). Some captured Italians worked on local farms, an example being Angelo Roggeri, who worked at Astwood Manor Farm (Skerratt 2001, 78).

Ministry of Aircraft Production

In the 1930s, and in an effort to reduce the effect of bombing on important war industries, notably those manufacturing military aircraft or their components, factories were moved away from potential target areas elsewhere into the Midlands, where it was considered that the skills developed by the motor industry could be adapted to that of aircraft manufacturing, and where the area was thought to be beyond the range of German bombers. One example of this was the Austin Aero Works, at Longbridge. When France was occupied in 1940 and enemy bombing of the Midlands started, a further dispersal of some of the aircraft component manufacturing processes into the surrounding counties was undertaken. Many of the motor repair garages in Worcestershire were requisitioned by the Ministry of Aircraft Production for this purpose (Jones et al 2008). One of the garages affected by this policy was the Swan Garage (Skerratt 2001), in the north of Dodderhill parish, which manufactured aircraft components for the Austin Aero Works (Skerratt 2001).

Note on sources

The above owes much to the first-hand accounts of the following, as recorded during interviews with Mick Wilks (unless otherwise stated): John Phillips, former BBC Engineer (interviewed by Brian Boulby in 1996); Bill Allington, formerly of No 11 Platoon Home Guard (2001); R Curtiss, former BBC Engineer and member of No 13 Platoon Home Guard (2005); and Doug Harris, formerly of No 11 Platoon Home Guard (2005).

National farm survey during the Second World War (*by Kate Allan*)

When the Second World War began in September 1939, Britain was faced with the urgent need to drastically increase the production of food, as well as to assess its storage and distribution, since imports of food and fertilizers were severely reduced by the war at sea. And so the Ministry of Food was established that same month, and the Ministry of Agriculture and Fisheries (MAF) set up County War Agricultural Executive Committees (CWAECs) to oversee improvements in food production.

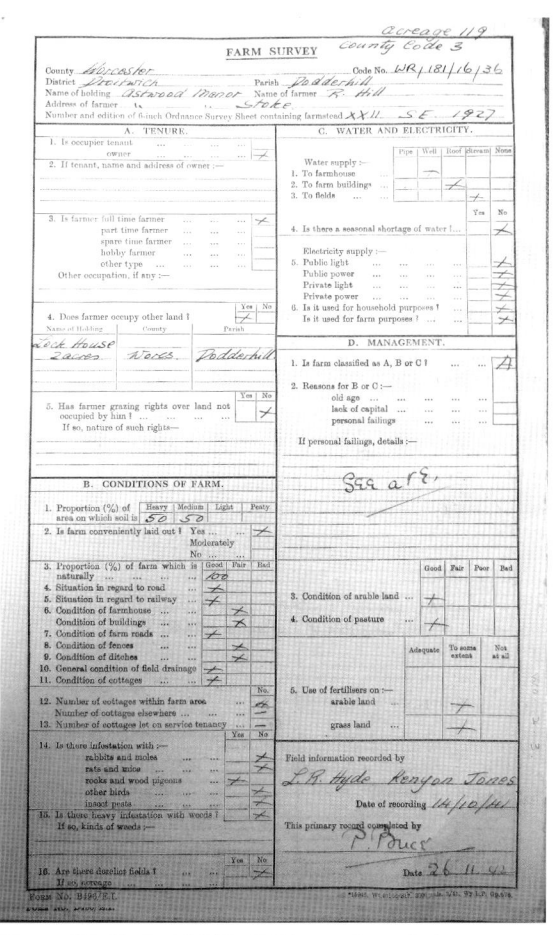

Figure 85 Typical 1941–2 Primary Farm Return record: Astwood Manor Farm (WR/181/16/36; NA MAF 32/60/16) (photograph by D Hurst)

In June 1940 the first war-time farm survey was undertaken to assess the productive state of farms (based on the annual agricultural census first held in June 1866), with the principal aim being to increase food production. By October 1940 this first survey had still not been completed, and it soon became apparent that the counties and districts had used very different standards in their data collection and recording. Ten counties even appear to have returned no information whatsoever (and none has yet been found for Dodderhill). As a result MAF realised that 'a uniform form of record' was required, and so the *National Farm Survey* of 1941–2 was born (records released in January 1992). This census also continued to be carried out every year after the war until 1995, when it was reduced to a sample survey.

As part of this National Farm Survey all holdings of five acres or more came under the scrutiny of the CWAECs which had the power to inspect land, direct what was grown, terminate tenancies, take possession of land, and assess the ability of each farmer to meet their aims, and this included mapping each holding. The records of 38 properties in and around the parish of Dodderhill (farms and smaller holdings covering a total of 2706 acres; eg Fig 85), and the corresponding maps survive (NA MAF 32/60/16; eg Fig 86), but, of these, only 29 are complete returns, the remaining nine being only partial. There is no way of knowing whether the latter were ever fully completed, or if pages have since become detached and lost. Some areas were incompletely mapped, particularly the western edge of the golf course and its border with Park Farm (Fig 87, holdings 2 and 3). There were also blank areas which may have been collections of small holdings of less than 5 acres and, therefore, not included in the survey.

Figure 86 National Farm Survey map showing 1941–2 land holdings in the vicinity of Brine Pits Farm (NA MAF 32/60/16) (photograph by D Hurst)

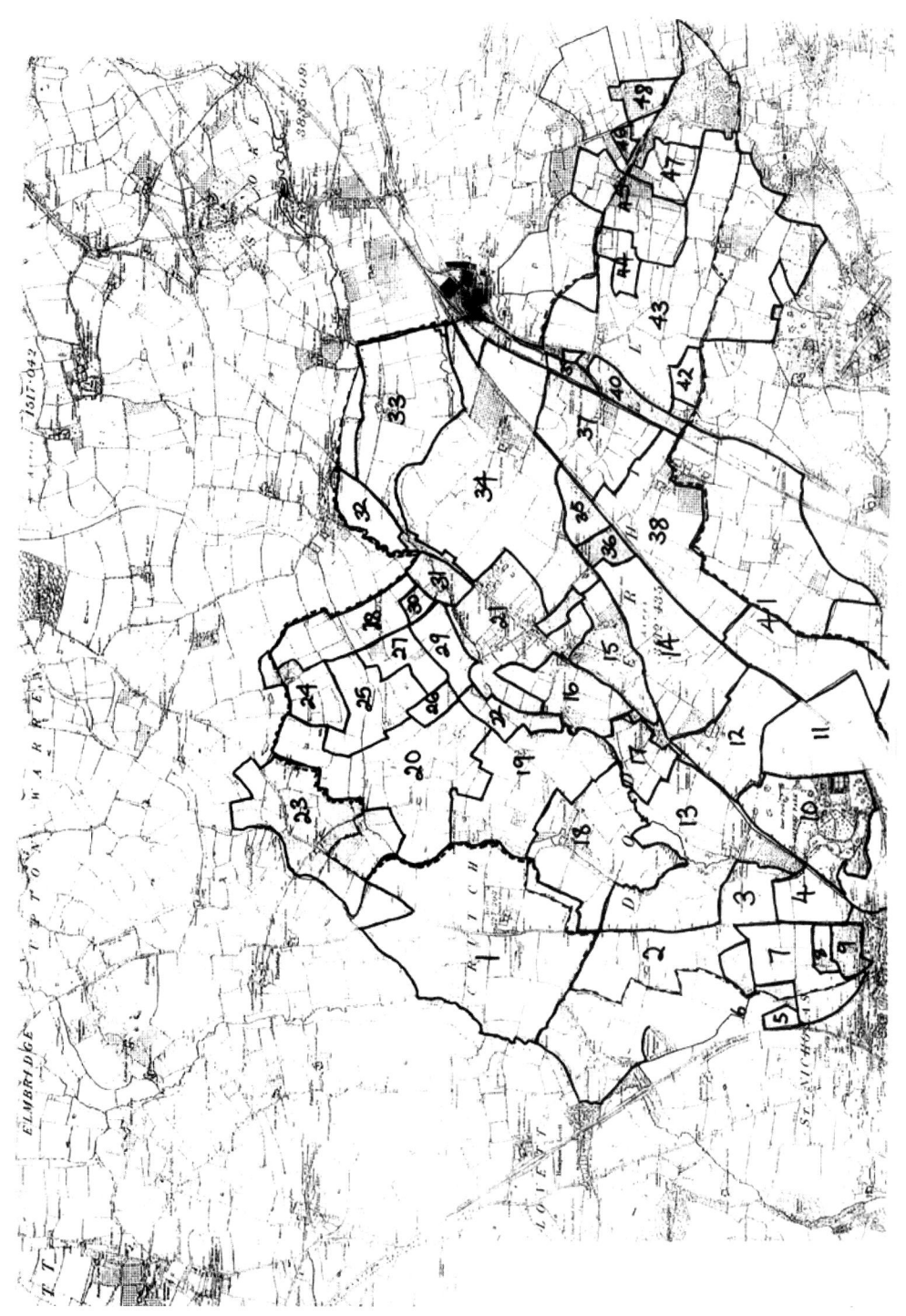

Figure 87 Plot of Dodderhill land holdings as mapped by the National Farm Survey of 1941–2

Holdings mapped by the survey were as follows (see Fig 87 for locations):

1	Crutch Farm	25	Withy Furlong
2	Park Farm	26	Wychbold Farm (part)
3	Golf Course	27	Brookhouse Farm
4	Spittal Close	28	Kingsland Hill Farm
5	Berry Hill	29	Wychbold Court
6	Egghill Farm	30	?Overfield [illegible]
7	Dodderhill Court (Yeats)	31	Geo. Jackson
8	Dodderhill Court	32	Webbs
9	Hill Court	33	Hobden Hall Farm
10	Impney Park	34	Wychbold Court Farm
11	Impney Farm	35	Little Astwood
12	Rashwood Farm	36	G. Howells
13	Ford Farm	37	Causeway Meadow
14	Yew Tree Farm	38	Astwood Manor
15	Wychbold Hall	39	Redhouse Farm
16	Walkmills Farm	40	Little Astwood
17	Rashwood Court	41	Walmer Farm
18	Brinepits Farm	42	E. Webbs & Sons
19	Ridgeway Court Farm	43	Astwood Bank
20	Ridgeway and Coney Farm	44	Hill Farm
21	Wychbold Farm	45	The Poplars
22	Wyken	46	Little Elms
23	Grange Farm	47	Hill Fields
24	Colley Pits	48	The Firs

Tenure

There was a total of 31 farms in Dodderhill as listed in the *Primary Farm Return* of the National Farm Survey of June 1941 (form B496/E1) as follows:

NA ref no	holding	owned by	farmed by
WR/181 16/2	Walk Mills	S N Part	W H Simpson
WR/181 16/5	Ridgeway Farm	D Brown	C H Richardson
WR/181 16/7	Ford Farm	R J Quinney	R J Quinney
WR/181 16/8	Poplars Farm	G A Grazier	G A Grazier
WR/181 16/9	Kingsland Hill	E S Crawford	E S Crawford
WR/181 16/10	Crutch Farm	Westwood Trustees	A F Perkins
WR/181 16/11	Impney Farm	Droitwich Spa Ltd	P Mc Hale
WR/181 16/12	Ridgeway Court Farm	Exors (*sic*) of E J.Harvey	Exors (*sic*) of E J Harvey
WR/181 16/15	Brine Pits Farm	A Hill	A Hill
WR/181 16/16	Wychbold Farm	G Pardoe	H Pardoe
WR/181 16/17	The Firs	Impney Hotel Co Ltd.	C W Horton
WR/181 16/18	Spitall Close	Droitwich Spa Ltd	T Garstone
WR/181 16/19	The Grange Farm	F Smith	F Smith
WR/181 16/20	Little Astwood	H de la Hay	H de la Hay
WR/181 16/21	Hill Farm	W J Reeves	S J Jones
WR/181 16/23	Yew Tree	H Sumner	H Sumner
WR/181 16/24	Rashwood	E Cowan	W Clowes
WR/181 16/25	Notts Farm	W A Steele	O S Bluner
WR/181 16/26	Causeway Meadow	H Lacey	H Lacey
WR/181 16/27	Hobden Hall Farm	J W Tibbetts (*sic*)	S C Tibbets
WR/181 16/28	Astwood	J de la Hay	C Allington
WR/181 16/30	Park Farm	Westwood Trustees	S Price
WR/181 16/31	Astwood & Walmer Farms	Messrs E Webb & Sons	Messrs E Webb & Sons
WR/181 16/32	Hill Court	Mrs E M Hollyer	Mrs E.M Hollyer
WR/181 16/33	Pipers Hill	H Cartwright, Rev G D Blois	W H Weaver
WR/181 16/36	Astwood Manor	R Hill	R Hill
WR/181 16/37	Rashwood Cottage	Powell, Mrs White (*sic*)	Mrs Ellen Houseman
WR/181 16/39	Sunny Hill	Mrs F M Wilson	Mrs F M Wilson
WR/181 16/43	Withy Furlong	A Cockbill	A Cockbill
no code given	Coney Green	Exors of Mrs Dugard	H Sumner
WR/181 13/63	Sharpway Gate	C Shaw	G A Grazier

Of these holdings twelve were farmed by their owners and seventeen by tenant farmers. Two returns had both the tenant and owner boxes ticked, indicating that the occupier had both ownership and tenancy of different parts of the holding, and these were the holdings of Little Astwood (WR/181 16/20) and Astwood and Walmer Farms (WR/181 16/31). Two returns show owner and tenant having the same surname: Wychbold Farm (WR/181 16/16) owned by G Pardoe but farmed by H Pardoe, and Hobden Hall Farm (WR/181 16/27) owned by G W Tibbets but farmed by S G Tibbets. This suggests that while one family member was responsible for the farming, another held the property. Three returns indicated joint ownership, and in these the acreage held by each was stated. However, it is impossible to ascertain from the survey where precisely these acres were. Yew Tree Farm (WR/181 16/23) and Coney Green (no reference number) were both farmed by H Sumner and a return for each completed, resulting, in part at least, in a duplication of data.

In Dodderhill 38.7% of the holdings were farmed by owner-occupiers, while tenanted holdings accounted for 54.8%, and mixed holdings for the remaining 6.5%. This ratio was broadly similar to the 22.7% of owner-occupiers, 65.9% tenanted, and 11.5% mixed tenure for the overall Midlands (Short 2000, 166).

Full-time or part-time farmers?

Twenty farms, about two-thirds of the total, were run by full-time farmers. Amongst the remainder there were two cattle transporters, a cattle dealer, a haulier, a seedsman, a boarding-house keeper, and a company director. This is similar to the picture that emerged from the overall national survey data where a little over two-thirds were classed as full-time (Short 2000). As for Dodderhill, so nationally most of the other occupations were related to agriculture.

Other land?

The farm survey return provided space for details of other land occupied by the farmer. Thirteen returns gave such information, sometimes in some detail. For instance in the case of Grange Farm (WR/181 16/19) the farmer had 'Oakfield, half tenancy, Chaddesley', or in the case of Yew Tree (WR/181 16/23) 'Soldens, Bag End, Himbleton', but other entries are less helpful such as in the case of G A Grazier at Poplars Farm (WR/1181 16/8), who also farmed land at Sharpway Gate but the survey does not detail this additional holding. Generally it is clear that most of the other land worked was either in Dodderhill, or its neighbouring parishes, but in two cases it was a considerable distance away: J de la Hay at Astwood (WR/181 16/28) occupying a farm in Cotheridge, and Webbs (WR/181 16/31), besides its trial grounds at Upton Warren, occupying Harcarse Farm in Duns, Berwickshire, Scotland. Nationally 20.8% stated that they occupied other land, and in Dodderhill the figure was twice that at 41.9%. This may reflect the accrual of land through marriage or its purchase for business investment.

Grazing rights

Five farmers had grazing rights on land not occupied by themselves, but again the detail is lacking in such entries as 'summer grazing 6 acres', and 'summer grazing 10 acres at Wychbold'. H Sumner, however, had 20 acres of summer grazing at Coney Green in Elmbridge and 2 acres at Bradley Green.

Surveying the condition of the farm

In the survey there were three possible responses ('good/fair/bad') about the condition of a farm, and Dodderhill had remarkably few aspects assessed as 'bad'. These were generally for the state of field drainage, ditches or fences. In general the condition of the farmhouse, the buildings, and the layout were 'good', sometimes 'fair'. Only Piper's Hill Farm and Notts Farm had what the CWAEC considered to be a bad situation regarding access to road and railway.

The precise criteria used to determine the grade given are unknown, and seem to have been determined by the surveyors themselves. This has resulted in widely differing results. In Devon, for instance, one whole district had a 98% 'A' grading, and it seems the surveyors had no idea of any national standards, or even standards within their own county. Unfortunately, this makes it impossible to compare Dodderhill with the rest of the country, or indeed with the rest of Worcestershire.

Cottages

If cottages were within the farm area or elsewhere these were counted, and their condition assessed – after the condition of fences, ditches and field drainage, and almost, therefore, as an afterthought. Again, there were three possible responses ('good/fair/poor'). Remarkably, almost all the cottages were classed as 'good'. Three individual cottages at Ridgeway Court Farm, Impney Farm and Hobden Hall, were rated a 'fair' grade, and only one farm cottage, which was at Piper's Hill Farm, received a 'poor' assessment. Of these four not given a 'good' grade, three were on tenanted holdings, suggesting that the owner was letting standards slide. According to the survey, therefore, housing conditions were generally of a high standard.

Pests

Animal, bird and insect pests were assessed on a 'yes/no' basis. It was not possible, on the form, to state any degree of infestation, or which fields were affected, although it was possible to name the species. Problems with weeds were treated similarly. Rooks and wood pigeons (grouped together in the survey) were widespread pests, mentioned in half the returns. Insect pests, unfortunately unnamed, were similarly widespread, and thistles were the most common weeds. A lack of detail makes it impossible to map the infested areas of the parish in any useful way.

Derelict fields

The survey required derelict fields to be recorded with their acreages, as in war time these were very much frowned upon, but, in the case of Dodderhill, there were none.

Water and electricity

Survey data for Dodderhill suggests that the supply of water was good. The farmhouses had either piped water or relied on a well, and some farms had both. Most of the farm buildings had piped water too, occasionally supplemented by a well, and four collected water from the roofs. As would be expected the water supply to fields came mainly from streams and ponds. Only three farms (widely scattered geographically) noted a seasonal shortage of water. These were Kingsland Hill Farm, which relied on streams, Piper's Hill Farm, relying on ponds, and Astwood and Walmer Farms held by Webbs. The latter would have needed a greater water supply for their horticultural trial grounds than the more usual agricultural activities.

Nine holdings reported having no electricity in either house or buildings. Four, namely The Firs, Yew Tree Farm, Hill Court, and Sunny Hill had a public supply of electricity for light in the farmhouse, while Grange Farm had a private supply. Wychbold Farm, Little Astwood, Rashwood Farm, Causeway Meadows Farm, Hobden, and Astwood had a public supply of light and power to both house and buildings, and from this point of view appear to have been the most modernised. Ford Farm had a public supply of electricity for lighting but strangely this was apparently used for neither house nor buildings! – possibly because it was faulty or had been cut off at the time of the survey.

Surveying the management of the farm

Each farm was classified in terms of the quality of its management as 'A, B or C'. In Dodderhill 13 farms were given an 'A' grade and the remainder a 'B'. No farm received a 'C' grading. Of the farms given a 'B' grade, one-third of them had a shortage of labour. In two further cases the reason given was 'lacks experience', while 'poor health' and 'short of capital' were also given as reasons. The condition of arable and pasture land was also assessed, and only one Dodderhill farm, Impney, received a 'bad' grade for its arable and a 'poor' for pasture. The use of fertilisers on both arable and pasture land was also assessed, the vast majority of farms being judged to be using fertiliser 'adequately' or 'to some extent', though pasture land was occasionally being left unfertilised.

A separate form (NA C47/SSY) also had to be completed with its 89 questions, covering 'crops and grass', 'livestock', and 'labour'.

Crops and grass

Crops grown for animal fodder and those for human consumption were detailed individually, and are summarised in Figures 88–90).

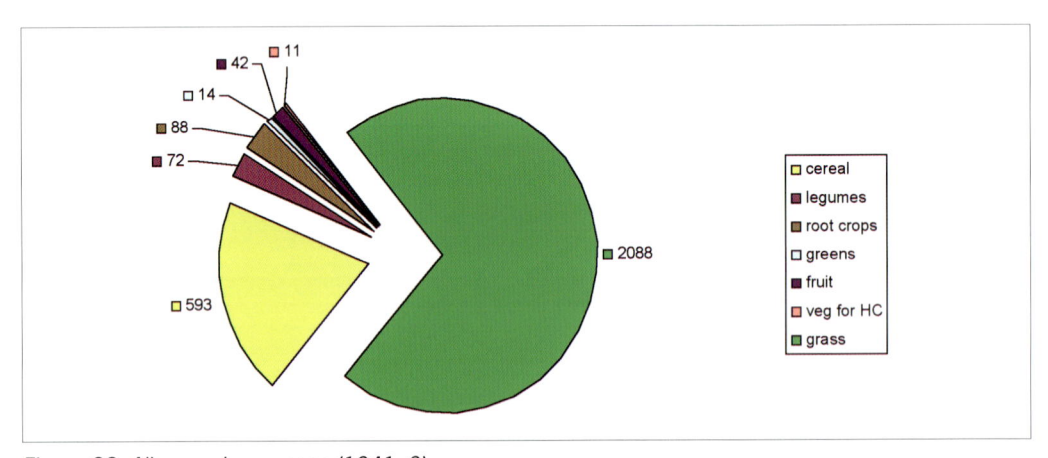

Figure 88 All crops by acreage (1941–2)

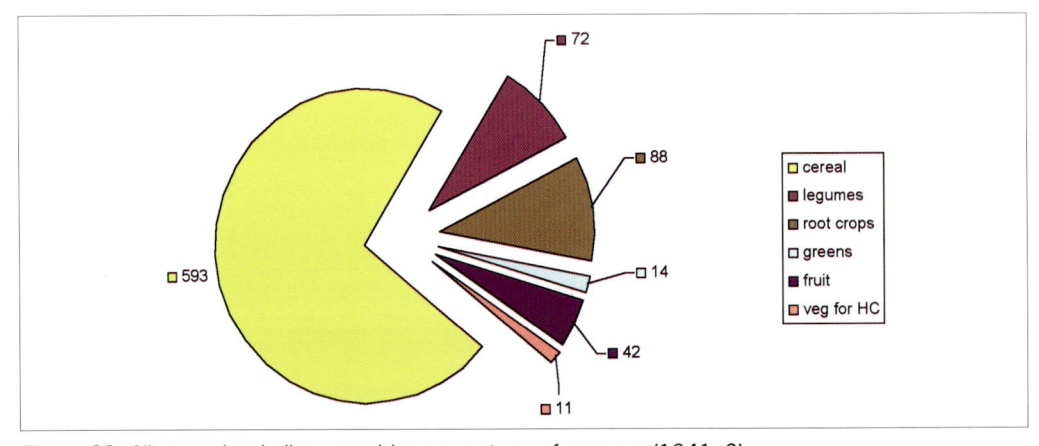

Figure 89 All crops (excluding grass) by percentage of acreage (1941–2)

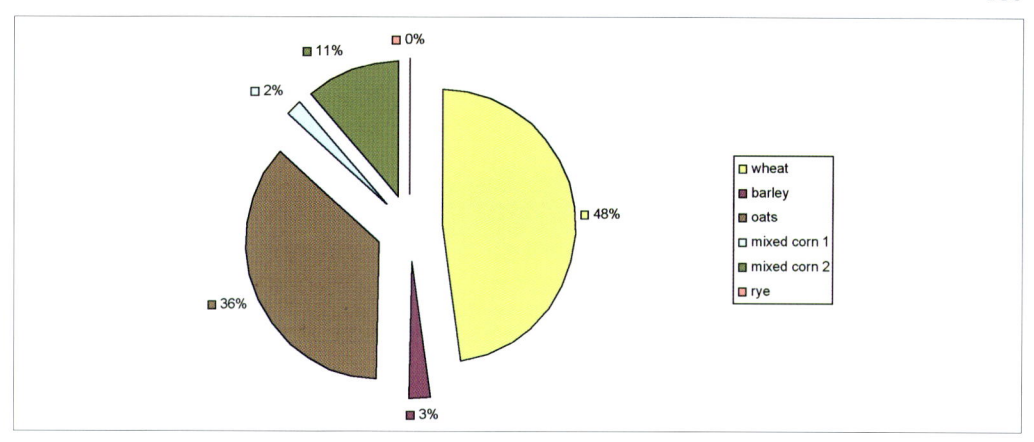

Figure 90 Type of cereals by percentage of acreage (1941–2)

Livestock

Questions 43 to 72 of the survey detailed the livestock, cattle, sheep and pigs (Figs 91–4). The 'other cattle' and 'other sheep' categories concerned animals too young to enter the food chain or breeding programmes. There was only one (rather lonely!) goat in the Dodderhill returns – at Poplars Farm.

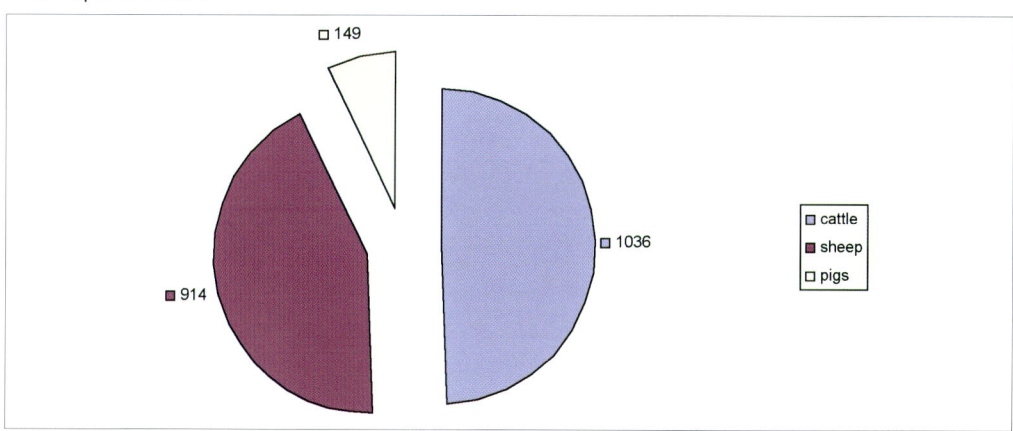

Figure 91 All livestock (1941–2)

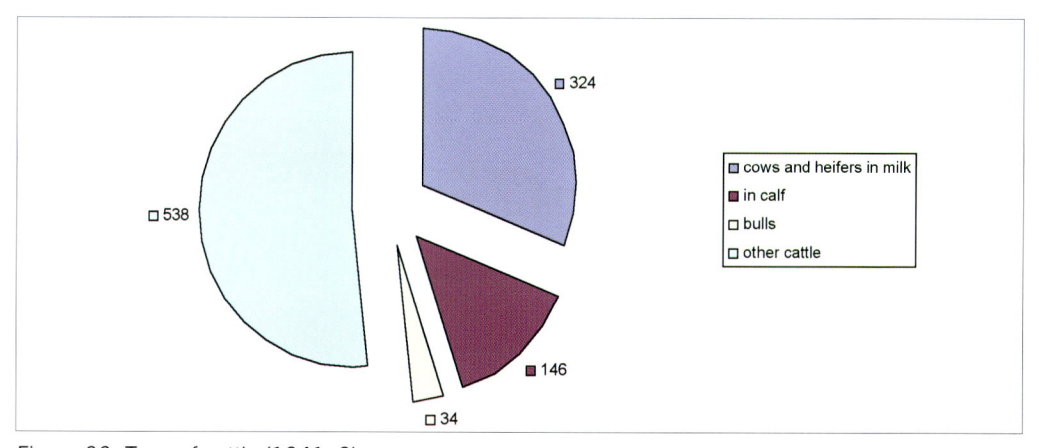

Figure 92 Type of cattle (1941–2)

186 DODDERHILL THROUGH THE AGES

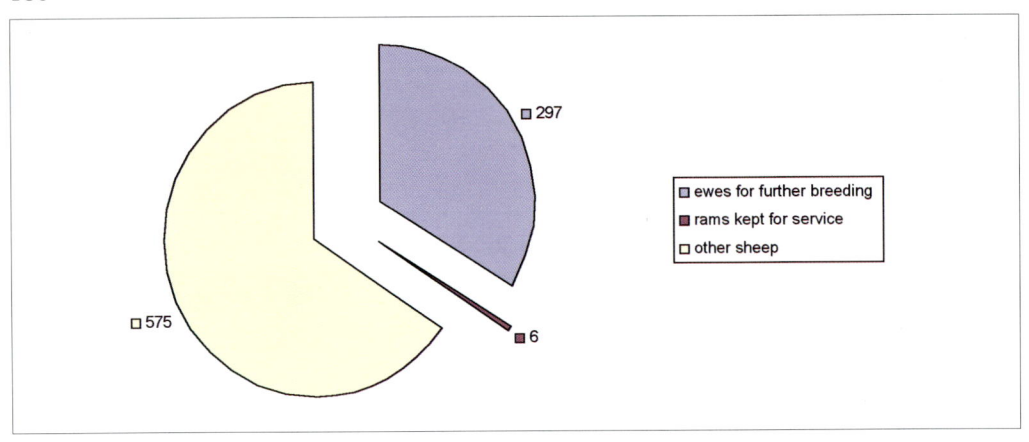

Figure 93 Type of sheep (1941–2)

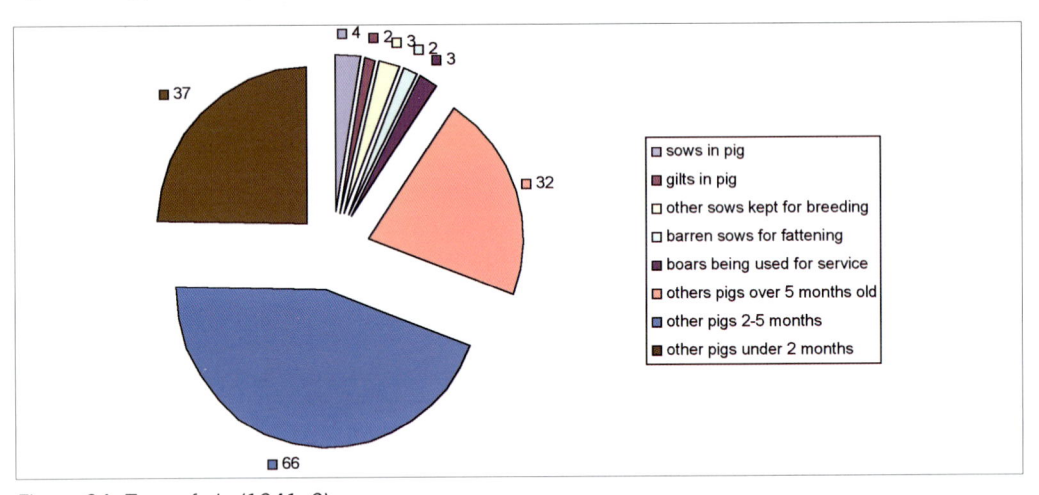

Figure 94 Type of pig (1941–2)

Poultry

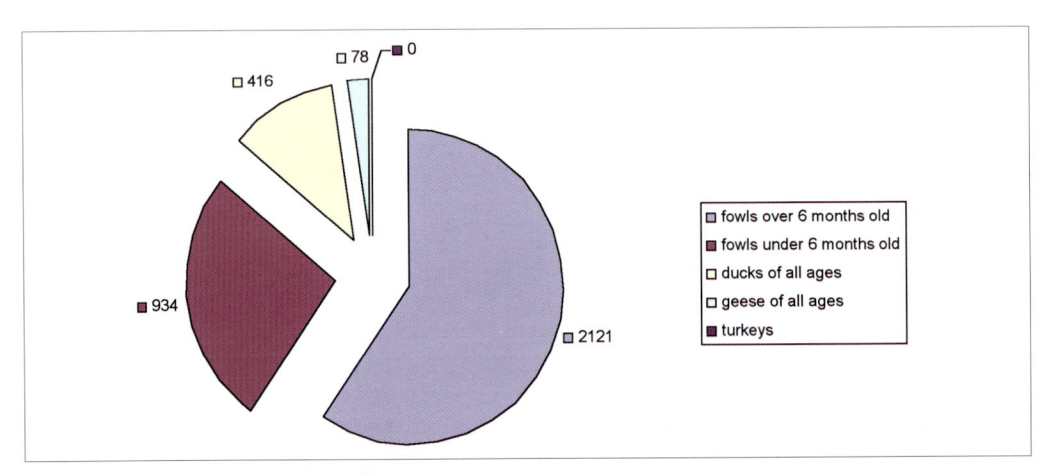

Figure 95 Type of poultry (1941–2)

Horses

Questions 81–9 of the survey enquired about horses, and many of the Dodderhill farms kept a horse or horses 'for agricultural use' – any more specific information was not recorded. In Dodderhill there were 33 mares and 23 geldings in this category. There were also six light horses, one heavy horse under one year old, and one stallion being kept for service. Fifteen horses were stated to be unbroken, and 23 further horses were entered under 'all other categories, not entered above'. Hunters and ponies possibly fell into this latter group. In total, therefore, there were 102 horses recorded in the parish of Dodderhill.

Labour

There were two groups of questions in the survey regarding labour on the farm. The first set were on the census return and the others on the supplementary form. The latter asked whether the workers returned under the former were family workers. The forms did not make clear how family members working on the farm were to be recorded, leaving individual farmers scope to interpret the question how they thought best. An assessment of a national sample found the greatest inconsistencies between answers given for labour were in the census returns (Short *et al* 2000, 135), perhaps due to a number of possible interpretations arising for this question.

Twelve Dodderhill farms recorded that they employed no regular workers. Of these only one reported that they hired one male and one female worker on a casual, seasonal part-time basis. Thirteen farmers stated that they employed just one person. The largest number of employees was at Hill Court, where eight men over the age of 21, one male under 18, and one woman were employed on a regular basis, and another woman hired seasonally. It is striking how little agricultural labour there appears to be, as in a rural parish it appears that only 65 people were employed by farmers. Perhaps farmers were hoping to get more help, but no members of The Women's Land Army ('land girls') are recorded in the Dodderhill returns. The absence of prisoners of war as farm labour is not surprising, as it was not until the beginning of 1943 that this source of manpower began to be used.

Rents

Again there was a considerable amount of confusion in the completion of the questions relating to rents. Some returns stated an annual rent, others the rent per acre (without stating the total acreage), and some gave an estimated rental value. Annual rents varied from £70 to £300 per annum, but no acreages were given so no values can be worked out proportional to the size of the farm. Two farmers paid a rent of 40s (£2) per acre, while another farmer of 247 acres estimated its rental value at £247 or £1 per acre.

Length of occupation of the holding

Nationally, this question produced a wide range of responses. There was confusion between the length of time a holding had been in a family's possession rather than that of the present family member. For Dodderhill farms the longest recorded occupation was 25 years, and the shortest 9 months. One return was nicely detailed as it stated '139 acres for 22 years, 108 acres for 7 years, 14 acres for 10 years, 43 acres for 9 years'. Unfortunately the name of the farm and its code number were both missing from the return! – though its particular pattern of tenure may allow it to be identified one day.

Horticultural survey

Only two horticultural returns detailing 'small fruit and vegetables' and 'stocks of hay and straw' (Form No C51/SSY) were found in the Dodderhill folder: Kingsland Hill (WR/181 16/9); and Rashwood (WR/181 16/24). Kingsland Hill returned as follows:

Brussels sprouts	1½ acres
Cabbages, savoys, kale and sprouting broccoli	2½ acres
Beetroot	½ acres
Onions	¼ acres
Beans, runner and French	1 acre
Peas, green for market	3¾ acres

and this farm was also storing five tons of hay. By way of contrast Rashwood recorded just one acre of peas, two tons of hay and one of straw.

Mechanisation on farms

Included in the Dodderhill folder were twelve separate sheets detailing answers to survey questions 129–48, but it is not easy to match these returns to individual farms, and the low number of sheets make this an unreliable sample. Despite care being taken with the records to keep them in their folder in their original order, there was no possible way of knowing if the returns were, in fact, in the correct sequence. Assuming that these pages do belong to the parish of Dodderhill but making no attempt to assign returns to individual holdings the following information was obtained:

a) Nine farms had at least one oil or petrol engine of between 1 and 9 horsepower (HP). Two farms each had an electric motor, one of 3 HP, and the other one of 10 HP. These were mainly used for pumping or for lifting, although electric motors could also be used for milking machines. Only one holding was recorded as having no motive power.

b) All twelve of these holdings had a tractor: all Fordsons, except for one Allis Chalmers, and a tractor described as a 'converted car'. In the national sample 21% of the holdings returned one or more tractors (Short 2000), where the Midlands sample returned the figure of 19.7%. As so many of the Dodderhill returns are missing it is impossible to assess fully the extent of farming mechanisation, but from the data available it appears to be higher than in both the national and Midlands samples.

The use of machinery on British farms increased dramatically during the war. Propelled by the shortage of labour, the use of tractors, combine harvesters and thrashing machines increased during these years, as did the use of tractor ploughs, disc harrows, drills, milking machines etc, and the cost of, and dependence on, imported oil was thought a price well paid for the extra acreage of food production (Short *et al* 2000, 135).

Overall view of Dodderhill farming in 1942 based on the national survey data

Clearly the survey was far from perfect both in design and execution, which perhaps in the circumstances was not surprising. The ambiguity of some questions and responses, and the variable qualitative judgements made by the assessors, and variable extent of answers, all make statistical analysis very difficult, but, as a snapshot of farming in 1942, it is a unique and valuable source of information for historians, despite its serious flaws (Short *et al* 2000, 234).

Several conclusions can be drawn about Dodderhill farming practices from the detailed data collected in the survey. A high proportion of land in Dodderhill in 1941–2 was given over to grass and, therefore, to dairying and/or beef farming which must have accounted for much of the farming activity in the early years of the war. Strangely the survey appears to give little emphasis to pastoral farming, and so there is, for instance, no reference to the quantity of milk being produced, and neither is there any reference to cheese making, which at this time was still farm-based or in small-scale production. It is tempting to see this as indicative of a developing government focus on arable as being more easily mechanised in an era of labour shortage, with cereals being a staple produce, and many farmers were encouraged in this period to plough up old pastures to this end. The survey may have, therefore, been directed to gathering preliminary information prior to mounting this campaign to change farming direction. One by-product of this move away from traditional farming was that the 'the Second World War resulted in the end of cheese production on the farm and it was only re-started at the end of rationing in 1953 by the MMB' (http://www.britishcheese.com).

There must have been some fruit grown in the area (eg apples, pears, plums, damsons etc), but no part of the survey recorded this in any detail. There were questions about other 'small fruit' (raspberries, strawberries, currants, cultivated blackberries, and rhubarb), but none of these were recorded in Dodderhill. Some useful rural resources were, therefore, seen as of little value, probably because of the difficulties of preserving large quantities. This may be further evidence of the survey focusing on how much land might be available with a view to converting it to cereal production. The purpose of the survey seems also to have been to ensure that no productive land was being actively wasted, and, by putting down a marker, that farms did not unknowingly deteriorate during the war due to pressures such as the lack of labour.

The national farm survey had not been without its critics at the time. By September 1941 it had become clear that the proportion of the census returns (4 June) which could be judged to be accurate was not much above 50%, and it was estimated that there were perhaps half a million errors to correct. Some farmers had refused to answer the questions, and others complained about wasting their time as a result of a mushrooming bureaucracy (the thorough coverage led to its being known as the second Domesday Book). In Dodderhill progress had been solid and the returns of all but four farms were completed by September 1941, and two more, Astwood Manor and Rashwood by the end of the year. Curiously the returns of Hill Court and Notts Farm were not completed until September of 1942, but in the end no Dodderhill farmer refused to answer any of the questions. And the records of the farm survey now stand as a tangible link with a dark time when the mobilisation of all resources was needed to defeat the enemy in an all-out war for national survival.

Education (*by* Carolyn Morris)

Increasing State involvement from 1902

The pupil experience

Prior to the 20th century the only medical input into education was the vaccination of all children against smallpox, which is first noted in the log of Overstreet school as early as October 1869. However, children's health began to interest government at the beginning of the 20th century, when it was discovered that two-thirds of the men who volunteered for army service during the Boer War were medically unfit for active service. Health screening was subsequently introduced for all school children and the first medical inspections took place at Rashwood on 31 August 1908, with routine medical examinations eventually taking place at the ages of 5, 8, and 12 years. After 1918 school clinics were set up, in order to teach parents treatments for common ailments, and the basic facts of hygiene necessary to good health. A full-time dentist was appointed for schools in Worcestershire by 1926 together with a part-time oculist. J W Willis-Bund, the first chairman of the Education Committee for Worcestershire, who served from 1903–23, said 'The school doctor and the school clinic are accomplishing a beneficent revolution in the health and physical well-being of the community, and nowhere is this being done more resolutely than in Worcestershire' (Priestley 1926). The gradual, but almost total, eradication of childhood diseases, through better health care and vaccination, took place throughout the 20th century, and has transformed children's lives, leading to an improvement in their school attendance and, therefore, education.

Conditions in the early schoolroom at Rashwood were at best uncomfortable for pupils and staff alike, with little heating, poor lighting, and no internal sanitation (Fig 96). The term 'class'

Figure 96 The schoolroom at Rashwood in 1913 (Robin Skerratt Collection)

meant a group of children linked by age or ability, and grouped into their own area of the schoolroom, and did not always signify that they enjoyed the luxury of their own teacher. In country schools it was common for all the teaching staff to work with all the children in one large room, and the infants' department was often a gallery above the main classroom, or an area separated by a curtain from the rest of the school. The head teacher surveyed all from a high desk from where he/she would teach the older children, and oversee the pupil teachers and monitors with their groups. Children were expected to sit obediently for hours on hard backless benches, often with their hands behind their backs, while they listened to the teacher reciting lists, and tracts for them to learn by rote, or copied items from the board to their slates or copybooks. Of necessity progress was uniformly slow.

Lighting at the outset was by oil lamps, and, when the oil ran out, the children had to be sent home, as it was too dark to work. New lamps were delivered in 1909 which gave 200 candle-power, and electricity was eventually installed in the early 1930s. From the log books it is apparent that heating was always a problem, and there were constant complaints that the caretaker had failed to light the fires in the winter before school commenced each morning. In February 1895 'It was so severely cold in school that some of the children in standards 1 and 2 were crying. Large fires were burning in the room, but they seemed to have no effect on the temperature, and it was very late in the day before we could use the ink, as it was frozen into a solid mass in the inkwells'! And again later that month 'It is impossible to make the room warm. In spite of all our efforts the thermometer only registered 30 degrees (F) at 11 o'clock' (ie it was still freezing).

A 'Tortoise' stove was installed in 1901 (together with pipework for a basic central heating system, which was of no use as the school had no water supply at that time, and it was not fully operational until 1942!), but this did improve matters somewhat. On 7 October it was noted that 'The new stove [was] lighted today – very greatly appreciated'. In February 1904, however, the school inspector said that 'The stove is excessively large and overheats the room. It requires a vaporizer as the dry heat which it gives off is unwholesome'. It can be wondered whether the teachers and pupils agreed with him!

In these harsh and uncomfortable conditions it is perhaps surprising that the pupils managed to retain any knowledge at all. The curriculum was still focused on the 3 Rs, and strict rules were laid down about lesson content and teaching methods. Poems were learned for recitation, and learning by rote (where the teacher makes a statement and the pupils repeat it parrot-fashion without any emphasis on comprehension) was the norm, with many hours being spent in repetition and practice. Good clear handwriting was an important part of a pupil's education in the days when all correspondence had to be handwritten, and ledgers were made up using pen and ink. Copy books were used daily, and the children were taught to write slowly and carefully with untidiness being regularly punished. The adage 'Don't blot your copy book' comes from this era, as does the saying to 'Start your day with a clean slate', the younger children doing their initial writing practice on slates.

As well as reading, writing and arithmetic, there were lessons in scripture, singing, and drawing, and also what were known as 'object lessons'. The latter were the forerunners of science and other practical subjects, and were very popular. The method used was to have a text to read, and a set of answers to learn by rote. No experiments, or deviation from the set text, were expected or allowed, and each topic was covered in one or two lessons. A different range of subjects was covered each year, with the objects (or pictures of them) kept in a special object box, and there are comprehensive lists in the log books. For example, the list of lessons to be prepared for examination in 1886 was listed as:

object	**animal**
sealing wax	eagle
bread	parrot
an egg	song-birds
a tablecloth	camel
bee hive	monkey
honey	whale
wax	shark
a bed	birds
a clock	
a candle	

natural phenomena	**moral lessons**
clouds	truthfulness
rain	honesty
wind	
snow	

the trades, as on pictures
tailor, bricklayer, painter, carpenter, baker, blacksmith

A great deal of time was also spent by the girls in learning to sew and embroider, and the results of their labours were sold off at sales of work to raise funds for the school. The boys spent part of their day undertaking drill. This was a highly regimented form of physical exercise, and was based upon the kind of exercises which would have been part of army training. It took place on the playground, and involved marching and lining up to be instructed in actions by the teacher, which were then performed in unison. It was intended to encourage 'Habits of obedience, quickness to hear and quickness to obey' (Boynton 1990, 118), and was considered by the educationalists of the day to be most important for preparing the children for their adult lives in service, as field or factory workers, or in the armed forces. It continued into the 1930s, when it fell out of favour.

Teaching had to be strict and formal in the circumstances of the open schoolroom, and a teacher was usually judged by their powers as a disciplinarian, and their ability to drive facts into the minds of their pupils. The passivity of the children was accepted as proof of the teacher's skill in dealing with them, and there were no opportunities given for the development of initiative or self-control. Any spontaneity was quashed, and enjoyment was frowned upon. Punishment was both frequent and severe. The punishment book for the period 1901–5 lists many misdemeanours which today would pass virtually unnoticed. For example, Arthur Thomas, aged 7, received two strokes of the cane for 'Contrived idleness and inattention'. Other crimes listed were: disobedience, impertinence, swearing, untruthfulness, slovenly work, copying, lateness, talking, cheating, truancy, smoking, and more interestingly, climbing doors, stealing gooseberries from the garden at Upper Ford House, and pushing Mary Diddiwell into a pond. Other punishments were lines and the dunce's cap, but caning was undoubtedly the favourite form of retribution, and often used to excess. On 8 May 1896 it was recorded that 'George Marshall was punished for disorderly conduct. He afterwards became sullen, and as his behaviour almost bordered on insubordination, I was compelled to punish him until he was thoroughly subdued'.

Perhaps if we were able to take these punishments in context and compare them to contemporary court sentences, they would not seem so extreme, for in the log dated 10 September 1897 it was recorded that the head teacher 'Had to attend the Police Court on Friday when the 3 Birmingham lads were sentenced to a month and the other 2 to 21 days hard labour for stealing (2 bottles of tea) from the girls' porch'. This was the cold tea that pupils brought with them for their lunch if they lived too far away from school to go home at lunchtimes – not really such a terrible crime in today's world, but life was much tougher in Victorian times. Corporal punishment was used widely as a deterrent to bad behaviour, possibly with some effect, since from 1886 onwards the annual inspectors' reports state consistently that 'The order is good', and the standard of education achieved seems to improve as well, since 'The teaching is satisfactory and promising in all respects'. In 1887 the report states that 'Order and teaching are both good. In reading there is some drawling, and in answering on objects and number children answer unequally. But these blemishes are slight in comparison with the general satisfactory results, and if they were removed the class would be excellent'. In any case, corporal punishment continued to be used in state schools throughout England for another 100 years, only finally being outlawed by the Education Act of 1986.

School life did have some lighter moments, with various outings and treats taking place throughout the year, and possibly the rarity of these events made them more valued. Major local and national events were often celebrated by the granting of a day's holiday. For example, on 31 August 1888 school closed 'On the occasion of the opening of the new church at Wychbold', and, when education became free for all in 1891, a day's holiday was granted to mark the occasion. On 7 July 1893 a holiday was granted to celebrate 'The royal wedding [and] by the kindness of Mr Corbett and Mr R.H.Amphlett the children from the 4 schools of Stoke Prior school board were entertained to tea at Wychbold Park'. This was the occasion of the wedding between the Duke of York and Mary of Teck. And on 21 June 1897 'A holiday [was] granted from Monday to Thursday in order to commemorate the queen's diamond jubilee'. There were also various day trips recorded: in 1906 there was a Baptist Sunday school treat at Droitwich, a fete in Brine Bath Park, and a choir outing to Llandudno, together with a picnic in the Lickey Hills paid for by 'donations and concert revenue'. As horizons widened and transport improved, these trips became increasingly more adventurous, until by 1965 the juniors were taken to the Commonwealth Institute in London, while the infants visited the Wildfowl Trust at Slimbridge. And in 1966 the first overseas excursion was made with a day trip to Holland for 35 children, parents and staff, who left home at 5am to fly from Castle Donnington (Leics) to Rotterdam, and did not return until 11pm. Quite an experience at the time, long before package holidays and cheap air travel.

School organisation

The early village school depended on four groups of individuals for its operation: teaching staff, inspectors, managers, and clergy. The teaching pyramid usually consisted of the headmaster at the helm, often with his wife by his side, as certified teachers, then lower down the scale came the assistant teachers, usually women, and usually uncertified. These assistants were unqualified because they had not completed a course at a recognised training college, but they were still allowed to teach, and were often very experienced due to having spent years previously as monitors and pupil teachers. They received lower salaries than the qualified staff and were, therefore, in demand by managers trying to economise on their school budgets. There was an almost incessant turnover of these junior staff, who were very poorly paid and worked long hours in the schoolroom.

Monitors were older children attempting to teach the younger ones what they had themselves learned, and their jobs included supporting the other teachers in the classroom, preparing materials, and giving out books and equipment when it was needed. They would also receive full-time education. Monitors were paid a very small amount for their work, but this was increased if they agreed to stay for 5 years as an apprentice. Pupil teachers were older, brighter children attempting to rise through the ranks before entering college to become fully qualified teachers. These latter continued to receive part-time tuition themselves (7½ hours each week) from the teaching staff within the school, generally at the end of the school day. In the early days of universal education there was an acute shortage of qualified teaching staff, and the use of monitors and pupil teachers was the best that could be expected until the numbers of fully trained and proficient teachers could be built up over the years. Teacher training colleges at Cheltenham and Saltley (in Birmingham) were amongst the earliest to be built by the Church of England in the 1840s, and these quickly became established as models of excellence.

Lack of any national, or even locally agreed pay scales meant that each school set the salary of each teacher on appointment, and the absence of any effective teacher organisations meant that many teachers (especially young and inexperienced females) were at the mercy of the appointing managers. A 'Schedule of Salaries and Allowances' to be paid to female teachers employed in 1886, recorded in the Rashwood log, shows the following salary scales: monitors (females) £5 4s (first year), £6 10s (second year), £8 (third year); certificated head mistress in schools having an average attendance of 50–75 (£40 pa), 75–100 (£45 pa), 100–125 (£50 pa), 125–150 (£55 pa), and 150–175 (£60 pa).

There was also a bonus of £6 to be paid to each head teacher obtaining a 'Good Merit Grant', and a bonus of £15 for the 'Excellent Merit Grant'; these were big incentives as the payments represented a large proportion of the salary. On the downside of this system, it was recorded by the headmaster in February 1895 that 'The Chairman greatly sympathised with me inasmuch as only the principal grant of 12/6 had been awarded thus decreasing my salary by over £7'.

Women teachers were automatically awarded less pay than their male counterparts, and were almost always in the lower ranks of their profession. Not until the Burnham Scale was adopted in 1926 did teachers' pay become fixed, the same salaries being paid throughout all local education authorities.

School managers remained largely anonymous in the log books, but they were an important part of the organisation of the early schools because they held the purse strings. The managing body usually consisted largely of local worthies, who were appointed due to their wealth and social position within the community, and this state of affairs persisted into the late 20th century. Knowledge of education was not a qualification, and while the best of them took an active and kindly interest, the worst were said to 'Meddle shamelessly in matters about which they knew little' (Boynton 1990, 108), but the same could be said of many politicians. Managers were in charge of appointing staff and determining pay, and were supposed to oversee the curriculum and training of the indentured pupil teachers. Normally the head teacher was not a school manager, and was only invited to their meetings as a courtesy, and the chairman of the managers was usually the local clergyman. The days of school governors being elected by parent ballot, or appointed by council co-option, were far in the future.

Following the Education Act of 1902, which abolished the school boards and gave responsibility for educational provision to the county councils, huge changes were gradually forthcoming in the power structure within the elementary schools. A quote from J W Willis-Bund neatly sums this up (Priestley 1926):

> I had the honour of being the first chairman of the Worcestershire Education Committee and remained so for a considerable period. (1903–1923) There have been times … when I felt thankful not only that I remained a Christian, but that I was not sent to an asylum either for lunatics or idiots. The difficulties in getting business done were great, so divergent were the views that the members of the committee took upon the various questions that arose, each member, including myself, showed his ignorance of the task before him by his conviction that he, and he alone, knew all about education, and what line of policy should be adopted. The chairmen of the various school boards considered that they were in sole possession of the necessary knowledge, and rather regarded the teachers as their hired servants … The clergy considered that the schools were their own property, and that they could do as they pleased with them, both as to teaching the children and controlling the teachers, as well as dictating what should be taught, while the teachers considered themselves in the position in which the English Church consider the sovereign as regards the State, that they were in these schools, and in all other places in matters connected with the schools 'over all persons and in all causes, ecclesiastical as well as civil, supreme'.

What a battle it must have been! But eventually the administration of the local education authorities took over the reins from the Church of England authorities, and huge progress was made in all fields of education. From a small voluntary service, as it was before the Act of 1870, education became a vast nationalised affair. The work of the local education authority (LEA), and their control by government departments has become a matter of the first magnitude in both local and national politics. Throughout the 20th century it became increasingly clear that education was of vital importance both to the individual and to the nation, and legislation necessarily reflected this conviction.

Butler Education Act of 1944 and beyond

The Butler Education Act was one of the most far-reaching and revolutionary Acts of the 20th century. It replaced all previous legislation relating to education, and established a nationwide system of free compulsory education for all children aged between 5 and 15, with provision for raising the leaving age to 16, as soon as was practicable. There were also proposals made to extend education to the under 5s and those past school-leaving age, and local education authorities were to set local policies and allocate resources, while head teachers and school governors were to set individual school policies and allocate resources within their own schools. There was to be set up a tri-partite system for children after the age of 11, when all pupils would move into a secondary school (either grammar, secondary modern, or technical), and the 11+ examination was introduced in order to enable children to be classified, so that they could be matched to type of school.

Elementary schools began to consider preparation of pupils for the 11+ as their main function, and the schools' reputations depended mainly on their success rates at this examination. It led to class divisions within schools, where streaming was introduced to enable the most able children to be taught in separate groups, and to social divisions between the grammar schools, which were considered to be middle-class institutions, and the rest, where children were often seen as having failed in some way. Whatever the arguments were for and against the 11+, it is true that the future educational life of a child was largely decided at the age of 11, as the system intended. Pupils who did not sit, or who failed the 11+ examination, could only gain access to a secondary modern school (generally considered to be second rate, though mainly because the LEAs did not get sufficient funding to develop these as originally intended ie to further more practical skills), and later perhaps to a technical school. There have never been any state-controlled secondary schools in Dodderhill, and children from here have always had to travel to either Droitwich or Bromsgrove for the later stages of their education.

Another important change, which the 1944 Act introduced, was the move towards child-centred education. It stated that 'It shall be the duty of the Local Education Authority for every area, so far as their powers extend, to continue towards the spiritual, mental and physical developments of the community' (1944 Education Act Part II, 7). The view was shared by all social classes and political parties that there was a need for a broadly based curriculum, which would promote the spiritual, moral, cultural, mental, and physical development of pupils, both at school and within the community. This philosophy resulted in a change in teaching methods, as it heralded the end of class instruction by rote, and the introduction of individual tuition, oral and team study, and individual practical application. Class sizes were reduced, and one class in one room with one teacher became the norm.

Figure 97 A class at Rashwood in 1952 (Robin Skerratt Collection)

At Rashwood School a new head teacher was appointed on 1 July 1946, J R Pointer, who was to remain at the helm until the school closed in 1971. In line with the new thinking on education, which the 1944 Act had outlined, he initiated many advancements, including the establishment of a school garden, which was developed to an extremely high standard of horticulture. This became a very great attraction for other schools in the area to visit. The school library was enhanced, school dinners were introduced, and a school uniform was approved at a managers' meeting on 13 November 1961. This was to consist of a navy blue blazer and a scarlet tie, together with grey shorts and a scarlet cap for the boys, or together with a skirt/pinafore and a scarlet beret for the girls. No doubt there are plenty of local residents who remember this very well!

In 1955 the schools in this area were reorganised, and senior children from Rashwood were transferred to secondary schools in Droitwich. Rashwood was divided into smaller units so that the average class size would be less than 30, and it was re-classified as a junior school. In 1957 an accommodation figure of 190 was agreed and plans began for an extension to the school buildings in order to provide two extra classrooms and a toilet block, though this new block was not available until 1960.

In 1964 it was reported that 'A new departure [was] made in asking groups of parents to attend school for discussions on educational problems eg the 11+ selection tests and the modern way of teaching mathematics. Held in the evenings these meetings have been very well attended'. Such an event is commonplace today, but would have been unheard of in the early days of education. The setting up of parent teacher associations and parents' evenings enabled parents to be truly involved in the education of their children for the very first time.

It seems from the log books that the brand-new school buildings at Rashwood (Fig 98) were never satisfactory, with cracks appearing in the plasterwork as early as March 1962. By 1966 they were 'Badly in need of re-decoration and repair', and in 1967 only one of the new classrooms was being used 'With Elsan toilets put in the old kitchen area' as 'School repairs

Figure 98 Rashwood School in 1965 showing the new extension (Robin Skerratt Collection)

still not carried out'. In that same year the managers passed a resolution 'That as the present school is situated in an isolated and very dangerous position on trunk road A38, the Worcestershire Education Committee be requested to seriously consider the reservation of a site for a new school on land recently acquired in Wychbold by the Droitwich Rural District Council. There has been considerable development of the housing estate in the village and some further 200 or more houses are planned. It is considered therefore that the time is now opportune to secure a site for a new school'. The site of Rashwood School, which had been so suitable at the centre of its catchment in 1885, had now become isolated by the construction of the M5 motorway which split the village asunder in the 1960s.

The extension was eventually declared to be unsafe (only 11 years after its erection), and Rashwood School was closed on Wednesday 16 July 1971. It was demolished in 1986, and today a Little Chef restaurant and Travelodge hotel stand on the site. Mr Pointer and his staff and pupils were then temporarily accommodated at St Peter's School in Droitwich, until the new school at Wychbold was ready for occupation in 1972.

Education is now regarded as a partnership between the parents, teachers, students and the community, and no-one today would dispute its importance. Recent legislation has given parents the right to choose a school for their child, and to make decisions about how their local schools are run, while governing bodies have become more inclusive, and the local education authorities have lost much of their power.

Prior to 1914 most rural children could only hope to follow in the footsteps of their parents when they left school – the boys would become farm labourers, toiling on the land for little pay, living in tied cottages with no security of tenure and at the mercy of both their employer and their continuing good health. The best that most girls could hope for before marriage was to enter service as a housemaid, with food and accommodation provided in return for one day off a month and a pittance of £10 per annum as reward for their labours. Very few children born around 1900 would have been able to benefit from higher education, and the chance to progress from being a pupil teacher to a fully qualified schoolteacher by gaining a Queen's Scholarship place at a teacher training college was probably the first opportunity available to young people from a rural background. Those born around the year 2000 will have many opportunities to carry on with their training past the age of 16, and many will go on to college or university. They will be able to determine their own way of life and their own future, and so the opportunity for education has transformed young people's expectations for the better.

Where the one school once provided education for all the local children, students are now able to travel far and wide in search of the best available education, and any school community may have pupils from many different parishes. School visits, which once only went as far afield as Droitwich, have been replaced by twinning and exchange visits to far-flung destinations. Wooden desks with fixed bench seats, slates and slate pencils, dipping pens and inkwells, have been replaced by individual chairs and tables, computers and interactive white boards. There are well-stocked libraries and science laboratories, televisions, properly functioning lighting and heating, indoor toilets and proper facilities for physical exercise and games. This all adds up to a much greater investment in the future generation, and should provide greater scope for fulfilment of both personal and community aspirations, in accordance with the hopes enshrined in the 1944 Act. The history of education in Dodderhill has, therefore, closely reflected the political and economic changes of the times, and in most ways can be considered to be typical of many an English rural parish, and education itself can be seen to have been a powerful force shaping society for the better.

Primary sources used

Census returns 1841–1911
Infants log book 1885–1912 – WRO BA 1618/14
Log books Rashwood School 1894–1906 – WRO BA 1618/15
Admissions registers Rashwood School 1889–1935 – WRO BA 1618/20
Punishment book Rashwood School 1901–53 – WRO BA 6331/2
Log books/photos 1906–72 – WRO BA 6331/1
Correspondence about building of Wychbold School 1949–72 – WRO BA 12710(viii)

Conclusions (*by* Derek Hurst)

In many ways, on the face of it, the archaeology of Dodderhill parish is typical of that of much of Worcestershire, for instance in its scatters of worked flint and the rather ubiquitous Roman pottery sherds. But, on closer scrutiny, as a result of a study like the one presented here, it can also be seen to be distinctive, for instance in that the flint scatters include a preponderance of Mesolithic material, suggesting that the terrain of central/north Worcestershire perhaps especially favoured human activity at that time.

Aside from the archaeology, the history of Dodderhill might also be considered to be little different from that of other rural parishes in the area, but, again, it is possible to point to features of history that mark Dodderhill out as distinctive, and this especially relates to the special significance of Wychbold. The nearby presence of Droitwich has also clearly impacted on its history, not least in the planting of the chief focus of institutions such as the Church firmly within the orbit of the town and salt production, and so causing at least a portion of the fledgling town (and including the main brine well) to fall under its ecclesiastical mantle. However, unlike much of the land surrounding Droitwich and generally elsewhere in Worcestershire, Wychbold was not under the control of the Church as lord of the manor.

But there were also other factors which individually shaped the character of Dodderhill's past, which are not as obvious since they consist of purely ordinary features, easily taken for granted. One is that it was well served by the best roads of the age, originally, of course, the Roman road that carved its way straight through the middle of the area. Such roads were essential to the Roman subjugation of Britain but they also gave back benefits in peaceful times when the same roads brought prosperity to the salt trade and, therefore, generally improved the economy of the area by facilitating a constant stream of goods and travellers. This endowment of Wychbold has continued in the modern day with the building of the M5 motorway, so that the transport theme still features prominently in the life of the place.

Returning to the past, most of the Droitwich brine wells were on the north bank of the River Salwarpe, the largest of all, Upwich, being within Wychbold (later Dodderhill) territory. This ensured that, in the days when the salt industry was taking shape, it became the location of the principal base for this enterprise, namely the royal residence which is still so elusive. Then in later times both the manor and the church became the subjects of disputes, as both lay and spiritual magnates sought to control these resources. Gradually the significance of these holdings was eroded by being granted away generally to more distant locations, so that the unusual and highly valuable local resource of salt eventually brought only limited wealth to this part of Worcestershire.

Though the principal holdings might have been lost the presence of a thriving industrial town, with its appetites and thirsts whetted by physical work, ensured that some benefit remained for others to reap locally, thereby enhancing the local rural economy. In ages when animals did most of the heavy haulage the production of grain and its milling would also have been boosted in this area due to the need to move salt long distances. The economy of Dodderhill, therefore, with its five mills in 1086, must have long been connected with that of Droitwich as part of the fertile hinterland supplying its earthly necessities. The parish was, therefore, much shaped by its links with Droitwich.

Meanwhile the majority of locals tended to live ordinary lives, mainly by tending the land. However, even here the connected nature of Wychbold, and the ease with which new ideas would have reached the area along the main road, may have had a subtle influence by encouraging the early take-up of new trends, such as enclosure of land for private farming which was contrary to the traditional communal practice. Then, with the exploiting of these new pastures, there were signs of new impetus in farming with a specialisation in dairying, from which some local families particularly prospered, especially with the advantages of the ready markets for more perishable goods at Droitwich and, later on, Bromsgrove. The fine houses built in the 16th–17th centuries in Dodderhill parish seem to be a very visible statement of new success in farming, and so the culmination of this refocusing of farming effort.

Even though the modern world marches on, many places and features of the medieval era can still be seen to be located in our 21st century landscape revealing the still existing historic framework within which we are living. And, despite the research, in some cases an air of mystery lingers on, such as why was a bridge named 'Leather Bridge', and, of course, just where is that mid Saxon royal residence to be found?

From about the Second World War up to the modern day the lives of many of the more recent inhabitants of Wychbold have been commemorated and wonderfully preserved for posterity by Robin Skerratt (2001) in his *Memories of Wychbold before the motorway*, which is a model study of a working community in a changing world, all (importantly) viewed from within and so with personal and local knowledge. If such projects had been possible for every century in the past, we would probably never have finished our research and so perhaps we should be thankful that we were only left a few archaeological finds and snippets of historical documents with which to tell this larger story of Wychbold and Dodderhill through the ages. Although, in the case of historical documents there are unlikely to be any new ones brought to light, in the case of archaeology there is every chance that more finds will come to light in future, and these could well make a great contribution to our better understanding of the past. Perhaps paradoxically, therefore, we should remain optimistic that this is not the whole story and that there is more to be unearthed in future.

Figure 99 Members of the Dodderhill Parish Survey Project with Mick Aston at the Making Time Team *lecture event at Avoncroft Museum*

Bibliography

Abbreviated references

Cal LPFD: *Calendar of Letters and Papers Foreign and Domestic*
CPR: *Calendar of Patent Rolls*
CSSPD: *Calendar of State Papers Domestic*
DBR: *De Banco Rolls*
FF: *Feet of Fines*, Worcestershire
Hampton Pap(ers): available at WRO and previously at BCA
HE: Bede, *Historia ecclesiastica*, ed by J McClure and R Collins, 1994 (reissued 1999). Oxford: Oxford Univ Press
IPM: *Calendar of inquisitions post mortem*. London: HMSO
QS: *The Quarter Sessions Rolls pt II: kalendar of the sessions rolls, 1591–1643*, ed by J W Willis-Bund, 1900. Worcester County Records
SLB: *The Stoneleigh leger book*, ed by R H Hilton, 1960, Dug Soc
Talbot Pap(ers): *Calendar of Talbot papers*, ed by E S Scroggs. Typescript held by British Library
Valor: *Valor Ecclesiasticus Temp Hen VIII*, vol 3, 1817

Digital primary sources

Anglo-Saxon charters: www.aschart.kcl.ac.uk, accessed 22 August 2010
Dodderhill tithe map: www.worcestershiremaps.org.uk
Prosopography of Anglo-Saxon England: www.pase.ac.uk, accessed 21 August 2010
Sawyer: www.esawyer.org.uk, accessed 22 August 2010

Other sources

Alcock, N W, 2006 The hearth tax in Warwickshire, in P S Barnwell and M Airs, *Houses and the hearth tax: the late Stuart house and society*, CBA Res Rep **150**, 106–19
Amphlett, J (ed), 1895–9 *A survey of Worcestershire by T Habington*, Worcestershire Hist Soc (2 vols)
Amphlett, J (ed), 1901 *Lay subsidy roll, AD 1603*, Worcestershire Hist Soc
Anon 1910, *Notes and queries for Bromsgrove and the district of central Worcestershire*, **II**
Anon, 1921 *Reports by the Joint War Committee and the Joint War Finance Committee of the British Red Cross Society and The Order of St John of Jerusalem in England on voluntary aid rendered to the sick and wounded at home and abroad and to British prisoners of war, 1914–1919, with appendices*. London: HMSO
Austin, D, 2002 The archaeology of the Domesday vill, in A Williams (ed), *The Digital Domesday*. Editions Alecto (Domesday) Ltd

Barber, A, and Watts, M, 2008 Excavations at Saxon's Lode Farm, Ripple, 2001–2: Iron Age, Romano-British and Anglo-Saxon rural settlement in the Severn valley, *Trans Worcestershire Archaeol Soc 3 ser*, **21**, 1–90

Barfield, L, 2006 Bays Meadow villa, Droitwich: excavations 1967–77, in Hurst, 78–242

Barker, P A, and Cubberley, A L, 1974 Two burials under the refectory of Worcester Cathedral, *Med Archaeol*, **17**, 146–50

Bassett, S, 1989 Churches in Worcester before and after the conversion of the Anglo-Saxons, *Antiq J*, **69**, 225–56

Bassett, S, 1992 Church and diocese in the West Midlands: the transition from British to Anglo-Saxon control, in J Blair and R Sharpe (eds), *Pastoral care before the parish*, 13–40

Bassett, S, 2008a Sitting above the salt: the origins of the borough of Droitwich, in O Padel and D Parsons (eds), *A commodity of good names. Essays in honour of Margaret Gelling*, 3–27. Shaun Tyas

Bassett, S, 2008b The medieval boundary of the Borough of Droitwich and its origins, *Trans Worcestershire Archaeol Soc 3 ser*, **21**, 219–42

Bassett, S, 2010 The earliest map of Droitwich, *Trans Worcestershire Archaeol Soc 3 ser*, **22**, 167–73

Benson, A C, 1894 *Genealogy of the family of Benson of Banger House and Northwoods, in the parish of Ripon and Chapelry of Pateley Bridge*

Bewdley Historical Research Group, 1999 *Bewdley in its golden age. Vol 2: trades and industries, 1660–1760*

Birrell, J, 2006 Procuring, preparing, and serving venison in late medieval England, in C M Woolgar, D Serjeantson, and T Waldron (eds), *Food in medieval England: diet and nutrition*, 176–88. Oxford: Oxford Univ Press

Blair, J, 2005 *The church in Anglo-Saxon society*. Oxford: Oxford Univ Press

Blewitt, L, 2002 Results of fieldwalking at Crutch Farm, *Dodderhill Parish History Notes* **1**, 14

Blewitt, L, 2006 From manor to mansion – the 19th century ownership of Impney: appendix 2, *Dodderhill History Notes* **2**, 51–4

Blewitt, L, and Field, B, 1994 *Droitwich: a pictorial history*. Chichester: Phillimore

Bond, C J, and Babb, L, 1971 Crutch Lane, Droitwich (SO 90346392), *Worcestershire Archaeology Newsletter*, **7**, 7

Boynton, J, 1990 *Three times table: the diary of an English village school 1863–1948*. Upton on Severn: The Self Publishing Assn Ltd

Bradley, P J, 1989 *Bays Meadow, Droitwich: the flint*, unpublished MA dissertation, Leicester Univ

Bridges, T, 2000 *Churches of Worcestershire*. Almeley: Logaston Press

Bromhead, J, 1996 *Droitwich Golf Club, 1897–1997*. Droitwich: Grant Books

Brooks, A, and Pevsner, N, 2007 *The buildings of England: Worcestershire*. New Haven and London: Yale Univ Press

Brown, A G, 1984 The Flandrian vegetational history of Hartlebury Common, Worcestershire, *Proc Birmingham Natur Hist Phil Soc*, **25**(2), 89–98

Buchanan, K M, 1944 *The land of Britain: the report of the land utilisation survey of Britain; part 68 Worcestershire*. London

Burgess, C, 1974 The bronze age, in C Renfrew (ed), *British prehistory: a new outline*. London: Duckworth

Butler, L, 1986 Church dedications and the cults of Anglo-Saxon saints in England, in L A S Butler and R K Morris (eds) *The Anglo-Saxon Church*, CBA Res Rep **60**, 44–50

Byard-Jones, J, 2007 *A history of Wollaston schools 1859–1984*. Stourbridge: History of Wollaston Group

Carpenter, J, 1995 *Wartime Worcestershire*. Studley: Brewin Books

Chaddesley Corbett Local History Group, 1988 *17th century Chaddesley Corbett wills and inventories*, Chaddesley Corbett Local History Group

Coates, R, 2007 Invisible Britons: linguistics, in N Higham (ed), *Britons in Anglo-Saxon England*, 172–91. Woodbridge: Boydell Press

Cook, M, Hurst, D, and Pearson, E, 1998 *Evaluation of land at St Mary's Church, Hanbury*, Worcestershire County Council Archaeological Service rep **678**

Cool, H, 2006 Bays Meadow villa, Droitwich excavations 1967–77: personal ornaments, in Hurst, 191–6

Coope, G R, Shotton, F W, and Strachan, I, 1961 A late Pleistocene fauna and flora from Upton Warren, Worcestershire, *Phil Trans B*, **244**, 379–421

Copeland, G W, 1960 Devonshire church houses, *Devonshire Archaeol Trans*, **92**, 116–41

Cudlip, D, 2009 *Wychbold Hall, Stoke Lane, Wychbold, Worcestershire: archaeological evaluation*, Cotswold Archaeology rep **09038**

Demidowicz, G, and Price, S, 2009 *King's Norton, a history*. Chichester: Phillimore

Dinn, J, and Hemingway, J A, 1992 Archaeology on the Blackstone to Astley aqueduct, *Trans Worcestershire Archaeol Soc 3 ser*, **13**, 105–119

Driver, E, 1909 *Cheshire: its cheesemakers, their homes, landlords and supporters*. Bradford: Derwent

Dyer, C, 1980 *Lords and peasants in a changing society. The estates of the bishopric of Worcester, 680–1540*. Cambridge: Cambridge Univ Press

Dyer, C, 1989 *Standards of living in the later Middle Ages: social change in England c 1200–1520*. Cambridge: Cambridge Univ Press

Dyer, C, 1991 *Hanbury: settlement and society in a woodland landscape*, Department of English Local History Occas Pap 4th ser **4**. Leicester: Leicester Univ Press

Dyer, C, 2000 *Bromsgrove: a small town in Worcestershire in the Middle Ages*, Worcestershire Hist Soc Occas pub **7**

Dyer, C, 2002 *Making a living in the Middle Ages: the people of Britain 850–1520*. Yale Univ Press

Edlin, H L, 1966 *Trees, woods and Man*, 2 ed. London: Collins

Eld, F J (ed), 1895 *Lay subsidy roll for the County of Worcester 1 Edward I[II]*, Worcestershire Hist Soc

English Heritage, 1989 *Monuments Protection Programme: monument class descriptions*. Available at www.eng-h.gov.uk/mpp/mcd/mcdtop1.htm, accessed 25 June 2011

Evison, V I, and Hill, P, 1996 *Two Anglo-Saxon cemeteries at Beckford, Hereford and Worcester*, CBA Res Rep **103**

Fagan, B, 2000 *The Little Ice Age*. New York: Basic Books

Faraday, M A, 2003 *Worcestershire taxes in the 1520s: the military survey and forced loans of 1522–3 and the lay subsidy of 1524–7*, Worcestershire Hist Soc new ser, **19**

Farwell, D, and Barnes, I, 1994 The ESSO Birmingham Airport link: archaeological investigations at Astwood, Dodderhill, *Trans Worcestershire Archaeol Soc 3 ser*, **14**, 173–80

Fegan, E S (ed), 1914 *Journal of Prior William More*. Worcestershire Hist Soc

Finberg, H P R, 1972 *The early charters of the West Midlands*, 2 edn

Gaut, R C, 1939 *A history of Worcestershire agriculture and rural evolution*. Worcester

Gelling, M, 1978 *Signposts to the past*. London: J M Dent & Sons

Gelling, M, 1979 *The early charters of the Thames valley.* Liverpool: Liverpool Univ Press
Gelling, M, and Cole, A, 2000 *The landscape of place-names.* Stamford: Shaun Tyas
Greig, J, 2005 Pollen and radiocarbon dating, in P Williams, D Hurst, E Pearson, and J Greig, *Archaeological watching brief and building recording at Impney Farm, Dodderhill, Worcestershire,* Worcestershire Historic Environment & Archaeology Service rep **991**, 7–12. Available at www.worcestershire.gov.uk/archaeology/library
Griffin, S, Hurst, D, Jones, L C, and Pearson, E, 1999 *Evaluation at Impney Farm, Dodderhill, Worcestershire,* Worcestershire County Council Archaeological Service rep **786**. Available at www.worcestershire.gov.uk/archaeology/library
Griffith, G, 1852 *The free schools of Worcestershire and their fulfilment.* London: Chas Gilpin
Grundy, M, 1994 *Memory Lane,* **5**. Worcester Evening News
GSB, 2009 *Land between Crutch Lane and Ford Lane (WSM 41757), Dodderhill, near Droitwich,* Geophysical Survey Report **2009/55**. GSB Prospection Ltd

Haines, R M, 1965 *The administration of the Diocese of Worcester in the first half of the fourteenth century.* London: SPCK
Hamilton, S G (ed), 1912 *Collectanea.* Worcestershire Hist Soc
Hart, J, 1633 *Klinike or diet of the diseased* (3 vols)
Hilton, R, 1966 *A medieval society: the West Midlands at the end of the thirteenth century,* new ed. Cambridge: Cambridge Univ Press
Hilton, R H, 1985 Medieval market towns, *Past and Present,* **109**, 3–23
Holyoake, A V, 1977 *Dear little Droitwich.* Bromsgrove: Market Place Press
Hooke, D, 1981 The Droitwich salt industry: an examination of the West Midland charter evidence, in J Campbell, D Brown and S Hawkes (eds), *Anglo-Saxon Studies in Archaeology and History* **2**, BAR Brit Ser **92**, 123–69. Oxford: British Archaeological Reports
Hooke, D, 1985a *The Anglo-Saxon landscape. The kingdom of the Hwicce* (reprinted 2009). Manchester: Manchester Univ Press
Hooke, D, 1985b Village development in the West Midlands, in D Hooke (ed), *Medieval villages, a review of current work,* Oxford Univ Comm Archaeol Monogr **5**, 125–54. Oxford
Hooke, D, 1990 *Worcestershire Anglo-Saxon charter-bounds.* Woodbridge: Boydell Press
Hooke, D, 1998a *The landscape of Anglo-Saxon England.* London: Leicester Univ Press
Hooke, D, 1998b Medieval forests and parks in southern and central England, in C Watkins (ed), *European woods and forests, studies in cultural history,* 19–32. New York: CAB International
Hooke, D, 2008a Early medieval woodland and the place-name term *leah,* in O J Padel and D N Parsons (eds), *A commodity of good names. Essays in honour of Margaret Gelling,* 365–76. Donington: Shaun Tyas
Hooke, D, 2008b Recent views on the Worcestershire landscape, *Trans Worcestershire Archaeol Soc 3 ser,* **21**, 91–106
Hooke, D, 2010. *Trees in Anglo-Saxon England: literature, lore and landscape.* Woodbridge: Boydell Press
Hooke, D, forthcoming Place-name hierarchies and interpretations in parts of Mercia, in R Jones and S Semple, *Sense of place in Anglo-Saxon England.* Shaun Tyas
Houghton, F T S, 1929–30 Salt-ways, *Birmingham Archaeol Soc Trans and Proceedings,* **LIV**, 1–17
Hughes, J, 2006 Hanbury Street, Droitwich; excavations 1980–82, in Hurst, 46–77
Hughes, J, and Hunt, A, 1992 Friar Street: the excavation, in S G Woodiwiss (ed), *Iron Age and Roman salt production and the medieval town of Droitwich,* CBA Res Rep **81**, 115–31

Hurst, J D (ed), 1997a *A multi-period salt production site at Droitwich: excavations at Upwich*, CBA Res Rep **107**. York: Council for British Archaeology

Hurst, J D, 1997b Wooden artefacts, in Hurst 1997a, 106–11

Hurst, J D, 1998 *Evaluation of land off Church Lane, Wychbold, Worcestershire*, Worcestershire County Council Archaeological Service rep **686**

Hurst, J D, 2004, Fuel supply and the medieval salt industry in Droitwich, *Trans Worcestershire Archaeol Soc 3 ser*, **19**, 111–32

Hurst, D, 2005 *Sheep in the Cotswolds: the medieval wool trade*. Stroud: Tempus

Hurst, J D (ed), 2006 *Roman Droitwich: Dodderhill fort, Bays Meadow villa, and roadside settlement*, CBA Res Rep **146**. York: Council for British Archaeology

Hurst, D, 2010a *Trial pits at Astwood New House field (WSM 39898; SO 93296506), Hanbury*, unpublished report

Hurst, D, 2010b *Fieldwalking (WSM 27163, 34766) and geophysical survey (WSM 27164, 33537) to east of Ford Cottages (SO 90456535), Dodderhill*, unpublished report

Hurst, D, 2010c *Fieldwalking and geophysical survey in field at junction of Crutch Lane and Ford Lane (WSM 38360; SO 913647), Dodderhill*, unpublished report

Hurst, D, 2010d *Fieldwalk on field to east of Crutch Lane (WSM 38361), Dodderhill*, unpublished report

Hurst, D, 2010e *Fieldwalk on field adjacent A38 (WSM 42423; SO 913647) near Rashwood Farm, Dodderhill*, unpublished report

Hurst, D, 2010f *Fieldwalk at Rashwood (WSM 42424; SO 915645), Dodderhill*, unpublished report

Hurst, J D, and Hemingway, J A, 1997 The excavation, in Hurst 1997a, 9–67

Hurst, D, Hunt, A, and Davenport, P, 2010 Iron Age settlement at Blackstone, Worcestershire: excavations 1972, 1973, and 1977, *Internet Archaeology*, **28**. Online access, http://intarch.ac.uk/journal/issue28/hurst_index.html

Hurst, D, Roberts, R, and Woodiwiss, S, 1988 A possible second Roman fort at Droitwich (HWCM 4154), *Trans Worcestershire Archaeol Soc 3 ser*, **11**, 75–80

Jones, C, Lowry, B, and Wilks, M, 2008 *20th century defences in Britain: the West Midlands area*. Almeley: Logaston Press

Jones, L, and Evans, C J, 2006 The excavation of an Iron Age and Romano-British site at Stoke Lane, Wychbold, *Trans Worcestershire Archaeol Soc 3 ser*, **20**, 11–35

Ker, N R, 1948 Hemming's Cartulary. A description of the two Worcester cartularies in Cotton Tiberius A. xiii, in R W Hunt, W A Pantin and R W Southern (eds), *Studies in medieval history presented to Frederick Maurice Powicke*. Oxford: Clarendon Press

Kerr, B, 1999 *Religious life for women c 1100–c 1350*. Oxford: Oxford Univ Press

Lacey, J, 1774 *Notes written by John Lacy of Bromsgrove in answer to queries proposed for promoting Parochial History of Britain*. London: The Society of Antiquaries

Lamb, H H, 1995 *Climate, history and the modern world*, 2 ed. Routledge

Langdon, J, and Masschaele, J, 2006 Commercial activity and population growth in medieval England, *Past & Present*, **190**, 35–81

Lentowicz, I J, 1997 Pottery, in Hurst 1997a, 68–89

Lentowicz, I, and Seaby, W, 1997 Coins, in Hurst 1997a, 96

Lipson, E, 1949 *The economic history of England, vol 1: the Middle Ages*

Littlebury, 1879 *Littlebury's directory and gazetteer of Worcester & District*, 3 ed. Ballantyne, Hanson & Co

Lucas, G, 1998 A medieval fishery on Whittlesea Mere Cambridgeshire, *Med Archaeol*, **30**, 19–44

McAvoy, F, 2006 Dodderhill, Droitwich: excavations 1977–85, in Hurst, 3–45
McClintock, D, and Fitter, R S R, 1956 *The pocket guide to wild flowers*. London: Collins
Maddicott, J R, 2005 London and Droitwich, *c* 650–750: trade, industry and the rise of Mercia, *Anglo-Saxon England*, **34**, 7–58. Cambridge: Cambridge Univ Press
Mann, A, 2007 *Archaeological evaluation on land off Hanbury Road, Droitwich, Worcestershire*, Worcestershire Historic Environment & Archaeology Service rep **1532**. Available at www.worcestershire.gov.uk/archaeology/library
Margary, I D, 1973 *Roman roads in Britain*, 3 ed. London: John Baker
Mattingley, J, 2009 Church houses: an under-recognised building type, *Local History News*, **93**, 16–17
Mawer, A, and Stenton, F M, with Houghton, F T S, 1927 *The place-names of Worcestershire*, English Place-Name Soc, **IV**. Cambridge: Cambridge Univ Press
Meeson, R A, and Alcock, N W, 2005 *Mere Hall, Hanbury, Worcestershire*, Rep **05/06** (produced for private circulation)
Mercer, E, 1975 *English vernacular houses: a study of traditional farmhouses and cottages*, Royal Commission on Historical Monuments. HMSO
Middlemass, B, and Hunt, J, 1985 *John Corbett, pillar of salt, 1817–1901*. Droitwich: Saltway Press
Mitchell, G H, Pocock R W and Taylor J H, 1961 *Geology of the country around Droitwich, Abberley and Kidderminster*, Memoirs of the Geological Survey of Great Britain. HMSO
Monkhouse, F J, 1971 Worcestershire, in H C Darby and I B Terrett (eds), *The Domesday geography of Midland England*, 217–72. Cambridge: Cambridge Univ Press
Moran, M, 2003 *Vernacular buildings of Shropshire*. Almeley: Logaston Press
Morris, E L, 1985 Prehistoric salt distributions: two case studies from western Britain, *Bull Board Celtic Stud*, **XXXII**, 336–79
Morris, E, 1992 Friar Street, Droitwich: petrology report on the prehistoric pottery, in S G Woodiwiss (ed), *Iron Age and Roman salt production and the medieval town of Droitwich*, CBA Res Rep **81** (microfiche)
Morris, E L, 1994 Finds, in D Farwell and I Barnes, The ESSO Birmingham Airport link: archaeological investigations at Astwood, Dodderhill, *Trans Worcestershire Archaeol Soc 3 ser*, **14**, 176–9
Muir, R, 2000 *The new reading of the landscape: fieldwork in landscape history*. Exeter: Exeter Univ Press
Myres, J N L, 1986 *The English settlements*. Oxford; Oxford Univ Press

Nash, T R, 1781–2 *Collections for the history of Worcestershire*, 2 vols
Newman, J, and Pevsner, N, 2006 *The buildings of England: Shropshire*. Yale Univ Press
Noake, J, 1856 *Notes and queries for Worcestershire*. London: Longman & Co

Orme, N, 1978 The medieval schools of Worcestershire, *Trans Worcestershire Archaeol Soc 3 ser*, **6**, 43–51
Owen, W, 1756 *An authentic account published by the king's authority of all the fairs in England and Wales*. London

Patrick, C, and Hurst, J D, 2004 *Archaeological survey and excavation along the Cotswold Spring Supply Trunk Main: archive report*, Worcestershire County Archaeological Service rep **1140**. Available at www.worcestershire.gov.uk/archaeology/library

Pearson, E, 1999 Environmental evidence, in Griffin *et al*, 8–10

Pearson, E, 2005 Plant macrofossils, in P Williams, D Hurst, E Pearson, and J Grieg, *Archaeological watching brief and building recording at Impney Farm, Dodderhill, Worcestershire*, Worcestershire County Council Archaeological Service rep **991**, 12–13. Available at www.worcestershire.gov.uk/archaeology/library

Percival, J, 1985 The precursors of Domesday: Roman and Carolingian land registers, in P Sawyer (ed), *Domesday Book: a reassessment*, 5–27. London

Pitt, W, 1796 *General view of the agriculture of the County of Stafford*

Pitt, W, 1813 *General view of the agriculture of the County of Worcester*

Pollard, E, Hooper, M D, and Moore, N W, 1974 *Hedges*. London: Collins

Price, S, 2010a *Wychbold Court, Wychbold, Worcestershire: historic building report*, Stephen Price Associates Ltd

Price, S, 2010b *Astwood Court Farm, Dodderhill, Worcestershire: historic building report*, Stephen Price Associates Ltd

Price, S, 2010c *Tudor Cottage, Droitwich, Worcestershire: historic building report*, Stephen Price Associates Ltd

Priestley, A W, 1926 *Education in Worcestershire: handbook prepared for the education weekend held in Malvern May 14–15th 1926*

Rackham, O, 1980 *Ancient woodland: its history, vegetation and uses in England*

Rackham, O, 1990 *Trees and woodland in the British landscape* (revised edition). London: Weidenfeld & Nicolson

Rastel, T, 1678 An account of the salt waters of Droytwich in Worcestershire, *Phil Trans Royal Soc London*, A, **12**, 1059–64

Rees, U, 1985 *The cartulary of Haughmond Abbey*, Shropshire Archaeol Soc. Cardiff: Univ Wales Press

Reynolds, A, 2003 The early medieval period, in N Holbrook and J Jurica, *Twenty-five years of archaeology in Gloucestershire: a review of new discoveries and new thinking in Gloucestershire, south Gloucestershire and Bristol*, Bristol and Gloucestershire Archaeol rep **3**, 133–65

Robson, S, and Hurst, D, 2000 Watching brief at St Augustine's Church, Dodderhill, *Trans Worcestershire Archaeol Soc 3 ser*, **17**, 207–14

Robson-Glyde, S, 2005 *Dodderhill building recording: Mill Cottage, Mill Lane, Wychbold, Worcestershire*, Worcestershire Historic Environment & Archaeology Service rep **1347**

Robson-Glyde, S, 2006a *Dodderhill building recording: Ridgeway Court, Wychbold, Worcestershire*, Worcestershire Historic Environment & Archaeology Service rep **1415**

Robson-Glyde, S, 2006b *Dodderhill building recording: Wychbold Court, Dodderhill*, Worcestershire Historic Environment & Archaeology Service rep **1416**

Rogers, J E T, 1866 *A history of agriculture and prices in England, vol 1: 1259–1400*. Oxford

Rogers, J E T, 1882 *A history of agriculture and prices in England, vol 2: 1401–1582*. Oxford

Röhrkasten, J, 2008 *The Worcester eyre of 1275*, Worcestershire Hist Soc new ser **22**

Round, J H, 1901 Introduction to the Domesday Survey, *VCH Worcestershire* **I**, 235–80

St Joseph, J K S, 1938 The Roman fort at Dodderhill (interim report), *Trans Birmingham Archaeol Soc*, **62**, 27–31

Sawyer, P H, 1968 *Anglo-Saxon charters. An annotated list and bibliography.* London: Royal Hist Soc

Sawyer, P H, 1983 The royal *tun* in pre-Conquest England, in P Wormald with D Bullough and R Collins (eds), *Ideal and reality in Frankish and Anglo-Saxon society. Studies presented to J M Wallace-Hadrill*, 273–99. Oxford: Basil Blackwell

Short, B, 2000 *The national farm survey, 1941–1943: state surveillance and the countryside in England and Wales in the Second World War.* Wallingford: CABI Publishing

Sims-Williams, P, 1990 *Religion and literature in western England, 600–800*, (reprinted 2005). Cambridge: Cambridge Univ Press

Skerratt, R, 2001 *Memories of Wychbold before the motorway.* Worcester: privately published

Smith, J, 2010 *Dodderhill and Pipershill Common (also called Hanbury Woods – Nash 1791): an incomplete history of the common and its trees*, Worcestershire Wildlife Trust unpublished report

Smith, L T (ed), 1964, *The itinerary of John Leland in or about the years 1535–1545 (new ed).* London: Centaur Press Ltd

Stenton, D M, 1934 *Rolls of the justices in Eyre being the rolls of pleas and assizes for Lincolnshire 1218–9 and Worcestershire 1221*, 53, Selden Soc

Stenton, F, 1971 *Anglo-Saxon England*, 3 ed. Oxford: Oxford Univ Press

Sutton, A F, 2005 *The mercery of London: trade, goods and people 1130–1578.* Ashgate

Thorn, F, and Thorn, C (eds), 1982 *Domesday Book: Worcestershire.* Chichester: Phillimore

Toomey, J, 2001 *Records of Hanley Castle Worcestershire* c *1147–1547*, Worcestershire Hist Soc new ser, **18**

Townshend, J, 2000 *17th century wills and inventories of Bromsgrove*, unpublished report

Trevelyan, G M, 1944 *English social history: a survey of six centuries.* London: Longman, Green and Co

Trinder, B, and Cox, J (eds), 1980 *Yeomen and Colliers of Telford: probate inventories for Dawley, Lilleshall, Wellington and Wrockwardine 1660–1750.* London: Phillimore

Tusser, T, 1580 *Five hundred points of good husbandry*, (1580 edition, reprinted 1984). Oxford: Oxford Univ Press

Unwin, G, 1957 *Industrial organisation in the 16th and 17th centuries.* London: Cass

Urquhart, J, 1983 *Animals on the Farm.* London: MacDonald

VCH Buckinghamshire II, 1908 *Victoria County History of Buckinghamshire* **II**, W Page (ed)

VCH Worcestershire II, 1906 *Victoria County History of the County of Worcester* **II**, J W Willis-Bund and W Page (eds) (reprinted 1971)

VCH Worcestershire III, 1913 *Victoria County History of the County of Worcester* **III**, J W Willis-Bund (ed) (reprinted 1971)

VCH Worcestershire IV, 1924 *Victoria County History of the County of Worcester* **IV**, J W Willis-Bund (ed) (reprinted 1971)

Wade Martins, S, 2004 *Farmers, landlords and landscapes: rural Britain, 1720–1870.* Macclesfield: Windgather Press

Warren, G, 1991 *Worcestershire at War.* Privately printed

Watkins, A, 1998 Peasants in Arden, in R Britnell (ed), *Daily life in the later Middle Ages*, 83–101. Stroud: Sutton publishing

Watts, V, 2004 *The Cambridge dictionary of English place-names.* Cambridge: Cambridge Univ Press

Webster, P V, 1977 Severn Valley ware on the Antonine frontier, in J Dore and K Greene, *Roman pottery studies in Britain and beyond*, Brit Archaeol Rep Suppl Ser **30**

Wells-Cole, A, 1997 *Art and decoration in Elizabethan and Jacobean England: the influence of continental prints, 1558–1625*. Yale Univ Press

West, J, 1962 *Village records*. London: Macmillan & Co

West, J, 1964a The forest offenders of medieval Worcestershire, *Folk Life* **2**, 80–115

West, J, 1964b *The administration and economy of the Forest of Feckenham during the early Middle Ages*, unpub MA thesis, Birmingham Univ

White, A, 1996 *Worcestershire salt: a history of Stoke Prior salt works*. Bromsgrove: Halfshire Books

White, R, 2007, *Britannia Prima: Britain's last Roman province*. Stroud: Tempus

White, R and Barker, P, 1998 *Wroxeter: life and death of a Roman city*. Stroud: Tempus

Whitehouse, D B, 1962 A note on excavation of the Roman fort at Dodderhill, Droitwich, 1961–62, *Trans Worcestershire Archaeol Soc*, **39**, 55–7

Whitworth, A, Hurst, D, Jones, L, and Pearson, E, 2001 *Evaluation at Baxenden Chemicals Ltd, Union Lane, Droitwich, Worcestershire*, Worcestershire County Council Archaeological Service rep **905**. Available at www.worcestershire.gov.uk/archaeology/library

Wilks, M, 2007 *The defence of Worcestershire and the southern approaches to Birmingham in World War II*. Almeley: Logaston Press

Williams, A (ed), 2002 *The Digital Domesday*. Editions Alecto (Domesday) Ltd

Williams, D, 1997 *Late Saxon stirrup-strap mounts: a classification and catalogue*, CBA Res Rep **111**. York: Council for British Archaeology

Williams, P, Hurst, D, Pearson, E, and Grieg, J, 2005 *Archaeological watching brief and building recording at Impney Farm, Dodderhill, Worcestershire*, Worcestershire Historic Environment & Archaeology Service rep **991**. Available at www.worcestershire.gov.uk/archaeology/library

Williams, P, and Price, S, 2008a *Appraisal of timber-framing at Old Cottage, Sharpway Gate, Dodderhill, Worcestershire*, Stephen Price Associates & Mercian Archaeology

Williams, P, and Price, S, 2008b *Historic building assessment of Redhouse Farm, Shaw Lane, Stoke Prior, Worcestershire*, Stephen Price Associates & Mercian Archaeology

Williams, P, and Price, S, 2008c *Historic building assessment of Crown Cottage, Wychbold, Worcestershire*, Stephen Price Associates & Mercian Archaeology

Willis-Bund, J W, 1894 *The inquisitiones post mortem for the County of Worcester. Part 1: from their commencement in 1242 to the end of the 13th century*

Willis-Bund, J W, and Amphlett, J, 1893 *Lay subsidy roll for the County of Worcester circ 1280*, Worcestershire Hist Soc

Wood, M, 1986 *Domesday: a search for the roots of England*. London: BBC Enterprises Ltd

Woodiwiss, S G, 1992 Old Bowling Green, the excavation, in S G Woodiwiss (ed), *Iron Age and Roman salt production and the medieval town of Droitwich*, CBA Res Rep **81**, 8–34

Yelling, J A, 1977 *Common field and enclosure in England 1450–1850*. London: Macmillan Press Ltd

Zaluckyj, S, 2001 *Mercia: the Anglo-Saxon kingdom of central England*. Almeley: Logaston Press

Index

Places are generally in Worcestershire unless otherwise indicated. Major themes are shown in capital letters.

Aethelbald, King 45, 50, 52
Aethelflaed 36, 51
Aethelred, king of Mercia 26, 48, 52
Aethelred, married to daughter of King Alfred 36, 49, 51
Aethelred II, king of England 56
Alms Houses 172, 176
Alvechurch 2, 32–3, 34–8, 139
Anglo-Saxon 25–35 passim, 38–53 passim, see also coins; pottery; roads; Wic; Wicbold; Wychbold and royal estate
    charters 26–30, 32–6, 41–6, 48–52
Astwood 2, 6, 12, 14, 22, 64–5, 67, 69, 70, 71, 79–80, 87–90, 100–5, 107, 110, 115, 117, 121–2, 125, 129, 130–1, 133–5, 138–41, 147, 158, 163, 172–3, 177, 180–3, 189, see also Dodderhill; yields
Astwood Court Farm 89–90, 100–2, 107, 117, 120–2, 134–5, 138–41, 147
Astwood Lane 89, 146, 158, 172–3
Astwood Manor Farm 65, 67, 90, 103–5, 140, 158, 163, 177
Astwood Meynill 88–9
Astwood New House 6, 22
Astwood Robert 89, 103–7
Astwood Savage 88–9, 90–103

Bays Meadow villa see Droitwich
bees 35, 97, 130
Black Death 63, 66–7, 74, 127
Body Brook 19, 64, 116
Brine Pits Farm 5, 115–6, 121, 128–9, 132, 178, 181
brine run 4, 5, 116
brine springs 4, 9–10, 20, 47, 57
briquetage 13–14
British Alkali Company (Stoke Prior) 93
British Broadcasting Corporation (BBC) 169–72, 174–7
    transmitter 170–2
Bromsgrove 2–3, 28, 30, 31–4, 36–7, 42, 46, 62–3, 68, 71, 74, 79, 84–5, 92–4, 98–9, 101, 109, 113–14, 118–24, 126–7, 132, 135, 142, 150, 172, 174, 196
    bank 93
Brookhouse Farm 65, 180
Brummel Court 172
BUILDINGS 134–47 passim, see also individual houses
    brick 98, 101, 107, 122, 135, 138–42, 144–6, 162
    open hall 131, 135–8, 141
    smoke bay 131, 136–8
    stone for 42, 71, 75, 80, 95, 97–8, 102, 107, 109, 122, 138, 140–2, 144–6, 152
    timber for 89–109 passim, 135–47 passim
        elm 92, 135, 137, 146–7
        oak 93, 146–7
    wall painting inside 74, 93, 136
burials 25, 38, 40, 41, 45, 77
    Roman 21
    Quaker 113–4
Burial Lane see Droitwich
butter 123, see also food

canal 87, 150–1, 158, 174
Capel Ditch 116
Causeway Meadows Farm 89, 102, 105–7, 180–1, 183
Ceolwulf, King 30, 49
Chaddesley Corbett 16, 36, 79, 118–19, 120–1, 132, 182
Chapel Bridge see Droitwich
Chapel House 158
Chateau Impney 17, 151, 171, 176
    park 153, 155–6, 180
cheese 44, 49, 85, 122–4, 130–1, 141, 189
    equipment for making 96–7, 122–3
    storage of 96–7, 100–1, 104, 122–3, 134, 141
Christmas Cottage 140–1
church court 65, 72
church house, of Dodderhill see Dodderhill and parish house
Church Lane 66, 175
CHURCHES see individual parish names/places
Civil War 38, 82, 84–5, 95, 101, 111–2, 119–20, 124
climate 5, 10, 12, 61, 82, 116
cloth making 62, 68, 78–9, 124–8 passim, see also occupations
Cofton Hackett 32, 34–5, 37
COINS
    Iron Age 15
    Roman 18–19
    Alfred the Great penny 51
Colley Pit(s) 65, 180
Colley Pits Lane 95, 135
Colman, Abbot 26, 42–3, 51
Corbett, John 79, 91, 93, 98, 100, 102, 105, 107–8, 146, 151–6 passim, 161–2, 169
Coventry Hospital 148, 157
Croft, The 172–3, 175
CROPS 116–21 passim, 184–5
    acorns 161
    barley 82, 117–18, 133, 184
    beans 96, 110, 118–19, 125, 132–3, 161, 188
    clover 118–9, 123
    corn 77, 117–18, 124, 184
        chamber 130
    dredge 133
    flax 68, 97, 101, 110, 115, 126–7
    hay 44, 57, 69, 75, 99, 116, 119, 125, 188
    hemp 97, 126–7
    muncorn 82, 96, 117–18
    oats 82, 101, 117–18, 130, 133, 184
    peas 101, 110, 118–19, 125, 132–3, 188
    pulses 82, 118
    rye 82, 110, 117–18, 184

vetches 119
wheat 11, 27, 33, 82, 96, 110, 117–18, 184
Crowle 36, 108
Crown Cottage 135, 142
Crown Lane 80, 85, 141, 173, 176
Crutch 2, 25, 38, 45, 63, 71, 80, 166
Crutch Cottages 146
Crutch Farm 22, 87, 180, 181
Crutch Hill 16, 48
Crutch Lane 12, 16, 22–3, 74, 152 *see also* roads
    Roman road 3, 16

dairying 122–4 *passim*, 81–2, 85, 120, 189, 201
Dissolution 73, 75, 77–8, 80, 103, 108, 127, 152
Dobunni 14
Dodder 6
Dodderhill 151, *passim*; *see also* Astwood; Droitwich; Wychbold
    common 59, 67, 89, 117, 140, 146, 169
    parish, detached parts of 2–3, 45, 58, 63, 71, 79, 116
    parish house 73, 76–7
    Roman fort 17, 26, 38, 42
    Roman marching camp 16–17
    St Augustine's 38–53 *passim*, 64, 71–5 *passim*, 77, 79, 83, 111–13 *passim*, 151–2
        bells 73, 112–3
        civil war damage at 84, 111–2
    St Mary's/Dodderhill Hospital 64, 72–5, 87, 89
Domesday Book 5, 30–1, 33, 36–8 *passim*, 43, 45–6, 49, 52–3, 55–60 *passim*, 68, 77, 88
DOMESTIC LIFE
    cooking 17, 21–2, 82, 123, 128–31 *passim*, *see also* food
dovecote 68–9, 87, 113
DRINK *see also* food
    ale 49, 62, 65, 73, 76, 116, 129, 133
    beer 129, 133
    cider 130, 133
        mill 133
    coffee 134
    perry 133
        mill 133
    tea 134, 193
    wine 17, 44, 62, 116, 132–3
DROITWICH 3, 83, *see also* Coventry Hospital; Dodderhill; *Salinae*; *Wic*; Wich
    Bays Meadow villa 19–21, 24, 46, 54, 150
    brine baths 108–9, 151
    burgesses 36, 55–6, 58–9
    Burial Lane 152
    Chapel Bridge 58, 74, 152, 173
    friary, Augustinian 73, 75–6, 113
    In Liberties 71, 151, 155, 157
    market 45, 50–1, 58, 62, 65, 72, 151, 201
    mill, town *see* mills
    Middlewich 29, 36
    Netherwich 29
    St Andrew 38, 45, 152
    St Nicholas 20, 38–9, 45, 152, 154
    salt making *see* salt production
    schools *see* education; schools
    Upwich 4, 13, 20, 25–6, 28, 29, 36, 38, 44–7, 48, 51–2, 55, 57–8, 62, 72, 83, 115, 200
    Vines Lane 21, 74, 114

    also see Witton
Droitwich Golf Club 102, 158, 169, 174

EDUCATION 87, 148–9, 156–68 *passim*, 190–9 *passim*, *see also* schools
    board school 158, 163–8, 190–5 *passim*
    British school 157–8
    charity school 148–9
    grammar school 148, 195–6
    national school 158–60, 162–5, 168
Edwin, Earl 30–1, 36, 46, 54
Elmbridge 2, 37, 38, 66, 69, 70–1, 81, 84, 88–9, 114, 126, 150, 152, 182
    chapel 63, 72–3
Elm Court 89, 93–5
enclosure 32, 66–8, 70, 81–2, 85, 90, 110, 120, 127, 147, 201

fairs 61, 127–8
    cheese 124
    linen cloth 127
    hats 127
    sheep 127
    wool 127
FARMING *see also* crops; fowl; grassland; livestock; ridge and furrow; WWII and National Farm Survey
    engines 188
    tractors 188
Feckenham 30, 36, 78, 87–8, 139, 148
Feckenham Forest 31, 37–8, 61, 67, 71, 78, 88, 117
FISH 44, 65, 132
Fladbury 52
FOOD *see also* cheese; drink; fish; fruit; fowl; vegetables
    bacon 96, 104, 131
    bread 116–18, 130, 192
    butter 44, 49, 122–3, 134
    fish 44, 65, 132
    meat 44, 50, 82, 124–5, 127–32
    venison 36, 67
Ford 64, 66, 75, 80, 103, 169, 192
Ford Cottages 21
Ford Farm 65, 101–2, 108, 115, 117, 120–2, 124–5, 129, 131, 133, 156, 180–1, 183
Ford Lane 80, 158, 174, 176
FOWL 132, 186
    ducks 132
    geese 49, 132, 186
    peacocks 132
    poultry 128, 130–2, 186
    turkeys 132, 186
Fownes Cottage 135
FRUIT 130, 132–3, 161, 184, 188–9; *see* orchards
    apples 101, 130, 132, 189
    pears 132–3, 189
FUEL 18, 28, 30–1, 46, 48, 52, 59, 69, 128
    coal 107, 128, 154
    firewood 18, 80, 147

geology 4, 116
Godwin, Earl of Wessex 31, 46, 55–7, 68
grass(land) 9, 10, 57, 66, 75, 110, 117, 125, 184, 189
Greenes 91, 99–100

INDEX

Grimley 35

Hadzor 38, 71, 108
Hampton Lovett 2–3, 36–8, 45–6, 70, 78, 154, 176
Hanbury 2–3, 14, 16, 22–7, 34, 36–8, 46, 63, 65–8, 71, 74, 88–9, 94, 100–1, 103–4, 117, 139–40, 147, 155, 175
    hillfort 13, 15
    minster 26–7, 29, 36, 42–3, 49, 51, 152
Hartlebury 11, 36, 101
Haughmond Abbey (Shrops) 63, 77
hedges 9, 32, 71, 110, 150
    dating of 67
Helperic (Helpridge) 5, 36, 65, 99, 110, 115, 118
Hen Brook 27, 64, 103, 116
Hill Court 73, 92, 108–9, 113, 169, 180–1, 183, 187, 189
Hill End 64, 67, 70, 76–7, 84, 100, 110, 115, 126, 135, 152, 154–5, 167
Hill Farm 65, 180–1
Himbleton 51, 182
Hobden *see* Obden
Hobden Hall 80, 95–8, 102–3, 144, 180–1, 183
Hollow Court 34, 37
Holmes Lane 67
hospitals 148, 169, *see also* Coventry Hospital
    St Mary's *see* Dodderhill
Huntingdrop 2, 63, 67, 71, 109, 110, 116, 118
Huntingthrop 65
Hutt Bridge (Tunbridge) 84
Hwicce 25, 29, 36, 38, 40–3, 45, 47–50, 52

Ice Age 9–10
Impney 10–11, 19, 22, 64–5, 69, 70, 81, 84, 87, 89, 107–8, 110, 117, 153–6, *see also* Chateau Impney; mills; yields
    Court 154
    Lodge 79, 153, 156
    lordship of manor 154–5
    Park 155, 180
Impney End 67
Impney Farm 134, 141, 145, 154–5, 180–1, 183–4
In Liberties *see* Droitwich
Inkberrow 30, 88, 106
Iron Age *see also* coins; pottery; roads
    farmstead at Wychbold 12–13
    salt *see* briquetage; salt production
Ivy Cottage 93–5

Kennets Hall 11
Kidderminster 28–9, 36, 62, 68, 84, 105, 119, 124, 127, 152, 165, 174
Kingsland 61, 64, 69, 110
Kingsland Hill Farm 65, 180–1, 183, 188
King's Norton 2, 34, 36, 37

Laburnum Cottage 140
Leather Bridge 61, 64–5, 84, 100, 110, 201
LIVESTOCK
    cows 49, 119–22 *passim*, 173, 184, *see also* dairying
    horses 44, 49, 81, 110, 119–20, 128, 130, 133, 187
        stealing 87
    oxen 57, 82, 119–20
    pigs 29, 31, 69, 71, 97, 130–1, 184–6

    sheep 5, 49, 51, 57, 62–3, 66, 71, 82, 85, 97, 115, 119, 124–8 *passim*, 130, 184–6
London 44, 50, 77, 79, 91, 95, 130, 148, 157, 170, 193
Lumbarde Cottage 146

Malverns 18
Martin Hussingtree 32–8, 46
Mercia 25–6, 29–30, 41–52 *passim*
Magonsæte 41, 49
Mere Hall (Hanbury) 100, 139–40, 147
Merewalh 40
Middlewich *see* Droitwich
milk *see* dairying
Mill Cottage 135, 166
mills 2, 44, 68, 77–80 *passim*, *see also* drink
    Astwood 102–3
    Briar mill 58, 103
    Droitwich town mill 58, 63, 79
    Impney mill(s) 58, 62, 79, 133, 153
    Paper mill 58, 61, 78, 100
    Rudgway mill 79
    Walkmill 68, 78–9, 115–16, 126, 130
    Wharf mill 79
    Wychbold mill(s) 58, 63, 70–1, 77–8, 93–4
Moors Farm 89, 98–9, 115

Netherwich *see* Droitwich

Obden 64–5, 89–90, 95
OCCUPATIONS (in Wychbold) 115
    blacksmith 81, 115
    cap maker 81
    carpenter 115
    clothier/cloth making 78, 93
    coal merchant 107, 154
    dairy-maid 94
    farmer *passim*, *see also* crops; dairying; livestock
    fuller *see* walker
    governess 93
    hatter 115, 127
    locksmith 115
    maltster 93
    mason 115
    mercer 115, 130, 148
    merchant 81
    miller 77, 79, 81, 93–4, 120, 133, 153, *see also* mills
    needle milling 78
    paper making 78, 100, *see also* mills and Paper mill
    rate collector 107
    servants 93, 101, 115
    shepherd 66, 81
    shoemaker 115
    tailor 115
    toll keeper *see* toll; toll house
    verderer 67
    walker 62, 79, *see also* mills and Walkmill, Wharf mill
    weaver 115
Old Astwood Farm (Hanbury) 89, 140
Old Cottage, The 135, 141
orchards 70
Osbern fitz Richard 31, 36, 55–6, 68, 71

Overstreet Cottages 158, 160

Pakington, John 70, 109
Papermill Lane 61
Park Farm 87, 178, 180–1
Parsonage House 108, 113
peat 10, 11, 44
Penda, King 40
Pershore Abbey 35
Piper's Hill 27, 34, 67, 85, 110–11, 117
Piper's Hill Farm 118, 144, 182–3
POTTERY 6, 12
    Iron Age 14, 123
    Roman 17–18, 19, 21–4, 200
    Anglo-Saxon 25–6, 28
    late Saxon 54
    medieval 23, 65–7, 89–90, 129–30
    post-medieval 23, 85
Purshill 70, 84

rabbits 61
railway 75, 151–2, 155, 173, 182
    station 150
Rashwood 22, 64–5, 67, 73, 83–4, 88–9, 110, 115–6, 121, 144–5, 150, 156, 181, 183, 188–9, 190, 194, 197–8
Rashwood Court 171, 173, 180
Rashwood Farm 107, 144–5, 180, 183, 188–9
Rashwood Lodge 173
Rashwood School *see* schools
Red House Farm 107, 140–1
RELIGION
    chapel, congregational 150
    chapel, house 89–90
    churches 71–4, 111–13, 151–2, *see also* individual parish names/places
    dissenters/non-conformists 85, 113, 157
    pagan 35, 41
    papists 85
    Protestantism 74
    Puritans 111–12
    Quakers 113–14
        burial ground 113–14
ridge and furrow 65–6, 89
Ridgeway 92, 115, 121, 131, 180–1
Ridgeway Court Farm 79, 83, 135, 141–2, 146, 180–1, 183
ROADS
    ridgeway (?prehistoric) 12, 16
    Roman 2–4, 16, 19, 21–2
    (Anglo-)Saxon 28–9, 31–3, 36, 50, 52, 54
    medieval 62, 80–1
    turnpike 114, 150
    motorway (M5) 198, 200
Robin Hood, The 150
Roman 16–24 *passim*, *see also* coins; pottery; roads
    farmstead at Wychbold 18, 21–2
    fort *see* Dodderhill
    marching camp *see* Dodderhill
    soldiers 17–18
    villa *see* Droitwich and Bays Meadow villa
Romsley 80
Rosemary Cottage 140
royal residence *see* Wychbold and royal estate

Sagebury 64, 85, 89–90, 92, 94–6, 98, 103, 110, 115, 121–4, 129
Sagebury Cottages 99–100
Sagebury Farm 65, 67, 89, 90–1, 94
St Augustine, church of *see* Dodderhill
St Mary de Wyche, church of *see* Wychbold
Salinae 20, 29, 48
SALT PRODUCTION
    Iron Age 13–14
    Roman 17–18, 20
    Saxon 26–30, 32–3, 36–7, 46–52, 54
    medieval 58–9, 62, 72, 80, 83
salt-ways 28, 33, 36, 50, 54
Saltwic 29
Salty Brook 12, 64, 116
Salwarpe 32–3, 35, 37–8, 45–6, 58, 102, 154
Salwarpe, River 2, 4, 6, 9–10, 12, 20–1, 26, 29, 33–4, 48, 54, 68, 78, 80, 89, 94, 102, 114, 116, 200
SCHOOLS *see also* education
    Baptist Sunday school 193
    dame school 160
    Dodderhill School for girls 16, 109
    Droitwich Free School 148, 156–7
    Droitwich National Girls' School 165
    Glenhyng 109
    John Corbett School (Stoke Works) 161–2
    Overstreet School 158–63, 190, *see also* Upper Street School
    Rashwood School 160, 163–8 *passim*, 190–9 *passim*
        Attendance Officer 165–6
        disease at 166–8, 190
        Nuisance Officer 167
    Upper Street School 158; *see also* Overstreet School
    West Ford House 158, 169
    Wychbold First School ix, xi, 6, 198
Sharpway 27, 34, 117, 141
Sharpway Gate Farm 145, 181–2
Shaw Lane 90, 103, 158, 175
sheep *see* livestock
Stoke Lane 12–14, 16, 19, 165
Stoke Prior 3–4, 27, 32–5, 37, 67, 71, 91, 93–5, 98, 100–1, 116–17, 138–9, 150–1, 163, 165–6, 173, 193
Stonehouse Farm 34
Stoppingas 40
Swan Garage 171, 177

Tardebigge 32–6, 94
Time Team ix, 201
toll, at Wychbold 2, 52, 62, 69–70, 80–1, 84
Toll, The 69, 116, 130, 132
toll house 2
Tudor Cottage 135–6, 141, 147

Upton Warren 3, 9, 36–8, 73, 92, 95, 98–9, 105, 182
Upwich *see* Droitwich

Vale of Evesham 32, 36
VEGETABLES 184, *see* crops
Vikings 54
vill/*villa regalis* *see* Wychbold and royal estate

INDEX

Warren House 146
Webbs 180, 182–3
Westwood 2, 33, 38, 45, 62–3, 80, 110, 133, 181
Westwood Nunnery/Priory 2, 45, 61, 71, 73–8, 80, 102, 127
Wic 26, 29, 42, 45–8, 50–2, *see also* Droitwich
Wicbald 54
Wicbold 1, 26, 29, 38–53 *passim*, 65, *see also* Wychbold and royal estate
Wicelbold 52–3, 55, *see also* Wychbold
Wich 1–2, 26–7, 29, 55, 80, 84
Wiglaf, King 27, 49
William I, King 55–6, *see also* Domesday Book
Witton 36, 58, 173
    Witton St Mary 38–9, 45, 75, 114
    Witton St Peter 38–9, 45, 152
woodland/woods 10, 24, 26–7, 29, 31–5, 36–8, 42, 50–1, 56–7, 59, 61, 63, 65–71, 82, 84, 90, 141, 147, *see also* Feckenham Forest
wool 62–3, 66, 82, 96, 101, 115, 124–7 *passim*
    scales 125
WORCESTER
    Roman 18–9, 29, 34
    Anglo-Saxon 33–4, 36, 51, 54
        church of Worcester 26, 30, 33–4, 36, 39–40, 43–6, 48–52, 54, 71
        St Helen's church 39–40
    medieval 61–2, 68, 72, 76, 78, 88–9, 127
        church of Worcester 55, 61–2, 69, 71–6, 103
    post-medieval 93, 100, 104, 111, 113, 121, 124, 127, 132, 134, 140, 150, 155–6, 165–6, 173
        church of Worcester 76, 84, 112
WORLD WARS 169–77 *passim*
    First 108–9, 169–70
        Red Cross Hospital 169, 171
    Second *see also* BBC
        air defences 175–6
        air raid shelters 170–2, 176
        Auxiliary Fire Service 176
        Auxiliary Hospital 109
        First Aid Point 176
        Home Guard 171, 173–5, 177
        Luftwaffe 170, 172, 175
        Military Police 170
        National Farm Survey 1941–2 177–89 *passim*
        prisoners of war 171, 175–7, 187
        Royal Warwickshire Regiment, The 170
        Wardens' Post 176
Wroxeter (Shrops) 19, 25, 40–1
Wulfhere, King 42–3, 51
Wychbold 3, 65, 68–71 *passim*, 84, *see also* Dodderhill; Droitwich and burgesses; toll; *Wic*; *Wicbald*; *Wic(el)bold*; Wich; yields; *passim*
    bailiff, of manor 57, 68–71, 80–1, 89
    church (St Mary de Wyche) 152
    Domesday Book, in 36–7, 55–60 *passim*
    manor court 70, 79, 84, 93, 105, 109–11
        location of 81
    mill *see* mills
    Post and Telegraph Office 94

royal estate 2, 21, 26, 27–9, 30, 36, 46–53 *passim*
school *see* education; schools (especially schools and Overstreet School, Rashwood School, Wychbold First School)
village 12, 23, 150, 173, *see also passim*
village hall 76, 173, 176
workhouse 77
Wychbold Court 78, 81, 84, 89, 91–5, 123, 131, 134–5, 137–8, 141, 169, 180
Wychbold Hall 94–5, 176, 180
Wyken *see* Helpridge

Yew Tree Farm 89, 144, 180–3
yields 2, 70, 87
    Astwood 2, 64, 87, 115
    Impney 2, 64, 87, 115
    Wychbold 2, 64, 87, 115